CORRUPTION AND DEMOCRACY IN BRAZIL

CORRUPTION AND DEMOCRACY IN BRAZIL

The Struggle for Accountability

edited by

Timothy J. Power *and* **Matthew M. Taylor**

University of Notre Dame Press

Notre Dame, Indiana

Manufactured in the United States of America

Library of Congress Cataloging-in-Publication Data

Corruption and democracy in Brazil : the struggle for accountability / edited by
Timothy J. Power and Matthew M. Taylor.
  p.   cm. — (From the Helen Kellogg Institute for International Studies)
  Includes bibliographical references and index.
  ISBN-13: 978-0-268-03894-6 (pbk. : alk. paper)
  ISBN-10: 0-268-03894-5 (pbk. : alk. paper)
  1. Political corruption—Brazil.   2. Political corruption—Brazil—
Prevention.   3. Political culture—Brazil.   4. Administrative responsibility—
Brazil.   5. Democracy—Brazil.   6. Brazil—Politics and government—
21st century.   7. Mass media—Political aspects—Brazil.   I. Power, Timothy J.
(Timothy Joseph), 1962–   II. Taylor, Matthew MacLeod.
  JL2429.C6C69   2011
  320.981—dc22
                                                        2010049970

Contents

PART TWO
Postelectoral Dimensions of Accountability

Acknowledgments

A volume such as this is a result of the labors of many others besides the editors, and this is the appropriate place to recognize and thank those who have generously assisted us along the road to publication.

This volume grew out of a workshop organized by the Brazilian Studies Programme (BSP) of the University of Oxford, held at St. Antony's College on May 23, 2008. The BSP, successor to the former Centre for Brazilian Studies at Oxford, has a long-standing program of research and publication on the comparative politics of Brazilian democracy. The editors are grateful to Joe Foweraker, director of the University's Latin American Centre at the time, and Margaret MacMillan, warden of St. Antony's College, for their support of the workshop. The workshop—and the resultant edited volume—benefited tremendously from the astute comments offered by our three discussants: Alfred P. Montero, Anthony W. Pereira, and Laurence Whitehead.

Timothy Power would like to thank Leslie Bethell, former director of Brazilian Studies at Oxford, and Andrew Hurrell, chair of the BSP management committee, for their roles in making the workshop possible. He owes a debt of gratitude to Susannah Bartholomew, former administrator of the BSP, and Maria Elvira Ryan, secretary of the Latin American Centre, for their excellent logistical support.

Matthew Taylor would like to thank Tim and Valéria Power for their hospitality at Oxford, where they set the perfect collegial tone for the enterprise ahead. It is not often that such productive intellectual pursuits are preceded by Brazilian delicacies and followed by both High Table and softball on the banks of the Thames. Bruno Speck helped shape the agenda for the workshop through his insightful comments on our initial framework document. Steve Morris and Chris Blake were kind enough to share their own work on corruption in Latin America while it was still in manuscript form, enabling us to build from a much stronger theoretical foundation.

Together, the editors would like to thank the eight other contributors for providing us with insightful, provocative, and scholarly chapters that are also highly germane to our central theme. We are grateful to Scott Mainwaring, director of the Helen Kellogg Institute for International Studies, for his strong support of this volume. Scott's own work on democratic accountability in Latin America was and remains a reference point for the editors and the contributors to this volume, as is evident from the chapters that follow. Finally, we are deeply appreciative of two anonymous reviewers whose comments greatly improved the book, as well as all of the editorial staff at the University of Notre Dame Press, for their wise counsel and guidance of the publication process.

Abbreviations

Acronym	Portuguese	Approximate English Translation
ABIN	Agência Brasileira de Inteligência	Brazilian Intelligence Agency
AGU	Advocacia Geral da União	Federal Attorney General's Office, or Federal Solicitor General's Office
AMB	Associação dos Magistrados Brasileiros	Association of Brazilian Magistrates
CGU	Controladoria Geral da União	Federal Comptroller's Office
CIDE	Contribuição de Intervenção no Domínio Econômico	Contribution for Intervention in the Economic Domain
CNJ	Conselho Nacional de Justiça	National Judicial Council
COAF	Conselho de Controle de Atividades Financeiras	Council for the Oversight of Financial Activities
CONAMP	Conselho Nacional do Ministério Público	National Council of the Ministério Público
CPI	Comissão Parlamentar de Inquérito	Congressional Committee of Inquiry
CPMF	Contribuição Provisória sobre Movimentação Financeira	Temporary Contribution on Financial Transactions
DFSP	Departamento Federal de Segurança Pública	Federal Public Security Department

DOI	Destacamento de Operações de Informações	Division of Information Operations
DOPS	Departamento de Ordem Política e Social	Department of Political and Social Order
DRU	Desvinculação dos Recursos da União	Disentailment of Federal Resources
ENCCLA	Estratégia Nacional de Combate à Corrupção e à Lavagem de Dinheiro	National Strategy for Combating Corruption and Money Laundering
ESEB	Estudo Eleitoral Brasileiro	Brazilian Electoral Study
FENAPEF	Federação Nacional dos Policiais Federais	National Federation of Federal Police Officers
FPM	Fundo de Participação dos Municípios	Municipal Participation Fund
FUNDEF	Fundo de Manutenção e Desenvolvimento do Ensino Fundamental e de Valorização do Magistério	Fund for Maintaining and Developing Elementary Education and Improving Educators
IBAMA	Instituto Brasileiro do Meio Ambiente e dos Recursos Naturais Renováveis	Brazilian Institute for the Environment and Renewable Natural Resources
INSS	Instituto Nacional do Seguro Social	National Social Security Agency
MP	Ministério Público	Public Prosecutorial Service
MPF	Ministério Público Federal	Federal Public Prosecutorial Service
OAB	Ordem dos Advogados do Brasil	Brazilian Bar Association
PAC	Programa de Aceleração do Crescimento	Program for Accelerating Growth
PCdoB	Partido Comunista do Brasil	Communist Party of Brazil
PDS	Partido Democrático Social	Democratic Social Party

PDT	Partido Democrático Trabalhista	Democratic Labor Party
PF	Polícia Federal	Federal Police
PFL	Partido da Frente Liberal	Liberal Front Party
PL	Partido Liberal	Liberal Party
PMDB	Partido do Movimento Democrático Brasileiro	Brazilian Democratic Movement Party
PPB	Partido Progressista Brasileiro	Brazilian Progressive Party
PPR	Partido Progressista Reformador	Progressive Reform Party
PPS	Partido Popular Socialista	Socialist People's Party
PRN	Partido da Reconstrução Nacional	National Reconstruction Party
PRONAF	Programa Nacional de Fortalecimento da Agricultura Familiar	National Program for Strengthening Family Farming
PSB	Partido Socialista Brasileiro	Brazilian Socialist Party
PSDB	Partido da Social Democracia Brasileira	Brazilian Social Democracy Party
PSOL	Partido Socialismo e Liberdade	Socialism and Liberty Party
PT	Partido dos Trabalhadores	Workers' Party
PTB	Partido Trabalhista Brasileiro	Brazilian Labor Party
SENASP	Secretaria Nacional de Segurança Pública	National Secretariat of Public Security
SIAFI	Sistema Integrado de Administração Financeira do Governo	Federal Integrated System for the Financial Administration of the Federal Government
SINESP	Sistema Nacional de Estatísticas de Segurança Pública e Justiça Criminal	National System of Statistics on Public Security and Criminal Justice

SISBACEN	Sistema de Informações do Banco Central	Central Bank Information System
SNI	Serviço Nacional de Informações	National Information Service
STF	Supremo Tribunal Federal	Supreme Federal Tribunal
STJ	Superior Tribunal de Justiça	Superior Justice Tribunal
TC	Tribunal de Contas	Accounting Tribunal (may be federal, state, or municipal)*
TCU	Tribunal de Contas da União	Federal Accounting Tribunal*
TJ	Tribunal de Justiça	Justice Tribunal
TRE	Tribunal Regional Eleitoral	Regional Electoral Tribunal
TRF	Tribunal Regional Federal	Federal Regional Tribunal
TSE	Tribunal Superior Eleitoral	Superior Electoral Tribunal

*Although the TCU and TCs are denominated as "tribunals," they are not judicial institutions but instead are auxiliary to the legislative branch.

Chapter One

Introduction

Accountability Institutions and Political Corruption in Brazil

TIMOTHY J. POWER *&* MATTHEW M. TAYLOR

Corruption is a troubling constant in the Brazilian political system, with instances of corrupt behavior readily apparent at the federal, state, and municipal levels and across all branches of government. Although the transition to democracy in 1985 raised expectations of increased transparency and accountability, each of the five postauthoritarian presidential administrations has been sullied by accusations of corruption (table 1.1), with important consequences in terms of both the policy-making process and public views of democracy. But accountability—defined here as the answerability of public officials for the public-regarding nature and probity of their actions—has been inadequate.[1] Existing accountability institutions have proven unable either to formally punish or to clear the names of the accused. Scandals come and go, but the political system remains largely intact, with the same players and institutions robustly ensconced and seemingly impervious to even the most credible accusations of wrongdoing.

Almost by definition, the costs of corruption cannot be measured. But recent estimates suggest that corruption in Brazil may eat up somewhere between 1.35% of GDP (FIESP 2006) and 5% of GDP (*Época* 2008).[2] Whatever their true scale, the costs are high enough that international organizations have called for new measures to fight corruption (e.g., OECD 2007), and organized domestic initiatives against corruption have become increasingly widespread (e.g., AMB 2007; Instituto Ethos 2006). But the economic costs are perhaps the least important aspect of corruption's effects: polls, for example, suggest that there has been a steady decline in trust in political

1

Table 1.1. Prominent Episodes of Alleged Federal Political Corruption, 1988–2008

Episode	Description
Ferrovia Norte-Sul	Allegations of irregularities in public bidding for this US$2.5 billion railroad were dramatically unveiled in a series of stories published by the *Folha de São Paulo* newspaper in 1987, leading to a congressional inquiry and cancellation of the bidding.
CPI da Corrupção	This 1988 congressional committee of inquiry (CPI) was created to look into alleged irregularities in the disbursement of federal funds to municipalities. The CPI filed accusations of abuse of power *(crime de responsabilidade)* against President Sarney and several ministers, but these were shelved by the acting president of the Chamber of Deputies.
P. C./Collorgate	A political operative close to President Collor, Paulo César ("P.C.") Farias, was accused of administering a kickback scheme totaling millions of dollars. The scandal led to Farias's conviction, and to Collor's impeachment in 1992.
Budget "dwarves"	In 1993, congressmen were found to be systematically defrauding the Treasury in the preparation of the annual budget. The scheme was run by congressmen whose short stature gave rise to the scandal's name. They allegedly defrauded the Treasury by writing amendments that benefited specific construction companies in exchange for bribes, as well as amendments that transferred funds to fake charities.
São Paulo Regional Labor Court (TRT)	The cost of building the Regional Labor Court in São Paulo during the 1990s was inflated nearly fourfold, with proceeds on the order of US$100 million allegedly appropriated by Judge Nicolau dos Santos Neto (commonly referred to as "Lalau"), with the participation of a senator, Luiz Estevão, and the president and vice president of the construction company that won the building contract.
SUDAM	In 2000, questions arose regarding the use of nearly R$2 billion controlled by the federal Amazonian Development Superintendency (SUDAM), a regional development program. Investigations uncovered a system of side payments to politicians and SUDAM officials. As a direct result of the scandal, SUDAM was closed in May 2001 and its responsibilities were transferred to a new Amazonian Development Agency. One implicated senator was forced to resign but soon thereafter ran successfully for deputy.
Operation Anaconda	An operation code-named "Anaconda" and run jointly by the Ministério Público and the Federal Police in 2003 broke up a ring of lawyers, detectives, and judges who were accused of selling judicial decisions.

Operation Sanguessuga	The CGU in 2004 uncovered the fraudulent purchase of ambulances. A 2006 Federal Police operation code-named "Sanguessuga" ("leech" or "bloodsucker"), found that congressional aides had been bribed to write individual budget amendments financing the purchase of these ambulances with Health Ministry funds. The group then allegedly rigged the local bidding processes. A CPI created in June 2006 recommended the expulsion *(cassação)* of seventy-two members of Congress.
Mensalão	Late in President Lula's first term, it was alleged that his government had provided members of Congress payments in exchange for their legislative support. The scandal also revealed kickbacks from public-sector purchases being used for both electoral and personal ends. The scandal led to the resignation of much of Lula's inner circle and the indictment of thirteen members of Congress.

Sources: Dimenstein (1988); J. Freitas (1987); Flynn (1993, 2005); Schilling (1999); Speck and Nagel (2002); Taylor and Buranelli (2007); Weyland (1998).

actors over the past decade and a half. In the run-up to the impeachment of former president Fernando Collor de Mello in 1992, confidence in politicians stood at 31% and confidence in parties stood at 26%. Driven at least in part by recurring scandals, the corresponding figures by late 2005 were only 8% and 9% (*Opinião Pública* 2006).

Brazil's performance in cross-national corruption indices, meanwhile, is not dreadful, but it does raise many red flags. The World Bank's Worldwide Governance Indicators, for example, show Brazil doing better than most countries in its income category on three relevant indicators: "voice and accountability," "rule of law," and "control of corruption." Brazil places second among the largest Latin American economies on all of these variables, after Chile. But other data sources offer a dimmer picture. Transparency International's well-known Corruption Perceptions Index in 2008 placed Brazil eightieth in the world in terms of perceptions of corruption, and eighteenth out of the thirty-two countries in the Americas, behind Mexico and Peru and only slightly ahead of Panama and Guatemala.[3]

International rankings of Brazilian corruption are considerably more optimistic than the views of ordinary Brazilian citizens. Transparency International's Global Corruption Barometer, a survey of fifty-two thousand individuals across the world, notes that Brazilians were the nationality displaying the greatest overall concern with corruption, with "99 per cent of respondents regard[ing] both petty and grand corruption as very or fairly big problems" (Transparency International 2004, 7–8).[4] Brazilians also led the survey in saying that corruption in their country affected political life "to a large extent," and they ranked political parties as the most corrupt institutions in society. Similarly, the Americas Barometer survey of 2006 asked Latin Americans in eighteen countries to spontaneously name what they thought was the most serious problem facing their country. Brazil tied for first (with Ecuador) in the percentage of citizens naming corruption in first place and was one of only two countries (along with Paraguay) where corruption was cited more frequently than either the economy or personal security (table 1.2). A survey by the DataFolha organization in August 2009 broke new ground by asking ordinary Brazilians to define corruption in their own terms. Some 43% immediately made reference to the public sector and politicians, leading the researchers to conclude that "the majority of Brazilians associates corruption with government." For example, the same survey found that 92% of citizens believed that there was corruption in the National Congress and in the party system, and 88% said the same about the presidency and the federal ministries. A third of the respondents said it was impossible to practice politics in Brazil without engaging in some degree of corruption (Fraga 2009).

These findings may seem troubling in light of recent research, which has shown consistently that—throughout Latin America as a whole—perceptions of corruption are strongly and negatively related to regime legitimacy (Booth and Seligson 2009; Power and Cyr 2009). And yet, as is so often the case in Brazil, for all these worries, the glass is half full. Brazil offers an important lesson about accountability not only because it is the fourth-largest democracy in the world and the largest in Latin America but also because of its remarkable institutional evolution over its most recent—and longest—experience with democracy. The development of accountability institutions in Brazil has been broad, dynamic, and continuous since the transition from authoritarian rule began in earnest in 1982. Several anticorruption bureaucracies, such as the Controladoria Geral da União (CGU), an executive auditing body, have been created out of whole cloth. Others, such as the Ministério Público prosecutorial service and the Federal Police, have been transformed to such a degree that they no longer resemble their predemocratic incarnations. Simultaneously, the body of legisla-

Table 1.2. Citizen Perceptions of Most Severe National Problem, Americas Barometer 2006 *(% spontaneously citing problem as the single most serious)*

Country	Pervasiveness of Corruption	Economic Security	Personal Security
Brazil	13	1	4
Ecuador	13	32	3
Honduras	10	13	32
Paraguay	10	7	5
Nicaragua	9	15	2
Panama	9	8	17
Bolivia	7	24	2
Costa Rica	7	18	16
Guyana	7	5	20
Mexico	6	11	15
Peru	6	15	7
Haiti	4	6	13
Guatemala	3	6	39
Colombia	2	4	5
Jamaica	2	4	50
Chile	1	3	39
El Salvador	1	22	38
Uruguay	1	15	6

Source: Americas Barometer 2006 data set, cited in Olsen (2007).
Note: The question's wording is: "To begin with, in your opinion, what is the most serious problem the country faces?" For each country, the Latin American Public Opinion Project used a national probability sample of 1,500 adult citizens.

tion that governs the entire system has shifted considerably, adapting to changing circumstances, previous scandals, and a new institutional order.

More broadly, a number of structural changes have influenced the environment in which political corruption takes place. The return to democracy in the 1980s, and a subsequent reduction in the government's direct economic role in the 1990s, may not have necessarily reduced corruption as much as anticipated (Morris 2009; Rose-Ackerman 2000, 275; Geddes and Ribeiro Neto 1999; Weyland 1998; Whitehead 2000),[5] but they have dramatically changed the conditions under which corruption occurs. As

Morris and Blake (2009, 3) note, democracy provides new opportunities for corruption but also nourishes pressures for accountability and "lofts corruption high onto the political and the analytical agendas." Increasing freedom of the press and greater potential for civil society mobilization provide opportunities both for more public debate over corruption and, potentially, for great public disappointment with the absence of accountability. On the economic front, events that have little direct connection to corruption per se (such as the end of hyperinflation in 1994) have nonetheless had a significant effect in improving the transparency of public accounts and making corruption more apparent.[6]

In sum, the picture that emerges of both political corruption and accountability is complex and merits sober assessment in light of the significant changes wrought over the past twenty-five years. That is the purpose of this volume.

The Importance of Accountability

It is no longer believed that political corruption—commonly defined as the misuse of public office for private gain—may "grease the wheels" of developing economies (e.g., Huntington 1968; Leff 1964; Nye 1967). Rather, a broad consensus has emerged that corruption distorts the criteria by which public policies are chosen and thereby undermines the efficiency, efficacy, and public-regardingness of those policies. As a result, in the economic realm, corruption worsens investment and business conditions and reduces aggregate well-being (e.g., Lederman, Loayza, and Soares 2005; Kaufmann, Kraay, and Zoido-Lobatón 1999; Mauro 1995; Rose-Ackerman 1999; Bardhan 1997).

At the level of individual citizens, meanwhile, corruption is equally pernicious, weakening the basic trust in other citizens, as well as in the government, that is at the core of most conceptions of robust, high-quality democracy (e.g., Bailey and Paras 2006; Seligson 2002, 2006). By eroding trust, corruption leads citizens to withdraw from the public sphere and instead attend to their narrowest self-interest. In so doing, it "diminishes the scope of collective actions" and "shrinks the domain of democracy" (Warren 2004, 328–29; Warren 2006). Political corruption thus matters "more" in democracies, and may be a greater threat to legitimacy than it is in other regime types, because it erodes two basic supports of democratic regimes: the equality of citizens and the openness of decision making (Heywood 1997, 421–22).

Bailey (2009) points to corruption's potential effects in three principal arenas of democracy: (1) interest articulation and aggregation; (2) policy making; and (3) policy implementation and adjudication. Examples of corruption in each arena are readily apparent in contemporary Brazil. The first arena, interest articulation and aggregation, encompasses "inputs" to democracy such as voting and party competition. Examples of corruption in this arena include illicit campaign finance schemes, which underlie many of the scandals in table 1.1, such as the revelations of the Comissão Parlamentar de Inquérito (CPI) da Corrupção and the Collorgate scandal.

Within the policy-making arena, at least three types of potential corruption exist: grand corruption, "cash for policy," and "policy for cash" schemes. Grand corruption is perhaps the simplest and most commonly recognized form of corruption, visible clearly in Judge "Lalau's" multimillion-dollar heist in the construction of the São Paulo Labor Court and the bilking of the Amazonian Development Superintendency (SUDAM) (see table 1.1 for details on these scandals). "Cash for policy" schemes subvert the policy process by offering personal rewards to legislators in return for their support of determined policy objectives and are perhaps best exemplified by the *mensalão* scandal, in which the government expanded its coalition by "renting" members of Congress. "Policy for cash" schemes reverse this logic, with policy choices driven by the likely rents that will accrue to policy makers. Examples include both the budget "dwarves" scandal of 1993–94 (Krieger, Rodrigues, and Bonassa 1994) and the *sanguessuga* ("bloodsucker") scandal, in which decisions about budget allocation were taken with an eye to private gains. In all of these cases, the supposed emphasis of policy on achieving the "public good" was subverted.

The third arena, rule implementation and rule adjudication, permits a variety of potential forms of corruption, ranging from the sale of administrative or judicial decisions to the misuse of privileged information. Rule implementation may be keyed to specific individuals either punitively *(para meus inimigos a lei)* or beneficially (for example, privileges extended to influential businesspeople). Rule adjudication may likewise be lopsided, as in the elaborate scheme for the sale of judicial decisions uncovered in Operação Anaconda. Examples of last-minute "flexibility" in the implementation of rules range from the high-profile scandals mentioned here to more quotidian corruption within administrative bureaucracies such as the social security agency (INSS) or motor vehicle bureaus, both of which have been the subject of repeated scandals in the past decade.

In light of corruption's effects in these three arenas of the democratic regime, it is not surprising that corruption has emerged as a significant theme in recent scholarly work on Latin America (e.g., Rosenn and Downes 1999; Tulchin and Espach 2000; Blake and Morris 2009; Morris and Blake 2010; Morris 2009), as well as more broadly (e.g., Johnston 2005; Treisman 2007). There are many posited facilitators of corruption, including history, culture, levels of education, economic inequality, the size of government, and institutional design (for an overview of the cross-national literature, see Treisman 2007 and Morris and Blake 2009). Taken as a whole, they suggest that corruption will never be completely uprooted from any polity. But the degree to which corruption is perceived to be effectively and earnestly combated by the powers-that-be has valuable effects in curbing future abuses and enhancing trust in the political system.

Impunity has appropriately been labeled corruption's "brother" and, perhaps even more appropriately, "evil twin" (Morris 2009, 9). For if corruption is destructive of the trust that is needed for both markets and democracies to function smoothly, the pernicious inertia of revealed but unaddressed corruption may be doubly so. An absence of accountability means that corruption may be fleetingly exposed but its practitioners will remain in the game. As a result, exposed but unpunished political corruption will erode confidence in all politicians—whether corrupt or not—and perhaps even in the political system itself.

Accountability processes by which political corruption is uncovered, investigated, and punished are therefore crucial for at least three reasons. First, they may have a salutary effect in extracting corrupt practices and corrupt practitioners from public office, leading to the restoration of the "link between collective decision making and people's powers to influence collective decisions" (Warren 2004, 328). Removing these dirty players and practices may also, by the same process, lead to improvements in the efficiency, efficacy, and impartiality of public goods provision (Della Porta and Vannucci 1997).

Second, through effective punishment, accountability signals the potential costs of corrupt behavior and the efficacy of the state to "contingent consenters" who might otherwise be tempted to engage in corrupt activities themselves (Levi 1999). Effective punishment not only discourages future transgressions but may boost voluntary compliance with other formal and informal rules, since there will be less perceived gain from flaunting these rules.

Third, and as a result of the foregoing, accountability may help to restore public trust in political institutions and the policy process after malfeasance has been uncovered. Accountability allows citizens in a democracy to "discern representative from unrepresentative governments" and sanction them appropriately (Manin, Przeworski, and Stokes 1999, 10). More broadly, the full accountability process may set in motion corrective measures by helping to identify institutional flaws, as well as by building political consensus around reforms designed to prevent a recurrence of specific forms of corruption.

In sum, because political corruption "matters more" in democracies than in other political regimes, it follows that effective accountability matters more too.

The Web of Accountability Institutions in Brazil

The study of accountability and political corruption poses a great challenge to political scientists. For academics accustomed to inhabiting narrow institutional bailiwicks—the study of specific institutions such as Congress or the courts, or specific approaches such as the study of judicial or electoral behavior—the question of how to fight corruption requires a major readjustment of analytical perspective.

Rather than focusing on institutions in isolation, we are forced to switch to a wide-angle lens and a more broadly systemic approach. Successful accountability requires the cooperation of institutions across various branches of government, as well as the private sector and society more broadly. The vibrant academic debate engaged over the past decade about various adjectives associated with democratic accountability—for example, "vertical," "horizontal," "intrastate" and "social" accountability—both illuminates and obscures this complementarity.[7] For while these distinctions enable us to distinguish different types of relational hierarchies and distinct relations of answerability, a robust accountability process requires all actors to be both principals and agents, objects of oversight and overseers themselves. In sum, a comprehensive approach to accountability must encompass what has been variously termed the "web" of accountability institutions (Mainwaring 2003, 29–30) or "national integrity systems" (Pope 2000).

Because of the broad comparative pretensions of much contemporary research, the extant literature provides equally broad prescriptions for fighting corruption: "The prevailing approach stresses the need for economic reform, the strengthening of the protection of private property and the rule of law; the reduction of state regulations, the elimination of red tape and the downsizing and professionalizing of the bureaucracy; the broadening of press freedoms and electoral competition; and greater citizen involvement to apply the needed pressures for reform and to alter public tolerance of corruption" (Morris and Blake 2009, 9–10).

Such prescriptions often take the form of one-size-fits-all admonitions. As such, they ignore country-specific interactions and idiosyncrasies. A collaborative case study such as the present volume on Brazil allows us to delve more deeply into the multifaceted accountability process in all its complexity, without concern—at least initially—for the distractions and simplifications that might be posed by cross-national comparison. Our focus on a single nation also allows us to hold the analytically troublesome variable of culture largely constant.

There is a long tradition of explaining corruption in Brazil as the result of cultural traditions, whether it is the absence of a clear separation between public and private, as in Faoro's depiction of patrimonialism (Faoro [1958] 1996; see also Domingues 2008; Fernandes 1975; Roett 1999); Sergio Buarque de Holanda's ([1936] 1971) discussion of the transplanted Iberian traditions of trust conditional on family networks; Da Matta's (1979) discussion of the figure of the *malandro;* or the frequent invocation of the *jeitinho* as a particularly Brazilian form of social adaptation.[8]

Indeed, there is undoubtedly some justification for appeals to culture in the Brazilian case. Recent research illustrates that Brazilian elites act in ways that reveal a cross-culturally high level of abuse of the perks of public office, even by Latin American standards: under equivalent enforcement conditions, for example, Brazilian diplomats outperformed all of the countries in the region in their abuse of diplomatic parking privileges in New York City (Fisman and Miguel 2006).[9] Recent survey research finds that informal practices such as the *jeitinho* are closely linked to tolerance for corruption more broadly (Almeida 2001, 2007, 2008)[10] and that "social acceptance of corruption influences citizens' perceptions of important aspects of democracy" in Brazil (Moisés 2009, 5). Others find evidence of "neopatrimonialism," by which the state and its civil servants have adopted patrimonial practices in a more modernizing guise that nonetheless benefits actors within the state at the expense of society more broadly (Schwartzman, cited in Domingues 2008).

These culturally oriented arguments are a wise reminder that institutions can never be analyzed out of context. Effective norms require some correspondence with popular beliefs if they are to stick (F. Reis 2008, 391–92), and government institutions do not operate in a vacuum: their rules and members draw on popular beliefs and values both for their normative bearings and to legitimate their decisions. But what we perceive as culture may also reflect beliefs about status. There is a saying in Brazil that each monkey has his branch *(Cada macaco em seu lugar):* in other words, a low-status person has no business meddling in the affairs of the elite. As Vieira (2008, 52) notes, that phrase has practical implications: those who are low on the totem pole may not feel they can exercise the social controls needed to impede the abuse of power. As a result, in a country long marked by tremendous social inequalities, perhaps we should not be surprised that the elite have historically allocated themselves special privileges, whether formally, through special standing for politicians in the legal system or separate jail cells for college graduates, or informally, through nepotistic hiring practices that blur the lines between private and public.

But throwing up our hands in the face of these phenomena and arguing that they are the outcome of an intractable "culture" seems overwrought, especially given recent improvements in overall structural conditions, and especially in light of democratization's important effects in ameliorating the lockhold of elites on power and in reducing economic inequality.[11] Perhaps as a result, as Carvalho (2008, 242) notes, rising education, declining poverty, and increased civic consciousness mean that Brazilian voters today are less dependent on government favors and more demanding of political reforms and accountability than ever before.

Further, while institutions are deeply embedded in society, and it is thus difficult to isolate the prevalence of corruption or the absence of accountability from the predominant culture, the opposite is also true: culture may well respond to shifting institutional performance. Moisés and

Carneiro (2008, 2; see also Moisés 2008) note that survey research around the world shows a close association between attitudes about the legitimacy of democracy and clusters of beliefs about the effectiveness of democratic institutions, as well as about satisfaction with regime performance. Brazil is no different; and although this may be troubling when we observe how low public confidence in many democratic institutions such as Congress has sunk, it also suggests that institutional improvements can contribute to improving attitudes about institutions and the democratic regime. Apathy, mistrust, and other traits of citizen involvement in politics are not static but may well respond to improvements in institutional operation. A virtuous cycle may be possible, whereby institutional gains translate into greater citizen involvement in accountability, greater accountability strengthens institutions, and this in turn increases diffuse societal trust, both in individuals and in institutions.[12]

In sum, we cannot ignore culture entirely, nor do we wish to do so. But in framing our analysis, we have chosen to focus primarily on the institutional component of accountability. We are helped in this regard by our decision to conduct a single-country study. In a country that has long been painted as sui generis because of its supposed cultural predisposition to various forms of informal and frequently corrupt behaviors, holding cultural factors constant may enable us to avoid needless simplification and elicit specific recommendations of direct relevance to policy makers.

Because Brazil has long been tagged as a nation where informal institutions play a significant role in the political game (e.g., Desposato 2006a; Geddes and Ribeiro Neto 1999; Roett 1999; Samuels 2006a), it also poses interesting theoretical questions of wider interest, complementing research on the role of informal institutions in Latin America (e.g., Fernandez-Kelly and Shefner 2006; Helmke and Levitsky 2006) and elsewhere around the world (e.g., Tsai 2006; Kitschelt and Wilkinson 2007). The definitional elasticity of corruption poses complex questions in the Brazilian case because of the presence of informal behaviors such as exchange politics and clientelism that are normatively troublesome but not necessarily illegal. For example, if a leading politician bargains vigorously with the federal government for funding to build an oversized airport in his home state, names it after his deceased son, and then locates it near an avenue that is named after himself, is this corrupt? Surely it qualifies as "misuse of public resources for private gain" (a common definition of corruption), and most observers would find this case—drawn from the real-life experience of the late Senator Antonio Carlos Magalhães of Bahia—to be highly questionable. But it is not technically illegal.

In this book we have thus walked a fine line. On the one hand, we analyze real cases of accountability only when *formally* illegal behavior—that is, corruption that breaks an existing law—is allegedly present. But we do not shy away from discussing related gray areas, in part because they are theoretically interesting and in part because of a suspicion that weak accountability for *formally* corrupt behavior carries over into tolerance for *informal* practices, such as clientelism, that may not be illegal but are questionable from a normative democratic perspective.

A second reason for a single-country study, alluded to earlier, is substantive. Brazil is the world's fourth-largest democracy, the fifth-largest country by population, and source of more than a third of Latin American regional GDP. As Brazilian democracy evolves past some of the simpler institutional threats of its early transition, political corruption increasingly appears to be one of the main hurdles to achieving the promise of a consolidated and robust democratic polity. Under these conditions, a sustained investigation of the accountability process at the federal level stands to offer important new knowledge about politics in a country that is one of the leading objects of comparative research.

Third, because our case study of Brazil is both intensive and extensive, we are able to develop the theme of *interdependence*. We focus especially on three aspects of interdependence: the interdependence of phases of the accountability process; the interdependence between institutions in the accountability system; and the interdependence of sanctions in the accountability system. Reflecting briefly on each for purposes of illustration:

- Consider the likelihood of an effective accountability process if the principal phases of the accountability process—oversight, investigation, and sanction—are out of sync. In the absence of competent oversight of potential wrongdoing, or if there is no effective investigation of red flags raised in regular audits, it is doubtful that corruption can be effectively targeted. Likewise, without effective punishment, oversight is unlikely to be robust, especially if the targets of monitoring efforts remain in a position to threaten those charged with overseeing them. And in the absence of effective oversight, the universe of cases investigated is likely to be highly contingent on chance and the appearance of the occasional whistle-blower.

- In terms of the interdependence between institutions, each institution in the accountability process relies heavily on the others to complete its work, whether this link is direct and formal (such as the relation between police and prosecutors) or indirect and informal (such as the link between media and prosecutors). Without independent media, for example, what are the chances of corruption coming to light and being effectively prosecuted? Without an efficient judicial process, will police investigators or prosecutors alone be able to effectively hold the line against corruption? Without effective audits, will congressional investigators be able to track corruption networks and effectively uproot them?

- Finally, in terms of the interdependence of sanctions, at least four types of overlapping sanctions may contribute to curbing political corruption:[13] electoral sanctions, such as failure to win reelection; political but nonelectoral sanctions, such as congressional censure or removal from office; reputational sanctions, such as negative media coverage; and legal sanctions, such as criminal or civil judgments. Once again, the various types of sanctions are interdependent. Can we really expect congressional representatives to stick their necks out and force their peers from office if these political sanctions do not result in later electoral or judicial punishments that permanently remove wrongdoers from the political game? Likewise, will auditing bodies or police investigators actively pursue corrupt political targets if there is little chance of these targets being removed from office?

With these issues of interdependence in mind, we pursue accountability here from the perspective of the full web of accountability institutions at the federal level. As figure 1.1 illustrates, even at its simplest—without taking into account specific component bureaucracies—the web of accountability is quite complex. (Note that our model here is highly stylized: the connections between the nodes are a goal, not necessarily a reality, as this volume makes abundantly clear.) Accountability institutions operate within each of the three branches of government, with further support from autonomous institutions such as the Ministério Público and the media.

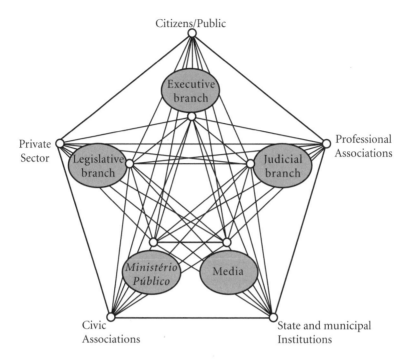

Figure 1.1. The Web of Accountability Institutions in Brazil

They are helped along by individual citizens, acting in diverse roles (e.g., as individual voters or as whistle-blowers). Private-sector businesses and state and municipal institutions clearly play roles as well, whether in denouncing corruption, creating codes of ethics for their operations, or pressuring federal agencies for resolution of specific issues. Nongovernmental civic associations and watchdog groups with an interest in corruption have also proliferated over the past two decades, with groups such as Transparência Brasil, Congresso em Foco, and Movimento Voto Consciente compiling, analyzing, and publicizing information about politicians and corruption. Meanwhile, professional associations such as the bar association (Ordem dos Advogados do Brasil, OAB) and the national association of judges (Associação dos Magistrados Brasileiros, AMB) have spearheaded public awareness campaigns, as well as leading public campaigns for reform.

The interdependence of institutions, accountability processes, and sanctions in the web of accountability is shaped by four important dimensions of each individual institution listed in table 1.3.

Three broad issues raised by the table are apparent in the contributions to this volume. First, the degree of institutional autonomy is important because accusations of corruption so often can be used as a political tool. Some institutions (e.g., the Federal Police, which is subordinate to the executive branch) are much more highly susceptible to politicization in this regard, so even when they are acting on the best of intentions, their motives can be easily questioned. But autonomy also plays an important role in determining how far individual members of each accountability institution can and will go in pursuing potential targets, since one common way of restricting autonomy is by threatening individual bureaucrats' career prospects.

Second, our framework stresses the importance of proximate institutions—those with which any given institution is required to interact regularly. One question raised by many of the contributors to this volume is to what extent Brazilian institutions of accountability are competing, overlapping, and noncooperative. Some degree of institutional friction is a sine qua non of interaction between bureaucracies, of course. But in a relatively young democracy, such conflict may be particularly apparent and unresolved, with potential drawbacks for the accountability process. Further, as several scholars have noted, the strength of formal institutions may be inversely related to support for governments perceived to be corrupt (Manzetti and Wilson 2008; Stokes 2005). In other words, practices such as clientelism may garner electoral support if formal institutions are weak. The concept of proximate institutions expands this perspective, illustrating that even if formal institutions are strong, friction between them may contribute to a weak overall institutional framework; as a result, even individually strong institutions—if they are embedded in a weak overall accountability system—may coexist with public tolerance and support for corrupt behaviors.

Third, both figure 1.1 and table 1.3 point to a central pitfall of trying to evaluate accountability solely in terms of principal-agent relationships: given the multiplicity and overlapping nature of such relationships—which include interdependent phases of accountability, interdependent institutions, and interdependent sanctioning processes—any attempt to

Table 1.3. Key Dimensions of Institutions within the Web of Accountability

Dimension	Definition
Scope	The responsibilities attributed to an institution and the effect these have on the institution's reach. Some institutions may have broad mandates (e.g., the media), while others have very narrow mandates (e.g., audit institutions). Some institutions may focus largely on the political class (e.g., congressional boards of inquiry), while others have a broader remit (e.g., federal courts). Scope is therefore an important consideration in terms of the possibilities for effective action by any single institution.
Autonomy	An institution's ability to choose what cases to address and how to prioritize its efforts, as well as its ability to act without undue concern for the reactions of other institutions. Some institutions may be able to act with considerable autonomy (e.g., the Ministério Público), while others are hierarchically subordinate (e.g., the Federal Police to the executive).[a]
Proximate institutions	Institutions with which a given institution must closely and frequently interact. Some institutions in the web of accountability have no proximate institutions: the media, for example. Others are greatly constrained by their relation with proximate institutions: the Federal Police cannot prosecute crimes directly in the courts, for example, but instead relies on the Ministério Público to carry its cases forward.
Activation	Whether an institution can act proactively or whether it instead reacts directly to others. Audit institutions, for example, may proactively determine what institutions should be audited, just as the Federal Police can proactively determine what cases to investigate. Courts, on the other hand, tend to be reactive, requiring activation by an external actor before they can take on particular cases.

[a] Even for nominally autonomous institutions, however, autonomy is of course a relative concept: a formally independent institution such as the Supreme Court may well restrain itself and act cautiously to avoid triggering a hostile reaction from other institutions or the broader public.

reduce the interactions to simple dyadic relationships may ignore significant complexity.[14]

Even more institutions are involved in the accountability process at the federal level than figure 1.1 can illustrate. Within the executive branch alone, a host of institutions can potentially play a role in the accountability process. There are advisory boards, such as the Public Ethics Committee (Comissão de Ética Pública), which directly advises the president and his staff. The Federal Police have played an increasingly important role as a major investigative body in recent years, helping to disrupt nests of organized crime and corruption. The Central Bank and the Federal Revenue Service perform an important oversight role in tracking financial flows, aided by cross-bureaucracy working groups such as the Council for the Oversight of Financial Activities (COAF). Lawyers in various bureaucracies such as the Revenue Service, the social security bureaucracy, the Advocacia Geral da União (AGU), and the Justice Ministry share duties in pursuing corruption investigations.[15] And the Controladoria Geral da Uniao (CGU) has been an important oversight and auditing body since its creation in 2001. Although the CGU has tended to focus its efforts primarily at the state and municipal level, often its investigations lead back to the federal level, as in the 2006 *sanguessuga* scandal, when national congressmen were found to be receiving kickbacks in transactions that were being audited at the municipal level.[16] Most of these executive bureaucracies are by design not very autonomous of political pressures, are fairly reactive, and tend to have a narrow scope of action. Also by design, all rely on proximate institutions to carry forward any corruption investigation, especially if it involves prosecution in the courts, in which case the Ministério Público must perforce be involved.

The legislative branch also contains a number of overlapping bodies, in addition to the elected representatives themselves. Each house of Congress has its own permanent ethics committee, and with approval of a third of their members both the Senate and the Chamber of Deputies can create an ad hoc investigatory committee, known as a *comissão parlamentar de inquérito* (congressional committee of inquiry; CPI).[17] These CPIs have been one of the most active components of the overall accountability process at the federal level, bringing to light a great number of accusations of political corruption and murky dealings. Also tied to the Congress, but somewhat autonomous from the day-to-day politics of legislators, is the

Federal Accounting Tribunal (Tribunal de Contas da União, TCU), an accounting body that has played an important role in monitoring spending at the federal level.

Congressional accountability institutions are a mixed bag with regard to the four dimensions of scope, autonomy, proximate institutions, and activation. The TCU, for example, is proactive, but its scope is restricted by strictly regimented audit procedures. Further, the TCU has historically had little practical autonomy from politicians and relies heavily on proximate institutions to carry forward any investigation. Congressional investigations by CPIs, on the other hand, have almost unrestricted scope and can theoretically occur autonomously, although the executive branch's strong influence over legislative majorities has restricted their effectiveness considerably. Further, given the inherently political nature of CPIs, their results seldom are of great consequence in terms of imposing legal sanctions against wrongdoers.

One of the most unusual accountability institutions in Brazil is the Ministério Público. Under the 1988 Constitution, this prosecutorial body is formally independent of the other three branches of government, with guaranteed budgets and career incentives set with little outside interference. As a result of this almost complete autonomy, the federal Ministério Público has been called a "fourth" branch of government and has played a fundamental role in choosing cases to investigate and prosecute (Arantes, this volume; Arantes 2002; Kerche 2007; Mazzilli 1993; Sadek and Cavalcanti 2003; Sadek 2008). Although our focus here is largely on the federal Ministério Público, it is worth noting that all of Brazil's twenty-six states, as well as the Federal District, have their own state Ministérios Públicos, which also often play a significant role in prosecuting corruption. The autonomy of the federal Ministério Público (and many of its local counterparts) is remarkable, and the scope of its prosecutorial work is almost unlimited. But although it is not as reactive institutionally as the judiciary, the small size of the federal Ministério Público has somewhat restricted its role, while its reliance on proximate institutions such as the Federal Police (for investigation) and the courts (for trials) has also limited its efficacy, as later chapters will demonstrate.

The federal judiciary and the electoral courts are the recipients of much of the Ministério Público's effort. Within the federal judiciary, most cases begin at the level of the federal trial courts and then work their way up through the regional federal courts (TRFs) to the Superior Justice Tribunal (STJ) and the Supreme Federal Tribunal (STF).[18] In the electoral courts, likewise, there are local level courts, regional electoral courts (TREs), and the Superior Electoral Tribunal (TSE), which has played the greatest role in regulating federal politicians' behavior during campaigns and elections. Both court systems are quite autonomous from other branches of government: the Brazilian judiciary is one of a handful of Latin American court systems considered truly independent (Kapiszewski and Taylor 2008). It also has a broad mandate to intervene in a number of potential arenas. But like courts elsewhere, the Brazilian judiciary is largely reactive, and its effectiveness in the accountability process relies heavily on proximate institutions, and especially on the quality of cases forwarded to it by the Ministério Público, with contributions from antecedent institutions such as CPIs and the Federal Police.

Finally, of the five institutions at the center of figure 1.1, the Brazilian media have been one of the most effective forces in bringing some types of corruption to light: the *mensalão* scandal, for example, took off when disgruntled politicians in the government's congressional alliance tipped off the press to bribes collected in the Postal Service. A surveillance film of a bribe being paid to a political appointee in the Postal Service was aired on national television, fueling widespread public indignation. Despite their shortcomings, the multiplicity and dynamism of national media have allowed the press to play a crucial role in the federal accountability process, proactively investigating, triggering reactions by other accountability bodies, and serving as an important link to society more broadly. While not all media organizations are autonomous of political pressures, the pluralism of the national press is a useful antidote: the scope of media coverage is broad, and the media cooperate closely with both central institutions and civil society organizations (as depicted in figure 1.1).

The Book Ahead

In sum, Brazil's maturing democracy contains a variety of actors who play a dynamic role in monitoring, investigating, and punishing political corruption. Perhaps as a result, public awareness of corruption has probably never been greater, which is both a reason for celebration and a cause for concern. Celebration, because it offers the opportunity for potentially meaningful reform. Concern, because there may well be a limit to citizens' patience with political corruption and impunity, and because comparative research on Latin America shows that experience with corruption effectively undermines the legitimacy of democratic institutions (Seligson 2006). With these limits in mind, this collection considers the performance of the Brazilian federal accountability system with an eye to (1) diagnosing the system's strengths, weaknesses, and areas of potential improvement; (2) taking stock of recent micro- and macro-level reforms; and (3) pointing toward the implications of the various dimensions of the accountability process for Brazil's young democracy.

The book is divided into two sections with different foci and approaches. The first three chapters investigate the complex relationships among representative institutions, electoral dynamics, and public opinion. Because of their concern with the interaction between voters and politicians, these chapters adopt an approach much more closely focused on individual actors than the second section, which is broadly institutional in approach. The five chapters in the second section focus largely on nonelectoral dimensions of accountability: the media, accounting institutions, police, prosecutors, and courts.

The rather banal corruption at the heart of the rather shocking *mensalão* scandal was hardly a rarity in Brazilian democratic politics, as table 1.1 makes abundantly clear. In chapter 2, Carlos Pereira, Timothy Power, and Eric Raile dissect the sensational *mensalão*, which absorbed the attentions of President Lula's administration between 2004 and 2005 and briefly seemed to threaten Lula's chances of reelection, as a case study of "cash for policy" political corruption. As they point out, a number of factors may have contributed to the government's need to provide its allies side payments (or "allowances"; hence the name *mensalão*) in order to keep its coalition together and govern effectively. Among these were institutional factors, such as the unique patterns of executive-branch dominance of legislative coalitions that have evolved in Brazilian democracy. Also present were contingent factors, such as the ideological distance between the incumbent Workers' Party (PT) and its coalition partners and the PT's insistence on filling many ministerial slots with its own members. But perhaps the most intriguing findings here refer to the broader lessons that can be drawn from this specific scandal. The configuration of political institutions is a contributing but not a determining factor: other Brazilian presidents have operated in the same basic matrix of coalitional presidentialism without resorting to side payments. Leadership and strategic bargaining also matter, as does the transparency of transactions between coalitional partners.

But once corrupt behavior has been uncovered, what repercussions do allegedly corrupt politicians face? In chapter 3, Lucio Rennó points to the extraordinary difficulty of imposing electoral accountability for political corruption. Through a study of voters' responses to the *mensalão* in the 2006 presidential elections, Rennó shows that corruption can influence voters' decisions but does so in highly uncertain and contingent ways. The multidimensionality of retrospective voting means that corruption is not the only factor voters weigh in voting decisions, and while scandal increases ambivalence toward candidates, such uncertainty may be balanced out by other issues, as well as by long-term ideological leanings.

Brazil's double-ballot majoritarian presidential election system, however, provides voters with an additional means of illustrating their displeasure and castigating presidential candidates: by voting punitively in the first round while reserving the right to vote strategically in the second. Using individual voting data, Rennó shows that the *mensalão* scandal indeed had an effect on the presidential election, but largely because left-of-center voters had two chances to voice their opinion: first, by voting their displeasure over the scandal and denying Lula a first-round victory; but second, by voting strategically to avoid a less desirable alternative, the election of a center-right candidate. Voters were thus able to send a message and punish the incumbent in the first round without defying their aggregate ideological preference in the second.

In chapter 4, Pereira, Rennó, and David Samuels similarly ponder the effectiveness of "vertical" or "electoral" accountability in a political system that has long been marked by tolerance for corruption at both the mass and the elite levels, but they focus specifically on congressional elections. Survey research (e.g., Almeida 2007) suggests that "delegative" voters among the Brazilian public may tolerate corruption because they believe politicians' purpose is to resolve citizens' individual problems, in personalistic or clientelistic ways. But the authors point to a puzzle posed by the 2003–6 legislature: federal deputies involved in scandal had a lower probability of running for reelection, as well as lower chances of winning reelection when they ran. Although impunity sometimes prevailed in the congressional arena (a number of deputies were absolved by their peers), it did not reign in the electoral arena.

What causal mechanisms are at work here? The authors go beyond voting behavior alone, testing hypotheses about the interactions between electoral institutions and two other components in the web of accountability: business elites and the media. To what extent is electoral accountability enhanced by elite mechanisms, such as punishment via the withholding of campaign funds? And to what extent are such punishments reinforced at the mass level by media exposure? The authors' conclusions suggest a variety of dimensions of electoral accountability that go far beyond individual voting behavior alone.

The second section of the book, on nonelectoral institutions of accountability, kicks off with a look at an institution that appears at the crossroads of many, if not most, institutional interactions in the web of accountability: the media. As Mauro Porto notes in chapter 5, the media serve as a central clearinghouse between governmental institutions, helping to build complex narratives from fragmentary shards of evidence emerging in the public sphere. By providing visibility to issues, claims, and individuals, and by focusing public attention on certain events, the media have become a central institution in the accountability system.

Yet despite an increase in the number of exposés of political corruption over the past generation, the media's role within the accountability system is ambiguous. News organizations are not well designed to cover all types of corruption, and they tend to assign priority to sensational scandals while ignoring less dramatic but equally pernicious forms of corruption. More importantly, the media have grown increasingly professional, autonomous, and assertive, but government institutions increasingly recognize the media's importance and have shaped their actions and institutional strategies accordingly. The media themselves now rely heavily on government institutions for stories, leading the press to lean on the crutch of "journalism about investigations," rather than engaging in the far more demanding task of "investigative journalism." As a result, despite vital improvements in media independence over the past generation, Porto argues, there is a significant risk that corruption coverage will be politicized, manipulated, or incomplete.

Accounting is a dreary profession, and accounting institutions are perhaps as a result understudied. But as Bruno Speck illustrates dynamically in chapter 6, they are vital players in retrospectively holding public officials responsible for misconduct, as well as in prospectively driving public administration reforms. After developing a broadly applicable general framework for understanding the autonomy and various roles of audit institutions, Speck uses it to evaluate the strengths and weaknesses of Brazil's most important government accounting agency, the TCU.

Speck finds that in comparison with many of its peers in the rest of Latin America the TCU is institutionally quite strong and its audits are technically quite rigorous. However, he also finds flaws, highlighting the politicization of top leadership posts, the TCU's inability to impose sanctions without the active engagement of its peer institutions, and the TCU's resulting reliance on weaker types of sanction that require little cooperation with peer institutions. The result of this interaction with the TCU's proximate institutions is that despite the TCU's laudable role in monitoring and investigating allegations and in proposing reforms, its effects on accountability in the political system as a whole are weaker than might be expected.

What explains the apparent legal impunity of politicians charged in political scandals? In chapter 7, Matthew Taylor points to two central weaknesses of the court system. First, the electoral courts that oversee campaigns and elections are in many ways an elaborate fiction, by which political parties agree to turn a blind eye to each other's worst lapses. Second, the difficulty in holding corrupt politicians accountable is a direct result of the federal judiciary's broader institutional deficiencies: the system is delay ridden and formalistic, and it provides special protections to public officials. Yet—and in this regard Brazil is to some extent idiosyncratic—the problem is not usually the willful breaching of the law by judges or prosecutors. Instead, it is precisely the strong adherence to law and procedure as they appear on the books that weakens accountability by binding judges to stringent and often unhelpful legislation.

Courts have a direct effect in providing legal sanctions, but they also have indirect effects in strengthening the likelihood of the imposition of sanctions elsewhere in the political system. As a result, Taylor argues, even if it were possible to approve an ideal political-electoral reform that unambiguously improved accountability between citizens and their representatives, in the absence of changes in the judicial-legal framework the pursuit of probity would likely continue to be undermined by the weakness of the punishments forthcoming from judicial institutions.

Two other accountability institutions have been dramatically reshaped over the past generation in Brazil: the Ministério Público and the Federal Police. As Rogério Arantes describes in chapter 8, the Ministério Público, Brazil's prosecutorial body, has been charged with defending broad societal interests and has gained such autonomy from the other branches of government under the 1988 Constitution that it has become a "fourth branch" of government. More recently, the Federal Police has become an increasingly active and potent force in investigating and rooting out corruption in the public arena, both at the federal level and, increasingly, at the state level.

As Arantes notes, the Ministério Público and the Federal Police are increasingly working with each other and the judiciary in a triangular fashion to impose accountability. But there are procedural choices involved in any strategy to reduce corruption, and the tactical choices between political, civil, and criminal proceedings can often lead to different types of accountability, ranging from public "reputational" shaming to the disruption of criminal networks, and from civil punishments such as fines to criminal jail sentences. Prosecutors and police are forced to make a tough choice between tactics on the basis of their perceived effectiveness and the probability that they will actually have some effect on corrupt players. Further, while there has been considerable improvement in the triangular game between the Ministério Público, the Federal Police, and the courts, their cooperation is nonetheless marked by ongoing tensions and rivalry.

So far, the analyses have focused primarily on the federal government, and rightly so, as this is the focus of the volume. Fiona Macaulay, however, points to one shortcoming of this approach in Brazil's decentralized federal system. As she emphasizes in chapter 9, although federal agencies are playing an increasingly active role in fighting political corruption at all levels of the federation, much of the effort is still carried out by state police, state prosecutors, and state courts.

Because these institutions are largely autonomous of their federal counterparts and respond to local political contexts, they introduce a wild card into the accountability process. They play an essential role at the federal level, and not always for the better: perhaps most important, they may introduce state-level "networks of influence and corruption" into already complicated federal accountability processes and further complicate interinstitutional coordination and cooperation. Macaulay's chapter is an important reminder that the complex web of accountability extends beyond the federal government, and indeed, that many corrupt acts originate much further down, whence they often rise by tortuous paths to the three branches of the federal government.

Our final chapter aims to tie the diverse strands together, producing two sets of conclusions. In the first, we contemplate the policy implications of our study, considering more closely recommendations that may contribute to the effective fight against political corruption and for ongoing accountability in Latin America's largest democracy. In the second, we draw analytical lessons that will be of special interest to social scientists interested in the functioning of accountability networks, pointing as well to some of the comparative implications that emerge from this comprehensive study of the Brazilian federal case.

Notes

1. Accountability has many meanings and many ends. At its broadest, accountability simply "implies that some actors have the right to hold other actors to a set of standards" (Grant and Keohane 2005, 29), such as the efficiency or efficacy of public policies. Given this volume's interest in unlawful *political* corruption, the standard we employ is accountability to ensure the probity and public-regarding nature of policy and the policy-making process. We recognize, however, that there may be tensions between the various criteria of accountability, including between criteria of probity, efficacy, and efficiency.

2. Given the size of the Brazilian economy, these estimates are staggering in absolute terms. To give some regional perspective, in 2007 the GDP of Ecuador was equivalent to 3.5% of the Brazilian economy; the Dominican Republic, 3.1%; Guatemala, 2.6%; and Costa Rica, 2.0%. If the conservative estimate by the Federação das Industrias do Estado de Sao Paulo (FIESP) is correct, this would imply that Brazilian corruption amounts "only" to the GDP of Panama (1.5% of the Brazilian GDP) (International Monetary Fund 2008).

3. Transparency International's index has been criticized on a number of fronts, including the fact that it ignores whether a country is democratic, so that countries like Qatar, Taiwan, and the UAE do better than Brazil, Mexico, or Argentina on the index; it does not take into account historical context or evolution over time; and, from a purely methodological perspective, it is very imprecise, with large confidence intervals around the estimates, and estimates that are strongly correlated to GDP per capita. For these and other critiques, see Abramo (2006) and Avritzer (2008).

4. The year 2004 was the last that the Global Corruption Barometer included Brazil in its survey group.

5. Indeed, as Montinola and Jackman (2002, 169) point out, "Countries like Argentina, Brazil and Peru . . . adopted neoliberal economic reforms, including reductions in government expenditures, and encountered apparent increases in corruption" (see also Manzetti and Blake 1996; Weyland 1998). It is worth emphasizing that the economic role of the Brazil state shifted in the 1990s through privatization and stabilization, so that the state is no longer as involved in day-to-day business decisions regarding telephony or electricity distribution. But contrary to the common assertion, the state did not shrink: on the contrary, the total tax take by all levels of government rose from under 25% of GDP in 1991 to over 37% in 2008.

6. For a discussion of the relationship between inflation and public ethics with great relevance to the Brazilian case, see Giannetti (1993).

7. A particularly useful and comprehensive discussion of accountability that addresses its many dimensions and tensions can be found in the first four chapters of Mainwaring and Welna (2003); see also Przeworski, Stokes, and Manin (1999) on electoral accountability and Schedler, Diamond, and Plattner (1999) for a mixed approach. In addition to focusing on *both* electoral and nonelectoral dimensions of accountability, our use of the term here differs from Mainwaring's definition in that we focus not only on formal accountability relations but also on broader informal controls by actors that do not necessarily have a *formalized* relationship of "oversight and/or sanction relative to public officials" (Mainwaring 2003, 7). Our conceptualization further incorporates actors from the media and civil society organizations that Mainwaring would prefer to exclude (although the Mainwaring and Welna volume does include a useful synopsis of Smulovitz and Peruzzotti's arguments regarding "social accountability"; see also Smulovitz and Peruzzotti 2006). While pursuing this broader conceptualization of accountability may blur definitional boundaries, it is necessary if we are to accurately portray the Brazilian accountability process. Indeed, as later chapters will illustrate, because formal controls are often quite weak, accountability in Brazil frequently relies on nonformal accountability relations, as well as informal "reputational" sanctions.

8. A *malandro* can be defined as a charming but streetwise rogue; at its core the concept reflects the notion of a person who goes around formal rules to get things done, often winking at the law in the process. Keith Rosenn defines the *jeito* (*jeitinho* is the diminutive form) as "the practice of bending legal rules to expediency." As he notes, the existence of the *jeito* "enables a society to continue individualistic, traditional patterns of behavior despite the state's attempt to substitute more progressive, achievement-oriented patterns of behavior via the formal legal structure" (1984, 43).

9. There were 29.9 violations for each Brazilian diplomat, by comparison with 16.5 per Chilean, 4.0 per Mexican, and 3.9 per Argentine.

10. But see the forceful critique in Vieira (2008).

11. The Gini coefficient for Brazil hit a high of 0.64 in 1989 but has declined continuously since 1993, reaching 0.548 in 2008. Data accessed at "IPEA Data: Renda—Desigualdade—Índice de Gini," www.ipeadata.gov.br, under "Social," "Temas," "Renda," and then, in the list "Series," "Desigualdade—Índice de Gini," July 11, 2009.

12. As Philp states the ideal, "One way of characterizing integrity-based systems is to say that they are ones in which we trust those holding public office. . . . Without trust we would be demanding strict compliance, not accountability. Indeed, the key issue is not whether we trust a particular individual (binary trust) but whether there are high levels of diffuse institutional trust, so that we trust the individual because we trust the institutional framework, not the other way around" (41).

13. Discussion of various types of sanctions can be found in Taylor and Buranelli (2007) and Grant and Keohane (2005).

14. See Philp (2009) for a critique of the principal-agent approach to accountability.

15. The Justice Ministry, however, has traditionally had the greatest role in setting legal policy within the executive, coordinating investigations across bureaucracies and choosing reform priorities.

16. There are more than 5,500 municipal jurisdictions in Brazil, and the legal status of municipalities is constitutionally recognized.

17. Joint CPIs are also a possibility, with approval from one-third of the members of both houses.

18. As later chapters will illustrate, however, many politicians' cases jump the queue and are heard directly at the STF. Taylor's chapter in this volume explains that the STF and STJ are not formally a part of the federal judiciary, although for our purposes we can bundle them under this term, since these courts sit at the apex of the judicial system.

PART ONE

Representative Institutions, Electoral Accountability, and Public Opinion

Chapter Two

Presidentialism, Coalitions, and Accountability

CARLOS PEREIRA, TIMOTHY J. POWER, & ERIC D. RAILE

He seemingly had everything going for him. He had handily won the presidency of the largest country in Latin America, despite a history of radical views that had compromised his four previous unsuccessful campaigns. He had assumed an office that vested in him extraordinary constitutional powers. Even the financial markets had decided that he was a palatable choice, again despite a profile that seemed to conflict with the fiscal austerity programs required by international donors. He had rapidly received the support of eight political parties in Congress and had just earned the backing of a large majority in the lower house. To top it all off, he was wildly popular with the general public. Why, then, did the administration of President Luiz Inácio Lula da Silva resort to illegal side payments in order to generate legislative support? If anything, legislators should have been paying *him* for the privilege of hanging from his coattails. To explain this puzzle, we argue that governmental bargaining conditions and suboptimal bargaining strategies were the primary causes of the *mensalão* bribery scheme that took place in Brazil from early 2004 through May 2005.[1]

Our argument emphasizes both institutional constraints and the relative autonomy of presidential leadership. A substantial literature has identified numerous linkages between characteristics of political institutions and public corruption. This literature has generally proposed and found that presidentialism (Panizza 2001; Gerring and Thacker 2004; Kunicová and Rose-Ackerman 2005; Lederman, Loayza, and Soares 2005), federalism (Treisman 2000; Panizza 2001; Gerring and Thacker 2004; Kunicová and

Rose-Ackerman 2005), and proportional representation electoral systems (Persson, Tabellini, and Trebbi 2003; Kunicová and Rose-Ackerman 2005) are associated with greater levels of perceived corruption, though Treisman's (2007) review of the literature raises some questions about whether these institutions have an impact on the *actual frequency* of corrupt activities. This literature has not yet investigated in much detail how such institutions work in conjunction with one another or how combinations of institutions structure the intragovernmental bargaining game—questions difficult to answer with aggregated cross-national data.

Brazil is one of four countries in Latin America to possess all three of these institutional characteristics (i.e., presidentialism, federalism, and a proportional representation electoral system for the national legislature),[2] and over time Brazil has refined a model of *coalitional presidentialism* to compensate for the fragmenting effects of this constitutional environment (Power 2010). Though important differences also exist, coalitional presidents often must behave similarly to European prime ministers in multiparty systems to achieve long-term success. Simply put, these presidents need to put together broad-based coalitions in order to pass legislation on an ongoing and legitimate basis. We contribute to the literature linking corruption and political institutions by highlighting the coalitional dimension of Brazilian governance and by examining the earlier-mentioned issues of bargaining conditions and strategies.

Briefly summarized, our argument is that political corruption occurs when official intragovernmental bargaining resources fall short of overcoming the difficulties in the bargaining environment. In the case of the Brazilian *mensalão,* the bargaining environment was extremely complex because of (1) the bargaining constraints imposed by the particular configuration of Brazilian political institutions, with its tense combination of strong centralizing and decentralizing forces; and (2) the particular bargaining context facing Lula, including the distribution of legislative preferences, the policy agenda, and the historical trajectory of Lula and his Workers' Party (PT). Lula's party had spent more than two decades as firmly entrenched government outsiders. When their time to govern arrived, some on-the-job learning was unavoidable. While Lula also commanded tremendous official resources to deal with these complications, the strategic choices made by Lula's administration reduced the effectiveness of these resources. Ultimately, corruption filled the gap when the misused official resources fell short of meeting the challenges posed by a very difficult bargaining environment.

This chapter proceeds as follows. We begin by offering some basic information about the *mensalão* scandal. We then examine the structure of the executive-legislative political game under the Brazilian variant of coalitional presidentialism, as well as the strategic options for the executive, the lead player in this game. Next, we offer a brief history of coalition management in Brazil before turning to the contextual issues facing Lula beginning in 2003. Subsequently, we examine Lula's strategic choices both in his first year of governance (2003) and in the period of the *mensalão* (early 2004 to mid-2005). Our examination supports the assertion that choices in the management of interparty coalitions were strong contributors to the *mensalão* scandal. We conclude by discussing the ramifications for our understanding of corruption and accountability in Brazil.

The *Mensalão* Scandal

For reasons of space, we will not go into the details of the several intersecting investigations in 2004–5 (mostly centered on the Postal Service and the regulation of gambling) that led to the uncovering of the *mensalão* affair. Suffice it to say that mounting political pressures on one of the congressmen implicated in the Postal Service inquiry led him to make an explosive announcement that changed the political game altogether. On June 6, 2005, federal deputy Roberto Jefferson of the Brazilian Labor Party (PTB) revealed a scheme in which aides to President Lula used illegal side payments to win votes in Congress. Within days, the legislature had established two parallel investigatory committees that made further spectacular revelations. Members of these *comissões parlamentares de inquérito* (CPIs) were designated according to long-standing conventions of proportional representation, and thus allies of Lula dominated the committees. This, however, made no difference to the outcome once financial evidence began to roll in and prominent witnesses took the stand, some with detailed confessions and some armed with impressive paper trails. Investigators linked payments of specific amounts to individual legislators and their staffers, and these payments were clearly synchronized with important legislative roll-call votes over the previous two years. The political consequences were immediate and, for some, dire. In late 2005, Congress expelled Jefferson and José Dirceu, the former chief of staff to Lula. These two also lost their political rights for eight years. Several other legislators resigned their seats preemptively to avoid the same fate.

On April 5, 2006, a special joint congressional committee released its final report in which it named eighteen deputies (and one former deputy) who had received *mensalão* payments. The committee, with Sen. Delcídio Amaral of Lula's own party (the PT) as chairperson and with respected attorney Dep. Osmar Serraglio of the Brazilian Democratic Movement Party (PMDB, the largest party in Lula's support coalition) as rapporteur, won praise for its impartiality and for the detail of its report. The committee declared bluntly that the *mensalão* was a form of vote buying in Congress operated by aides to the president, but the committee spared President Lula from direct responsibility for the affair. The committee approved the report by a 17-4 vote and referred it to the congressional leadership. Subsequently, the full Chamber of Deputies absolved some of the accused, each of whom received a separate secret vote.

Parallel to the internal congressional investigations, the former federal public prosecutor (Procurador Geral da República), Antônio Fernando de Souza, launched an independent criminal investigation. In March 2006, Souza asked the Supreme Court to open criminal proceedings against forty individuals linked to the *mensalão* affair, including some who had already been judged by their political peers. Roberto Jefferson, for example, was formally accused of money laundering, even two years after being expelled from the Chamber of Deputies. José Dirceu, along with former PT president José Genoino and party treasurer Delúbio Soares, were accused both of racketeering and of intent to corrupt others *(corrupção ativa)*. All in all, Souza's brief identified a so-called "Gang of Forty," including four senior PT officials, ten federal deputies in the PT and allied parties, a dozen members of legislative staff, and several bank employees who had allegedly operated the *mensalão* scheme. Spectacularly, in August 2007 the Supreme Court (Supremo Tribunal Federal, STF) announced that it would approve all forty indictments and that each of the accused would have to stand trial in the STF.[3] According to STF judge Joaquim Barbosa, who is responsible for managing the *mensalão* case, the trial has moved relatively quickly because the STF has decided to decentralize the witness hearings via courts of first instance. Yet most verdicts are not expected before 2011.

We note that allies of Lula dominated the congressional investigatory committees; that the full Chamber of Deputies, controlled by progovernment forces, expelled key political aides to Lula based on the committee reports; and that Lula himself appointed the federal prosecutor, Souza, as well as six of the ten STF justices who approved the 2007 indictments.[4] This is to say nothing of the mountains of investigatory journalism that have accumulated since early 2005, all of which point strongly to the same conclusions. In fairness to President Lula, we note that the investigations uncovered evidence that the opposition Brazilian Social Democracy Party (PSDB) in the state of Minas Gerais had enlisted the same illegal financier (Marcos Valério de Souza) in the elections of 1998 and, moreover, that no official government process has implicated the president himself directly in the scandal. President Lula has been accused of sins of omission rather than sins of commission.

The objective of this chapter is not to demonstrate whether Lula did or did not have direct knowledge of the *mensalão* affair (an issue that is likely to remain unresolved) but rather to discuss the institutional and political variables that apparently led his administration to initiate the scheme of illegal side payments. Like astronomers studying a black hole, we cannot directly see our phenomenon of interest; we can only infer that it exists by constructing a theory that can be tested indirectly by marshalling various lateral bodies of evidence. Our theory relies on coalitional politics and presidential strategy. Our bodies of indirect evidence include cabinet representation, political ideology, and transfers of particularistic resources ("pork") between the executive branch and its backers. If the empirical implications of our theory "follow the money" and match up well with the conclusions reached by independent investigations, we gain confidence that we have correctly identified some of the important factors at work.

The Structure of the Political Game

The extensive institutional powers and resources of the Brazilian president add considerably to the "clarity of responsibility" (Powell 2000) for government actions, a crucial piece in the accountability relationship between government and the citizenry. However, from the executive's perspective the political game is not always so clear. The institutions that strongly centralize power in the office of the executive are counterbalanced by strong decentralizing forces. Certain Brazilian institutions disperse power and individualize incentives, thereby complicating the executive's job of generating legislative support through official channels—to the point that Brazilian presidents may sometimes feel like their job is not so different from herding cats.

Chief among these complicating features are Brazil's electoral institutions (Ames 1995a, 1995b), which detract from policy-making efficiency. Brazil uses an open-list proportional representation electoral system with virtually no effective national threshold for party representation in the legislature. These electoral institutions produce excessive party fragmentation. In fact, Brazil's multiparty political system is one of the most fragmented in the world (Mainwaring 1999). The party of the president has not held more than 25% of the lower house seats since 1990. Compounding the issue of fragmentation, party switching by legislators is a common occurrence in Brazil (Melo 2004; Desposato 2006b),[5] and coalition voting discipline is not particularly high (Amorim Neto 2002).

Open-list proportional representation systems also encourage voters to support candidates on the basis of personal qualities and activities (Mainwaring 1991; Ames 1995b). Consequently, individual legislators have incentives to cultivate direct relationships with local constituencies rather than doing so through national parties. This cultivation typically takes the form of personalistic politics and support for geographically oriented pork-barrel policies. The system also gives state parties (rather than national parties) influence in the selection of legislative candidates. In sum, the political party system makes building stable and reliable coalitions difficult (Samuels 2000) and prevents the executive from generating legislative support by assisting legislators with reelection efforts.

The federal structure of government and the existence of an independent judiciary also disperse power in ways relevant for bargaining outcomes. These institutions further increase the number of veto players in a country, meaning that the number of actors capable of blocking any particular policy initiative is larger. As the number of veto players increases, the ability of the executive to create policies directly reflective of her personal preferences tends to decrease (Tsebelis 2002).

If this were the end of the story, the plight of the Brazilian executive in a highly decentralized system might seem bleak indeed. However, as

mentioned at the outset of this section, the Brazilian executive also benefits from various institutions that centralize power and resources. A number of studies have shown that variables internal to the decision-making
process (e.g., the rules by which the Congress operates, the degree of cabinet proportionality) and the institutional legislative powers held by the
president (e.g., decree and veto powers, the right to introduce new legislation, permission to request urgency time limits on certain bills, and discretionary powers over budget appropriation) influence the behavior of
legislators in ways that promote governability (see A. Figueiredo and Limongi 2000; Amorim Neto 2002; Amorim Neto, Cox, and McCubbins
2003; Pereira and Mueller 2004; Alston and Mueller 2006). In addition to
these centralizing tendencies in government, the high degree of fragmentation in the legislature can also be positive in that the executive has many
potential partners and allies. Furthermore, the low degree of party loyalty
and discipline means that monetary benefits are likely to be persuasive for
a substantial number of legislators.

The upshot for the executive is that certain political institutions hinder
the executive in implementing her policy preferences, while other political
institutions increase her ability to do so. The former constitute bargaining
obstacles for the executive (or in some cases bargaining assets for legislators), and the latter constitute sources of bargaining leverage. The president
stands at the intersection of these centralizing and decentralizing institutions, charged with creating and maintaining a governing coalition in this
complicated and contradictory environment.

Strategic Governance Options

Standing as he does at this intersection, a Brazilian executive must develop
an integrated governing strategy that balances political transfers (i.e., cabinet posts, other patronage), monetary transfers (i.e., legal pork or illicit
payments), and concessions on policy preferences within the overall systemic constraints. Ideally, an executive will develop an integrated strategic
approach that minimizes total costs to utility. The strategy chosen will also
depend on the distribution of preferences and baseline support in the legislature, what types of policies the executive hopes to pass and implement,
and the president's popularity with the public. The executive can trade on

public popularity when bargaining with the legislature, though this technique is less effective in a regime like that of Brazil in which partisan identification is relatively weak and legislators are elected more on a personalistic basis. Such conditions limit the link between legislators and the president in the minds of the voters.

The distribution of political benefits itself is multifaceted, since the executive must determine the number of parties in the formal governing coalition, the ideological spread of those parties, and the proportionality of the seat distribution within the cabinet. Again, he does so within an overall system of constraints. These choices constitute the executive's "coalition management" approach, which we define as *the strategic manipulation of coalition characteristics over time to achieve legislative objectives.* Smaller and more ideologically homogeneous governing coalitions are easier to manage internally; however, a governing coalition with a smaller number of political parties, especially if these parties include a minority or a bare majority of legislators, can create substantial difficulties with getting legislation passed. Furthermore, excluding certain parties raises the risk of alienating those parties, and the appearance of an unfairly small governing coalition could otherwise generate ill will.

A cabinet constituted disproportionately of an executive's own partisans may also create external animosity, but the larger effect would be to disrupt relationships within the governing coalition. Commitment to the governing coalition generally carries with it an expectation that the political party will have access to cabinet posts, as well as the associated resources and policy-making capabilities. Ignoring such expectations can undermine support from within the governing coalition.

In addition to political transfers, the executive may also obtain legislative support using monetary benefits. The Brazilian executive has the authority to choose which individual pork requests (i.e., individual budgetary amendments) and which state-based pork requests will actually be executed and disbursed. Monetary benefits are particularly valuable in a political system like that of Brazil, in which ideological commitments tend to be weak and in which pork is a highly effective tool for getting reelected (Pereira and Rennó 2003).

Pork is not, however, a guaranteed means of generating legislative support. The relative bargaining leverage of the executive and the distribution of legislative seats are important considerations when executives design pork disbursement strategies, and these pork expenditures suffer from diminishing marginal returns in producing legislative support (Raile, Pereira, and Power 2011). Furthermore, political transfers (like cabinet seats) are relatively cheaper than pork under certain circumstances, such as when the executive needs the support of factions ideologically similar to his own party (Araujo, Pereira, and Raile 2008).

The number of moving parts here is daunting, but one should also consider the issue of what an executive intends to *do* with legislative support. All other things held constant, an executive can be less accommodating with noncontroversial and minor policy changes. The importance of particular legislative efforts to the executive is also relevant. The executive will be more disposed to give ground on policies over which she has weak preferences. Finally, the executive must consider nontraditional legislative options. The Brazilian president has substantial unilateral decree powers that can serve as a credible threat when he is bargaining with the legislature (Pereira, Power, and Rennó 2005, 2008). However, an executive must exercise care with these unilateral powers, since they too can generate animosity in the legislature.

A Brief History of Brazilian Coalition Management

In 1992, Brazilian President Fernando Collor de Mello became the first popularly elected president to be impeached and removed from office in all of Latin America. At first glance, the impeachment seemed like one more chapter in the traumatic story of Brazil's fledgling democratic institutions. However, this episode—complex and distressing as it was—illustrated how the Brazilian presidential system that emerged from the 1988 Constitution was flexible enough to allow adjustments under democratic rule. The democratically elected legislature, rather than the military using extra-constitutional means, decided to remove Collor from office on the basis of charges of corruption. From this perspective, the impeachment process supplied evidence that Brazilian democratic institutions could effectively check opportunistic behavior on the part of a very institutionally powerful and resource-laden executive.

Accusations and evidence of corruption against Brazilian presidents are not rare, so why was Collor impeached and removed from office but not others? Why was Collor unable to trade pork, local policies, and cabinet portfolios for his political survival? Prior to Lula's first year, the Collor government had been the only administration since redemocratization in which a president governed without a stable, multiparty, majority governing coalition supporting him within Congress. Collor preferred instead to build ad hoc coalitions, relying mostly on his high popularity and a strategy of "going public" to achieve majority support.

Collor (1990–92) had an initial governing coalition that consisted of only three political parties (Liberal Front Party [PFL], PMDB, and National Reconstruction Party [PRN]). Collor's coalition began with 245 seats, which was about 49% of the Chamber of Deputies at the time; this was clearly a minority coalition government. His coalition size quickly dropped to 144 seats by the end of the first year of his administration when the PMDB quit the cabinet and was replaced by the Democratic Social Party/ Progressive Reform Party (PDS/PPR). Collor's first cabinet straddled the center and right ideologically, but his second and third cabinets were the most homogeneous coalition governments of the democratic period, featuring exclusively right-wing parties. Further, his cabinets were extremely disproportional—the coalition parties apart from his own small party (PRN) were underrepresented within the cabinet. Similar to his previous cabinets, Collor's fourth and final minority cabinet (shown in table 2.1), which did not include his own party, was highly disproportionate (per the "coalescence" measure of Amorim Neto 2002) and awarded over half of the cabinet seats to nonpartisan ministers. He did not share power with parties that could support him in times of need. By 1992, when he was facing massive popular protests around the country without a credible and sustainable coalition in Congress, the cost of "buying" support had caught up with Collor. Partly as a consequence of this political choice, he was impeached and removed from office.

Fernando Henrique Cardoso (1995–2002), on the other hand, learned quickly that governing without a sustainable coalition in Congress would be too risky even with an impressive range of presidential powers and resources for trade with legislators. He initially included only four parties in his governing coalition (PSDB, PFL, PTB, and PMDB). However, Cardoso recruited two additional parties (the Brazilian Progressive Party [PPB] and the Socialist People's Party [PPS]) into his government in order to accelerate approval of his many proposed constitutional reforms, which required

Table 2.1. Cabinet Representation under Collor, Cardoso, and Lula

Party	Collor (Apr. 1992) Chamber Seats	Collor (Apr. 1992) Cabinet Posts	Cardoso (Apr. 1999) Chamber Seats	Cardoso (Apr. 1999) Cabinet Posts	Lula (Feb. 2003) Chamber Seats	Lula (Feb. 2003) Cabinet Posts	Lula (Feb. 2004) Chamber Seats	Lula (Feb. 2004) Cabinet Posts	Lula (Apr. 2007) Chamber Seats	Lula (Apr. 2007) Cabinet Posts
PC do B					11 (4%)	1 (3%)	9 (3%)	2 (6%)	13 (4%)	1 (3%)
PDS/PPR	44 (20%)									
PDT					16 (6%)	1 (3%)			23 (7%)	2 (6%)
PFL	88 (40%)	2 (18%)	107 (29%)	4 (20%)			43 (13%)	1 (3%)		
PL	17 (8%)	1 (9%)			34 (14%)	1 (3%)				
PMDB			100 (27%)	2 (10%)			78 (24%)	2 (6%)	90 (26%)	5 (15%)
PP/PPB			52 (14%)	2 (10%)					41 (12%)	1 (3%)
PPS			5 (1%)	1 (5%)	21 (8%)	1 (3%)	20 (6%)	1 (3%)		
PR									34 (10%)	1 (3%)
PRB									1 (1%)	
PSB	40 (18%)	1 (9%)			28 (11%)	1 (3%)	20 (6%)	1 (3%)	28 (8%)	2 (6%)
PSDB			101 (28%)	6 (30%)		1 (3%)		1 (3%)		1 (3%)
PT					91 (36%)	20 (59%)	91 (29%)	21 (58%)	83 (24%)	16 (46%)
PTB	31 (14%)	1 (9%)			44 (18%)	1 (3%)	52 (16%)	1 (3%)	21 (6%)	1 (3%)
PV					6 (2%)	1 (3%)	6 (2%)	1 (3%)	13 (4%)	1 (3%)
Ind.		6 (55%)		5 (25%)		6 (18%)		5 (14%)		4 (11%)
Totals	220	11	365	20	251	34	319	36	347	35
	Coalescence = 0.44		Coalescence = 0.69		Coalescence = 0.56		Coalescence = 0.51		Coalescence = 0.64	

Sources: primary sources for cabinet and Chamber data, Amorim Neto (2007), Amorim Neto and Coelho (2008), and O. Amaral (forthcoming).

Notes: The percentage accompanying "Chamber Seats" is the percentage of intracoalition seats held by a party within the Chamber of Deputies. Cabinet "coalescence" is Amorim Neto's (2002) measure scaled from 0 (perfectly disproportional mapping from Chamber seats to cabinet posts) to 1 (perfectly proportional). The total number of seats in the Chamber under Collor was 503; the figure under Cardoso and Lula was 513. Column totals for percentages may not be exactly 100% because of rounding. Data are for the fourth cabinet of Collor's term, the first postelection cabinet of Cardoso's second term, the first (2003) and second (2004) cabinets of Lula's first term, and the first postelection cabinet (2007) of Lula's second term.

supermajorities in both houses of Congress. The additions brought the coalition size up to 381 seats, or almost 75% of the Chamber of Deputies. Cardoso maintained a supermajority coalition even in his second term, as shown in table 2.1. Though large, the Cardoso coalition was not endangered by internal ideological differences. It was a focused center-right coalition in which the constituent parties shared considerable agreement about the president's agenda of constitutional reforms. A notable feature of the Cardoso coalition was the high level of coalescence of his cabinets.[6] Cardoso's coalition management choices were decisive elements in helping him sustain his majority coalition for almost eight years at a comparatively low cost.

The Specific Context for Lula's Game

As mentioned earlier, systemic institutional features are important for setting the bargaining parameters and stakes, but these broad features do not constitute the entire set of information relevant to the executive-legislative bargaining game. Certain features of the game facing any executive are contextual. One important contextual feature for Lula was the nature of his political party. The PT was a house divided. Born in 1979–80 as an unusual alliance of workers, intellectuals, and social movements, the PT had always had multiple factions or *tendências*. In 2002, the dominant faction was the Campo Majoritário, which itself was a merger of sorts between Lula's historic group known as the Articulação and its ally Democracia Radical, the two elements considered to represent the pragmatic wing of the party. However, several smaller factions such as Democracia Socialista, Força Socialista, and O Trabalho were on the left. Lula could not ignore the radicals, and he had to respect the party's tradition of reaching out to ideological minorities. In this sense, we emphasize that *the PT is utterly unlike any other party that has captured the Brazilian presidency in the past.* Most analysts have called attention to the role of ideological stretching *across* parties within the Lula coalition; we draw attention to the role of ideological diversity *within* the president's party. In sum, the PT is the only large Brazilian party in which internal ideological struggles actually matter, and this feature could not help but affect the approach to allocating executive power.

Another important piece of contextual information is that Lula's traditional leftist leanings put social welfare programs and policies squarely on the agenda. However, social programs are very costly, and U.S.-style deficit spending was not an option. As a consequence, Lula needed to find ways to cut other costs and/or to enhance government revenues. The clearest options for freeing up funds were reforms to the tax and pension systems— reforms that would create controversy and offend his core partisan supporters. Just as importantly, such reforms would require constitutional amendments, with the approval of a concomitant 60% majority in each house of Congress. A more fiscally conservative approach was also necessary to enhance Lula's credibility with external funding organizations and markets, as well as with a nontrivial portion of the electorate (Martínez and Santiso 2003; Spanakos and Rennó 2006). A record of leftist rhetoric raised questions about whether Lula would continue the fiscal austerity programs that had helped Brazil's economy grow. Satisfying these actors was essential to continued growth and prosperity, but it would require a delicate balancing act between fiscal conservatism and social leftism.

Yet another bargaining-relevant difficulty facing Lula was the distribution of ideological preferences within the legislature. The top panel of figure 2.1 shows the ideological positions of the parties and the number of seats each party held in the Chamber of Deputies in March 2003, shortly after Lula and the new deputies assumed office.[7] The ideological location of Lula's political party, PT, was rather distant from the ideological positions of the parties that held the bulk of the seats in the Chamber of Deputies (328 of 513 seats, as shown in the figure from PMDB rightward). While we have indicated Lula's position along with PT, this is not to say that his ideal point was equivalent to the average of his party.[8] Instead, this point was the natural departure point for bargaining. As a candidate in a nationwide election, Lula needed to appear more centrist and needed to obtain some support from the right side of the distribution in figure 2.1. As the figure shows, one of Lula's electoral alliance partners was the Liberal Party (PL), a party well to the right of PT. The inclusion of the PL in the 2002 campaign was the first sign that the president would build a disconnected coalition.[9]

The central point here is that bargaining with the legislature over controversial legislation would be expensive for Lula, given the initial gap between his party's ideology and the ideology of the strong majority of

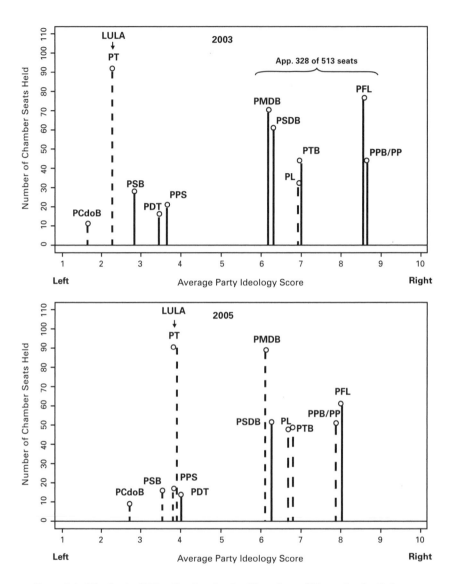

Figure 2.1. Ideological Distribution in the Chamber of Deputies for Lula

Notes: Average ideology scores are from surveys of legislators in 2001 (top panel) and 2005 (bottom). Seat figures in the top panel are averages for March 2003, the month after installation of the new legislature and two months after Lula's inauguration. Seat figures in the bottom panel are averages for March 2005. The seat figures are weighted for party switching. Some small parties are excluded. Dashed lines indicate Lula's electoral alliance (top) and Lula's legislative voting alliance (bottom).

Chamber members (even if we allow for some individual-member variance around each party's ideal point). Any policies at or near the executive's ideal point would create substantial disutility for many non-PT legislators. Lula's previous identity as a firm opponent of government would further serve to increase the price of bargaining.

Lula's Strategic Decisions

This section examines Lula's strategic decision making, especially with regard to coalition management in his first year as president and during the period of the *mensalão*. The section also considers the difficult constitutional reforms of Lula's first year and the ramifications of these reforms.

The First Year

Partially in response to these contextual factors, Lula adopted a different coalition management approach from that of his predecessor Cardoso. Shortly after Cardoso began his second term in 1999, he had a coalition of five parties and a coalescence rate (i.e., a seats-ministries proportionality rate) of 0.69 on a 0–1 scale (with a score of 1 representing perfect proportionality). Following his inauguration in 2003, Lula formed a coalition of eight parties, with a much lower coalescence rate of 0.56 (see table 2.1).

Legislators, as professional politicians, are perhaps more likely to observe a more conspicuous statistic: the share of cabinet ministries controlled by the party of the president. This is a simple, intuitive measure of monopolistic behavior that is easily calculated by glancing at any photo of the weekly cabinet meeting, is broadly disseminated by the media, and is frequently discussed on the floor of Congress. Upon taking office, Lula immediately expanded the number of cabinet-level posts from twenty-one to thirty-four. Ostensibly, the purpose of expanding the cabinet upon taking office was to include several new ministries with responsibilities for different dimensions of social policies, but the bulk of the new positions went to loyalists of the president's own Workers' Party. The PT was awarded no fewer than twenty portfolios (59% of the total), despite holding only about a third of the intracoalitional seats in the Chamber of Deputies. In early 2003 Lula had not yet seduced his preferred coalition partner, the PMDB, which was the second-largest party in the Chamber at the time. In December of that year, in a major political coup for Lula, the PMDB joined the coalition as the eighth party in the cabinet, replacing the departing Democratic Labor Party (PDT). However, by that time the cabinet was basically full and Lula had already firmly established the principle of PT overdominance.

In the first year of government, cabinet expansion and the rewarding of PT members were necessary for Lula to satisfy the internal factions within the party. As noted above, the expanded cabinet size created space for minority factions (e.g., Trotskyists and agrarian social movements) while preserving the dominance of Lula's own Campo Majoritário. After two decades of leading the PT through the political wilderness, upon arriving to power Lula had to give as much attention to proportionality *within* the party as to proportionality *across* parties. Yet the data show that Lula did not provide fair representation of intra-PT diversity in his first cabinet. In the 2001 internal party elections, the Campo Majoritário had received the support of 52% of the PT rank and file, as compared to 33% who voted for the leftist factions. However, the 2003 cabinet distribution was quite different: of the twenty portfolios awarded to the PT, some thirteen (65%) went to the Campo and only three (15%) went to the leftist factions.[10] Thus Lula overrepresented precisely those PT *tendências* most amenable to forming a governing coalition with right-wing and centrist parties; the leftist factions had historically opposed such an alliance strategy.

In thinking through these intra-PT dilemmas, the president wanted to appease the hard left while at the same time positioning the Campo Majoritário for the long haul. The "easy way out" was simply to expand the total size of the cabinet, a mathematical distraction that would gloss over the central fact of Campo hegemony. The end result was the appointment of twenty PT ministers, which left the allied parties perplexed and dismayed. This is a classic case of a "nested games" problem (Tsebelis 1990) in which observation of apparently nonrational behavior is the fault of the observer rather than the actor. Lula's benchmark was simply different from the one that outside observers might have used.

In terms of coalition size, the number of governing coalition parties was greater under Lula; his governing coalition included eight parties every month from the start of his term through the *mensalão* scandal, as compared to a high of six parties for Cardoso (Amorim Neto 2007). Even so,

Lula's initial minority coalition fell far short of the 60% supermajority in the lower house necessary for constitutional amendments. Lula surpassed this threshold only after adding the PMDB to his alliance in December 2003. Moreover, the ideological spectrum of Lula's coalition was much more diverse than was that of Cardoso, spanning from left-wing to right-wing parties. In sum, Lula had a more ideologically diverse coalition with a greater number of parties but with less baseline support in the Chamber — not a promising combination.

As mentioned earlier, some very difficult constitutional amendments were on the agenda for Lula's first year in office. He would pursue pension reforms (see Alston and Mueller 2006) and tax reforms as signals to the international finance community and as a means of freeing funds for certain social programs. Somewhat surprisingly, Lula pursued such reforms in basically identical terms to those of Cardoso, though he changed the focus of the tax reforms and broke the reforms into more palatable pieces. The pension and tax reforms represented extreme reversals of position for Lula, since the PT had been a main source of opposition to Cardoso's reform attempts.

The pension reforms passed in August 2003 with proreform votes from 357 members (70% of the total members) in the Chamber of Deputies in two rounds. However, similar to what had happened with Cardoso, Lula's initial tax reform proposal never reached the floor. The governing coalition abandoned its original proposal and decided to focus instead on aspects related to increased taxation via social contributions (CPMF, DRU, and CIDE), which would not require sharing new tax resources with states and municipalities. The main source of revenue would be the existing tax on financial transactions (CPMF). The DRU, on the other hand, was created in 2000 to provide the executive with flexibility in spending revenues from the taxation of manufactured goods, while the CIDE was a tax on gasoline consumption. The CPMF and DRU votes occurred in September 2003, while the vote on the less controversial CIDE occurred the following year. The more controversial reforms passed with the requisite supermajority in the Chamber of Deputies.

Lula's distribution of monetary benefits involved a substitution of these benefits for political benefits (Raile, Pereira, and Power 2011), reflecting the relative costs of each. Lula had focused political benefits primarily on his partisans, which is the relatively cheaper strategy (Araujo, Pereira, and Raile 2008). Handing political benefits over to ideologically distant parties would cede some policy control to ideological opponents; sending pork to these parties is less politically costly. Lula purchased outside support for the difficult constitutional reforms by sending the lion's share of pork to parties *outside* the governing coalition. Of the individual pork, 76% of the total value went to individuals from noncoalition parties in 2003, and 41% of the total went to the core opposition parties (the PSDB and PFL). Even more of the state-based pork went outside the coalition, with 89% disbursed to states run by noncoalition parties (and 34% of the overall total going to states controlled by the PSDB and PFL).

Neither set of reforms would have passed without positive votes from outside the formal governing coalition. Lula received only 213 votes from within the coalition for the pension reforms, a number well below the 308 required. Within the PT itself, four members voted against the reforms and another seven abstained from voting. Both the PSDB and the PFL, the government coalition's primary opponents, were split about evenly in supporting Lula's pension reforms. Lula received decent support from the PSDB and PFL because the reforms were basically what these parties had proposed earlier and because of the relative volume of pork being sent their way. Similarly, Lula received 215 supportive votes from within the coalition for the CPMF and DRU tax reforms, though the support from the opposition PSDB and PFL parties was less for these reforms.

The painful transition period of Lula's inaugural year had left its scars. Though preemptively rewarded with a windfall of cabinet posts, Lula's own party remained fractured, and elements of the party resented the policy directions of the necessary constitutional reforms. The seemingly unfair distribution of cabinet seats within the PT likely enhanced that resentment. Furthermore, the PT received only 22% of the intracoalitional pork in 2003, despite contributing an average of 36% of the coalition's seats in the Chamber that year. The other parties in the governing coalition were left unsettled by the cabinet expansion and over-rewarding of the PT. Yet another slap in the face for these other coalition parties was that the vast majority of overall pork had gone to noncoalition parties in an effort to pass the constitutional reforms. Finally, the general public had not made matters any easier for Lula. His popularity steadily plunged during that first year in office from a high of about 54% to a low of about 27% (figure 2.2).[11] This trend, too, severely eroded Lula's political capital.

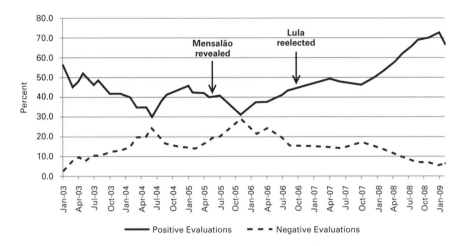

Figure 2.2. Popularity of Lula Government, 2003–2009

Source: the data are from CNT/Sensus (http://sistemacnt.cnt.org.br/).
Notes: Data points are marginal percentages from mass surveys. Positive is the sum of *ótimo* and *bom* evaluations, while negative is the sum of *ruim* and *péssimo* evaluations. Neutral evaluations (*regular*) are excluded. Data points have been linearly interpolated for months without surveys.

Mensalão

Lula had learned in that first year that managing the PT's internal factions would be extraordinarily difficult. He had also learned that dealing with the opposition would be an expensive endeavor; gaining PSDB and PFL votes for the constitutional reforms had been quite costly despite the ideological satisfaction of these parties with the legislative measures. Yet another important lesson was that the general public could be somewhat fickle, as the honeymoon ended quickly because of unhappiness over the constitutional reforms and natural erosion in support. The most important lesson for Lula may have been that he was dealing primarily with weakly ideological, opportunistic, and clientelistic political parties—a context that historically had lent itself to an extreme form of "exchange politics" (Geddes and Ribeiro Neto 1999).

Lula did take some corrective measures after that rough first year. He cleaned house within the PT by expelling several members who had not voted with him, and he even further increased the ideological heterogeneity of the formal governing coalition through the addition of the PMDB in December 2003. The PMDB's large size (seventy-eight seats in the Chamber) pushed the government's coalition beyond the 60% supermajority threshold. However, the PT did not "make room" for the PMDB, allocating only two cabinet seats to this new partner in early 2004. This skewed allocation increased the PT's dominance over its governing coalition partners at exactly the same time that the *mensalão* is alleged to have begun. In February 2004, the PT controlled 58% of the cabinet portfolios while supplying only 29% of the coalition's seats in the Chamber of Deputies (see table 2.1).

Lula also realized the power of pork (especially with eroded public support) and increased the use of this tool substantially, with individual pork disbursements going from under twenty-seven billion *reais* in 2003 to over forty-four billion in 2004 and over fifty billion in 2005. In addition, Lula significantly increased the proportion of the pork staying within the coalition (from 24% of the total in 2003 to 56% in 2004). He particularly ensured that the more ideologically distant members of the government coalition (like the PMDB, PL, and PTB) who were shortchanged in cabinet seats, as shown in table 2.1, received a disproportionately large share of that pork. Lula also spent a much smaller proportion of the intracoalitional pork on his party, the PT, though the new amount represented a substantial increase in absolute terms.

Maintaining majority support is difficult, and this was particularly so for Lula given the distribution of preferences shown in figure 2.1 and the strategic miscalculations made early in the administration. According to investigators, illicit monthly payments to legislators began in January 2004 and spread across the political spectrum in the legislature. The scale of the scandal became clear when Roberto Jefferson of the PTB found himself trapped by evidence and blew the whistle in mid-2005.[12]

Again, we return to the key question of why the *mensalão* occurred. Perhaps too many legislators had learned to play the blackmail game and needed a cut of the payment arrangements in return for keeping quiet. Another possibility is that the price of legislative support had increased dramatically after that difficult first year, and key legislators knew they could extract a substantial ransom in return for their support.

Our analysis suggests a more complete, though fully compatible, explanation: the *mensalão* compensated for prior and present deficiencies in the very complex bargaining environment. Payments to the legislature from early 2004 through mid-2005 took three major forms: pork, cabinet seats, and the *mensalão*. Though showered with cabinet seats, Lula's PT continued to suffer from fractionalization and internal squabbles. Further, while the absolute value of pork going to the PT increased, PT pork as a percentage of the overall intracoalitional total plummeted. Interestingly, some of the legislators implicated in the *mensalão* scandal were PT members. *Mensalão* certainly would have been a means of dealing with the squabbles and shortfalls. Conversely, the parties in the government coalition most dissimilar to the PT ideologically (the PMDB, PL, and PTB) received cabinet seats far below the proportional level. As compensation, these parties received a disproportionately large share of the intracoalitional pork. Certain members of these parties also received compensation in the form of *mensalão*.

Implications of the Analysis

In conclusion, we relate our analysis back to the two major themes of this volume—corruption and accountability. In particular, we summarize the ways that coalition management can create conditions permissive to corruption. We also consider multiple meanings of accountability, including a president's accountability to his own coalition.

Corruption

What have we learned about political corruption from our examination of the causes of the *mensalão* scandal in Brazil? Perhaps most importantly, we have identified conditions ripe for corrupt activities. In particular, corruption is one of the few viable "solutions" when official bargaining resources fall short of overcoming the difficulties (some self-inflicted in this case) in the bargaining environment. The strong contradicting institutional forces in Brazilian government contribute to the complexity of the bargaining environment. The coalitional presidency in Brazil is almost schizoid in its extreme mixture of "consensual" and "majoritarian" institutions (Lijphart 1999). Further, the institutional framework provides incentives for corruption, while giving the president ample power to funnel government proceeds illicitly.

However, our explanation does not rely on institutional explanations alone, because to do so would imply that every administration would engage in large-scale vote-buying scandals. This has not happened. Therefore, we also emphasize the importance of strategic bargaining. Specifically, we point to the ways misused bargaining resources can also leave an executive short of overcoming a difficult bargaining environment. Even given institutional constraints, the president has some room to maneuver. Much like an architect who builds a house on shaky foundations, bad initial decisions by the president in cementing his coalition will later compromise the structural soundness of the edifice. In constructing governing coalitions, Brazilian executives face choices about ideological range and heterogeneity, about transfers of budgetary resources, and about access to the all-important presidential cabinet. These choices influence the demands that fickle legislators will later make against the executive.

Our analysis points to some pitfalls to avoid in coalition management. One such pitfall is disproportionality in the allocation of cabinet portfolios. Access to executive power is the lifeblood of Brazilian politics, and politicians prize it greatly (Samuels 2003). Other things being equal, greater cabinet coalescence means a more satisfied coalition arrayed behind the president, while a more monopolistic approach is sure to engender internal dissatisfaction. Lula's packing of the cabinet with members of his own party is understandable in the historical and political context of PT politics (as the party had waited twenty-two years for access to the federal government and was characterized by various internal factions that had to be appeased), but it was almost certainly an unwise choice in terms of coalition management.

We have suggested that this cabinet disproportionality combined with Lula's (perhaps necessary) decision to create an ideologically heterogeneous, disconnected coalition to generate the conditions that led to the *mensalão* scandal of 2004–5. In another respect, Lula's policy agenda also contributed to the scandal. The constitutional amendments necessary both to appease outside observers and to free funds for social spending alienated core supporters. These reforms also required that Lula send the majority of pork outside the governing coalition, thereby further upsetting the internal cohesion of the coalition. Therefore, circumstances of policy making indirectly also led to the illicit payments.

The story we have told is not moralistic, yet there is a moral to the story. If politicians pledge support for a president and are subsequently given only limited access to the executive branch, they will seek compensation in other ways. *Presidencialismo de coalizão* cannot be *presidencialismo de exclusão.*

Accountability

What does the aftermath of the *mensalão* scandal teach us about accountability? Despite the regime's schizoid nature, the accountability mechanisms have worked reasonably well in some respects. The previously mentioned resignations, expulsions, and prosecutions all testify to the effectiveness of Brazilian accountability mechanisms at the level of national government. Though some fact-finding and decision-making processes were less transparent than full accountability would seem to require, many government officials did receive punishment for their actions.

The issue of accountability through electoral mechanisms is more complex. Does "accountability" mean giving the people what they want, or does it mean punishing all public officials associated with improper behavior? As is well known, Lula made a full political recovery from the scandal and went on to win a convincing reelection in October 2006.

While various potential explanations for this recovery exist, observers commonly cite three factors: (1) Lula's enduring personal popularity, which fortuitously insulated him from scandals affecting his party and allies (despite short-term erosion in public support during his first year); (2) his innovative social policies, especially the conditional cash transfer program known as Bolsa Família (Hall 2006); and (3) the acceleration of the strong economic recovery which began in mid-2004 (Hunter and Power 2007). Seen against the backdrop of improving economic conditions and Lula's popularity (see figure 2.2), the *mensalão* crisis now appears only a temporary downturn in the president's fortunes. He was reelected with a 61% majority in 2006, has close to a 70% majority in the Chamber of Deputies in 2009, and is supported by twenty of twenty-seven governors in his second term. He is the most popular president since the advent of modern political polling in Brazil, and few other world leaders can match his level of popular support.

Regardless of one's take on the issue of electoral accountability, the aftermath of the scandal has forced President Lula's hand in other respects. In his second term, Lula has adjusted his coalitional strategy in a more inclusive and less monopolistic direction. While the PT is still key to the coalition, its dominance over its partners is much less pronounced than in the first term (see table 2.1). Lula has also done a better job of making room in the cabinet for the large PMDB, giving the party five posts by early 2007.

Other factors that contributed to the *mensalão* scandal have also changed. The decisive rebranding of the PT as a pragmatic, promarket, center-left party after 2003 greatly reduced the perceived ideological distance between the PT and its alliance partners (see the bottom panel in figure 2.1). Also, partly because of the corruption scandals, Lula ran for reelection with a far higher degree of autonomy from his own party than was the case in 2002 (Hunter and Power 2007). Lula seems to have adjusted his personal approach to the management of coalitional presidentialism, but the question that remains is whether the lessons of the *mensalão* scandal will be internalized by other actors in Brazilian politics. Given that coalitional presidentialism exists not only at the national level but also within each of Brazil's twenty-seven states, we venture that we have not seen the last of this volatile connection between corruption and coalition building.

Notes

1. In Portuguese, the word *mensalão* literally implies monthly payments, or figuratively a "monthly retainer." In reality, the payments were not monthly but timed around crucial roll-call votes in Congress. Nonetheless, when the scandal broke the media seized on the monthly concept and the *mensalão* term stuck.

2. The other three countries are Argentina, Venezuela, and Mexico; a mixed electoral system attenuates the fragmenting effect of proportional representation in Mexico, however.

3. Silvio Pereira, a former secretary general of the PT, reached a plea-bargain agreement with the Procurador Geral da República in January 2008 and will no longer have to stand trial.

4. There was one vacancy at the time of the August 2007 STF deliberations.

5. In the last two decades, up to one-third of federal legislators have typically switched parties during the quadrennial legislative sessions, but court decisions have recently restricted the practice. In August 2007, a resolution by the Tribunal Superior Eleitoral (TSE), later confirmed by the Supreme Court, established the principle that elective mandates belong to parties, not individuals, and that party defectors would lose their seats in legislative bodies. These rulings have been challenged in several hundred court cases in the past two years, with some politi-

cians claiming just cause for defection. Currently, the Lula government is sponsoring a constitutional amendment that would open up a "window" for party switching six months prior to elections.

6. An exception to this trend was the last few months of Cardoso's final term. Partisan ministers often resign to pursue elective office as the end of a president's service nears. As a consequence, presidents tend to have more disproportionate cabinets during this lame-duck phase.

7. The ideology data in the top panel of figure 2.1 are drawn from a survey conducted by Power in mid-2001, about eighteen months before the 2002 election, so they represent the reputational positions of the parties on the eve of the Lula presidency. The ideology data in the bottom panel are drawn from a 2005 survey, thus representing the updated ideological reputations of the parties after two years of the Lula presidency.

8. The survey of experts by Wiesehomeier and Benoit (2007) finds that analysts of Brazilian politics generally see President Lula as being slightly to the right of his own party.

9. Disconnected coalitions are those that include parties occupying noncontiguous spaces on the left-right spectrum. As figure 2.1 shows, the leftist PT "skipped over" the most influential center party (Cardoso's PSDB) in order to ally with smaller parties on the center-right. In the 1988–93 period, the PT and PSDB had frequently allied at the subnational level.

10. The remaining four PT ministers were not linked to internal factions; three had technocratic backgrounds, and the fourth (Waldir Pires) made his career in other parties. Notably, of the three ministries awarded to the left, two (Cities and Fisheries) were created only in 2003. Amaral generously provided information regarding factional affiliations; for further analysis, see Amaral (forthcoming). On the Campo Majoritário, see Hunter (2007).

11. Presidential popularity is calculated as the percentage of positive evaluations minus the percentage of negative evaluations of the president.

12. Roberto Jefferson's political trajectory is typical of many members of the clientelistic parties of the center-right, which tend to support the government of the day. During the 1970s military regime, Jefferson belonged to both the government and opposition parties at different times. In 1992, as a PTB deputy, he led the so-called "shock troops" who attempted to protect President Collor from impeachment. In 1994, he was implicated in a budget scandal involving twenty-nine members of Congress (Krieger, Rodrigues, and Bonassa 1994) but escaped formal prosecution. He supported Cardoso in his first term though not in his second term, when as president of the PTB Jefferson aligned the party behind Lula. When Jefferson was expelled from Congress in 2005 as result of the *mensalão* scandal, he was only fifty-two years old yet already in his sixth four-year term in Congress. He remains president of the PTB today.

Chapter Three

Corruption and Voting

LUCIO R. RENNÓ

Corruption was a central theme in the 2006 Brazilian elections. Public opinion data from the Brazilian Electoral Study (Estudo Eleitoral Brasileiro, ESEB) leave no doubt: 30% of voters mentioned corruption scandals as "the key" campaign issue in 2006. The economy came in a distant second place, with 10%. Hence, it is impossible to understand the Brazilian election without considering the impact of corruption and scandals on vote choice. In fact, the main puzzle of the 2006 elections is how the incumbent president, Luiz Inácio Lula da Silva, won reelection despite a first term marked by so many scandals (Rennó 2007b, 2007c). Does this represent a breakdown of electoral channels of accountability?

In a chapter about voting, I will use the term *accountability* in a relatively narrow sense to denote voters' ability to punish incumbents in elections for wrongdoing while in office (e.g., Przeworski, Stokes, and Manin 1999). The central question is: Does Lula's reelection in 2006, in spite of corruption accusations that dogged the president for eighteen months prior to the election, indicate that voters tolerate corrupt behavior? Or better yet, *reward* such behavior? Clearly, the 2006 electoral process and its outcome touch on a long-standing debate about voting behavior in Brazil: Do voters tend to prefer the candidate who "steals, but get things done" *(rouba mas faz)*?[1] If yes, then accountability in Brazil is at stake. Therefore, uncovering the criteria that voters employ in their electoral decisions is fundamental to understanding the microfoundations of accountability.

Uncovering the answer is not a simple task. It is complicated by the multiplicity of competing vote calculi, especially the possible multidimensionality of voting based on retrospective evaluations of the incumbent administration. Retrospective voting is the essence of accountability because it is based on a calculus in which voters look back at how the incumbent performed in office and decide if they are satisfied with the incumbent's actions. If the answer is yes, the incumbent is rewarded with votes. If the answer is no, the voters turn to another candidate.

However, there are many facets of incumbents' performance that a voter can take into consideration. Evaluation of the incumbent's management of the economy is a classic element of performance, but it is certainly not the only one. The subject of the present volume, corruption, is a structural part of everyday life in much of the developing world and in many new democracies. We read about it in the news, watch it on television, and observe it in our daily lives. Yet it would be simplistic to assume that corruption alone determines vote choice. The real issue is: How do views about corruption affect vote choice *in contrast to other possible aspects of performance in office,* such as the management of the macroeconomy? Evaluating how voters *balance* competing dimensions of retrospective evaluations aids in understanding the mechanisms of accountability at the individual level. Voters need to sort through various cross-pressing dimensions—such as long-term loyalties to parties and ideological preferences—before they can arrive at a final choice (Zaller 1992). The puzzle, then, is how voters solve these complex dilemmas.

In tackling this question with reference to the 2002 and 2006 Brazilian elections, this chapter makes three main points. First, I argue that retrospective evaluations of the government are *multidimensional* and can be framed by various distinct events that involve incumbents' performance. Hence, the traditionally studied dimension—economic voting—must be complemented by other factors that voters may consider when judging incumbents' performance. Previous literature on retrospective voting has often ignored such multidimensionality (Fiorina 1981; Kinder and Kiewiet 1981). Retrospective evaluations of the government can also be based on the administration's probity and integrity, its posture toward international security and global issues, its performance on public security, and its positions on other domestic policy issues. We need a more complete picture of the criteria voters employ in order to hold their representatives accountable.

Second, I claim that corruption was decisive in the 2006 presidential race. Were it not for the corruption scandals, President Lula would have

easily won reelection in the first round of the election. Because Brazilian presidential elections use double-ballot majoritarian rules, voters were
able to punish the incumbent in the first round. I claim that because of corruption scandals surrounding his government, Lula became the second-
best option for a significant number of voters. These voters were strongly
cross-pressured by corruption on the one hand and ideological sympathies
and/or positive evaluations of social and economic policies on the other. As
a consequence, a number of such left-wing voters who had traditionally
voted for Lula opted instead for Heloísa Helena or Cristovam Buarque (former Lula allies, and candidates from other left-wing parties) in the first
round of balloting. This phenomenon was sufficient to deprive Lula of an
outright victory on election day, forcing him into a runoff three weeks later
with the center-right Geraldo Alckmin. But in the second round, "when
push came to shove" as it were, left-leaning voters returned home to Lula.
For left-wing voters there was no doubt that Lula was a better option than
Alckmin. In sum, corruption mattered, but its effects were filtered by the
double-ballot majoritarian format adopted in Brazilian races for the executive branch.[2]

Third, a theoretical proposition generated by my research is that ideology, long-term loyalties, and partisanship can "shield" incumbents from
accusations of corruption.[3] Accusations of wrongdoing generate cognitive
dissonance for otherwise loyal voters, forcing them to consider whether
they should continue supporting their natural candidate. However, doubts
are put aside when the accused candidate is juxtaposed against a least-
preferred option, which often happens in runoff elections. In such cases,
voters opt for the candidate that is closer to their preferred ideological or
policy positions, even if they have doubts about that candidate's possible
wrongdoings while in office. As will be shown in this chapter, such behavior
occurs even among the left, which has always carried the anticorruption
banner in Brazil but still is willing to support a candidate that is closer ideologically in spite of involvement in corruption.

The following section provides a more in-depth theoretical account
of the relationship between voters and representatives, attempting to relate accountability to the multidimensional nature of retrospective voting. I then discuss the Brazilian elections of 2002 and 2006. From the theoretical discussion and the characteristics of the Brazilian case, I derive
some testable propositions. The middle sections of the chapter describe

the data set and engage in hypothesis testing. My results indicate that corruption was an important factor in the 2006 elections but played no role in the 2002 contests, which first vaulted Lula into the presidency.

Accountability and the Multidimensional Nature of Electoral Calculi

Accountability is but one aspect of *delegation,* a relationship in which one actor grants another the responsibility for making decisions and acting on her behalf. Delegation, therefore, poses an inherent tension: Will the delegates truly act on behalf of those who granted the authority?

This relationship has been exhaustively investigated by principal-agent theory, according to which the principal actor entrusts the agent tasks that must be completed and goals that must be achieved, and the agent acts accordingly. Tasks and goals are delegated for many reasons. The classic example is that the agent has expertise that the principal lacks. Agents, therefore, have more information than principals and more control over the outcomes. If principals do not know what agents will be doing in detail, the possibility for shirking by agents is high. This leads to our question above: How can the principal restrain opportunistic (understood as self-interested and dishonest) behavior by the agent?

Key to curbing opportunistic behavior is the threat of sanctions. If the goal is not achieved or if the principal is dissatisfied with the agent's performance, then she can punish the agent. Obviously, punishment will require some additional gathering of information, through monitoring.[4] But ultimately it is the threat of punishment that controls the agent's behavior. Punishment, in most cases, is based on some form of retrospective evaluation. Accountability refers to this post hoc judging and punishing procedure (Przeworski, Stokes, and Manin 1999). In summary, delegation requires accountability, which is based on monitoring and retrospective evaluations of performance.

Representative democratic regimes, widespread throughout the entire Western world, are based on relations of delegation of power. Consequently, information gathering, monitoring, and accountability are fundamental aspects of democratic governance. Delegation, monitoring, and accountability are present in the relationship between voters and representatives, between politicians and bureaucrats, and between the executive, legislative, and judiciary branches. The spirit of democracy's institutional design is one of stimulating control in order to reduce the likelihood of arbitrary, unilateral decisions. Regimes in which accountability is not present cannot be considered fully democratic.[5]

Guillermo O'Donnell (1994) has advanced the idea of vertical and horizontal accountability to elucidate two key types of relationships that involve delegation in democracies. The vertical dimension refers to the relationship between voters and elected representatives, while the horizontal dimension refers to the relationship between distinct branches of government and between politicians and bureaucrats. Vertical accountability— my exclusive focus in this chapter—often hinges on evaluations of the past performance of the incumbent administration. This occurs most obviously when the officeholder himself runs for reelection, but it also occurs in open-seat races (e.g., the presidential elections in Brazil in 2002 or in the United States in 2008) whenever there is a candidate who clearly represents the governing party or coalition (in these examples, José Serra and John McCain, respectively). In such a case, voters can look back and evaluate the record of the incumbent and/or her intended successor.

This is the essence of retrospective voting, in which voters look back and judge the past performance of the incumbent (Fiorina 1981; Kinder and Kiewiet 1981). If voters are satisfied with the performance of the incumbent, they will likely vote for him or his designated candidate. If not, they will consider voting for a challenger. Therefore, accountability and retrospective voting are inherently linked, and identifying what factors voters employ when voting retrospectively is a form of elucidating the microfoundations of accountability.

However, most studies that analyze retrospective voting focus on a single dimension: evaluations of the economy (Stokes 2001; Fiorina 1981; Kinder and Kiewiet 1981). This monocausal approach is simplistic and ignores the multidimensional process of decision making that voters must face—a complex process that may leave voters in various states of ambivalence or contradiction. Voters weigh multiple elements of an incumbent's performance when voting retrospectively, not just the management of the economy, as the literature on retrospective voting would have it. Voters also focus on other elements of an incumbent's record, such as performance in combating or being involved in corruption. Given the centrality of corruption in political rhetoric in the developing world, corruption can be understood as an inertial trait of political regimes. Corruption scandals are even more damaging in nascent democracies because they can erode the public's trust on democratic institutions and lead to skepticism toward the regime (Seligson 2002, 2006; Power and González 2003). In transitional democracies marked by repeated scandals—such as the case of Brazil analyzed in this volume—how an administration deals with corruption and how clearly it may be linked to wrongdoing become structural components of elections and a consistent criterion for voters' evaluations.[6]

Yet not all voting is retrospective (Stokes 2001). Voters may also rely on *prospective* evaluations, where they look at candidates' proposals for the future. To this, one could add the short-term determinants of vote choice related to campaign events and day-to-day developments, such as an equivocal declaration by a candidate, an obvious gaffe, or a poor performance in a debate (Holbrook 1994; Green and Palmquist 1994). In sum, the possible determinants of vote choice are multiple and commonly in contradiction with one another, generating ambivalence among voters.

In addition to retrospective voting, prospective voting, and campaign effects, we must recognize partisanship and ideology as long-term loyalties that affect vote choice (Campbell et al. 1960; Green and Palmquist 1994; Pappi 1996). When strong long-term ties are present, deriving from childhood socialization or from adult life experiences with politics, vote choice is often predetermined and is relatively resistant to short-term shocks or even past performance. Retrospective voting may not influence electoral choices when ideological ties between voters and candidates are strong. Conversely, independent voters (those with no party identification) are largely immune to such attachments and are presumably more attuned to retrospective evaluations.

In new democracies, with undeveloped party systems, the number of independents is usually much higher than in regimes where parties have existed for a long time (Baker, Ames, and Rennó 2006). Where parties are inchoate, they do not have established reputations and do not have "brand names," to use the terminology of Lupia and McCubbins (2000). The results are low levels of partisanship and high electoral volatility (Mainwaring and Scully 1995; Roberts and Wibbels 1999). In such environments, then, long-term factors may be less important than short-term shocks and retrospective evaluations.

Vote choice, then, is affected by a large number of variables reflecting incumbent performance in office, expectations about the future, long-term socialization and partisanship, campaign effects, and contextual factors including the pervasiveness of corruption. If this model of voting seems complex, that is as it should be. The question, then, is, How do these distinct factors influence vote choice in Brazil?

Two Brazilian Presidential Elections: Sorting Out Competing Electoral Calculi

The elections of 2002 were a watershed event in Brazilian history. For the first time, a candidate from an authentic left-wing party ascended to the highest office of the republic. Luiz Inácio Lula da Silva, a survivor of the droughts of the destitute Northeast region of the country—whose inspiring personal story included moving as a child to São Paulo in search of a better life and becoming a lathe operator and later the leader of a labor union—was elected president on the strength of a diverse multiparty coalition led by the Workers' Party (PT), which he helped create. The 2002 election therefore generated the most significant processes of alternation in power and elite circulation ever seen in Brazil. The election brought to the federal administration groups that had never occupied such positions before and thus was pivotal to strengthening Brazilian democracy.

In spite of its historical relevance, the 2002 election was a smooth ride for Lula, as figure 3.1 shows. The campaign revolved around a sustained attack by three main opposition candidates (Lula, Anthony Garotinho, and Ciro Gomes) on the incumbent administration's candidate, José Serra of the Brazilian Social Democracy Party (PSDB). Lula's lead during the campaign was never threatened. The only real excitement was the guessing game about who would go to a possible runoff against Lula (and a second round at times seemed unlikely because of Lula's commanding advantage). The strongest competition took place between José Serra and Ciro Gomes. After a series of gaffes by Ciro, all of which were well exploited in Serra's negative campaign ads, Serra advanced to the runoff. Lula, meanwhile, stayed above the fray, adopting such a statesmanlike and nonconflictual posture that his nickname became "Lula Peace and

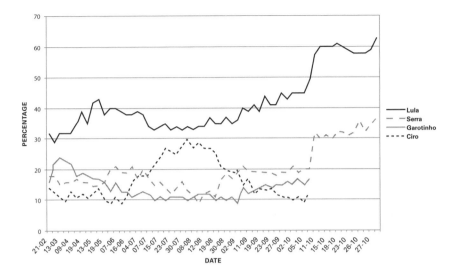

Figure 3.1. Vote Intention in the 2002 Elections

Source: Datafolha, Vox Populi, and IBOPE Vote Intention polls.
Note: first round on October 6, runoff on October 27.

Love." He easily dispatched Serra in the runoff, with a margin of victory of twenty-two points.

Lula's first term, however, was not as dull as his 2002 electoral victory. It was marked by three main characteristics. First, the president adopted a market-friendly macroeconomic policy, with strong results in strengthening the fundamentals of the Brazilian economy. Second, the new administration invested heavily in social policies, with the signature initiative being Bolsa Família, a conditional cash transfer program well targeted to the needs of Brazil's poor. Finally, on a more negative note, several key government personnel were involved in recurring corruption scandals.

This conjunction of factors generated mixed feelings about the Lula administration among critics as well as allies. Critics were surprised by the success of the economic policy directed by finance minister Antônio Palocci, who opted to follow the main lines of his Cardoso-era predecessor, Pedro Malan. A clear sign of Lula's economic pragmatism was the appointment of the market-friendly Henrique Meirelles, a former executive at FleetBoston Financial, to head the Central Bank. As under Cardoso, interest rates were kept high, and the government operated an inflation-targeting regime through the generation of a primary budgetary surplus. These policy continuities were disappointing to many on the left. On the other hand, long-time allies of Lula were satisfied with his investment in social policies. Bolsa Família proved very successful in combating inequality (S. Soares et al. 2007) as well as in winning votes (Hunter and Power 2007; G. Soares and Terron 2008; Zucco 2008; Licio, Rennó, and Castro 2009). Yet all were taken off guard by the eruption of several prominent corruption scandals. For supporters, the scandals were a source of deep frustration, which resulted in defections of important PT leaders to other parties. The formation of the Partido Socialismo e Liberdade (Socialism and Liberty Party, PSOL) by PT dissidents Heloísa Helena and Chico Alencar, among others, was a direct consequence of the scandals.

For the opposition, led by the two parties that had supported Cardoso in the 1990s (the PSDB and the Liberal Front Party, PFL]), the scandals—especially the *mensalão* scandal that erupted in June 2005 (see Pereira, Power, and Raile, this volume)—presented a major political opportunity. The initial expectation of opposition leaders was that Lula would be easily defeated in the 2006 elections, an assumption that seemed realistic as the president's popularity plummeted from June through November 2005. Although some argued that the proximity of the scandals to the presidential office constituted grounds for impeachment, the opposition preferred to try to keep Lula in a constant state of public accusation. The idea was that the lingering shadow of the scandals would ensure his defeat in 2006.

The 2006 electoral process was marked by this combination of factors. The campaign, as expected, started with serious attacks by the opposition accusing the incumbent either of direct complicity in corruption or of passive toleration of wrongdoing in his administration. Whereas in 2002 Lula had faced a comfortable situation in which he and the two other opposition candidates, Ciro Gomes and Anthony Garotinho, had "teamed up" to attack the progovernment candidate, José Serra, in 2006 it was Lula himself who was on the receiving end of a three-way attack. Making things worse was that two of the three main challengers were former Lula allies and historic PT leaders in their states: Cristovam Buarque of the Democratic Labor Party (PDT), who was Lula's first minister of education and also a senator from the Federal District, and Heloísa Helena of the PSOL, a

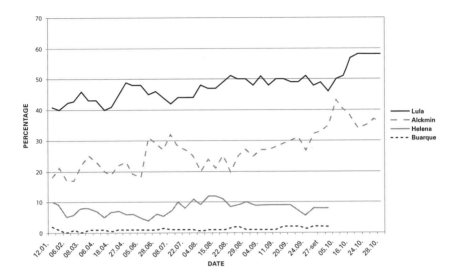

Figure 3.2. Vote Intention in the 2006 Elections

Source: Datafolha, Sensus, and IBOPE Vote Intention polls.
Note: First round on October 1, runoff on October 29.

senator from Alagoas expelled from the PT for voicing her frustration with Lula's pragmatic turn in 2003. However, the main critic of the government was Geraldo Alckmin, a former governor of São Paulo nominated by the centrist PSDB, who also received the support of the conservative PFL.

In spite of the corruption scandals and attacks by adversaries, Lula maintained a solid lead throughout the campaign, facing only one major downturn in the final week of the first round, as shown in figure 3.2. The dramatic increase in vote intentions for Alckmin was a direct consequence of the "dossier scandal" in late September, in which PT operatives were arrested with huge sums of unaccounted-for money while attempting to purchase a file of allegedly damaging information about José Serra, then a candidate for the governorship of São Paulo.[7] When the news media began showing the arrest of *petistas* with suitcases full of money in the last week of the campaign, Lula's vote intention dropped just enough to prevent his outright victory in the first round. However, Lula's runoff campaign was marked both by an effective strategy, which controlled the agenda and set the tone of media coverage, and by good performance in several debates (which he had skipped in the first round). Similarly to four years earlier, the runoff election held no surprises, and Lula won easily. In fact, Alckmin actually received fewer votes in the second round than in the first, suggesting defections from his camp to that of Lula.

On the basis of this brief historical account of the two elections, what are the main explanations for vote choice in each? In 2006, it is possible that corruption played a substantive role in the elections. Although Lula's popularity had been recovering throughout 2006, the last-minute dossier scandal apparently reactivated in voters' minds the continual allegations of corruption that had tarnished the president's first term. On the other hand, Lula's management of the economy and of social policy were widely seen as effective. Hence, Lula supporters faced a dilemma: Which factor[s] should weigh more heavily on their decision? Should it be Lula's "success" in economic and social policies or "failure" on issues of probity? PT party identification and/or left-wing ideology may have also limited voters' propensity to vote against Lula. For a core base of voters on the left, Lula and the PT are still the only possible choice, despite any errors they may have committed while in office.

As discussed earlier, voters can be ambivalent in weighting the different factors that influence vote choice (Feldman and Zaller 1992; Zaller 1992). Hence, it is necessary to place the distinct explanations side by side to evaluate their influence on vote choice. This calls for multivariate modeling of vote choice. What variables should enter the equation? In Brazil, the main explanations that have been hypothesized to explain vote choice are economic voting, PT partisanship, ideology, and views about the qualities and characteristics of candidates (Meneguello 1994; Singer 1999; Almeida 2001; Carreirão and Barbetta 2004; Carreirão and Kinzo 2004; Samuels 2006b; Carreirão 2007; Nicolau 2007; Rennó 2007b, 2007c; Baker, Ames, and Rennó 2006; Ames, Baker, and Rennó 2008). Hunter and Power (2007) have also added to the equation the impact of targeted social policy on vote choice, correlating election results with the implementation of the Bolsa Família program at the subnational level.

Interestingly enough, the subject of the present volume—corruption— has not been thoroughly explored in voting studies in Brazil. This chapter, therefore, tests some of the main contending explanations for vote choice in the 2002 and 2006 elections with a special emphasis on the effect of corruption. The main hypotheses are discussed below.

Hypothesis 1: The effect of corruption on vote choice will be stronger in 2006 than in 2002.   In the 2002 ESEB, corruption was mentioned by less than 5% of the voters as an important electoral issue. Because it was not a salient electoral theme, it will have a limited negative impact on vote choice for the candidate of the incumbent Cardoso administration. Also, two other factors—that José Serra distanced himself from Cardoso and that his supporting coalition was not identical to that of the president—will attenuate the impact of views on corruption on his voter profile. In 2006, Lula's vote will be affected by corruption more clearly.

Hypothesis 2: When corruption matters, as in the case of 2006, it will more strongly affect vote choice between candidates on the same side of the ideological spectrum.   If long-term affinities do play a role in elections, they will serve as a shield for candidates involved in corruption. Voters from different sides of the ideological aisle will not "cross over" because of accusations of malfeasance. Corruption will, therefore, lead to variation in choice between candidates of the same side of the ideological spectrum. In 2006, this means that corruption will more clearly affect the choice among Lula, Heloísa Helena, and Cristovam Buarque, favoring the last two.

Hypothesis 3: In the 2006 runoff between Alckmin and Lula, one should expect a transfer of votes to Lula from the eliminated left-wing candidates, Heloísa and Cristovam, even among their supporters who think corruption is a problem.   Voters who still think corruption is a problem are more likely to support Lula in the second round of the election because of ideological factors. In fact, Lula's campaign was rather clever to promote an ideological issue, privatization, as the main theme of the runoff campaign. Lula blamed Alckmin and the former Cardoso coalition for the 1990s privatizations in an attempt to convince disaffected left-wing voters to "come home" to the PT: his antineoliberal discourse was a way of signaling to these voters that Lula was closer to their ideological preferences than the opposition candidate. Evidence of second-round vote transfers implies that ideological and partisan loyalties created shields for the Lula administration.

Data and Variables

I use data from the 2002 and 2006 ESEBs. Data for 2002 are drawn from a national probability sample of 2,513 cases and were collected between

October 31 and December 28, 2002. ESEB 2006 is based on a similar sample of 1,000 cases collected between December 17 and December 27, 2006. I include in the analysis as many variables as possible without compromising the comparability between both periods. Therefore, the variables included were present in both waves of the ESEB.[8]

The dependent variable is the declared vote in the first and second round of each election. In all cases, the dependent variable is nominal, with more than two categories. In the first round of 2002, vote choice includes Lula, Serra, Anthony Garotinho, Ciro Gomes, and invalid votes (abstentions, null and blank votes). In the second round it is a trichotomous choice among Lula, Serra, and invalid voting. In the first round of 2006, vote choice includes Lula, Alckmin, Heloísa Helena, Cristovam Buarque, and invalid votes. In the runoff, only Lula da Silva and Alckmin along with invalid votes are analyzed. For both elections, candidates with an insignificant number of votes are omitted from the statistical analysis. The independent variables tested in both elections are:

(1) *Perceptions about corruption as a main national problem.* This is based on the response to an open-ended survey question asking the respondent to name the country's worst and second-worst problems. Responses related to corruption as the worst problem were coded as 2 and as second-worst problem coded as 1. All other responses were coded as 0. Hence, the variable has values 0, 1, and 2, indicating the increasing strength of opinions that corruption is the worst problem. This variable should have a stronger impact in 2006 than in 2002, and it should negatively affect the vote for Lula in his reelection campaign. Perception of corruption should be most significant in choices between Lula and Heloísa and Lula and Cristovam in 2006.

(2) *Perceptions about the economy as a main national problem.* This is drawn from the same open-ended item concerning the country's worst and second-worst problems and is coded identically to the corruption variable above. Voters who have a negative evaluation of the economy should vote against incumbents. Therefore, this variable should have a negative impact on the preference for José Serra in 2002 (when he was the candidate of the incumbent Cardoso administration), and also on Lula da Silva's reelection bid in 2006. It should be equally important in both elections, especially in vote choices between candidates on opposite poles of the ideological spectrum.

(3) *General retrospective evaluation of the incumbent administration,* using a five-point scale indicating how well the government performed. This is an indicator of overall satisfaction with the performance of the administration. This should favor Lula in 2006 and Serra in 2002: those who are happy with the incumbent administration generally support candidates who represent continuity. Given that other variables in the model capture specific views on corruption and the economy, this variable controls for other possible dimensions of retrospective evaluations. Hence, it is an important substitute for possibly excluded variables and aids in correctly specifying the model.

(4) *Vote for Lula in the previous election* measured as a dummy variable. Given that Lula was the only candidate that ran in both elections, as well as in 1998, I verify the stability of Lula votes by including in the equation the respondent's declared vote in the previous election. It is coded 1 if the respondent voted for Lula and 0 otherwise. Given that we also control for partisanship (see below), this binary variable is an indicator of attachment to the personality of Lula and as a proxy for the impact of his personal characteristics in the election. This variable should have a positive impact in Lula vote in all situations, except for the choice of Lula versus Heloísa Helena—a prominent dissident who was expelled from the PT and who may have stolen some of the traditional Lula supporters in 2006.

(5) *PT party identification.* Respondents identifying with the Workers' Party are coded as 1 and the rest as 0. This variable should have a positive impact on Lula da Silva's vote in both elections, with the same caveat about Heloísa Helena in 2006.

(6) *PT rejection,* coded as 1 for those who strongly reject the PT and 0 for all others. This variable is included in the analysis on the basis of Carreirão and Barbetta's (2004) arguments that the PT serves as an "anchor" for voting behavior in Brazil, affecting even those voters who do not identify with the party. Therefore, if only PT identification were included, the overall effect of partisanship would be underestimated.[9] PT rejection should have a negative impact on the Lula vote and should favor the two PSDB candidates, Serra in 2002 and Alckmin in 2006. The PSDB has catalyzed the anti-PT vote in all national elections since 1994.

(7) *Ideology* was assessed in two ways. First, I used voters' ideological self-placement on a five-point scale ranging from left to right. This is a

problematic measure because almost half of the 2002 and 2006 samples were unable to locate themselves on the scale, indicating the weakness of this kind of measure (Almeida 2001). To cope with the low response rate, I recoded this variable as a dummy variable differentiating between those who self-positioned on the left and everyone else. Even though this binary variable is potentially plagued with error, it is better to include the variable in the model than to run the risk of underspecification. In 2002, self-declared leftists should favor Lula. In 2006 there is less certainty, given that Heloísa positioned herself farther to the left than the president.

Given the frailties of this measure, I also used a distinct indicator of ideology based on the candidates' positions on the ideological spectrum. In 2002, Lula, Garotinho, and Ciro were all considered to stand to the left of José Serra. In 2006, Lula, Heloísa, and Cristovam are to the left of Geraldo Alckmin. Voters' choices between candidates should be affected by the candidates' ideological position, with vote shifts between left-leaning candidates more likely than transfers between left and right candidates. Therefore, the choice between Lula and Heloísa and between Lula and Cristovam (two dyads within the family of the historic left) should be affected by perceptions of corruption, negatively affecting the president. The choice between Lula and Alckmin should not be affected by corruption in the first round of 2006. Hence, the criteria used to choose between candidates vary depending on the choice set.

(8) *Controls for political information* (Lupia 1994; Luskin 2002; Delli Carpini and Keeter 1996), *age, gender, and educational level* were also included in the models. Political information is based on correct responses to a five-question quiz on political facts. Educational level is based on an eight-category variable ranging from illiteracy to a completed university degree. Age is a continuous variable, and gender is coded 1 for males.[10]

Analysis and Results

The analysis below is based on multinomial logistic regression (MNL) with robust standard errors. This is one of the most adequate estimation techniques for elections with multiple candidates. In each model, a vote for Lula provides the baseline category: therefore a negative value on a coefficient indicates that the independent variable in question *increases* the likelihood of voting for Lula. Conversely, positive coefficients signify an increase in the likelihood of voting for one of the *other* candidates (or casting an invalid ballot) in the paired comparisons with a vote for Lula. It is important to highlight that the inclusion of those who decided to abstain or to cast an invalid vote (blank or spoiled ballot) is important to correctly model the full range of decisions posed to voters in the elections.

We start with a comparison of the determinants of vote choice in the first rounds of the 2002 and 2006 elections (results displayed in tables 3.1 and 3.2). The first hypothesis, that corruption matters in 2006 but not in 2002, is confirmed by the data. None of the choices in 2002 are affected by perceptions of corruption, while in 2006 some choices are.

In 2006, the second hypothesis is also confirmed: perceptions of corruption matter only when it comes to choices between candidates on the same side of the ideological spectrum. This means that voters who thought corruption was a central problem of the country opted to vote against the incumbent Lula administration, but they registered their disapproval by voting for candidates drawn from alternative left-wing parties (i.e., other than the PT). When it came to the choice between Lula and Alckmin, two candidates from opposing sides of the ideological spectrum, perceptions of corruption were not significant in the first round. What did affect the choice between Lula and Alckmin in the first round were perceptions about the economy. Those who thought the main problems of the country were economic voted against the incumbent. Hence, views on corruption are secondary to those on the economy when the candidates possess sharply divergent ideological profiles.

In tables 3.3 and 3.4, we investigate the impact of the variables in the two runoff elections in order to test our third hypothesis about inter-round vote transfers. Again, in 2002, views on corruption and the economy did not matter much (table 3.3). In 2006, negative views of the economy favored Alckmin as expected (table 3.4), yet perceptions of corruption, interestingly enough, favored Lula. This provides strong evidence confirming the hypothesis of vote transfers within the family of the political left. Voters who preferred Heloísa and Cristovam in the first round, and who thought corruption was a problem, did in fact "come home" to Lula in the second round. Heloísa Helena voters massively transferred their support in the second round to Lula: 56% of her voters in the first round shifted to Lula in the second (as did 11% of Cristovam voters, and even an astonishing 7% of

Table 3.1. Vote in the First Round of the 2002 Brazilian Presidential Election

	Lula–Ciro Gomes	Lula–Serra	Lula–Garotinho	Lula–Invalid Vote
Corruption is the worst problem	-0.09	-0.08	0.02	-0.20
	(0.25)	(0.19)	(0.22)	(0.29)
Economy is the worst problem	-0.14	-0.02	0.09	-0.17
	(0.10)	(0.08)	(0.09)	(0.12)
Evaluation of incumbent administration	0.06	0.36***	0.01	-0.05
	(0.06)	(0.04)	(0.04)	(0.06)
Voted for Lula in 1998	-2.15***	-1.82***	-1.19***	-1.58***
	(0.44)	(0.30)	(0.25)	(0.41)
Workers' Party supporter	-1.62***	-1.96***	-1.58***	-0.54**
	(0.33)	(0.26)	(0.24)	(0.28)
Rejects Workers' Party	1.92***	2.24***	1.62***	2.00***
	(0.23)	(0.18)	(0.20)	(0.26)
Ideology—self-places as Left	-0.28	-0.90***	-0.46	-0.40
	(0.38)	(0.33)	(0.31)	(0.41)
General political information	0.21***	0.14**	-0.02	-0.05
	(0.08)	(0.06)	(0.07)	(0.10)
Age	0.02***	0.02***	0.00	0.00
	(0.01)	(0.00)	(0.01)	(0.01)
Gender	0.24	0.33**	0.16	-0.24
	(0.18)	(0.14)	(0.16)	(0.22)
Educational level	0.09***	0.05***	0.05***	0.03
	(0.02)	(0.02)	(0.02)	(0.02)
Constant	-4.18***	-3.94***	-1.96***	-1.62***
	(0.57)	(0.44)	(0.45)	(0.57)
Observations	2019	2019	2019	2019

Source: Estudo Eleitoral Brasileiro (Brazilian Electoral Study, ESEB), 2002.
Note: Robust standard errors in parentheses.
*significant at 10%; **significant at 5%; ***significant at 1%. $R^2 = 18\%$.

Table 3.2. Vote in the First Round of the 2006 Brazilian Presidential Election

	Lula – Alckmin	Lula – Helena	Lula – Cristovam	Lula – Invalid Vote
Corruption is the worst problem	−0.09	0.42*	0.84**	0.60
	(0.15)	(0.25)	(0.38)	(0.45)
Economy is the worst problem	0.39***	−0.14	0.26	−0.26
	(0.15)	(0.24)	(0.45)	(0.46)
Evaluation of incumbent administration	−1.47***	−1.27***	−0.71	−1.58***
	(0.23)	(0.30)	(0.67)	(0.35)
Voted for Lula in 2002	−1.77***	−0.45	−1.99**	−1.22**
	(0.26)	(0.40)	(0.88)	(0.54)
Workers' Party supporter	−1.86***	−0.38	−33.53***	0.46
	(0.61)	(0.56)	(0.59)	(1.07)
Rejects Workers' Party	1.75***	1.27***	0.56	3.11***
	(0.24)	(0.41)	(0.65)	(0.72)
Ideology—self-places as Left	−0.06	0.85*	0.04	−33.18***
	(0.48)	(0.51)	(1.13)	(0.49)
General political information	0.26**	0.02	0.32	−0.48*
	(0.13)	(0.17)	(0.59)	(0.26)
Age	0.38	0.52	0.04	0.33
	(0.24)	(0.36)	(0.63)	(0.52)
Gender	0.02**	0.03***	0.06*	0.02
	(0.01)	(0.01)	(0.03)	(0.02)
Educational level	0.27***	0.29***	0.68***	0.18
	(0.07)	(0.09)	(0.20)	(0.13)
Constant	−0.20	−2.92**	−8.40**	−1.56
	(0.98)	(1.25)	(3.36)	(2.05)
Observations	824	824	824	824

Source: Estudo Eleitoral Brasileiro (Brazilian Electoral Study, ESEB), 2006.
Note: Robust standard errors in parentheses.
*significant at 10%; **significant at 5%; ***significant at 1%. R^2 = 36%.

Table 3.3. Vote in the Second Round of the 2002 Brazilian Presidential Election

	Lula–Serra	*Lula–Invalid Vote*
Corruption is the worst problem	−0.01	−0.01
	(0.18)	(0.27)
Economy is the worst problem	0.03	−0.18
	(0.07)	(0.11)
Evaluation of incumbent administration	0.35***	0.00
	(0.04)	(0.06)
Voted for Lula in 1998	−1.60***	−0.69**
	(0.29)	(0.31)
Workers' Party supporter	−1.97***	−0.24
	(0.26)	(0.25)
Rejects Workers' Party	2.55***	2.06***
	(0.16)	(0.23)
Ideology—self-places as Left	−1.05***	−0.50
	(0.32)	(0.40)
General political information	0.14**	0.02
	(0.06)	(0.09)
Age	0.01**	0.00
	(0.00)	(0.01)
Gender	0.42***	−0.05
	(0.13)	(0.20)
Educational level	0.03**	0.03
	(0.01)	(0.02)
Constant	−3.84***	−2.57***
	(0.40)	(0.58)
Observations	2026	2026

Source: Estudo Eleitoral Brasileiro (Brazilian Electoral Study, ESEB), 2002.
Note: Robust standard errors in parentheses.
*significant at 10%; **significant at 5%; ***significant at 1%. R^2 = 28%.

Alckmin voters, which also helps understand why Alckmin received fewer valid votes in the runoff than in the first round). Therefore, the huge transfer of votes from Heloísa Helena to Lula—both candidates traditionally considered more to the left of the Brazilian spectrum than Cristovam or Alckmin—explains why negative views on corruption now favored Lula, in a reversal of the pattern uncovered in the first round. In sum, when "push

Table 3.4. Vote in the Second Round of the 2006 Brazilian Presidential Election

	Lula–Alckmin	Lula–Invalid Vote
Corruption is the worst problem	−0.25*	−0.01
	(0.15)	(0.19)
Economy is the worst problem	0.46***	0.40**
	(0.15)	(0.20)
Evaluation of incumbent administration	−1.45***	−0.65**
	(0.21)	(0.27)
Voted for Lula in 1998	−1.70***	−1.39***
	(0.24)	(0.31)
Workers' Party supporter	−1.80***	−0.97*
	(0.53)	(0.53)
Rejects Workers' Party	1.67***	1.46***
	(0.23)	(0.29)
Ideology—self-places as Left	0.06	0.17
	(0.38)	(0.50)
General political information	0.22*	−0.14
	(0.13)	(0.16)
Age	0.22	0.13
	(0.22)	(0.28)
Gender	0.01	−0.00
	(0.01)	(0.01)
Educational level	0.23***	−0.02
	(0.06)	(0.07)
Constant	0.72	0.01
	(0.87)	(1.15)
Observations	846	846

Source: Estudo Eleitoral Brasileiro (Brazilian Electoral Study, ESEB), 2006.
Note: Robust standard errors in parentheses.
*significant at 10%; **significant at 5%; ***significant at 1%. $R^2 = 36\%$.

came to shove," corruption became a secondary issue for voters who sought a close ideological substitute for an eliminated candidate.

Satisfaction with the incumbent president is also an important explanation for vote choice in both elections. The indicator of satisfaction with the incumbent administration has the expected effect, favoring Serra in 2002 and Lula in 2006, suggesting that Brazil conforms to patterns of retrospective voting observed in numerous other democracies. Results for both elections and all four rounds also are very consistent in pointing to the impact of long-term loyalties in shaping vote choice, as revealed by the coefficients for PT partisanship and PT rejection, prior support for Lula, and self-declared ideology. In all elections, PT identification is a positive predictor of a Lula vote—the only exception being the case of Heloísa Helena in 2006. Hence, it is clear that Heloísa and Lula were engaged in hand-to-hand combat for the same voters.

The models also highlight how PT rejection always favors the PSDB candidate more than any other. Partisanship is confirmed in other ways as well: the results also reveal Lula's supporters to be fairly stable over time. Having voted for Lula in the past strongly predicts another vote for Lula in the present—the exception once again owed to Heloísa Helena, who temporarily stole longtime Lula supporters in 2006, mostly those concerned with corruption.[11] Finally, self-described leftist ideology affected the Lula vote as expected in the two rounds of the 2002 elections but failed to do so in 2006. Left-wing voters in 2006 voted predominantly for Heloísa Helena. The Lula electorate in 2006, on the other hand, was not as monolithically leftist as was the case in 2002. The president seems to have attracted new voters into his camp, probably as a consequence of social policies and their economic impact (Hunter and Power 2007).

Last but not least, the controls for political information, age, gender, and educational level indicate that Lula voters are usually less informed on political issues, undereducated, younger, and more likely to be male, especially when in comparison to supporters of PSDB candidates. This is clearly true in 2002. The combination of less information and lower educational level indicates that the mean PT supporter is poorer, which also points to a possible social class differentiation among the supporters of the PSDB and the PT.

THE THREE MAIN HYPOTHESES OF THIS STUDY WERE CONFIRMED BY the data. Corruption did affect vote choice in 2006, as a consequence of repeated scandals that haunted the incumbent administration. Perceptions of corruption led to an increase in support of candidates who opposed Lula but who competed with him for ideological space on the left, especially Heloísa Helena of the radical PSOL. In fact, Heloísa "stole" many longtime

Lula supporters—or perhaps "borrowed" is the better word, since these voters gravitated back to Lula after Heloísa was eliminated from the race for the presidency. Radical leftists did not hesitate to back Lula in the runoff, even those who thought corruption was a central problem of the country.

The overall impression from a comparison of the two elections is that the 2002 elections were more ideologically divided and partisan than those in 2006. Partisanship, ideological preferences, and previous vote patterns were more important in 2002 than views on national problems and retrospective voting. In 2006, ideology and partisanship did not disappear, but they were less influential and lost ground to retrospective evaluations of the government, in all of their multiple dimensions. The results indicate that vote choice in Brazil involves many competing calculi and that these vary not only across elections but also across ideological camps. Choices between candidates on the same side of the ideological divide tend to be more influenced by distinct dimensions of retrospective evaluations. Because ideology and partisanship fade in choices between similar candidates on these aspects, other factors are more influential in vote choice. On the other hand, choices between candidates on different sides of the ideological spectrum are influenced more by long-term loyalties and less by evaluations of the incumbent's performance. Hence, if such choices are the predominant ones in elections, incumbents running for reelection can win some leeway during their terms to commit some mistakes and still avoid punishment.

What are the implications of these findings for delegation and accountability? Simply put, *prior loyalties in the form of partisanship, ideology, and charismatic ties may provide shields for incumbents who have less-than-perfect records, even on issues related to involvement in corruption.* Corruption did matter in the 2006 elections, but its impact was attenuated by retrospective voting based on the economy and general satisfaction with Lula's mandate in other dimensions, as well as by long-term attachments. This helps us understand the puzzle of how an administration so implicated in corruption scandals managed to win another four years in office.

The findings presented here also suggest that accountability is conditioned by the double-ballot majoritarian system, which affords voters the possibility of sending a clear message to incumbents in the first round. Historic leftists and PT supporters punished Lula in the first round by voting for Heloísa or Cristovam. The final outcome of the election, with Lula's resounding victory, hides the punishment suffered in the first round, giving a false impression that elections did not ensure accountability. Still, one cannot ignore that in the second round ideology and retrospective voting based on the economy sheltered Lula from the corruption scandals. So, it is also possible to claim that ideology trumps accountability, especially in first-past-the-post electoral systems without two rounds. In two-round systems such as the one in Brazil, the question is whether the message delivered in the first round was properly received, especially since the recipient was the victor in the second round.

Notes

I would like to thank Timothy Power and Matthew Taylor for comments and suggestions on earlier versions of this chapter. I would also like to thank the participants of the workshop on corruption held at the University of Oxford for extremely helpful comments that improved the current version. Last but not least, the careful reading of two anonymous reviewers helped clarify some points. Remaining errors are my responsibility.

1. This phrase is used ironically in Brazil to describe politicians who are seen as effective administrators but who are also thought to be corrupt. The expression is usually linked to the career of Adhemar de Barros (1901–69), who was both a mayor and a governor of São Paulo in the 1950s.

2. Still, the 2006 pattern does not imply that corruption, like other forms of retrospective evaluations, will affect vote choice in all elections. There are situations in which the visibility of corruption is heightened. For instance, when scandals occur with frequency, affecting prominent candidates and earning intense coverage from the media, it is very likely that corruption will influence vote choice. See Porto (this volume) on media, scandals, and corruption for an interesting discussion of how media coverage may also limit accountability by accusing and judging politicians without due process.

3. The concept of shielding is inspired by Pérez-Liñán's innovative idea of a "legislative shield" (2007). In his argument, presidents that avoided impeachment had a solid base of support in Congress that protected them. Similarly, I argue that incumbents' popularity, generated by factors other than corruption scandals, such as solid management of the economy, can shield them from possible wrongdoing.

4. See McCubbins and Schwartz (1984) for a discussion on monitoring devices. On agency theory and delegation, see Lupia (2001).

5. There is a long lineage of political theory that discusses democracy in such a way, leading back to ancient Greece. A very illuminating discussion of this view is *The Federalist Papers* (Hamilton, Jay, and Madison [1787–88] 1902).

6. For a review of the literature on corruption and development, see Bardhan (1997).

7. See the introduction to this volume for a summary of the different scandals in recent Brazilian history.

8. Because of this situation, some variables that are not present in both data sets were not analyzed. For instance, views on social programs, on ideological issues such as privatization, and on candidates' personal characteristics are not included in the models. Still, the models presented are the most adequately specified, given the data available.

9. By underestimation of partisanship, I claim that looking only at identification is not sufficient to understand the full impact that parties may have in Brazilian elections. Rejection of a party is also important to explain why a voter decided not to chose a specific candidate. Still, a better source of data about the role of partisanship would be based on a longitudinal or panel design over the span of a single election, where partisanship measured in early moments of the campaign process could be used to assess vote choice. This strategy would clearly avoid endogeneity problems that plague cross-sectional analysis. However, a detailed account of such issues is a topic for another paper. For a still incipient approach to this question in Brazil, see Mochel et al. (2006).

10. Collinearity between independent variables is always a problem in social, political, and economic analysis. However, perfect multicollinearity is rare. Obviously, some of the independent variables included in the model are correlated, but none to a degree that jeopardizes the analysis.

11. Rennó (2007c) shows that 95% of Helena voters thought corruption was the worst problem of the country. Of those who shifted to Lula in the second round, 68% thought corruption was a problem.

Chapter Four

Corruption, Campaign Finance, and Reelection

CARLOS PEREIRA, LUCIO R. RENNÓ, & DAVID J. SAMUELS

The conventional understanding of corruption in Brazil suggests that "impunity reigns." The media expose scandal after scandal; anticorruption activists form NGOs; yet little changes. The case of corruption under President Lula is instructive. During Lula's first term, the media delved deeply into the administration's numerous scandals. Lula's personal approval rating declined during the *mensalão* scandal in 2005, but such disapproval proved only superficial and fleeting—after all, Lula won reelection in 2006. One can tell a similar story at the municipal level, where Pereira, Melo, and Figueiredo (2009a, 2009b) found that mayors do not refrain from "rent seeking" because the probability of being caught—and thus punished at the polls—is very low. In short, corruption is widespread throughout the political class. Given the scandals of Lula's first term, even the PT, which many had regarded as less corrupt than other parties and which claimed "transparency in government" as a key element in its platform, is now regarded as just like the rest.

Accountability requires political competition, effective institutions able to check and constrain politicians' misbehavior, and a desire by voters for "clean government." Yet observers have long noted Brazilian citizens' tolerance of corruption across party lines. That is, despite their party's historical trajectory, even *petistas* apparently care relatively little about corruption (Samuels 2008). This fact perhaps explains why the PT's support in the 2006 legislative elections remained fairly stable compared against 2002, and why, despite mountains of evidence that party leaders had systematically violated their own stated principles, the PT's level of partisan identification in 2009 stood exactly where it had when Lula took office in 2003.

These examples suggest that the sources of impunity in Brazil lie at both the elite *and* the mass levels (for a review, see Taylor 2010). Political elites have historically felt free to blur the line between the public and private spheres, and voters tend either not to pay much attention to this activity or not to care. Indeed, public opinion surveys find that a majority of Brazilians accept or even support the notion of *rouba mas faz*—the idea that a politician "steals, but gets things done." According to the 2002 Brazilian National Electoral Study (ESEB) (Almeida 2007), 53% of voters with no education said they would vote for a politician who steals but gets things done. Support for *rouba mas faz* declines with education, but even so, 46% of Brazilians with an eighth-grade education would vote for such a politician. Among Brazilians with a high school education the percentage is 38%, and even among those with some college education the proportion is 25%.

Of course, relatively few Brazilians have a college degree, which suggests that tolerance of corruption remains fairly high among modal Brazilian voters (Cervellini 2006). Such findings echo those of anthropologists and sociologists who have long emphasized the difficulty in Brazilian culture of separating the public from the private sphere (e.g., da Matta 1979). Given this widespread tolerance of corruption, most voters are unlikely to punish *rouba mas faz* behavior as long as politicians continue to deliver on their personalistic promises of private goods. Thus, despite the occasional counterexample, observers of Brazilian politics tend to assume that politicians generally do not fear accusations of corruption simply because few are caught, fewer are prosecuted, and even fewer are ultimately punished. If electoral impunity is the norm and if the root of impunity lies not in an underfunded and perhaps similarly corrupt judiciary but rather in popular indifference or even acquiescence to corruption, then we should expect allegations of corruption to matter little for politicians' prospects of reelection.

This essay explores an empirical puzzle that confounds this conventional view. In the 2006 legislative elections, federal deputies who were accused of involvement in one of the many scandals that marked the 2003–6 legislature had a lower probability of *running* for reelection and a lower probability of *winning* reelection if they decided to run (Rennó 2007a).

Such a result suggests substantially greater optimism than the conventional wisdom allows.[1] If impunity reigns, why would corrupt politicians be reluctant to run for reelection? And why, if they did risk running, would corrupt politicians lose more frequently than ostensibly "clean" politicians?

Rennó's findings are especially intriguing because incumbent deputies accused of corruption spent more on average on their reelection campaigns than deputies who were not accused of corruption. In other words, it appears as if legislators must compensate for damage to their reputations by spending more in the next election—which implies that the impact of corruption on elections may pass through the critical conduit of campaign finance.[2]

Two Mechanisms of Electoral Accountability

Rennó's findings raise a series of questions about the connection between allegations of corruption, campaign finance, and "political survival" in Brazil. To what extent do allegations of corruption truly damage politicians' careers? If accusations of corruption are indeed harmful, then what is the *mechanism* by which electoral accountability works in Brazil? Given the importance of money to candidates' reelection prospects (Samuels 2001a, 2001b, 2001c), it may be that accusations have only an indirect effect on deputies' reelection chances by reducing their ability to raise funds, which in turn affects their competitiveness. Jacobson and Dimock (1994) found that corruption had a similar effect on incumbents' competitiveness in the United States. We should also entertain the hypothesis that Brazilian voters punish corruption directly by withdrawing support for politicians associated with scandal. Do allegations of corruptions affect voters' opinions *directly, indirectly,* or both?

This chapter explores the two potential mechanisms, implied above, by which accountability might operate in Brazil: an elite mechanism or a mass mechanism. First, accountability might work indirectly through an *elite* mechanism. This hypothesis suggests that *at least some members of the political and economic elite punish allegations of corruption by withholding campaign contributions,* which in turn discourages incumbents from running again and/or damages their reelection chances. This hypothesis follows from Samuels's (2001b) characterization of the Brazilian campaign-finance market as a network of relatively few highly capitalized financiers. Comparatively few individuals or corporations give money to politicians in Brazil, but when they do they tend to give huge sums. In contrast, in the United States most politicians do not personally know many of their donors, most of whom give small amounts.

The nature of the Brazilian campaign-finance market suggests that politicians are personally close to those who fund their campaigns. If financiers care about corruption, we should see sanctioning behavior levied against politicians whose behavior violates expected norms. As Samuels (2001b) posited, campaign financiers seek to develop long-term relationships with politicians by "investing" in their careers. Such relationships require trust. We do not need to assume that all campaign financiers are honest or that campaign financiers seek only honest politicians. Indeed, some donors may not care at all whether politicians are honest—but there may be some threshold past which political financiers may regard politicians as "too corrupt" and thus a threat to their "investment." There is no honor among thieves, but there must be some form of trust for even an illegal business partnership to flourish. Involvement in a public corruption scandal might be the signal that a politician has gone too far, suggesting that potential campaign financiers would be better off withholding their money and investing in other, potentially clean candidates.

If those who fund campaigns see accusations of corruption as a signal that they have "invested poorly" in a politician, then accusations of corruption should be followed by a decline in such investments. Successful business owners are not stupid—they will not throw good money after bad. After all, corruption suggests that the campaign finance investment has been poorly spent because the politician has not used his or her time and energy to protect the campaign financier's interests and has instead acted in his or her own interests exclusively. Exposure of corruption might also be "bad for business" in that it might bring the scrutiny of Brazil's tax authority down upon the financier's business operations. Wealthy contributors have no interest in giving a politician a free ride—they want to get their money's worth. If they detect that they are wasting their money, they will search elsewhere for a reliable investment.

Thus, to the extent that corruption affects incumbents' ability to raise funds for a campaign, corruption affects reelection through an elite mechanism because money is so important to winning reelection. Perhaps the elite hypothesis accounts for patterns of election and reelection in Brazil. Of course, we must entertain the possibility that Samuels's "elite accountability" mechanism is a chimera and that no elite accountability mechanism exists at all, which would leave Rennó's findings unexplained. That is, maybe wealthy elites care so little about corruption that they *do* throw money at clean and dirty politicians alike.

Rennó's findings also open up the possibility of a *mass* accountability mechanism. Even controlling for the impact of elite accountability, we must also ask whether *voters* directly punish allegations of corruption. Of course, voters might *not* punish corruption and might even reward *rouba mas faz* even as elites are punishing such behavior. However, as was said before, Rennó's chapter in this book points out that some voters did punish Lula in the first round of the presidential election if they perceived him or his administration as corrupt. Still, when they had to choose between Lula and Alckmin in the second round, left-wing voters who had abandoned Lula in the first round held their noses and voted for him anyway. Hence, voters are aware of corruption scandals, but when push comes to shove, ideology and evaluations of the economy trump corruption.

In any case, in the legislative elections either the elite or the mass mechanism—or both—must be at work. Thus our second hypothesis suggests that voters will punish politicians perceived as corrupt, even if elites do not.

We have hypothesized that the elite mechanism works through campaign finance by weakening incumbent politicians. Many thus retire, expecting to lose if they seek reelection. And for those who do risk reelection, elite withdrawal of campaign finance weakens their reelection prospects. Yet why would Brazilian voters punish corrupt deputies? What is the mechanism of accountability? Brazil's electoral system for legislative elections imposes huge information requirements on voters to learn about incumbent performance in office. How do voters figure out whom to reward or punish, given Brazil's complex open-list proportional representation system?

As others have suggested (e.g., Ferraz and Finan 2008; Porto, this volume), media exposure is key to exposing and ultimately punishing corruption. A free press is a key element of democracy precisely because it provides information about government activities to average citizens. A free flow of information is a necessary condition for accountability to function. In theory, a free press provides objective information about who has received an allegation of corruption. To be sure, and as Porto emphasizes in this volume, the press is not entirely "free" in many if not most of Brazil's states, since politicians themselves own many of the TV and radio stations and local newspapers.

However, media exposure might serve as the catalyst for the spread of negative publicity about an incumbent candidate for reelection. In Brazil, compared to other countries, rates for readership of newspapers are relatively low—but those who do read newspapers are likely to be among the "opinion leaders," people who enjoy talking about politics and to whom other people listen about politics. Such individuals may serve as the conduit for information in their neighborhood or workplaces (Baker, Ames, and Rennó 2006). Accusations of corruption in the media could tarnish a candidate's name among voters in general, negatively affecting the candidate's reelection prospects, *with or without an elite effect* through provision of campaign finance.

We suspect, however, that the *timing* of the release of information about politicians' misbehavior is also fundamental for voters to hold politicians accountable. Pereira et al. (forthcoming) demonstrate that the number of irregularities perpetrated by mayors and detected by an auditing agency during the electoral campaign (up to four months prior the election) negatively affects mayors' reelection chances. However, if the audit agency discovers and publicizes irregularities prior to that time, the accusations have no effect on election results. A similar effect may be at work in legislative elections.

To summarize, allegations of corruption might impede a candidate's ability to raise funds, or they could lead to voter backlash—or both. To the extent that allegations of corruption affect incumbents' ability to raise funds, we should see fewer corrupt incumbents running for reelection and fewer winning reelection. To the extent that allegations of corruption encourage voters to seek out "honest" politicians, corruption should reduce incumbents' ability to win votes, controlling for the effect of corruption on campaign finance.

In the next section we explore these hypotheses statistically. First, we explore the relationship between accusations of corruption and politicians' strategic decisions to *run for reelection* or not. Jacobson and Dimock (1994) showed that allegations of corruption reduce the likelihood that an incumbent member of the U.S. House of Representatives will run for reelection—precisely because "corrupt" incumbents believe they are vulnerable. We suspect a similar dynamic is at work in Brazil. "Corrupt" Brazilian deputies may desist from running precisely because they know they will be unable to raise sufficient funds and/or that they have lost the trust of their vote base. Second, we explore the impact of accusations of corruption on campaign finance. We find a weak relationship between corruption and candidates' ability to raise money, partly confirming our hypothesis. Finally, we explore the impact of allegations of corruption on the probability that an incumbent will *win reelection*, controlling for the impact of corruption on a candidate's ability to raise funds. Results from these regressions confirm that both mass *and* elite accountability mechanisms are at work in Brazil. Finally we explore the implications of our findings for scholarly understanding of corruption in contemporary Brazil.

Exploring the Elite Accountability Mechanism Indirectly

The elite accountability mechanism can work indirectly or directly. At the heart of this mechanism is a story about the nature of campaign financing in Brazil. Businesses that contribute "aboveboard" campaign funds have made a conscious decision to contribute legally, directly, and publicly to candidates' campaigns. Many Brazilian firms contribute to campaigns indirectly (with in-kind contributions of material or labor) or pay into *caixa dois*, off-the-books contributions. Business leaders who make on-the-books contributions are far less likely to tolerate corruption and are more likely to withdraw support from deputies accused of illegal activity.

Incumbents surely understand this and know that accusations of misbehavior will damage their fundraising prospects. Given the importance of campaign finance to deputies' reelection chances, incumbents who are accused of corruption will realize that accusations of corruption thus damage their chances of winning reelection. Many such deputies will realize that running again is futile, and they will desist from even trying. The raw numbers strongly support this idea. In 2006, there were 628 incumbents eligible for reelection, including *titulares* and *suplentes*.[3] Some 73% of these (456) ran for reelection. Breaking this down, we find a difference between deputies involved in scandal and those not involved. Of deputies impli-

Table 4.1. Impact of Scandal on Deputies' Decisions to Run for Reelection

Independent Variable	Run for Reelection
Scandal	−0.12
	(0.04)***
Titular	0.12
	(0.05)**
Pork	0.46
	(0.17)***
Member of Govt Coalition	0.03
	(0.04)
Legislation Approved	0.04
	(0.02)**
% of Votes in State 2002	−1.95
	(0.67)***
Constant	0.99
	(1.84)
Observations	624

Note: Probit regression reporting marginal effects of coefficients, with robust standard errors in parentheses.
*significant at 10%; **significant at 5%; ***significant at 1%.

cated in scandal, 61% (71 of 115) ran for reelection, while 75% (385 of 513) of deputies *not* implicated in scandal decided to run.

This is a statistically significant as well as substantial difference. Table 4.1 presents results of a probit regression exploring the impact of scandal on deputies' decisions to run for reelection, controlling for various other factors. Our main independent variable indicates whether an incumbent deputy was involved in corruption. To test our hypotheses we constructed a simple indicator of "media accusation of involvement in corruption." This variable counts deputies' involvement in the major scandals of Lula's first term. We read through the coverage of the national newsmagazine *Veja* and the widely circulated newspaper *Folha de S. Paulo* for the entire four-year period of the 2003–6 legislature to find any indication that a deputy (whether a *titular* or a *suplente*) was implicated in a corruption scandal. We compiled a list of all the names associated with the following major scandals—the *sanguessuga* or "bloodsucker" scandal, the "bingo" scandal, the "post office" scandal, and the *mensalão* or "monthly allowance" scandal—as well as any deputies who were accused of violations of parliamentary decorum or administrative improbity (see Power and Taylor's introduction to this volume for further details).[4] This indicator, which we call "scandal," can theoretically range from 0 to 6. Ninety-nine deputies were involved in one scandal, fourteen deputies were mentioned in two scandals, and two deputies were implicated in three scandals.[5]

As deputies who are electorally weak may need to spend more money in order to compensate for their weakness, one might argue that electoral weakness can be a cause of corruption. To deal with that possibility, we included a control for "titular" (source: TSE 2002b) and a variable designated "pork," which is the percentage of a deputy's pork-barrel budget amendment requests that the president "executed," averaged by year (source: Câmara dos Deputados 2003–6).[6] Deputies who are relatively successful at obtaining release of pork-barrel funds will have a higher value on this variable. We expect variables to be positively related to running for reelection.

We also included a variable that measures deputies' "legislative performance," the total number of pieces of legislation the deputy authored or coauthored that were eventually approved, and a variable indicating whether the deputy was a member of a party in the government coalition: the Workers' Party (PT), the Communist Party of Brazil (PCdoB), the Democratic Labor Party (PDT), the Liberal Party (PL), the Socialist People's Party (PPS), the Brazilian Socialist Party (PSB), the Brazilian Labor Party (PTB), and the Green Party (PV).[7] Finally, as a control we include the deputy's percentage of the total vote in the previous election (TSE 2002a). The legislative performance variables could have positive or negative effects. Deputies who have success *within* the legislature may use that success to further their progressive ambitions *outside* the legislature. As Samuels (2003) noted, the strongest incumbents are also the strongest candidates for higher office, and they thus might run for governor or senator. In any case, we are uninterested in the question of progressive ambition here and are primarily interested in the impact of scandal on whether deputies run for reelection.[8]

The numbers in each cell represent the impact in percent of a unit change on the independent variable. Thus the results provide strong support for our "elite indirect effect" hypothesis: controlling for the impact of other variables, deputies involved in one scandal are 12% less likely to run for reelection. Accusations of corruption tend to cull weakened incumbents from the herd, as in the United States. This is likely a function of deputies' reduced prospects of raising campaign finance. In the next section we bolster this "indirect" evidence with "direct" evidence that elites withdraw campaign finance from deputies involved in scandal.

Exploring the Elite Accountability Mechanism Directly

Our general hypothesis supposes that elites will actually withdraw funds from incumbents who are accused of corruption. The results in table 4.1 are indirect in that they show only that involvement in scandal affects deputies' strategic decisions to enter the race or not. We suggest that deputies involved in scandal realize that they will be unable to raise sufficient funds to win and thus that they opt out of the campaign. In this section we test a direct rather than indirect hypothesis: involvement in scandal negatively affects incumbents' actual ability to raise money.

We proceed directly to a statistical test. The universe of cases we explore includes all deputies (both *titulares* and *suplentes*) who were elected in 2002 and who subsequently ran for reelection as federal deputy in 2006 (N = 456). The dependent variable in this regression is the deputy's "percentage of all campaign finance revenue" in the deputy's home state in 2006. The source for this information is the Tribunal Superior Eleitoral (2007). We include controls for "titular" (we expect *titulares* to raise more funds, *ceteris paribus*) and "pork." Samuels (2002) hypothesized that porkbarreling helps deputies raise campaign funds, so we expect this variable to have a positive impact.

Table 4.2 displays results from two different OLS regression models (with robust standard errors)—one that includes a control for state-level competition (measured as the number of candidates for federal deputy in the state divided by the number of seats available) and one that does not. The first model supports our hypothesis. The main independent variable is signed correctly in the second model but is not statistically significant. This suggests that our results are sensitive to the inclusion of the control for state-level competition.

Table 4.2. "Elite" Accountability Mechanism: Scandal Affects
Campaign Finance

Independent Variable	% Total Campaign Finance Revenue in State 2006	
% of Total Campaign Finance Revenue in State 2002	0.57 (.07)***	0.55 (0.07)***
Scandal	−0.01 (0.00)*	−0.01 (0.00)
Titular	0.00 (0.00)	0.00 (0.00)
Pork	0.02 (0.02)	0.02 (0.02)
# Candidates per Seat	—	0.08 (0.03)**
Constant	0.01 (0.00)***	0.00 (0.00)
Observations	456	456
R-squared	0.35	0.36

Note: OLS regressions with robust standard errors in parentheses.
*significant at 10%; **significant at 5%; ***significant at 1%.

In model 1, note that the lagged dependent variable is (not surprisingly) highly correlated with the dependent variable, while neither "titular" nor "pork" is statistically significant. However, involvement in "one additional scandal" reduces deputies' ability to raise campaign finance by 1% (.01). This may seem like a small effect, but the mean for this variable is only 2% (.02). Thus, to illustrate this result, consider the following example: in states in which district magnitude is between 8 (the lowest value) and 10 (fourteen of twenty-seven states), the mean percentage of campaign finance is .05 or 5%. If one runs the same model as in table 4.1 just on cases in these states, the coefficient on "scandal" is .01—meaning that involvement in one scandal reduces access to campaign finance on average by 20%—a decline of .01 from .05 (the average) to .04. A similar ratio holds in larger states.

In short, these results provide some support for our hypothesis. However, we recognize that this result is sensitive to the inclusion of the control for state-level competition. Unfortunately our measure of state-level competition is constant within each state and thus controls for factors associated with politics in each state. Our results indicate that heightened competition tends (unsurprisingly) to increase incumbents' spending. When we include this variable, "scandal" remains negatively signed but loses significance.

We must point out, however, that even this limited support for our hypothesis is good evidence of an elite effect, since many deputies who might have otherwise run for reelection have dropped out of the sample—at least in part, we suggest, because of their difficulty raising campaign funds. If scandal reduces the likelihood that deputies will run for reelection, then we should *expect* a weak result on "scandal" in table 4.1, because deputies with reduced ability to raise campaign funds will have dropped out of the sample. The impact of corruption on incumbents' ability to raise funds would no doubt be stronger if all incumbents were "forced" to run for reelection, whether they were involved in scandal or not.

Exploring the Mass Accountability Mechanism Directly

Thus far we have provided evidence that corruption affects legislative turnover indirectly, through an elite effect. Deputies themselves pull out of the race at least partly because scandal affects their prospects for raising money. This is an important finding on its own—it implies that at least part of Brazil's political-economic elite is concerned about corruption enough to withhold money from incumbents accused of corruption. This dynamic merits further investigation. We now move to explore a third hypothesis, that voters themselves punish deputies accused of corruption, controlling for the "selection" effect of deputies who decide not to run, as well as for the effect of scandal on deputies' ability to raise campaign finance.

At first glance, it appears that involvement in scandal hurts deputies' chances of winning reelection. Overall, some 61% (279 of 456) of all incumbents (including *titulares* and *suplentes*) ran for reelection. Of those not involved in scandal, 75% won reelection (249 of 385), but only 42% (30 of 71) of those accused of corruption won. To confirm the effect of corruption and bolster our claim of a mass accountability mechanism, we statistically explored the factors that improved or harmed incumbents' reelection chances, again using probit analysis. We aim to explore the impact of scandal on reelection, controlling for the impact of scandal on campaign finance—that is, to test for the effect of scandal on deputies' reelection chances independently of their ability to raise money. By controlling for the impact of scandal on campaign finance, we can then test for the hypothesized impact of scandal directly on reelection—what we have called the mass effect—through voter punishment.

To accomplish this, we took the predicted values for each observation from table 4.2 and included them as an independent variable in a model predicting likelihood of reelection success, along with several other variables (model 1 below). This model controls for the effect of scandal on candidates' ability to raise campaign finance and thus does not include campaign finance directly as a variable in the equation. We then compare this against a second model that includes campaign finance. If we find that scandal affects reelection even when the impact of scandal on campaign finance is controlled for, then we gain confidence that scandal has an independent effect on voter behavior—what we have labeled the mass effect.

Table 4.3 presents results. The dependent variable here is a dummy for "win reelection" (as one of the 513 *titulares* for the subsequent legislature) or not. The main independent variable is "scandal," a dummy variable as defined above. The first model includes the predicted values of "campaign finance" "purged" of the effect of "scandal," while the second model includes "campaign finance" directly. The models also include several variables thought to be associated with legislative reelection in Brazil, as previously defined: the number of candidates competing per seat in each state; the dummy indicating whether the incumbent was a *titular* or a *suplente;* the percent of all votes in the state; pork; legislation approved; and the dummy indicating whether the incumbent was a member of the government coalition.

The results provide strong support for our mass accountability hypothesis. In the first model, having purged the effect of scandal on campaign finance, we find that involvement in one scandal substantially reduces an incumbent's chances of reelection—by 15%. Model 2 reveals how important it is to purge the effect of scandal on campaign finance: when one includes "campaign finance" directly in the equation, it is a very powerful predictor of reelection success, as is past vote performance and being a *titular*. Still, note that "scandal" remains significant and negative even

Table 4.3. "Mass" Accountability Mechanism: Impact of Scandal on Reelection

Independent Variable	Win Reelection	
Scandal	−0.15	−0.12
	(0.06)**	(.05)**
% of Total Campaign Finance Revenue in State 2006	—	4.08
		(1.31)***
(Predicted Values)	−2.33	—
	(1.59)	
# of Candidates per Seat	1.59	0.98
	(.79)**	(.75)
Titular	0.30	0.31
	(0.07)***	(0.06)***
% of All Votes in State 2002	3.02	−0.32
	(1.27)**	(1.25)
Pork	−0.02	−0.08
	(0.20)	(0.20)
Legislation Approved	0.02	0.02
	(0.02)	(0.02)
Member of Govt. Coalition	−0.11	−0.07
	(0.05)**	(0.05)
Observations	456	454

Note: Probit regression reporting marginal effects of coefficients, with robust standard errors.
*significant at 10%; **significant at 5%; ***significant at 1%.

when "campaign finance" is included in the second model. Another interesting result is that opposition politicians performed better than members of the government coalition—perhaps this represents a secondary measure of our mass accountability mechanism, punishing *all* members of Lula's coalition for the government's tolerance of corruption, even though Lula himself won a smashing reelection victory.[9]

We must add, however, that when we attempted to identity the impact of involvement in particular scandals, we found that only involvement in the "bloodsucker" scandal significantly reduced deputies' reelection chances. The main reason most other scandals did not significantly reduce reelection chances was that relatively few deputies were involved in each scandal, with the exception of the bloodsucker scandal and the famous *mensalão* scandal. However, involvement in the *mensalão* did not significantly reduce deputies' reelection chances.

As we noted at the outset, we suspect that the timing of different scandals determines the extent of their effect on voter opinion and thus on election outcomes. The *sanguessuga* scandal occurred close to the 2006 elections, while the others all occurred earlier in the legislature. Thus media exposure of scandal may matter, but only if it falls close enough to an election so that voters will remember (Pereira, Melo, and Figueiredo 2009a, 2009b). Unfortunately we cannot empirically confirm this hypothesis with the available data. Including a variable for the "proximity" of the scandal is no help because doing so is the same as putting in a dummy variable for each scandal—which would generate the same result as we have already described: involvement in the *sanguessuga* scandal affects deputies' reelection chances, while involvement in other scandals does not. This question merits additional research, perhaps using a panel survey.

Overall, our results tell a fairly clear story. Deputies accused of corruption are more likely to desist from running for reelection (table 4.1). Those accused of corruption who do run for reelection are weaker candidates, at least in part because at least some campaign financiers shy away (table 4.2). Yet many deputies (probably the truly and deeply corrupt ones) persist in their reelection efforts partly because if they lose office they also lose special parliamentary legal privileges. Nevertheless, at least in part because association with corruption has weakened their ability to raise money but also in part because voters appear to punish corruption, deputies who have been associated with scandal are far less likely to win reelection (table 4.3).

IN THIS STUDY, WE FIND SUPPORT FOR BOTH ELITE AND MASS MECHANISMS of accountability. The elite mechanism affects election results through campaign finance. Incumbent federal deputies who are accused of corruption receive less campaign financing than those who are not involved. This makes them far weaker candidates for reelection. Thus deputies involved in scandals are far less likely to attempt reelection. Those accused of corruption who do try their luck, because they have fewer resources or must scramble to find additional resources, are also less likely to win reelection. As Samuels (2001b) suspected, elites have created mechanisms to punish politicians who violate implicit campaign finance contracts.

Yet accountability is not simply a function of political elites' machinations. We also found that mass accountability mechanisms directly affect federal deputies' electoral success. Involvement in scandals reduces the likelihood of winning reelection, even when the indirect effect of scandals through campaign finance is controlled for. This effect seems to be a function of media priming, given that the effect of corruption on individual vote choice was apparently much more important in 2006 than it was in 2002 (Rennó, this volume). Thus it remains to be seen whether 2006 was an aberration or whether future surveys will show a decline in support for *rouba mas faz,* across education levels, even independently of media priming effects.

One might ask whether our *statistically* significant results are also *substantively* significant. It is true that involvement in scandal reduces incumbents' reelection chances. Yet a reelection rate of 42% is not a reelection rate of 4.2%. That is, the impact of scandal on voter retribution is not total, only partial. Given the conventional wisdom about voters' indifference to corruption, we believe this result is encouraging: the conventional wisdom expects little voter retribution, but we see some—which is surely better than none. The glass is half full rather than completely empty.

In our view, the statistical results are surprisingly optimistic regarding the possibility of purging corrupt legislators. However, this optimism must be tempered by the following fact: given that 42% of deputies accused of corruption do manage to win reelection, Brazil's legislature will always contain a large number of corrupt deputies unless (noncorrupt) deputies themselves create stronger institutional punishments for involvement in corruption. If Brazil's legislature lacks the will or institutional capacities to purge itself of corrupt members, we are not likely to see any improvement in the public's low opinion of legislators and political parties.

Given the conventional view of both elites' and masses' acceptance of corruption, our results raise two additional questions for students of Brazilian politics. First, what is the source of the elite effect? Why might campaign financiers punish allegations of corruption? At the elite level, elected politicians claim in interviews that they have felt increasing pressure to eliminate *caixa dois* and to report all contributions in the wake of the scandals of Lula's first administration.[10] Given the intense media coverage of the scandal and the obvious negative effects that association with scandal had on their colleagues' reelection chances, politicians are increasingly reluctant to accept under-the-table cash donations. This does not mean that *caixa dois* no longer exists, only that politicians and donors are turning more to off-the-books "in-kind" donations than to the storied and traditional brown paper bags full of cash. *Caixa dois* probably will never go away with the current electoral rules, but media scrutiny matters, and campaign finance irregularities now come under more and more immediate suspicion.

Taylor (2010) notes "important, if gradual" improvements in uncovering and prosecuting corruption. We would point particularly to the growing authority of the federal tax agency, the Receita Federal, in terms of its power to investigate individuals' and corporations' bank accounts and to detect irregular financial transactions. Taylor highlights several other measures that facilitate detection—if not prosecution—of corrupt political practices. Given these efforts toward reducing corruption through empowering agencies and enacting new or changing existing legislation, it should come as little surprise that campaign financiers would also respond by seeking to avoid any association with corrupt practices—after all, the effort to eliminate corruption also focuses on private-sector practices such as money laundering, tax evasion, and payment of bribes in exchange for political favors.

The key in this equation is the private sector. In terms of allegations of corruption, private-sector interests may not fear official investigation themselves. They have greater concerns about *losing their investment.* Business owners in Brazil are not tied to any particular party and prefer to spread their political "investments" around (see, e.g., Schneider 2004). They seek low-risk or secure investments and expect a high return. After all, they could simply put their money in a Brazilian bank and earn a healthy return after four years. A campaign-finance "investment" must have lower risk than any other investment that does not enjoy indexing against the inflation rate. In other words, all campaign finance investments are relatively high risk. Accusations of corruption, in our view, are analogous to international investment risk agencies' classification of countries' investment risk level. Accusations of corruption can be taken as a mark against a politician's trustworthiness—not to voters in general but to campaign financiers in particular. Because financiers are free to pick and choose among candidates, they pick the safer investments.

The second question has to do with Brazilian voters: Do enough Brazilian voters care about corruption to punish politicians, especially in Brazil's wide-open legislative races? And if the answer to that question is yes, is antipathy toward corrupt politicians a onetime phenomenon or a long-term development? There is mixed evidence for these questions. Hence, our responses here are preliminary. Rennó (this volume) shows that perceptions of corruption strongly affected vote choice for president in the 2006 elections but not in 2002. Of course, it is important to bear in mind that there were fewer high-profile corruption scandals immediately prior to 2002 compared against 2006. Corruption was important in the first round of the 2006 presidential elections, when many voters who viewed corruption as a national problem preferred candidates other than Lula, such as Heloísa Helena or Cristovam Buarque. Individuals who cast votes for these two leftist candidates mostly transferred their allegiance to Lula in the second round of the election, contributing to Lula's victory. As Rennó's chapter demonstrates, if these voters had supported Lula all along, he would have won in the first round. Perceptions of corruption prevented Lula from winning in the first round.

More detailed investigation of the 2006 ESEB shows that 10% of those individuals who supported Lula in 2002 abandoned him in 2006 for Geraldo Alckmin—the main *opposition* candidate—because of the importance they placed on corruption. Overall, only 80% of those who supported Lula in 2002 voted for him in the first round in 2006 (obviously he added votes, gaining the support of many who had voted for other candidates in 2002). This is a significant drop—and it is due mostly to perceptions of corruption as a national problem. Hence, corruption significantly affected vote choices in 2006.

We cannot conduct the same analysis for Chamber elections because of the high fragmentation of votes and because of high "I don't remember" answers to questions about vote choice for federal deputy in national surveys. Thus our conclusions are tentative. However, given the magnitude of the impact of corruption for presidential elections, it is quite likely that perceptions of corruption also influenced congressional elections. Clearly, the amount of media coverage and exposure of federal deputies involved in scandals increased the visibility of the issue in the races for the Chamber of Deputies. Brazil's open-list proportional representation system affords voters easy opportunities to shift their votes away from one candidate and onto another. Given the impact of corruption on vote choice in the presidential election, it is hardly unlikely that a similar dynamic occurred in the races for federal deputy. Still, even though our results tend to support such a hypothesis, we recognize that this question merits further research, perhaps using oversampling of particular states in national surveys.

As for the potential for long-term cultural change and the importance of corruption, Rennó's analysis of the 2002 and 2006 ESEB surveys suggests that corruption was not as significant a problem in 2002, so it could have been a onetime event because of the critical mass of coverage it received. Nonetheless, the possibility exists that the impact of corruption as an important factor in vote choice for legislative elections may linger on into the future. It is clear that if the media have primed voters with coverage of corruption, and if other issues such as the economy or violence are on the back burner (relatively speaking), then corruption can have a substantial impact on individual deputies' reelection chances. Politicians will have to pay attention to issues of corruption in the future, further strengthening the mass mechanisms of accountability.

Notes

1. Rennó (this volume), using public opinion data, also calls attention to how views on corruption may be more influential in vote choice than the conventional wisdom described above. He finds that perceptions of corruption as a national problem were much higher in 2006 than 2002 and that they affected vote choice for Lula, especially in the first round of the 2006 elections.

2. It might be the case that electoral weakness causes corruption, but this is unlikely here—after all, previous presidents of the Chamber of Deputies (Severino Cavalcanti and João Paulo), as well as leading members of Lula's own Workers' Party and other political parties, were caught up in these scandals, among other bigwigs. In the specific case of the *mensalão* scandal, party leaders of coalition parties were directly involved.

3. *Titulares* are incumbent deputies who were elected outright to their seats (the titular holders of each seat in the Chamber of Deputies), while *suplentes* are alternate members drawn from further down the electoral list. *Suplentes* are called to serve whenever vacancies arise, as when *titulares* die, resign, or take a cabinet position. Because most electoral lists are based on interparty coalitions, the *suplente* may not be from the same party as the *titular* who is being replaced.

4. We would like to thank Vitor Santana, Rodrigo Molino, Heloisa Bessa, and Felipe Assis for research assistance in the construction of the data set.

5. We also created a more nuanced variable for "corruption," using the number of times a deputy appeared in articles about corruption between 2004 and 2006 in the database of Transparency Brazil's Web site "Deu no Jornal" (www.deunojornal.org.br/busca.php). This Web site provides comprehensive coverage of newspaper and newsmagazine mentions of corruption from all of Brazil's states. We found no relationship between the raw number of media mentions in a deputy's home state or overall and any of our dependent variables, in contrast to the simpler measure employed in the text. The reason may be that we were unable to differentiate between "positive" and "negative" mentions (there are literally tens of thousands of articles in the database; we lacked resources to code them all). Another reason may be that some deputies are "shielded" from bad coverage in their home state because they either own the media outlet or are friendly with those who own the media outlets. This may bias any efforts to link media exposure to accountability. In any case, the "micro" mechanism connecting media exposure to accountability in Brazil merits further attention.

6. As suggested by an anonymous reviewer, we also considered controlling for electoral weakness. However, such a control is not useful without an interaction with a dummy for each state—after all, a deputy in position #25 on the list of all candidates in São Paulo is elected, while a deputy in position #25 on the list of all candidates in Sergipe is not even a *suplente*. There is no good way to control for electoral weakness without getting bogged down with state dummies. We also feel that dividing candidate votes by total number of votes (as the reviewer suggests) in the state would not be likely to solve the problem, given that a relatively small percentage of votes in São Paulo, Rio de Janeiro, or Mato Grosso is a good thing, while a small percentage of votes in a small state is a bad thing (from the candidate's perspective).

7. The variable "legislative performance" is the sum of *projetos de lei* (ordinary bills), *projetos de lei complementar* (bills intended to activate or regulate an article of the Constitution), and *projetos de emendas constitucionais* (constitutional amendments, which can be proposed by individual deputies).

8. We lack data for four cases because of missing data on one or another independent variable.

9. We tested for an interactive effect between "member of government coalition" and "scandal" but found none.

10. Samuels conducted several anonymous interviews with deputies in late April and May 2008 regarding campaign finance practices. Such earnestness must always be taken with a large grain of salt, but it is interesting to note the consistency of the (unprompted) response regarding incentives to shift away from *caixa dois*.

PART TWO

Postelectoral Dimensions of Accountability

Chapter Five

The Media and Political Accountability

MAURO P. PORTO

One of the most important trends in Brazilian journalism in the last twenty-five years has been the increase in the number of exposés about political corruption. Since the return of democracy in the mid-1980s, scandals about the probity of public officials have figured prominently in news headlines. In analyzing the journalism of the 1990s, a leading Brazilian reporter characterized it as a "journalism of denunciations" (Nassif 2003). The new trend has not been limited to Brazil, of course. Investigative journalism has gained unprecedented prominence all over Latin America in the same period (Waisbord 2000; Alves 2005; Peruzzotti and Smulovitz 2006).

The growing number of media exposés about the probity of public officials raises important questions. Does the increase of news stories about official wrongdoing mean that the Brazilian news media have become effective "watchdogs," fulfilling their role as a fourth branch of government? Do more denunciations necessarily mean better accountability? Or have the Brazilian media become loud but incoherent "barking dogs," inundating the public sphere with revelations that fail to establish effective accountability?

There are no easy answers to these questions, and the reality is frequently more complex than available analytical frameworks suggest. A well-known Brazilian saying states that barking dogs are not the ones that bite *(cão que ladra não morde)*. As I demonstrate in the following pages, extensive and dramatic news coverage of corruption does not necessarily lead to improvements in political accountability. Strident but muddled media scandals might damage the reputations of innocent people and erode public confidence in democracy, while failing to hold corrupt officials accountable. From this perspective, barking dogs don't really bite in terms of promoting efficient accountability. On the other hand, the recent investigative emphasis of the news media has had clear and lasting positive effects in countries like Brazil, with a long history of patrimonialism and official improbity. In such contexts, a free press tends to become a very effective tool in curbing corrupt behavior. Investigative journalism plays a variety of positive roles in the accountability process, including the exposure of corrupt officials and the reinforcement of the work of anticorruption offices (Macdonell and Pesic 2006). Those functions are strengthened when the news media become more autonomous from official control and more assertive. As several comparative studies have shown, countries with a free press tend to have more success in the struggle against corruption (Brunetti and Weder 2003; Chowdhury 2004; Freille, Haque, and Kneller 2007).

The aim of this chapter is to analyze the links between the news media and political accountability in Brazil, focusing on some basic questions: How do the news media affect the quality of political accountability in Brazil? In what ways do news organizations and professionals interact with the broader network of accountability agencies? How do these interactions shape the outcome of accountability processes? What conditions enhance the media's role as an agent of accountability? In other words, when do barking dogs really bite?

To advance the search for answers to these questions, this chapter situates the news media in terms of the broader "web of accountability institutions" (Mainwaring 2003). More specifically, I argue that to fully understand the role of the media in the struggle against corruption we need to develop analytical frameworks that specify the place of the news media within the specific "institutional architecture" (Waisbord 2006, 284) that characterizes the society or context under investigation.

Who Are the Barking Dogs? The Brazilian News Media

In this chapter I use the term *news media* in an admittedly narrow sense. The argument that follows focuses on the main news organizations, which include the newspapers and newsmagazines with the highest circulation levels, as well as the radio and television stations with the biggest audiences. In terms of print media, Brazil has a diversified newspaper market, with more than five hundred dailies, but only four of them sell more than two hundred thousand copies per day: *Folha de S. Paulo, O Globo, Extra,* and *O Estado de S. Paulo* (Grupo de Mídia 2006, 346). There are three main weekly newsmagazines, which have played an important role in uncovering recent political scandals: *Veja,* with an average of 1.1 million copies sold per week; *Época,* with 440,000 copies per week; and *Istoé,* with 360,000 copies per week (Grupo de Mídia 2006, 284). The penetration of print media is therefore low, but newspapers and newsmagazines play an active role in denouncing corruption and in defining the agenda of radio and television stations. They are also widely read by the national political elite and opinion leaders.

Broadcasting has a more significant penetration than print media. Radio is an important medium, with 1,681 AM stations and 1,987 FM stations nationwide (Grupo de Mídia 2006, 261). Several radio networks have strong journalism departments, including Rede Bandeirantes and CBN. Despite the significance of radio, television is the most important news source in Brazil, with more than 90% of households having at least one television set. The television market is dominated by Globo Organizations, the conglomerate that owns TV Globo (Rede Globo), the country's main network. In 2005, TV Globo was responsible for 52% of all TV viewership in Brazil, while SBT came in second with 19% and TV Record in third with 13% (Grupo de Mídia 2006, 163). TV Globo's main newscast, *Jornal Nacional,* is the most important source of political information among Brazilian citizens (Porto 2007a).

By focusing on the main news organizations, I do not consider the full range of communication technologies and genres that are relevant for discussions about corruption and political accountability in Brazil. For example, I do not analyze the role of new technologies, such as pay TV (cable and satellite television) and the Internet, given that these technologies currently reach only 12% of households (Azevedo 2006, 96; Grupo de Mídia 2006, 221). I also do not consider the large amount of free broadcasting airtime that political parties and candidates have access to in Brazil. From annual political party programs to candidates' state-sponsored advertising time during elections (Horário Gratuito de Propaganda Eleitoral), politicians enjoy free and unmediated access to prime-time radio and television. Such access to the national media has become an important democratizing force in the political process (Porto 2006). Moreover, candidates and parties have made extensive use of political advertising airtime to attack opponents, especially in terms of their probity. As a result, the regulations of the Supreme Electoral Court (TSE) about the "right of reply" *(direito de resposta)* to these attacks have figured prominently in the "judicialization" of political conflict in Brazil (Steibel 2007). Finally, I do not analyze the role of entertainment in the representation of political corruption and processes of accountability. As a result, I do not consider a broad range of studies that show the active role of Brazilian *telenovelas* in the discussion of these issues (e.g., Lima 1993; La Pastina 2004; Porto 2005).

This chapter therefore focuses on Brazil's main news organizations. It is not my purpose here to analyze the complex history of Brazilian journalism, but some aspects are important to note. In the years following Brazil's independence in 1822, newspapers tended to ally themselves to political factions and parties, functioning as tools of propaganda. Although the early partisan impulse of the press can still be felt to this day, newspapers went through an important process of modernization between the end of the nineteenth century and the Second World War. The processes of urbanization and industrialization that characterized this era created the conditions for the emergence of a more regular and stable press, with higher levels of journalistic professionalization and widespread adoption of new technologies (Ribeiro 2004; Albuquerque 2005; Luca 2008).

The period between the 1950s and 1980s was marked by the strengthening of the commercial and industrial nature of Brazil's media system, even though newspapers remained influenced by partisan or ideological interests (Taschner 1992; Ribeiro 2004; Albuquerque 2005; Matos 2008). The "Folha Project," which was established by the newspaper *Folha de S. Paulo* in the mid-1980s, exemplifies the changes that took place in the newsrooms during this period. The project had the stated purpose of imposing a more "professional" and "objective" journalistic culture and entailed a substantial reorganization of the company, with hundreds of journalists either fired or resigning from the newspaper (Lins da Silva 1988; Taschner 1992; Albuquerque 2005, 494–95). The Folha Project was the culmination of a long and complex process of consolidation of a modern cultural industry, one that emphasizes a business logic rather than traditional partisan interests (Taschner 1992).

As a result of these contradictory historical developments, Brazil's current media system is characterized by the presence of a vibrant commercial press with important levels of autonomy in relation to the state. It should be noted, though, that newspapers with higher circulation levels are owned by a handful of family groups and are concentrated in the most developed region of Brazil (the Southeast), while the press in the less developed states is usually owned by local political oligarchs that tend to manipulate news coverage for political purposes (R. Amaral and Guimarães 1994; Motter 1994; Lima 2001; Porto 2003; S. Santos and Capparelli 2005; Abramo 2007). Despite the persistence of political and ideological interests in the media system, the rise of a more autonomous and market-driven press is a major factor explaining the growth of investigative journalism in the 1980s.

In the case of television, instrumental manipulations of news coverage by owners and political elites have been more enduring. One explanation is that the allocation and renewal of television and radio licenses is an exclusive right of the executive branch, thus creating a basic relation of dependence between media owners and the federal government. Moreover, television became a nationally integrated medium during the authoritarian military regime (1964–85).[1] TV Globo's rise to the status of virtual monopoly in the late 1960s and early 1970s was a result, in part, of the military's policy of "national integration," which aimed at the creation of a national consumer market and of a platform to build the regime's legitimacy (Lima 1988; Mattos 2000; Jambeiro 2001). In this period, there was an important "coincidence of interests" and collusion between the policies of the regime and the commercial strategies of Roberto Marinho, the owner of Globo Organizations. TV Globo's tendency to ally with the government of the day and political bias continued after the transition to democracy (Porto 2003).

As a result of these and other factors, the growth of investigative journalism has been more pronounced in the print media, while TV Globo has frequently covered political scandals in a "passive" or "episodic" style.[2] It should be noted, though, that TV Globo undertook an important overhaul of its news division in the mid-1990s. The reform included fundamental changes in managerial positions and in TV Globo's model of journalism, leading to a more assertive style of reporting that relies less on official sources and presents a more balanced and pluralistic news coverage (Porto 2007b). In terms of assertiveness, the changes have been particularly dramatic in the realm of local news, where TV Globo journalists in the main urban areas have taken on new roles as "representatives of the people," confronting local officials and demanding accountability (Lima 2001, 253–67; Rêgo 2004). These changes in TV Globo's journalism, which led to an increase of exposés about the probity of officials, were a result of a clear attempt to recover the credibility that had been squandered in past political interventions (Rêgo 2004; Porto 2007b). As I show in more detail elsewhere (Porto 2007b), the deepening of democracy in Brazil, with the rise of a more active and organized civil society, forced TV Globo to change its journalism. As a result, Brazil's most powerful media company has improved its performance as an agent of accountability.

Why Did the Barking Get So Loud? The Roots of Media Scandals

The dramatic increase of media exposés in Brazil since the transition to democracy in the mid-1980s has been well documented (Campello de Souza 1989; Lins da Silva 2000; Porto 2000; Waisbord 2000; Chaia and Teixeira 2001; Nassif 2003; Chaia 2004; Rosa 2004; Lima 2006; Abramo 2007; Nascimento 2007). The purpose of this chapter is not to review the long list of corruption-driven media scandals over the last three decades, including the exposés that led to the impeachment of President Collor de Mello in 1992 (on the role of the media in the impeachment, see Lattman-Weltman, Carneiro, and Ramos 1994; Fausto Neto 1995; José 1996; Waisbord 1996; Conti 1999). In the discussion that follows, I focus on identifying the causes and consequences of media scandals and on evaluating their performance in the process of political accountability.

A number of reasons explain the rise of investigative journalism in Latin America in the 1980s. Here I would like to highlight the importance of four factors. First, *political democratization* has transformed the context within which the news media operate. For example, the downfall of authoritarian regimes and military dictatorships led to the end of official censorship and allowed the emergence of legal frameworks that are more protective of press freedom (Waisbord 2000; Peruzzotti 2006; Pérez-Liñán 2007, 69–71). Thus the general liberalization of political and legal environments created better conditions for the development of more assertive styles of reporting.

A second factor that explains the rise of investigative journalism is the emergence of *a stronger media market,* with greater levels of economic independence from the state (Waisbord 2000; Peruzzotti 2006; Pérez-Liñán 2007, 71–74; Matos 2008). On the one hand, the rise of a commercial media system, described in the previous section, meant that news organizations became more independent from government funds, including those distributed as subsidies or as advertising. Thus financial autonomy allowed greater political independence. On the other hand, the neoliberal reforms of the 1980s and 1990s, which included the privatization of major state-owned companies, had the unintended consequence of shrinking the pool of resources that governments had traditionally relied upon to control the press. Yet the impact of market reforms should not be overestimated: as Waisbord (2000, 66) notes, the Brazilian government still controls sizable advertising budgets and resources.

A third important factor was the *strengthening of journalistic professionalization.* The growing number of journalists with college degrees, improvements in salaries, and the rise of a new culture that defines exposure of politicians' misdeeds as part of journalists' professional mission are some of the factors that explain the rise of denunciations (Waisbord 2000; Pérez-Liñán 2007, 78–81; Matos 2008, 197–227). Overcoming the limits of traditional partisan alliances, news organizations have established a more independent and demarcated professional space, with its own norms and values.

Paradoxically, at the same time that news organizations became more autonomous, they also deepened their dependence on the political class. To explain this apparent contradiction, I introduce a fourth factor that, I believe, is essential to understand the nature of contemporary media scandals in Brazil: *the close relationships between journalists and government officials.* As Waisbord (2000, 93) notes, "Closeness between journalists and official sources is also indispensable for the media to delve into official wrongdoing." Since journalists tend to rely on government officials and political elites to obtain inside information and to get access to secrets and evidence, they develop an ambivalent relationship with the politicians they are supposed to monitor. On the one hand, investigations put journalists in an adversarial or even hostile position in relation to politicians. On the other hand, journalists need the cooperation of officials to uncover wrongdoing. As a result, the news media frequently "bark" on the command of certain officials who have particular political purposes in mind. In their search for scoops and the hottest headlines, the news media have become central stages of "intra-elite games" (Peruzzotti 2006, 255) in which journalists are sometimes willingly manipulated by outside sources or disregard basic ethical standards.

One example can illustrate the paradoxes of the relationship between reporters and officials. In his book about the role of the media in the rise and fall of President Collor, the journalist Mario Sergio Conti (1999) describes some of the investigations that were carried out by journalists during the wave of scandals that led ultimately to the president's impeachment. Hearing rumors that Cláudio Humberto, the president's press secretary, was spending more money than his income could justify, *Folha de S. Paulo* reporter Gustavo Krieger opted for some controversial investigative methods. First, he called Humberto's personal assistant claiming to be a staff member of American Express and managed to get the number of her employer's credit card. Then Krieger called American Express claiming to be Cláudio Humberto and was able to get information about the expenditures of the press secretary. On the basis of this information, Krieger published an exposé showing contradictions between Humberto's income and his expenses (Conti 1999, 349).

Conti, who was then the editor in chief of the newsmagazine *Veja*, also recounts that he telephoned Cláudio Humberto to let him know that he would not run another story based on Krieger's findings. According to Conti, the presidential press secretary expressed his gratitude for the gesture. Conti argued that he had decided to protect Humberto in that particular instance with the aim of improving his personal relationship with a key official source. As he put it: "*Veja* was not going to publish a good report that week, but would open the way to have as a source one of the most well-informed officials of the government" (Conti 1999, 483; my translation). In other words, the journalist protected an official from a denunciation in order to ensure his future collaboration.

This episode is revealing of the dilemmas of watchdog journalism. It illustrates the fact that Brazilian journalists frequently find it acceptable to use methods that might be considered unethical. A survey of 402 Brazilian journalists found that they were much more open to the use of questionable methods of information gathering than their U.S. and French counterparts (Herscovitz 2004). For example, while 61% of Brazilian journalists found it acceptable to claim to be somebody else, only 22% of American reporters and 40% of French reporters answered in the same way.

Collusion between journalists and officials frequently prevents watchdogs from barking when evidence of wrongdoing is available. Journalists' dependence on officials also allows some sources to avoid denunciation, while at the same ensuring that the media will publicize accusations against rivals. The close relationship between journalists and government officials demonstrates why we should not analyze the news media in isolation from the broader institutional framework. There is an evident need for analytical frameworks that specify the architecture of the accountability system and consider the patterns of interaction between journalists and officials that derive from this architecture. These frameworks should also evaluate the consequences of these interactions for the quality of political accountability. I contribute to this effort by proposing a theoretical framework that focuses on the concepts of media scandals, social accountability, and the "institutional architecture" that characterizes Brazil's accountability system. I start by defining political accountability and situating the role of the media in the process by which officials are held accountable for corrupt behavior.

The News Media and Political Accountability

There is no consensus in the literature on how to define accountability, and the meaning of the concept remains evasive, with fuzzy boundaries (Schedler 1999; Mainwaring 2003). Despite these difficulties, which I do not discuss here, I distinguish between three main types of political accountability: vertical, horizontal, and social.

Vertical accountability (VA) assumes that, in a democracy, representatives act in the best interest of the represented and should answer and be responsive to the preferences of the citizens they represent. VA further designates the mechanisms by which citizens hold officials accountable for their actions. In modern representative democracies, the most important VA mechanism is free and fair elections.[3]

Horizontal accountability (HA) refers to the existence of state agencies that are legally empowered to take action, from routine oversight to criminal sanctions or impeachment, in relation to actions or omissions by other agencies (Mainwaring and Welna 2003). In other words, HA refers to the process by which officials hold one another accountable.

Social accountability (SA) has been defined as a nonelectoral, yet vertical mechanism of control that rests on the actions of civic associations and the media, which expose governmental wrongdoing and activate the operation of horizontal agencies (Smulovitz and Peruzzotti 2000; Peruzzotti and Smulovitz 2006). Thus SA refers to the process by which civic groups and the media render public officials accountable.

The concept of social accountability is an important advance in the literature about the quality of political representation in Latin America. It broadens the focus of analysis by incorporating nonstate actors that play a central role in the process of political accountability, including the news media. Moreover, it highlights accountability mechanisms that have some advantages when compared to elections. First, social accountability does not depend on fixed calendars; second, it can be directed toward the monitoring of single issues or the oversight of nonelected public officials (Peruzzotti and Smulovitz 2006, 10).

Since the agents of social accountability (media and civic groups) lack the legal sanctioning powers that voters and state agencies enjoy, it has been argued that social accountability does not entail real checks on power (Schedler 1999). But as Peruzzotti and Smulovitz (2006, 16) note, social accountability has the potential of imposing reputational costs, and therefore public officials cannot easily disregard the actions of civic groups and the media; moreover, social mechanisms can activate horizontal accountability agencies, propelling them into action. For example, media exposés frequently push congressional and judiciary offices to prosecute officials involved in corruption (Waisbord 2000, 230–31; Lemos-Nelson and Zaverucha 2006).

Social accountability also has the potential to improve the quality of other forms of control. For example, news coverage of corrupt behavior can strengthen the role of elections as accountability mechanisms. In an interesting study that uses data from Brazil's recent anticorruption program that randomly audits municipal expenditures, Ferraz and Finan (2008) show that when voters learn about irregularities committed by mayors, the mayors' chances of reelection are reduced, especially in municipalities with radio stations.[4] By investigating the links between exposure to information about corruption and electoral performance, the authors demonstrate that the media have the potential to enhance the role of elections as accountability mechanisms. Nevertheless, the study has some problematic assumptions that need more careful investigation. For example, the authors assume that the mere presence of radio stations in the municipalities is an indicator of the extent to which voters had access to information about the audits. This assumption is particularly problematic when one considers the fact that the number of radio stations owned by politicians in Brazil is very high, especially in the less-developed states (R. Amaral and Guimarães 1994; Motter 1994; Lima 2001; S. Santos and Capparelli 2005; Abramo 2007). As a result, radio and television stations might fail to publicize allegations of corruption by officials because a significant number of them are controlled by local political elites.[5] Despite these limitations, Ferraz and Finan's study offers valuable findings that open a promising line of inquiry.

The difficulties in evaluating the links between media exposés and electoral outcomes became particularly evident during the reelection of President Luiz Inácio Lula da Silva in 2006. After all, the president was reelected with relative ease, despite the long list of media scandals involving high-ranking officials of his administration and several leaders of his party.[6] Does this mean that barking dogs are harmless? What does this election tell us about the links between denunciations and electoral accountability?

It would be a mistake to conclude that the 2006 election means that media exposés have no electoral consequences or that Brazilians tolerate corruption. Lucio Rennó's chapter in this volume demonstrates that although corruption mattered more in 2006 than in the previous presidential election, it was not the main factor influencing vote choice. The impact of scandals was attenuated by retrospective voting based on the economy and general satisfaction with Lula's administration.

The results of the 2006 presidential election suggest that voters might hold officials accountable for their performance in areas other than corruption, even when election news coverage is dominated by scandals.[7] Lula's reelection also demonstrates that citizens can interpret the significance of exposés in a variety of ways. As Waisbord (2006, 299) puts it, "Different publics experience scandals differently." In the case of the 2006 presidential election, voters with lower levels of income and from the less developed states tended to support the incumbent, independently of corruption allegations. As several studies have shown, Lula's social programs, especially the conditional cash transfer scheme that targets low-income families (Bolsa Família), are key to explaining his good performance among these voters (Oliveira 2006; Hunter and Power 2007). In other words, citizens do not always share the outrage that leads watchdogs to bark loudly. It is not clear yet if such cases of "disjuncture" between the news media and segments of their audience might contribute to the erosion of journalistic credibility.

Media Scandals and the Institutional Architecture of the Accountability System

This chapter argues that to fully understand the implications of investigative journalism for the quality of political representation in Brazil, it is necessary to inspect the architecture of the accountability system. My focus here is on the answerability of public officials for probity at the federal level. Although I believe that the framework is also useful for research about similar questions at the regional, state, or municipal levels, this chapter emphasizes the network of accountability institutions at the national level.

A first step in this direction has been put forward by the sociologist John Thompson (2000). In his analysis of modern political scandals, Thompson suggests that the visibility granted by the media to transgressions committed by public figures is central to understanding the nature of political scandals. He argues that since the media are the most fundamental agents in the process that transforms hidden transgressions into public knowledge, modern scandals are media phenomena by definition. Thompson defines the modern mediated scandal as "an event which involves the disclosure through the media of previously hidden and morally disreputable activities, the revelation of which sets in motion a sequence of further occurrences" (2000, 52). In his "social theory of scandals," Thompson defines them as struggles over symbolic power in which reputation and trust are at stake. Since scandals have the potential to destroy reputations or undermine trust, he argues that they have enormous political implications.

Because of their monopoly over the ability to give massive and immediate visibility to issues, claims, and individuals, the media have become central institutions of the accountability system. The federal agencies in charge of monitoring, investigating, and sanctioning public officials have long understood the centrality of news organizations and have shaped their actions and institutional strategies accordingly. It is therefore striking that studies of political accountability have frequently ignored or underestimated the role of the media. As Lattman-Weltman (2003) puts it, the lack of attention in these studies to the production and circulation of information is startling.

A central claim of this chapter is that the performance of a country's political accountability system is highly dependent on the type of relationship that is established between the accountability institutions of the state and the news media. As a result, the evaluation of mechanisms of control should consider the patterns of interaction that emerge between these two fields, instead of analyzing them in isolation.[8] But how do these two fields interact? On the one hand, the strategies of state accountability institutions are shaped by the organizational and cultural characteristics of the news media. On the other hand, news coverage of political corruption is highly dependent on the organizational and cultural characteristics of state accountability institutions.

Scholars have already identified the urgent need for more integrated approaches that focus on the *interrelationships* of state accountability institutions (Mainwaring 2003; Taylor 2010; Taylor and Buranelli 2007). This chapter proposes to advance this line of inquiry by highlighting the need to include the news media within the "institutional architecture" of accountability systems.[9] I define the "institutional architecture of accountability systems" as *the network of organizations that seek to monitor, investigate, and punish political corruption, including state agencies, the news media, and civil society groups.* Thus, contrary to previous integrated approaches, the concept of institutional architecture incorporates nongovernmental actors (the news media and civic groups) in the analysis of political accountability. A key assumption of the concept is that each organization of the system establishes specific patterns of interaction with other organizations and that the final output of the system is highly dependent on these patterns.

For the sake of simplicity, I will focus on interaction between the news media and state agencies, especially the Ministério Público (Public Prosecutor's Office). The preliminary theoretical model presented in this chapter needs further elaboration, and more comprehensive and systematic studies are necessary to demonstrate its analytical value. It is with these caveats in mind that I develop the analysis that follows.

As a starting point, let me present a brief and admittedly simplistic characterization of the network of state agencies in charge of monitoring, investigating, and punishing corruption in Brazil. Here are some examples of existing accountability agencies:[10]

- Agencies of the judiciary: Supremo Tribunal Federal (STF), Superior Tribunal de Justiça (STJ), Justiça Federal, Justiça Comum
- Agencies of the legislature: congressional committee of inquiry (Comissão Parlamentar de Inquérito, or CPI); Tribunal de Contas da União (TCU)
- Agencies of the executive: Polícia Federal (PF), Controladoria Geral da União (CGU)
- Independent agencies: Ministério Público (MP)

As this incomplete list demonstrates, a significant number of state agencies are involved in the accountability process, most of them analyzed elsewhere in this volume. When we think of possible obstacles in the struggle against corruption in Brazil, a shortage of institutional actors is certainly not one of them. All three traditional branches of the state boast anticorruption agencies, and a powerful and autonomous institution (the Ministério Público) works alongside them. Problems arise, though, in terms of overlapping responsibilities, lack of coordination between agencies, and weak performance in terms of sanctions. For example, the judiciary is not efficient in prosecuting corruption cases. Lawsuits take several years to go through the several appeal instances, and final convictions are rare, with high levels of impunity (see Taylor, this volume). While the system does not perform well in terms of sanctions, the numerous agencies focus instead on the investigative phase of the accountability process, with agencies competing vigorously for publicity (Taylor 2010; Taylor and Buranelli 2007).

These general features of the institutional architecture have two important consequences. First, state agencies fight with each other for visibility in the investigative phase. As we have seen, the mass media are the central institutions in determining which issues, institutions, and individuals will be granted higher levels of visibility. As a result, officials of state agencies actively seek the cooperation of journalists and news organizations to advance their own interests and to get their share of social visibility. They cannot achieve these aims without giving "incentives" to the media, which might include inside information or access to ongoing inquiries, including leaks of preliminary evidence. Needless to say, by attracting the sympathies of journalists in this way, officials not only often disregard ethical standards but also violate the law and individual rights.[11]

There is a second important consequence of the general features of the institutional architecture in Brazil. The competition for visibility and the presence of several overlapping investigations frequently create a complex and confusing scenario. In this context, the news media frequently play a central role in building a narrative that puts pieces together and allows citizens to make sense of the huge number of denunciations emerging in the public sphere. As Taylor and Buranelli (2007, 75) put it: "With no central coordinator or any significant institutionalized lines of communication between bureaucracies . . . the investigatory process tends to generate substantial amounts of pertinent information, but lacks a clear chain of command or filtering process by which such information could be effectively deployed. The media tend to be the only systematic aggregator of information, which means that once press attentions turn elsewhere, pressures for accountability and the collation of disparate information dissipate." The news media frequently become the only institution able to "piece together" an investigatory process that is by definition slow, dispersed, and complex. Nevertheless, the news media are not well prepared to perform this role. With their own interests in terms of the maximization of audiences and profit margins, news organizations tend to give priority to stories that include dramatic elements and titillating details ("sensationalism") and that focus on revelations involving elite actors, especially those in the center of state power ("personalization") (Waisbord 1996, 2000). These journalistic values tend to generate news narratives that treat political corruption as a result of personal failings rather than as an institutional or structural problem (Waisbord 1996; 2000, 239–40). Not surprisingly, journalists encounter major difficulties in covering corruption schemes that are institutionalized and that do not include surprising events or powerful, well-known actors.[12]

There is another important reason why the news media are not well prepared to play a coordinating role in the accountability process by aggregating dispersed information and interpreting it in a consistent way. The mythic image of the investigative journalist as an intrepid detective who digs up information and discovers evidence of wrongdoing is far from accurate. Although propagated since the days of Watergate, this traditional view of news-making practices is misleading. It ignores the fact that journalists increasingly depend on the work done by state accountability agencies or on inside information provided by government officials.

In his analysis of political scandals in Argentina, Peruzzotti (2006, 266) identifies two main forms of information gathering. The first category includes cases in which information that leads to a certain exposé is independently obtained, via either a journalistic investigation or the workings of civic groups. The second category includes cases in which information is the product of "leaks" obtained from official sources. According to Peruzzotti, one of the consequences of scandals that fall in the second category is that they leave the news media at the mercy of the dynamics of inter-elite conflicts.

The journalism that results from "off-the-record" leaks, instead of independent investigations, has become known in Latin America as *denuncismo.* The term designates a form of journalism that is characterized by facile denunciations that lack sufficient evidence and that are a result of information provided by official sources (Waisbord 2000, 103–10; see also Lattman-Weltman 2003; Peruzzotti 2006).

On the basis of similar categorizations of information-gathering practices, Nascimento (2007) distinguishes between *investigative journalism,* which results from investigations made by journalists themselves, and *journalism about investigations,* which disseminates information about investigations made by authorities. After analyzing news stories about political corruption published by Brazilian newsmagazines between 1989 and 2002, Nascimento identifies a significant increase in the number of reports about investigations, with a corresponding decline of investigative journalism.[13] According to the author, a major cause for the shift has been the close association between the news media and the Ministério Público, which has had its powers and autonomy strengthened by the 1988 Constitution (see also Abreu 2002; Lattman-Weltman 2003).

The concept of an institutional architecture of accountability systems provides new analytical tools to evaluate the "journalism about investigations." As we have seen, the concept suggests that the behavior of accountability officials is determined, to an important degree, by the organizational and cultural characteristics of the news media. A key factor that explains the media's growing emphasis on external investigations is the profound change that Brazilian news organizations went through in the last decades. Severe financial difficulties and the shrinking of their readership and of advertising revenues were some of the factors that led media companies to implement organizational reforms. The new management strategies included cutting costs and budgets at the same time that online versions of publications increased the demand for content. In a context of shrinking budgets, reduced staffs, and a growing demand for content, external investigations allowed news organizations to have access to a significant volume of information at a relatively small cost (Rosa 2004, 433–34).

The growth of "journalism about investigations" thus reveals several important features of the institutional architecture of Brazil's accountability system. First, it reflects the system's emphasis on the investigation phase and the corresponding neglect of the stages of oversight and sanction. Second, it shows that the reorganization of media companies has limited the ability of journalists to conduct their own investigations and increased the demand for information from investigations carried out by officials from state agencies of accountability. These officials, in turn, need the news media to succeed in the competition with other agencies for visibility. The clear "institutional fit" between the interests and organizational features of state accountability agencies and the interests and organizational features of the news media is the major factor that explains the news media's growing dependence on external investigations.

The Media and the Ministério Público: Barking Dogs on Short Leashes?

Before concluding the analysis of the institutional architecture of Brazil's political accountability system, I stress the importance of the relationship between the news media and the Ministério Público (MP). The focus on the interactions between these two actors results from the MP's new role in Brazil's institutional architecture. The 1988 Constitution strengthened the MP's powers and autonomy, transforming the office into a central element of Brazil's accountability system (Arantes 2002; Cavalcanti 2006; Kerche 2007).

The 1988 Constitution granted a significant level of autonomy to the MP by removing it from the jurisdiction of the executive power and by transforming it into a de facto fourth branch of government. Moreover, the MP has a decentralized hierarchy, in which the ability of individual prosecutors to open inquiries and carry out their own investigations is not limited by their superiors. The MP's high levels of autonomy and its wide range of attributions and powers are unprecedented in comparison with the accountability systems of other countries (Kerche 2007).

The MP and the news media have become central structures of the institutional architecture. On the one hand, the MP has achieved a new level of autonomy, with greater prosecutorial powers, while on the other hand, the mass media continue to have the monopoly of the ability to give massive and immediate visibility to issues, assertions, and individuals. The theoretical framework presented in this chapter suggests that the relationship between these two important actors is not random but follows certain patterns that derive from features of the institutional architecture itself.

The importance of the partnership between prosecutors and journalists has been highlighted by several authors.[14] For example, it has been noted that prosecutors see the news media as essential tools to build their own credibility and strengthen their institutional position in terms of funding and public support (Nascimento 2007, 160). There is some evidence suggesting that news coverage of the MP's activities enhances its level of social support. For example, when the MP's presence in the news media increases, more citizens contact the MP to denounce wrongdoing and to present complaints (Arantes 2002, 220; Rêgo 2004, 27). Some authors argue that in their permanent attempt to attract the media's spotlight prosecutors frequently abuse their power (Arantes 2002, 256; Taylor and Buranelli 2007, 64).

Sometimes prosecutors leak information about official wrongdoing to journalists and then use the resulting news exposé to open the inquiries that they wanted to start but for which they lacked sufficient evidence (Abreu 2002, 4; Nascimento 2007, 299). Since journalists can be prosecuted for violating the law in terms of the secrecy of judicial proceedings when they accept such leaks, they sometimes pass information received from prosecutors to politicians and then report that they received the materials from political sources (Rosa 2004, 449). One of the problems with these backstage negotiations is that preliminary evidence of the investigative phase is treated as "absolute truth" by the news media, building a type of social visibility for denunciations that is characterized by a monolithic interpretive frame in which the accused party's version of events is absent (Nassif 2003, 22–23).

The importance of the relationship between prosecutors and journalists is evident. But what explains the alliance between the news media and the MP? The concept of institutional architecture provides, I believe, important analytical tools to answer this question. As we have seen, the concept assumes that the strategies of state accountability institutions are shaped by the organizational and cultural characteristics of the news media, and vice versa. I conclude this brief discussion about the relationship between the MP and the news media by focusing on one particular *cultural* characteristic that helps explain their close relationship: the resonance between their internal cultures.

In his research with members of the MP, Arantes (2002) identifies a particular political culture. Drawing from an old tradition in Brazilian political thought that criticizes the "artificial nature" of the nation's political institutions, prosecutors have developed a negative interpretation of both the state and civil society. On the one hand, prosecutors blame representative institutions for the crisis and inefficiency of the judiciary. On the other hand, they view Brazilian society as weak and incapable of defending its own interests and legal rights. These assumptions have resulted in "political voluntarism," with the MP frequently assuming the role of a paternalistic guardian of society or of an external moderating power that seeks to correct deficiencies of the other branches of government.

As Afonso de Albuquerque (2005) demonstrates, Brazilian journalists think similarly. They also draw from the same aspects of political thought to develop a sense of social mission that resembles the "political voluntarism" of prosecutors. Also expressing an ambivalent attitude about liberal political institutions and procedures, journalists have begun to claim the role of *Poder Moderador,* or "moderating power,"[15] especially since the 1980s. According to Albuquerque, media organizations have frequently intervened as "arbiters" in disputes between the three constitutional branches in the name of political stability, supporting the executive branch in most cases (2005, 498). The congruence between the respective political cultures of prosecutors and journalists is therefore one of the key characteristics of the institutional architecture of Brazil's political accountability system.

SOLUTION

THE GROWING NUMBER OF MEDIA EXPOSÉS ABOUT POLITICAL CORRUPTION has contributed to improve political accountability in Brazil through a variety of means. Frequently, journalists' denunciations have exposed corrupt officials and imposed important reputational costs, a type of sanction that has important consequences in the political world. At other times, journalists have reinforced the work of anticorruption agencies or have goaded them into prosecuting dishonest government officials. The positive consequences of watchdog journalism are evident. Thus barking dogs frequently bite the wrongdoers, improving the quality of political accountability.

Nevertheless, it would be wrong to assume that more denunciations necessarily mean better accountability. The shortcomings of the "journalism of denunciations" have become clearer in recent years. Some journalists have collected systematic information about a significant number of cases of abuses committed in the name of curbing corruption, with political reputations destroyed after waves of denunciations that proved later to be false or misleading (Nassif 2003; Rosa 2004). One of the most serious problems of watchdog journalism is that barking dogs sometimes bite innocent people. The resulting wounds are frequently deep or incurable, causing irreversible damage to reputations. In the process, the news media do little to acknowledge mistakes or to prevent them from happening again.

What could be done to improve the news media's contribution to political accountability? Here I can only outline a few suggestions. Enacting a law that establishes rules for public access to government documents and information would strengthen journalists' investigative capabilities. Such a new statute, which is common in more advanced democracies, would have the important effect of diminishing journalists' dependence on information leaked by officials. As Waisbord (2000, xvi) remarks in reference to South American countries, "The absence of regulations that require filing public documents and authorize public access excludes the possibility of reporters obtaining official information without help from sources" (see also Ferraz and Finan 2008).

Democratic media regulations are also important. Brazil's current press law is an archaic and authoritarian legal instrument imposed in 1967 by the military dictatorship. Attempts to replace it by new regulations have proved controversial and have failed for several reasons. On the one hand, bills have died because of the powerful lobby established by media companies, which wrongly associate all attempts to establish communication regulations with limits to press freedom. On the other hand, bills have failed because politicians frequently try to use them to impose authoritarian forms of control over a more assertive or aggressive media system.[16] The lack of debate in political and social circles about the need for democratic media legislation is a major obstacle to progress in this field.

Media regulations are also important to alter fundamental aspects of the institutional architecture's internal structure, so as to improve its performance. As we have seen, the commercial logic of the media system, which has become more evident in the recent restructuring of media companies, tends to weaken the investigative capabilities of news organizations and to favor news stories that reflect the news values of sensationalism and personalization. Different types of regulation could create new incentives, limiting the concentration of ownership, creating public interest obligations to broadcasters, and preventing the control of radio and television stations by political elites. Finally, as Taylor and Buranelli (2007) suggest, the ideal solution might be a mix of private and public media, with a strong antitrust law.

State accountability agencies and the news media could also establish forms of self-regulation to strengthen their respective levels of professionalization and prevent abuses on the part of their members. The MP, for example, could establish clearer guidelines about how prosecutors should handle information and which limits should exist in their relations with journalists. Although MP staff are almost completely autonomous and there are no forms of public control over their activities, the MP created a national board (Conselho Nacional do Ministério Público) in 2005 with the aim of monitoring the financial and administrative management of the agency (Kerche 2007, 269–70). The oversight board includes MP prosecutors, members of the judiciary, one representative of the National Bar Association (Ordem dos Advogados do Brasil), and two eminent citizens appointed by Congress. This new Conselho Nacional could approve and monitor the implementation of new guidelines.

In the case of the news media, journalists could also develop clearer guidelines to orient the reporting of political corruption. Although, as we have seen, Brazilian journalism has gone through an important process of professionalization in the last decades, newsroom manuals still lack specific standards about the handling of investigations or about the handling of information leaked by officials (Rosa 2004, 449). In this normatization of new professional standards, special attention has to be given to the need of protecting individual rights, ensuring a minimum level of the accuracy of information, and making journalists' relationship with their sources more transparent (Peruzzotti 2006, 253).

Whatever the solutions that might be considered, it is important to promote changes in the incentives of the actors that make up the institutional structure of the political accountability system. If close attention is paid to the patterns of interaction that characterize the architecture, chances of finding more effective solutions will increase.

Notes

I would like to thank the participants in the workshop "Accountability Institutions and Political Corruption in Brazil" (Brazilian Studies Programme, Latin American Centre, St Antony's College, University of Oxford, May 23, 2008), especially Timothy Power, Matthew Taylor, and Alfred Montero, for their comments and criticisms. I am also grateful to Silvio Waisbord and Afonso de Albuquerque for the careful reading of an earlier version of this chapter. I am of course the only one responsible for its shortcomings.

1. Television was inaugurated in Brazil in 1950 when the press baron Assis Chateaubriand launched TV Tupi in the city of São Paulo. From 1950 to the mid-1960s, however, the number of households with TV sets remained relatively small and TV stations had a very limited range. Nationwide direct television broadcasting was initiated only after 1969 with the inauguration of the military dictatorship's national telecommunications infrastructure that allowed the interconnection of television stations by microwave and satellite systems (Lima 1988).

2. For example, while the print media played an active role in the impeachment of President Collor de Mello in 1992, TV Globo's main newscast, *Jornal Nacional*, adopted an "episodic" frame, focusing on events and failing to provide interpretations or commentary about the links between the president and the corruption scheme (Conti 1999, 626; Waisbord 2000, 76; Porto 2003, 301–3). One study about *Jornal Nacional*'s political coverage offers another example. Based on a content analysis of forty-four broadcasts aired in 1999, the study shows that political scandals took 45% of *Jornal Nacional*'s political coverage. Nevertheless, the

great majority of these reports adopted an "episodic frame," usually reporting the activities of CPIs in a rather descriptive way (Porto 2007a, ch. 6).

3. On the concept of vertical accountability, see Przeworski, Stokes, and Manin (1999). For a discussion of the connections between political scandals and the mechanisms of vertical/electoral accountability in Brazil, see Pereira, Rennó, and Samuels (this volume).

4. Using less consistent data, another study suggests that media exposés of corruption also affect the electoral performance of candidates to the Brazilian Congress (P. Santos 2008).

5. For example, a television station in the state of Pernambuco owned by the federal deputy José Inocêncio ignored the presence in the region of members of a CPI who were probing allegations that Inocêncio had ties to local drug planters (Lemos-Nelson and Zaverucha 2006, 97). In 2001, during the so-called *escândalo do painel* (referring to an intrusion into the electronic voting system used in Congress, which posts the outcome of roll-call votes on a display panel), Senators Antônio Carlos Magalhães and José Roberto Arruda resigned after it was revealed that they had violated the secrecy of the votes cast in the expulsion of their Senate colleague Luiz Estevão. When students organized demonstrations in the city of Salvador demanding Magalhães's resignation, police invaded the campus of the Federal University of Bahia and brutally attacked the protestors. TV Bahia, the local station owned by Magalhães and affiliated to TV Globo, did not broadcast images of the attack. TV Globo's newscast *Jornal Nacional* was able to air images of the violence only after obtaining footage made by members of a trade union (S. Santos and Capparelli 2005, 91).

6. For a more detailed discussion of the scandals that marked Lula's presidency, especially the *mensalão* scandal, see Pereira, Power, and Raile (this volume).

7. Evidence of this strong emphasis on scandals by the national media during the 2006 election can be found in TV Globo's campaign news coverage. In the two weeks that preceded the first round of the presidential election, the *escândalo do dossiê* (dossier scandal), which involved high-ranking officials of the president's party (the Workers' Party, PT), dominated the headlines (see Rennó's chapter in this volume). A content analysis of twelve broadcasts of TV Globo's newscast *Jornal Nacional* from this period demonstrated that 46% of the airtime devoted to the election by Brazilians' most important news source focused on scandals (Porto 2008).

8. As Waisbord (2000, 283), notes, the adoption of a media-centered approach to understanding scandals runs the risk of being insufficiently political or subsuming all scandals to media operations.

9. The concept of "institutional architecture of scandals" was proposed by Waisbord (2006) to characterize the myriad of institutions that make scandals possible. This chapter builds on this innovative conceptual work to develop the concept of an "institutional architecture of accountability systems." But while Waisbord focuses on identifying the web of institutions that make scandals possible, the focus

of this chapter is on the network of institutional relations that characterize national systems of political accountability.

10. For a detailed discussion of Brazil's accountability agencies, see other chapters in this volume: Taylor on the judiciary and electoral courts; Speck on the TCU; Arantes on the PF and MP.

11. Prosecutors from the MP, for example, have been frequently criticized for abusing power in their search for a share of media visibility. According to Arantes (2002, 256), several MP members are known for suffering from a "spotlight syndrome," which is characterized by a fascination with TV cameras and reporters that leads them to act irresponsibly. For example, prosecutors frequently leak information from preliminary inquiries in a way that violates the basic rights of the accused, including the right to due process and privacy rights.

12. In his excellent analysis of cases of corruption in the city of São Paulo, Arantes (2002, 221–22) shows that the news media faced major difficulties when covering the scandal of the Máfia das Reformas (Reforms Mafia). The scheme involved complex illegal transfers of funds from the municipality's budget, disguised as regular administrative procedures. Since the scheme lacked dramatic developments and no major official was prosecuted or imprisoned, the media spotlight moved to other scandals.

13. Lins da Silva (2000, 187) also notes that, with very few exceptions, newspapers rarely take the lead in denouncing corruption.

14. Space considerations prevent me from describing this relationship in depth. For a detailed analysis, see Arantes (2002, 206–24).

15. Historically, this term was applied to the Brazilian military, which often held the role of final arbiter in political crises, up to and including the events of 1964.

16. In her analysis of the disputes between Congress and the press over the definition of honor in Brazil, Carla Teixeira (2004, 33) highlights how politicians frequently respond to media attacks by trying to advance draconian pieces of legislation. Teixeira focuses on the controversies that followed a sarcastic commentary piece by filmmaker Arnaldo Jabor, aired by TV Globo's *Jornal Nacional* in 1996. In his satirical monologue, Jabor compared the Brazilian parliament to a market or a shopping center, suggesting that its members engaged in illegal transactions in exchange for their votes. The reaction of deputies and senators was strong, including attempts to expedite a new press bill that included harsher penalties for journalists violating the "rights of personality," including the "honor and the image of persons." The new press law did not pass, but the event illustrates the difficulties of building democratic media regulations in Brazil.

Chapter Six

Auditing Institutions

BRUNO W. SPECK

Government audit institutions play a central role in overseeing public spending, and the tradition of dedicating a specific agency to the task of reviewing how the government collects, manages, and spends public funds goes back to the early stages of modern state building. This function is vital to the accountability process because it provides benchmarks for evaluating public expenditures, as well as a regular means of monitoring them.

Many institutions play a role in government auditing in Brazil, but at the federal level the most significant is the Tribunal de Contas da União (Federal Accounting Tribunal, TCU). In this chapter, I first lay out an analytic model for analyzing government audit institutions more widely and then proceed to an analysis of the TCU itself, looking at both the formal rules that govern it as an institution and its performance in practice.

A Framework for Analysis

Government auditing is an essential function of modern political systems. Long before the recent quest for good governance, most modern political systems have considered oversight of public resource use, from the perspective of lawful and efficient budget allocation, to be a central government function.

The literature on audit institutions, however, is sparse. The broad literature on auditing itself, written by auditors for auditors, is rather technical and does not provide much guidance as to the purpose of auditing or any reflection on the most propitious institutional arrangements.[1] The few contributions on audit institutions from political scientists are very broad in scope and tend to compare audit institutions in a purely descriptive way.[2] Only recently has research on aid and development begun to produce valuable insights on the role of audit institutions in promoting good governance and fighting corruption.[3]

Given the absence of clear analytic tools, I start here by providing a simple analytic model that permits us to analyze audit institutions at a middle range between auditors' highly specific approaches and political scientists' rather broad perspective. The goal of this section is to better understand the role of audit institutions, the auditing process, and the independence of audit bodies in the abstract before applying this framework to the TCU later in the chapter.

What is the role of audit institutions? Audit institutions vary widely, not only in institutional design, but also in the overall tasks they perform. While some have broad powers to regulate, investigate, and sanction public officeholders, others are limited to producing reports on specific aspects of budget management. The main clients of audit agencies also vary but might include the legislature, the government, or the public. In some cases, it is not clear to what extent government auditing can be labeled as external or autonomous, since the institution maintains close links to one of the branches of government; in others, audit institutions are designed as formally independent institutions, with autonomy comparable to that of the central bank or regulatory agencies.

The history of audit institutions has generally followed two paths. Generalizing broadly, either the government has been interested in rationalizing and centralizing the management of scarce resources (the historic example being Prussia), or parliament has sought to ascertain that the government has spent tax money in accordance with the law (the historic example being the British parliament).[4] Today's audit institutions are often influenced by this historical path dependence, even though the process of government auditing has been modernized considerably in most countries. But government audit institutions of different origin today face similar challenges, both at the technical level of audit procedures and at the institutional level of audit politics.[5]

Analytically, it may be useful to shift the focus from audit institutions to government auditing. Borrowing from the functionalist approach, we can ask: What is the role of auditing in modern political systems?[6] My response is that auditing produces two outputs for the modern political system: (1) holding public officeholders responsible for misconduct and (2) improving budget management.[7] The issue of responsibility focuses on past behavior, with the core question being: To what extent should officeholders be held accountable for the lawfulness of their decisions? In some cases, responsibility also may be ascribed for inefficient (but not necessarily illegal) budget allocation. Expected outcomes when individual officeholders are held responsible for their past behavior are recovery of lost or stolen assets and application of civil, criminal, and political sanctions.[8] The second output of auditing regards public expenditure as a whole, rather than focusing on individual bureaucrats' behavior. The basic challenge is detecting systemic sources of diversion, waste, or inefficiency and translating these findings into recommendations for improving the integrity and efficiency of future spending. Although answering these questions requires an understanding of how budget management has worked in the past and draws on the results of government auditing, it has a different emphasis. It focuses on the future, aiming at reforming public administration by improving the probity and efficiency of public expenditure.

How are specific institutions tied into these functions of government auditing? All modern political systems have differentiated the auditing function so that government auditing is to a large extent centralized in one bureaucracy. This bureaucracy grounds its work on internationally recognized audit standards and commonly is afforded protection from external pressure. But despite this process of differentiation and specialization, audit institutions must work jointly with other institutions to produce the two central outputs mentioned above.

Internationally, one of the most important differences between audit institutions lies in their interaction with other bureaucracies in their particular political system. To what extent do they hold a monopoly over the auditing function? And what institutions do they rely upon to achieve the two functional outputs of holding public officeholders responsible for misconduct and improving budget management?

Understanding the institutional setting in which government auditing takes place is thus one of the key objectives of this chapter, in keeping with this volume's overall focus on the interactions between institutions within the "web" of accountability. Heuristically, I hope to provide a clearer picture of government auditing and a means of answering questions such as: If the audit institution does not punish wrongdoing, how are officeholders held accountable? If the audit institution falls short of identifying systemic risks, is this due to a flawed institutional design or due to poor performance by other institutions involved? If some functions of government auditing are carried out by a patchwork of different institutions and actors, are there missing links, overlapping responsibilities, or areas left uncovered?

To address these issues, I develop a four-stage model describing the processes that lead to sanctions and recommendations for reforming budget management. These stages are (1) detecting misconduct and leakage, (2) assessing the facts, (3) pinpointing individual responsibility and developing reform proposals, and (4) implementing both sanctions and reforms in practice (see table 6.1). This model permits us to differentiate the share each institution holds in developing specific subfunctions of auditing.

At each stage government auditing has to cope with different challenges on how to achieve the expected outcome. In addition, a country's achievements with regard to this outcome depend on the definition of the specific role of its audit agency as well as the role of other institutions. At the first stage, detecting misconduct, the strategies of audit institutions include legally required and regularly scheduled audits, selective approaches based on audit choices made by the auditing agency, or muddling through in reaction to scandals as they arise. In addition, external institutions can play an important role. Public institutions may hold the power to demand audits from the state agency. An audit system may also create incentives and channels for the public to report misconduct.

At the second stage, of assessing the facts, the challenges an audit institution faces include gaining enough power to inspect all aspects of budget management, as well as attaining the power and the training necessary to conduct audits in accordance with modern standards. External influence on audit agencies when performing these core activities of auditing tends to be negative. However, some audit institutions innovate by outsourcing audit activities to private firms.

At the third stage of translating audit findings into sanctions and reform recommendations, government auditing varies widely, ranging from audit institutions that hold a wide range of powers to sanction misconduct, to agencies that must report their findings to other institutions, including the executive branch itself, the legislature, or the judiciary.

Table 6.1. Government Auditing and Government Audit Institutions

Process and Outcomes	Government Audit Institution	Other Institutions
1. Identification of leakage and misconduct	*Different policies* - Legal routine tasks (policing) - Reacting to ongoing scandals - Annual thematic focus - System of warning signals (fire alarms)	- External demand for oversight? - Channels for whistle-blowers (discretionary)
2. Assessment of budget expenditures	*Scope of auditing* Are there off-limits areas? *Criteria of auditing* - Compliance with accounting standards and budget law - Performance along criteria of economy, efficiency, and effectiveness	- Outsourcing of audit tasks? - External influences on auditing process?
3. Translation of audit findings into (a) sanctions and (b) recommendations for reform	*Backward accountability (a)* - Civil (monetary and administrative) sanctions - Criminal sanctions - Political sanctions *Preventive measures (b)* - Power over ongoing budget expenditures - Recommendations for reforms	*Shared responsibilities with other institutions* - Executive branch - Prosecution and Courts - Congress *Channels for communicating recommendations* - Executive - Legislature - Media - Public
4. Implementation of outcomes	*Sanctions (a)* - Postponing of decisions *Prevention (b)* - Soundness of recommendations	*Main problems* - Overlapping powers - Missing links and loopholes *Major opportunities* - Shared responsibility for findings

Finally, it is a long path from ascribing sanctions and suggesting reforms to actually implementing these findings. In the case of sanctions, an audit agency's final decision may be questioned by other institutions with overlapping powers, or those blamed for malfeasance may appeal to other institutions so as to evade disciplinary measures. In the case of preventive reforms, implementation depends on convincing the lawmakers and administrators about the soundness of the audit findings. Audit agencies may also design special policies to follow up on past recommendations, thus strengthening the forward-looking character of government auditing.

As they attempt to carry out these four stages, a central question for modern government audit institutions is how they can be protected from political pressures. Audit institutions require a certain degree of independence from their clients to perform their role properly, but achieving such autonomy will always be a challenge, given that the government is the main target of auditing.[9]

Again, the institutional design of government institutions and their place within the political system of each country vary widely. But three features help audit institutions to develop into vigorous, autonomous institutions: functional autonomy, funding guarantees, and an independent directorship.[10] The functional autonomy of the institution is guaranteed when audit institutions have the power to plan and execute audit activities without external influence. These rights normally are enshrined in the constitution and in bylaws. Autonomous audit institutions should have the authority to initiate, conduct, and conclude the audit process without interference from the government or the legislative body.[11]

Questions of funding can subvert audit institutions by providing external institutions with leverage over their performance. Audit institutions must often negotiate their budget with the legislative and executive branches. In such negotiations, audit institutions that have been critical in their audit findings may find themselves strangled by budget cuts. A similar effect may result if lawmakers heap additional tasks on the audit institution without properly funding the new mandates.[12] Influence can also be brought to bear in the opposite direction when audit institutions are seduced into a softer approach to auditing by generous additional funding that translates into perks for the staff or the head of the institution. Finally, autonomous audit institutions must be able to fund their particular choice of auditing priorities. Otherwise, functional autonomy remains an empty promise. Functional autonomy thus requires that they be permitted to elaborate their own internal budget and implement it without external interference. Autonomous and strong audit institutions need an independent directorate if they are to conduct their audit tasks properly. The independence of audit institutions depends on the independence of their leadership from different clients in public administration, including, most importantly, the government in power. This independence can be generated in part by the method used to select directors, and by directors' protection from external pressures while in office. To assess this dimension of the independence of audit institutions, I present a model of the main institutional constraints that either foster or weaken the independence of the directors of audit institutions. I divide these factors into two groups, the first focusing on factors in the selection and nomination of directors, the second focusing on constraints on the leaders once they are in office.

During the selection process, a first factor that influences the independence of future directors is the professional requirements for the job. When virtually no qualifications are required of the candidates, political criteria tend to have the upper hand. When such qualifications are in place, and refer to professional criteria, the independence of future officeholders is fostered in two ways. First, professional requirements filter out many candidates with a political background, allowing only those who demonstrate additional qualifications to be candidates. Second, officeholders with a professional background in auditing or related fields are expected to place professional ethics over political loyalty. Thus technical prequalifications can be considered a protective mechanism, acting as a filter and as a way of introducing professional ethics into the audit body.

Second, candidate selection mechanisms are of paramount importance for the behavior of future officeholders. In practice, there is no country where auditors are selected by popular election or on merit criteria. The directors of government audit institutions, like those of other semiautonomous institutions, are appointed by other institutions, involving typically the legislative and executive branches but in some cases also the judiciary or civil society. The challenge consists in building mechanisms where this power of appointing the head of audit institutions does not translate into an enduring influence over the audit body. These mechanisms are discussed below.

In countries where the influence of the executive branch predominates in the selection of audit institution directors, there is a low degree of independence. For independent audit institutions, distance from the executive branch is more important than distance from the legislative body, since the former administers the bulk of public funds that need to be audited. Thus, where the legislative body holds the upper hand in selecting the directors, independence tends to be higher. However, since both legislators and the government are drawn from the political world, shifting the responsibility for selecting directors from one to the other institution will not eliminate political influence. In addition, in many countries the executive holds considerable sway over the legislative body, with the real division of power being between government and opposition. Therefore, additional factors such as veto powers for minorities (by means of qualified legislative majorities for approval of audit institution directors), mutual agreement of the executive and legislative branches (requiring approval of nominations by both branches), public hearings on nominations (involving civil society), or special rights for the opposition (in Argentina the head of the audit institution is nominated by the largest opposition party) may also contribute to building directors' autonomy from the outset.

Once the leading officials of audit institutions are in office, protections are important tools to foster their independence. The three most important are protection from removal from office, the duration of their term in office, and a collegial leadership structure. Regarding protection from removal from office, the criteria basically are the same as in the selection process. Removal should by all means be shielded against politicization. The weakest model is that in which the head of the audit institution can be removed by an act of the executive branch alone. The participation of the legislative body, especially if it requires a qualified majority, or due process before a high court, can protect heads of audit offices from political pressure.

For the directors of audit offices to gain independence from political pressures, the duration of the term in office also needs to be disassociated significantly from the political election cycle. When audit institutions' directors' terms coincide with the legislative or presidential election cycles, the risk of politicization and links to the political sphere remain high. The longer the directors' terms, the smaller the risk that independence will be curtailed. A lifetime term seems to be the institutional design that best allows officeholders to cut ties to the political sphere.[13]

Many audit institutions establish collegial rather than monocratic leadership structures to govern their audit institutions: that is, decisions are made by several directors rather than any single individual. A collegial leadership structure may not necessarily be more independent than one headed by a single individual. However, if individual members are nominated over time, the collegial model dilutes the executive branch's influence on the nomination process, with the leadership structure becoming more pluralistic with each new nomination, as nominees of both current and past governments are represented. Under these conditions, any political ties that individual members of the leadership hold will be diluted in collective decisions.[14]

Given this basic framework for understanding government auditing and the design of audit institutions, let us now analyze the Brazilian Tribunal de Contas da União (TCU) from the perspective of institutional design, as well as its performance in practice.

The Role of the TCU in Government Auditing in Brazil

Like all of the constitutions since 1946, the current 1988 Brazilian Constitution categorizes the Tribunal de Contas da União as part of the legislative branch. The Constitution states that Congress holds the power to exert control over the government, and it defines the TCU as the institution that supports Congress in this role. However, the Constitution also specifies in detail the powers and responsibilities of TCU, thus guaranteeing the agency considerable de facto autonomy from Congress as well.

Elements of government auditing in Brazil are carried out by a wide range of institutions, including different branches of government: the executive branch's Controladoria Geral da União (CGU), the Brazilian Congress, especially its Comissão de Fiscalizaçao Financeira e Controle (Committee for Financial Oversight and Control), the Ministério Público prosecutorial bodies at both the federal and state levels, the electoral courts, and the Attorney General's Office (AGU). But as in most countries, the TCU, as the leading government audit institution, holds the bulk of responsibility for overseeing public expenditures, punishing misconduct, and recommending reforms. While other control institutions play an important complementary role in auditing, the TCU is dedicated exclusively to this function, and its role therefore intersects with all of the other institutions mentioned here.

Drawing on the analytical framework developed in the previous section, I now turn specifically to the TCU, assessing the legal framework governing its role and its performance in practice. The TCU, which dates back to the founding of the Brazilian Republic in 1891, last saw its institutional design overhauled in the 1988 Constitution. Since then, the powers of the TCU have been altered slightly, including new responsibilities in procurement, in the law on fiscal responsibility, and in the law on budgeting procedures, among others.[15]

Compared to audit institutions in other countries, the TCU holds very broad powers in all phases of the auditing process. In Brazil, unlike many other countries, audit institutions are empowered to directly punish misconduct through imposition of fines and bans on public contracting. However, in many cases, the TCU reports misconduct to other institutions who are charged with imposing sanctions. Thus, despite its strong concentration of auditing powers, the TCU is required to interact closely with other institutions to achieve its goals of holding public officeholders responsible for misconduct and improving budget management.[16] The relation between autonomous action and interaction with other institutions varies, however, in each of the four stages of auditing, described in turn below.

Stage 1: Detecting Misconduct

Although there is great resemblance among government audit institutions in terms of investigatory procedure, audit institutions differ widely in terms of how investigations are triggered. System "leakages" might be unveiled by routine and legally mandatory inspections. Alternately, external institutions and actors might be allowed to request inspections and audits, or the audit institution itself might be allowed to choose and prioritize audit activities by itself. All three alternatives have specific consequences in terms of the efficiency with which the audit institution detects irregularities and in terms of its interaction with other institutions involved in the audit function.

The TCU is governed by a mix of all three forms of activation (although the mix has changed over time). A large part of the audit capacity of the institution is absorbed by routine tasks, with the bulk of the workload dedicated to three specific activities: (1) the preparation of an audit statement on the government's annual accounts, which must be endorsed or rejected by Congress; (2) inspection of annual financial reports from all officeholders managing public funds (roughly three thousand units of government each render separate accounts); and (3) approval of all civil servants' employment and retirement (several thousand cases per year).[17] These legal obligations consume much of the TCU staff's time, leaving limited resources to deploy on additional means of detecting irregularities.

Limited time and resources mean that audit institutions cannot inspect all aspects of public administration at every audit. Thus the prioritization of efforts is a very important element of government auditing and requires specific audit policies aimed at detecting misconduct and systemic leakage. Such policies may adopt different methods, such as employing sophisticated systems of indicators to detect irregularities, shifting annual audit priorities, or simply creating channels for whistle-blowers. All are present in Brazil.

The TCU annually chooses priorities for that year's auditing, such as a focus on social security programs or fund transfers to nongovernmental organizations. This selective approach is expressed in the annual report on the government's accounts, which focuses on a number of specific topics each year.[18] The TCU reacted to recent corruption scandals by opening new channels for the public to report misconduct.[19] In 2004, the TCU decided to open an additional channel to the public by creating an ombuds office, available via Web site, e-mail, phone, or letter.[20] In addition to the increased number of allegations reported to the TCU, creation of the ombuds office has led to increased reporting of irregularities.[21] It is not mandatory, though, for the TCU to follow up on allegations of misconduct received through the ombuds office or other channels. The discretionary power to drop or follow these tips is wide, and the same is true for allegations coming from public officeholders, members of Congress, and public institutions.

In contrast to this discretionary response to whistle-blowers, the law empowers Congress and congressional committees to demand inspections by the TCU.[22] Such demands mandate obligatory action by the TCU. In recent years, Congress has expanded its demands on the TCU to perform inspections and audits in critical areas. Congressional committees have also increasingly demanded technical support from the TCU for their own hearings and investigations. And individual members of Congress have filed allegations of malfeasance with the TCU. Thus the channel opened by law between the legislative body and the TCU has been widely used by Congress.

Stage 2: Assessing the Lawfulness and Efficiency of Public Budget Management

If audit institutions are to adequately fulfill their mission, they must have the power to investigate all aspects of government finances, including all revenues collected, exemptions offered, and disbursements made, up until the final allocation of funds. In many countries, the scope of government audit institutions in this regard is limited. Public investment in private companies, loans from international organizations, the defense budget, or special funds for the president are frequently excluded from scrutiny by audit institutions.

In Brazil, however, the 1988 Constitution defines audit powers broadly, leaving no significant legal loopholes that would put certain budget items out of reach of government auditing.[23] Congress holds the power to control public budgets, and the TCU is its primary auxiliary agency in this regard. The TCU is thus empowered to investigate all aspects of budget management, from revenue to expenditures. This comprises budget items managed directly by the executive branch as well as indirectly through foundations, agencies, or private companies in which the state holds a stake. The TCU also has the power to inspect federal fund transfers to states, municipalities, or entities outside the public sector. In addition, the TCU is entitled to inspect loans contracted by the government, as well as subsidies and tax relief. In sum, the scope of government auditing was defined widely by the 1988 Constitution, and the power of the TCU to audit any aspect of public budgeting is not significantly curtailed by legal constraints.

The two main criteria of modern government auditing are the lawfulness and efficiency of budgetary allocation.[24] While the question of compliance with the law and with accounting standards was at the origin of audit institutions, during the course of the twentieth century the focus of government auditing shifted to a new set of questions. In many countries today, a central question is whether public funds are spent in an economic, efficient, and effective manner, and the key criteria is increasingly performance as opposed to compliance. This shift requires the legal power to question such aspects of budget management and, more than that, the technical capacity to perform such audits.

In Brazil, the TCU is empowered explicitly by the 1988 Constitution to engage in audits focused on performance criteria. In practice, however, the TCU has a long tradition of compliance reviews (focused on lawfulness), and developed its capacity to engage in performance audits (focused on efficiency) only in the 1980s.[25] Reviews of audits performed in the last decade demonstrate that the TCU staff has the capacity to assess government programs in terms of program design, sound management, internal control mechanisms, and their impact on society.[26] However, it is not clear that the TCU should prioritize performance audits of this nature, given the reality of budget management in Brazil. From a technical standpoint, performance review requires more sophisticated methods and has produced valuable insights for improving management of public finances. But the results of compliance audits in Brazil demonstrate that violation of legal and accounting standards is still abundant. Audits performed by the TCU unveil that even in the last decade (1997–2006) between a third and three-quarters of the most cost-intensive government programs show severe irregularities (see table 6.2, the category "budget projects").[27]

Thus, given the reality of public budget management in Brazil, compliance audits are still a priority. More than a programmatic decision, the balance between compliance and performance audits by the TCU is a result of the patterns of budget management in Brazil. Given the environment it is working in, the TCU will be required for some time to come to focus more on compliance review and on holding officeholders responsible for misconduct.

Stage 3: Translating Audit Findings into Sanctions and Recommendations

If the leakage of public resources is detected, whether the cause is misconduct or simply bad administration, audit institutions are expected to contribute to or produce conclusive findings on two key questions of public

Table 6.2. TCU Functions

		1997	1998	1999	2000	2001	2002	2003	2004	2005	2006	2007
Sanction and recovery	Officeholders convicted	—	937	845	1,263	1,170	1,408	1,135	1,044	1,285	1,512	1,574
	Fines levied (in R$ million)	47.53	39.71	44.66	72.56	355.18	754.10	835.70	382.60	360.59	501.16	518.90
Civil service	Officeholders banned from higher positions (for 5–8 years)	—	—	—	17	13	21	23	18	14	13	130
Procurement	Companies banned from contracting with the state (for 3–5 years)	—	—	—	2	6	0	21	21	12	23	47
Elected officeholders	Officeholders banned from running for election	—	—	—	1,382	—	—	—	2,352	—	—	—
Budget projects	Value of funds inspected on request by Congress (in R$ million)	2,200	1,970	1,750	4,290	7,510	14,300	14,400	19,500	19,300	20,700	23,900
	Number of programs with severe irregularities	55%	32%	33%	34%	38%	38%	40%	33%	40%	73%	77%

budget management: Who should be held responsible for past misconduct, and how can the management of public funds be improved in the future?

Concerning past misconduct, audit institutions in many countries are limited to reporting unlawful behavior to other institutions, which then are responsible for allocating civil, administrative, criminal, or political responsibility. In these cases, typically the courts and legislative branch file charges based on audit findings, aimed at holding officeholders responsible.

The Brazilian TCU follows a different model. It has the power to define the financial loss caused by civil servants and to hold them directly responsible for damage caused to public well-being, to impose fines, and to demand the repayment of losses. No other institution is empowered to overturn this decision from a technical standpoint. The TCU has always made significant use of these powers and in recent years it even has expanded this role of holding civil servants responsible for losses. In 2007, the institution held 1,500 civil servants responsible for irregularities and damages caused to public administration, fining them a total of R$500 million (see table 6.2, the category "sanction and recovery"). This means each fined civil servant on average owes more than R$300,000, more than the annual income of even the highest echelon of public servants in Brazil.

Similarly, the TCU is empowered to ban companies involved in severe misconduct in public contracts from bidding for government business for a period of three to five years. While this power has been in place for the last three decades, only recently has the TCU seriously begun to employ such sanctions. While a decade ago no company was blacklisted by the TCU, in 2007 the number of companies that were barred from contracting with the federal government for three to five years was forty-seven. That said, the numbers still range significantly behind the extraordinary numbers of fines against civil servants mentioned above (table 6.2, the category "civil service").

A third form of sanction is ascribing political responsibility to officeholders by barring them from running for elected office or holding civil service positions. Here the TCU shares responsibility for imposing sanctions with other institutions. There are three modes of political sanctions. First, in addition to financial sanctions, the TCU is empowered to ban officeholders involved in cases of severe misconduct from higher positions in the civil service for a period of five to eight years. No other institution is involved in this decision. Again, the power has been there since 1988, but such sanctions only began to be applied in recent years. In 2007, 130 office-holders were sanctioned in this manner. This may seem a small number, but it is worth noting that a decade ago the TCU did not employ such sanctions at all.

Second, the TCU is required to prepare lists of all officeholders who have been involved in severe cases of misconduct and report them to the electoral courts. By law, the TCU's role in implementing this political sanction is different from the above mentioned blacklisting of officeholders. The TCU's role in the process ends once it has submitted the list to the electoral courts, who by law must block those names that have been black-listed by the TCU from running in federal, state, or municipal elections. The TCU's list builds on the results of past audits and is prepared in the June before each election. While these lists have played a minor role in the past and have not been widely publicized, recently the TCU began to pub-lish this information on its Web site, allowing watchdog organizations to make use of it.[28] The list published by the TCU for the 2008 municipal elections included more than four thousand names.

The third type of sanctions relate to the executive branch. After review-ing the annual financial report of the president, the TCU issues a conclu-sive technical statement on overall budget management, which could pre-sumably influence public perceptions of the president. The effect of this statement, however, is somewhat diluted because Congress is the only insti-tution that can hold the government responsible for eventual misconduct.[29] While the TCU usually manages to issue these reports on time, Congress frequently postpones its decision on final endorsement or rejection of the executive branch's annual accounts for years. In any case, the discussion of the annual financial report of the government does not have much politi-cal weight in the Brazilian Congress, especially in comparison with other countries.[30]

Finally, criminal sanctions are a matter for prosecutors and the courts. Although the TCU has its own in-house branch of prosecutors, the insti-tution is not empowered to indict officeholders for criminal offenses. They have a merely advisory role, providing legal advice to TCU directors. Fur-ther, despite the name "Tribunal," the TCU is not part of the Brazilian judi-ciary. Therefore, the TCU can only report criminal behavior to the Minis-tério Público prosecutorial body, which either charges the officeholders or drops the case. Beyond reporting to prosecutors, the TCU has no responsibility or power whatsoever in terms of carrying forward criminal sanctions against officeholders.

The TCU's role in holding officeholders responsible for past misconduct has institutional effects within the auditing institution itself. The auditing process is organized along quasi-judicial lines, and due process is an essential means of legitimizing the audits. TCU auditors produce a technical report, suggesting approval or rejection of financial reports. One of the nine "ministers" (senior directors) of the TCU acts as prosecutor, guiding the investigation and providing a conclusive statement, including possible charges against the officeholder. If charges are filed, the defendant is notified and has a chance to defend him- or herself against the accusations. In the subsequent "trial," all of the ministers discuss the case, either accepting or challenging their colleague's brief. The ministers make their final decision by a majority vote. The defendant can appeal the decision, and a new trial will be held in the TCU to offer a final verdict. Because this procedure is quasi-judicial, government audit institutions in Brazil are labeled as Tribunais de Contas (Tribunals of Accounts), for they respect officeholders' right to defend themselves, to raise objections, and to provide evidence in their favor. As noted earlier, however, the Tribunais de Contas are not part of the judiciary.

This institutional arrangement is responsible for the long delay in producing conclusive audit statements. It often takes years or even decades for the TCU to reach a final verdict. The TCU faces a challenge similar to that of the justice system in Brazil. One might rephrase a famous saying as "Accountability delayed is accountability denied." When it comes to holding officeholders accountable, the delay is doubled: since the TCU is not a part of the judiciary, defendants can appeal TCU verdicts before a court of law, beginning yet another procedure that can take years to reach a final conclusion.

Taking stock of the question of retrospective accountability, we can conclude that the TCU's main responsibility lies in reaching conclusive findings on civil responsibility. When it comes to allocating political responsibility, the TCU shares powers with Congress and the electoral courts. And establishing criminal responsibility is completely out of the hands of the TCU.

The second dimension of the TCU's role is the goal of improving future public budget administration. The TCU prepares recommendations for the executive branch in many of its audit statements. Recently, greater attention has been given to following up on these recommendations, but for the most part the exercise remains perfunctory.

I have argued elsewhere that the institutional design of the TCU and especially its decision-making process are tailored to foster its sanctioning power, to the detriment of its role in suggesting reform recommendations.[31] The legitimacy of sanctions depends on a set of procedures that govern the decision-making process. Reform recommendations, by contrast, draw their legitimacy not from procedure but from the accepted expertise of the authors of such proposals and the proposals' basic soundness.

Stage 4: Imposing Sanctions and Implementing Recommendations

The fourth stage involves both imposing sanctions and implementing recommendations for reform. When it comes to imposing sanctions, although the definition of civil and political responsibility lies with the TCU, for the most part the implementation of sanctions depends entirely on institutions other than the TCU. This is therefore the weakest link in the contemporary Brazilian system of government auditing. The TCU holds the power to assess the damage caused by misconduct and determine the necessary sanctions. But although the TCU makes broad use of this power to attempt asset recovery and to apply fines, in practice most of these fines—which, as noted earlier, totaled R$500 million in 2007 alone—are never paid. The reason lies in the institutional context: institutions other than the TCU have to take action if fined officeholders refuse to pay.

The effective sanctions forthcoming from the TCU are low for several reasons. First, decisions by the audit body frequently are questioned in court, as noted earlier. Though the TCU adopts quasi-judicial procedures, accused officeholders are entitled to question the TCU's findings in the "real" court system.[32] Several decisions by the Brazilian Supreme Federal Tribunal (STF) have limited the possibility of judicial appeals against the TCU's findings to questions of due process, and the STF has reaffirmed that audit statements of the TCU cannot be overturned by courts on purely technical grounds. But TCU decisions regarding the civil responsibility of officeholders can still be appealed in the courts, delaying the implementation of the TCU's decisions on the overall audit process. By the time a final verdict is reached in court, those held responsible frequently are no longer in office, have transferred the assets in question into safe havens, or have died. Again, delayed accountability means less effective accountability.

A second reason civil responsibility for improper administration seldom is properly ascribed is a lack of effectiveness and political will on the part of the Advocacia Geral da União (Federal Attorney General's Office, AGU), the institution in charge of prosecuting those who do not comply with TCU decisions at the federal level. Fewer than 1% of the fines levied by the TCU are effectively paid. At the municipal level, where portions of the federal budget are also spent, the picture can be even worse: it may be that the person whose job it is to press charges in court for noncompliance with TCU decisions is him- or herself the offender, or is a member of the local government that has been convicted. The central point is that when the executive branch is in charge of implementing decisions against its members, a conflict of interest tends to slow down or block effective civil sanctions.

For similar reasons, the power of the TCU to ban candidates from running for elected office when they are found to have misused public budgets does not have any effect in practice. Politicians blacklisted by the TCU before the electoral courts simply appeal their cases in the regular courts, which means that the validity of the TCU decision remains in limbo until the courts reach a final decision. This loophole allows candidates to successfully register and run for elected office, despite their questionable record in managing public funds. In many cases, elected officeholders have finished their term before the court reaches any decision on their electoral blacklisting.

As a result, only a handful of sanctions imposed by TCU decisions are really effective, largely because they do not require any follow-through by other institutions in the web of accountability. Civil servants can be blacklisted from promotion, for example, and companies can be banned from contracting with the state, with no further intermediation by another authority before these sanctions become effective.[33] Perhaps as a result, the TCU has broadened its use of these types of administrative sanctions, and the number of officeholders and companies banned has increased in recent years (table 6.2).

The second element of this fourth stage is the generation of recommendations for reform and their implementation. The two main institutions involved in the discussion and implementation of reform proposals concerning the design of public policies and institutions are the executive and Congress. The success of audit institutions' recommendations for preventing future misconduct thus depends largely on these institutions.

Audit institutions' recommendations for reform can be carried forward through three channels. The first is the government bureaucracy. After the auditing process, the TCU sends the audit report, including recommendations for change, to the officeholder responsible. While the TCU in some cases might request changed behavior (backed by the threat of further sanctions), in most cases the recommendations rest on nothing more than a convincing argument. But there is no guarantee that the TCU's recommendations will be heard. One reason is that retrospective accountability and prospective recommendations can conflict with each other. An officeholder fearing punishment by the TCU, for example, may provide minimal information and be reluctant to accept recommendations that are not legally binding. Regardless, no systematic studies are available on how TCU recommendations have fared or on the extent to which they have been accepted by bureaucracies.

One important development that may increase the distance between the TCU and the members of the executive branch is the creation of the Federal Comptroller's Office (CGU, Controladoria Geral da União). By law, the role of the TCU as a control institution, and especially its role in providing the government with recommendations from audit findings, has not changed with the creation of the CGU. In practice, however, the CGU's oversight of the public sector has changed the role of the TCU. The executive branch can now resort to its own audit institution to diagnose shortcomings and loopholes in the budget management cycle. Obviously, the executive branch is more likely to prefer the CGU's recommendations to those of a body like the TCU that answers to Congress.

Should recommendations and suggestions of preventive measures not be carried through by the government, the TCU can resort to a second channel, Congress. In theory, many TCU recommendations would be of specific interest to congressional committees charged with oversight of the ministries involved. However, in reality the interaction on this level is minimal. TCU auditors are only sporadically called to testify in congressional hearings or to advise congressional committees, and audit findings are not yet a key resource for members of Congress. Congressional requests for information about ongoing audits, which could be taken as one indicator of legislators' interest in the TCU's audit findings, have remained flat over the last decade.

Congress has, however, increased its other demands on the TCU. It has frequently required the TCU to allocate auditors temporarily to its own investigations, mostly in congressional committees of inquiry (*comissões parlamentares de inquérito*, CPIs). These demands increased considerably as congressional oversight of government bureaucracies has grown since 1989.[34] Most recently, it led the TCU to create a clearing center for congressional demands.

Another type of cooperation between the TCU and Congress that has proven successful has been the previously mentioned audits of long-term government programs, which have strengthened the interaction between these institutions and produced tangible effects. A turning point in the relationship between Congress and the TCU, however, was a new rule governing the budget process. The Budget Guidance Law (Lei de Diretrizes Orçamentárias) of 2001 enhanced the cooperation between the TCU and the Congressional Budget Committee (Comissão Mista de Orçamento). This new rule was created in reaction to a large corruption scandal in 1999, involving a public contract for a new court building in Sao Paulo. Despite early warnings from the TCU as early as 1997, and investigations by the Ministério Público in 1998, public funds continued to be siphoned away for many years by a ring headed by a corrupt judge, a senator, and construction company executives. Not until a congressional committee of inquiry set up by the Brazilian Congress in March 1999 concluded that the group had siphoned away R$169 million during the building of a new regional labor court was the project effectively stopped.

In response to this blatant proof of lack of interaction between different control institutions, the budget law was reformed, systematizing the cooperation between the TCU and Congress. Even before the new rule, the TCU reported to Congress on irregularities in ongoing projects, and the Joint Budget Committee (Comissão Mista de Orçamento) might take this information into account when discussing the next budget.

The new rules in place since 2001 have set up a clear structure and hence enhanced the cooperation between the budget committee and the audit agency. Now the TCU is required to report on irregularities in any major government projects with a clear recommendation regarding whether to block further fund transfers and to present these findings in a timely fashion before the government submits the budget proposal for the coming year to Congress. Again, the TCU does not take a final decision but rather provides expert advice to Congress. It is the budget committee that must decide whether to block further fund transfers to projects highlighted by the TCU as suffering from severe irregularities. The committee has not overturned the recommendations of the TCU to date. Instead, it requires that the TCU follow up on these projects and will not permit further fund transfers unless the TCU signals that all pending problems have been resolved.

This new type of audit covers a significant portion of the budget (around R$20 billion, see table 6.2). The shifting rules of cooperation between Congress and the TCU in auditing large government programs were a turning point in the effectiveness of external control of government, especially when compared to the previous practice of loose cooperation between the TCU and the Budget Committee. This new preventive measure has even changed the executive branch's relation with the TCU. In the past, officeholders worked hard to postpone a final verdict by the TCU; in many cases today, public administrators are eager to have the TCU reassess its projects as early as possible in order to have blocked funds released.

Finally, should the legislative body fail to take action, the last channel through which the TCU can obtain a hearing for its recommendations is the public. The TCU is often correctly questioned about its poor record in detecting misconduct early on, before misconduct erupts in corruption scandals. However, in many cases the TCU has raised warning flags but neither the government nor Congress has taken action. Making audit results as widely available as possible and maintaining a systematic dialogue with society are ways of fostering public recognition and trust. The Brazilian TCU invests in this area, albeit without a clear focus.[35] The recently created ombuds office and a program labeled "Public Dialogue" have intensified TCU contacts with civil society.[36] But the focus of these programs is still on trust building and on receiving allegations of misconduct. The TCU does not promote its audit findings actively in society at large, even when government and lawmakers fail to implement its proposals.

Taking Stock: The TCU's Role in Government Auditing in Brazil

We stated initially that government auditing has to be measured against two basic outcomes for the political system: holding public officeholders responsible for misconduct and producing recommendations that improve budget management. The first output is retrospective, focusing on past individual behavior and responsibilities. The latter is prospective, focusing on collective patterns of behavior, systemic corruption risks, and institutional design.

Table 6.3 summarizes the analysis so far, from the viewpoint of the basic outcomes of government auditing. It identifies government auditing as a cooperative task, unveiling the strengths and shortcomings in different areas from the viewpoint of institutional design and practice. Further, it focuses specifically on the TCU's share of responsibility in carrying out sanctions and providing recommendations, as well as how it develops these tasks in practice.

Comparative View of Institutional Arrangements for Independence

An important question for the performance of government audition institutions is how to keep them independent from the bureaucracies they must audit. Earlier I noted that this independence develops along three dimensions: functional autonomy, budget allocation and management, and the independence of its directors.

With regard to the first two dimensions, the TCU faces no significant constraints. The institution is self-governed, within the limits of its bylaws. Its nine ministers vote among themselves on a president who serves for two years and can run for a second term. The TCU's budget allocation has not fluctuated significantly since the 1988 Constitution. The TCU works out its annual budget plan autonomously and executes it without external interference. The TCU is functionally autonomous, within the limits set by law. It develops its own audit policy and receives mandatory requests only from Congress or through changes in the existing law.

The third dimension, regarding the independence of its ministers, is the source of much criticism of the TCU. Institutional constraints on the TCU's independence arise from two sources: the process of selecting the ministers and the mechanisms to protect these ministers from external

Table 6.3. The Role of the TCU: Assessing the Law and Practice

		Role of the TCU		Role of Other Institutions	
		Legal Framework	*Practice*	*Legal Framework*	*Practice*
Sanctions	Criminal	No involvement	TCU reports evidence of criminal misbehavior to Ministério Público	Main responsibility lies with the Ministerio Público (and courts)	Unknown
	Civil	TCU alone holds power to define damage caused and financial sanctions to be applied (based on annual accounts rendered by officeholders and investigations)	TCU always applied financial sanctions to officeholder and has increased the emphasis on this modality (1,500 officeholders convicted to pay 0.5 billion Reais in 2007)	Implementation of sanctions depends on Advocacia Geral da União, FUNDEF, and other government agencies (and on courts)	Effectiveness is low because of poor implementation by AGU and appeal to courts by officeholders
		TCU holds power to ban public servants from higher positions	TCU started banning servants recently, still moderate numbers (130 banned in 2007)	—	High effectiveness
		TCU holds power to ban companies from future contracting with state	TCU started banning companies recently, still moderate numbers (47 banned in 2007)	—	High effectiveness
	Political	TCU prepares a list of former officeholders to be banned from running in elections	TCU issues lists regularly before registration of candidates (including more than 4,000 names before 2008 municipal elections)	Implementation of sanctions depends on courts (electoral justice), without discretionary power	Effectiveness is low because of legal loophole (black-listed candidates appeal to courts, enabling them to run for office while no final decision is taken)
Prevention		TCU issues expert opinion on approval of annual accounts of the government	TCU provides conclusive statement on annual accounts	Congress takes final decision, either endorsing or overturning the TCU opinion	Congress delays debate on annual accounts for years, lessening the endorsement to the status of a symbolic act
	Civil service	TCU holds the power to endorse or reject process of contracting and retirement of permanent civil servants	TCU endorses thousands of processes of civil service annually	TCU endorsement is binding for administration	—
	Procurement	TCU holds the power to inspect all processes of contracting public jobs or public works	TCU follows hundreds of processes of public contracting, demanding adjustments	TCU recommendations are binding for administration	Administration is forced to apply the law on public procurement

Table 6.3. The Role of the TCU: Assessing the Law and Practice

		Role of the TCU		Role of Other Institutions	
		Legal Framework	*Practice*	*Legal Framework*	*Practice*
Prevention	Government programs	TCU inspects large government programs and may recommend blocking resource transfers	TCU issues conclusive statement on compliance with legal and accounting standards, recommending adjustments	Legislative branch implements blockage, without discretionary power	Effective blockage of further resource transfer to government programs with severe irregularities
	Recommendations	TCU audits performance of public resource management and recommends adjustments and reforms	TCU develops performance audits on selective issues, recommending adjustments and reforms	Implementation depends on administration obeying the recommendations, large discretionary power	Unknown

pressure once they are in office. Selecting and protecting the directors of audit institutions requires institutional safeguards to privilege independence, integrity, and professional qualification. However, taking the countries of Latin America as a reference, we see that the means of achieving these safeguards vary widely (table 6.4).

First, required prequalifications include formal criteria like citizenship and age, but also professional skills, political nonpartisanship, and, in some cases, previous public-sector employment experience. In many Latin American countries no prequalifications are required of the directors of audit institutions. Where such criteria are in place, they refer to specific professional skills or limit the range of candidates to a specific group of professionals. Nonpartisanship, where required, excludes political activists from running for office. Criteria concerning integrity are mentioned in a number of countries in the region; however, they are generally rather vague.

In the case of the TCU, the 1988 Constitution introduced strong professional prequalifications for some TCU ministers. Two of the nine ministers must be former staff members of the TCU (one selected from among the TCU's prosecutors, and the other from among the TCU's auditors). As career public servants they have a strong professional background

Table 6.4. Latin American Auditing Institutions

	Constitution	Name of Audit Institution	Chapter in Constitution	Autonomy	PREQUALIFICATION							Selection (Share Executive)	Selection (Share Legislative)	Selection (Share Other)	Head of Audit Institutions Term in Office in Comparison to Government	Governing Model
					Citizenship	Age	Education	Experience	Integrity	Audit Skills	Incompatibilities					
Argentina	1994	Auditoria General de la Nacion	Part of the legislative power	Functional autonomy (Art. 85)	x		x	x				None	High	None	Higher (2.0 times)	Collegial (7 members)
Brazil	1988	Tribunal de Contas da União	Part of the legislative power	Not mentioned		x		x	x	x		Low	High	None	Lifelong (until age 70)	Collegial (9 members)
Chile	1980	Contraloria General	Independent power	Autonomy (Art. 87)		x						High	Low	None	Lifelong (until age 75)	Monocratic
Uruguay	1967	Tribunal de Cuentas	Independent power	Functional autonomy (Art. 210)	x	x						None	High	None	Equal	Collegial (7 members)
Paraguay	1992	Contraloria General	Independent power	Functional and administrative autonomy (Art. 281)	x	x	x					None	High	None	Equal	Monocratic
Bolivia	1995	Contraloria General	Economic order	Not mentioned								Low	High	None	Higher (2.0 times)	Monocratic
Peru	1993	Contraloria General	Economic order	Autonomy (Art. 82)								High	Low	None	Higher (1.4 times)	Monocratic
Ecuador	1998	Contraloria General	Control institution	Administrative and budgetary autonomy (Art. 211)	x		x	x	x			Low	High	None	Equal	Monocratic
Colombia	1991	Contraloria General	Control institution	Functional budgetary autonomy (Art. 267)								Low	High	High	Equal	Monocratic

Table 6.4. Latin American Auditing Institutions (*cont.*)

Constitution	Name of Audit Institution	Chapter in Constitution	Autonomy	PREQUALIFICATION							Selection (Share Executive)	Selection (Share Legislative)	Selection (Share Other)	Head of Audit Institutions Term in Office in Comparison to Government	Governing Model
				Citizenship	Age	Education	Experience	Integrity	Skills	Incompatibilities					
Venezuela 1999	Contraloria General	Independent from other powers	Functional and administrative autonomy (Art. 281)								Undefined	Undefined	None	Higher (1.15 times)	Monocratic
Panama 1994	Contraloria General	Economic order	Independent (Art. 275)	x	x	x		x			None	High	None	Equal	Monocratic
Costa Rica 1949	Contraloria General	Economic order	Functional and administrative autonomy (Art. 183)								None	High	None	Higher (1.5 times)	Monocratic
Nicaragua 1987	Contraloria General	Independent from other powers	Functional and administrative autonomy (Art. 156)								None	High	None	Higher (1.2 times)	Monocratic
Honduras 1982	Contraloria General	Independent from other powers	Functional and administrative autonomy (Art. 222)	x	x		x	x			None	High	None	Higher (1.25 times)	Monocratic
El Salvador 1983	Corte de Cuentas	Independent from other powers	Independent from executive (Art. 195)	x	x		x	x			None	High	None	Higher (1.65 times)	Collegial (3 members)
Guatemala 1985	Contraloria General	Independent from other powers	Not mentioned	x	x		x	x			None	High	None	Lower (0.8 times)	Monocratic
Mexico 1917	Auditoria Superior de la Federación	Part of the legislative power	Functional and administrative autonomy (Art. 79)	x	x	x		x		x	None	High	None	Higher (1.5 times)	Monocratic

and usually do not have strong political ties. The president's influence over these ministers is therefore limited. However, the other seven ministers can be freely nominated if they satisfy the very formal criteria of age and citizenship, or the vague criteria of professional expertise and integrity. In the Latin American context, the Brazilian model of recruiting some directors of the audit institution from among career public servants of the institution is outstanding. Many countries require professional expertise but do not translate this requirement into an objective criterion. The link to the political world, however, can also be severed through incompatibilities or quarantine rules. In Mexico, for example, elected representatives and those who held high-level positions in government cannot be nominated to top positions in the audit office during a quarantine period of one year after leaving office. No such rule exists in Brazil.

Second, concerning the process of selection, in many Latin American countries the executive, the legislature, and (in one case) the judiciary share the power to appoint the head of audit institutions. The process can vary widely. Either the president selects and legislators endorse his nomination (e.g., Chile or Peru), or legislators select a list of three candidates and the president picks one of these three (e.g., Bolivia or Ecuador). The balance of power in the first model shifts to the president, while in the second case representatives have the upper hand. In contrast to these cases of shared power, in many countries the legislative branch has complete control. In these cases, variations in the simple majority rule can limit the politicization of the selection process. In Paraguay, for example, the Senate elaborates a triple list, and the House of Representatives holds the power to make the final choice. In Mexico and Uruguay, the nominees to head the audit institution require approval from a qualified majority (two-thirds) of the legislature, guaranteeing the minority some veto power in the selection process. Two interesting cases deserve mention. In Venezuela, the Constitution does not make clear who should select the head of the audit institution.[37] In Argentina, the main opposition party selects the person who will preside over the audit board, a solution that harnesses political competition in service of independent oversight.

In the case of the Brazilian TCU, the president selects three out of nine ministers. As mentioned earlier, two of these are chosen from the staff of the institution. The third candidate can be chosen freely, granted he or she meets the formal requirements. However, all nominations by the president require Senate endorsement. The remaining six ministers are chosen by Congress. Again, Congress has great leeway in choosing the candidates, as the requirements for candidates are a mix of formal (citizenship, age), low (education, experience), and vague (reputation). Six out of nine ministers in 2008 were elected representatives before they were nominated by their colleagues for the position. These political ties are not dissolved after their nomination to the TCU.

Third, the guarantees given to the head of audit institutions include tenure and protection from removal. Concerning the question of tenure, Latin American countries can be divided into three groups. In the first group, which includes most countries in the region, tenure coincides with presidential or congressional terms, implying a continued close link to the political sphere. Where the head of audit institutions stays in office significantly beyond the political cycle (e.g., Bolivia and Costa Rica), the separation tends to be more accentuated. Finally, in Brazil and Chile, the heads of audit offices are appointed for life, which should contribute to severing the link with the political world. In Brazil, however, politicians are frequently nominated to join the TCU at the height or the end of their political career, in what is sometimes seen as a kind of early retirement. Three of the current ministers were sixty years or older when they were nominated for the position.[38] Given the mandatory retirement age of seventy, this is far from a lengthy "life" term. Age and political background thus have a profound impact on ministers' connections to the political world and their commitment to their new institution.

Fourth, audit institutions can be organized on two models of leadership: monocratic or collegial leadership. Collegial governing per se does not guarantee more independence than monocratic models, as noted earlier. However, institutional designs that promote a varied composition and more mixed political ties may dilute the effects of individual members' political bias in a collegial body. Where the directors of audit institutions to be indicated by the legislative body need approval by a qualified majority (e.g., Uruguay), a mixed composition that results from negotiations with the opposition is highly probable. Another model that helps to ensure a variety of positions in collegial bodies is "stepwise" nomination. This is the case in Argentina, where Congress replaces half of the directors of the audit office every four years. The directors each have an eight-year term, ensuring that their terms extend beyond those of the nominating Congress.

In the case of the Brazilian TCU a similar model is in place, ensuring a variety of viewpoints. With a larger number of members of ministers and life terms (to age seventy), the TCU includes ministers selected a decade or more ago. The TCU ministers in September 2008 included one minister nominated by President Sarney, five by Cardoso, and three by Lula. The composition of the TCU, however, is a result of institutional design and political context: should a political party manage to stay in power for more than a decade, the ministers of the TCU will likely become increasingly politically aligned with its partisan views.

As stated initially, one of the main criticisms held against the TCU is its closeness to politics, a characteristic built into it from the beginning that was not challenged significantly in the last century. The rationale for this lack of independence is twofold: first, the selection as a member of the TCU is considered to be a perk for retiring politicians, including high remuneration, one's own staff, and allowances. Second, the nomination comes with strings attached, since the government with its majority in Congress does not expect any trouble from its former allies once they are transferred to the TCU. Thus, as long as the recruiting mechanism for the collegiums is biased toward members of the political elite, the TCU will not be able to sever its ties to government and opposition. The mechanisms of protection from political prosecution and lifetime tenure are of minor importance.

Once sufficient political will is accumulated to change this setting, an institutional bridge toward more independence could be to select all members of the TCU among auditors and prosecutors, thus tempering the negative impact of selection by the government and the legislature. Such selection, similar to the selection of the attorney general, would allow the TCU to evolve into a full-fledged external government auditing agency. Life tenure and collegial decisions would continue protecting the institution from censorship and guarantee balanced decisions when sanctions affect sensitive areas of the political system or touch upon the interests of the political elite.

GOVERNMENT AUDITING IS A CENTRAL COMPONENT OF MODERN POLITICAL systems, aimed at punishing misconduct and improving public budget management in the pursuit of greater efficiency and integrity. By design, the TCU is the most important but not the only institution involved in government auditing in Brazil. To assess the TCU's role and its ties with other institutions, this chapter presented a model of the government audit process. From this, it became clear that the TCU has broad control over the process of detecting misconduct. However, although the TCU has developed into a highly professional organization in assessing government behavior (in terms of both its probity and its efficiency), when translating these findings into sanctions or recommendations, the TCU faces an important question: Should government auditing continue to focus on sanctions for noncompliance, or is improving the system of budget management a better path toward greater efficiency and integrity?

Another key question at this point is to what extent the TCU is sufficiently independent of the political sphere to take decisions on sanctions and recommendations in a politically neutral way. Although the TCU looks quite good in comparison with the rest of Latin America, several factors drag it closer to the political sphere. The most important, of course, is that seven out of nine ministers are drawn from the political world and are seldom able to cut these ties during the short period they typically serve on the TCU before retirement.

Finally, government auditing in Brazil is characterized by a surprisingly wide gap between the decisions taken by the TCU and the implementation of sanctions that require cooperation with other institutions in the web of accountability. The ineffectiveness of sanctions that transcend the TCU is partly embedded in the institutional design, but it is also a result of the poor performance of the other institutions. Recent changes in the pattern of sanctions applied for misconduct have managed to bypass these obstacles partially: the TCU and Congress have explored ways of punishing and preventing system leakage that do not require the cooperation of other institutions, such as banning companies and officeholders from dealing with the state or blocking budget transfers to suspect government projects. Thus, although the pursuit of comprehensive government auditing will require fixing the missing links between the TCU and its peer institutions, the most effective strategy in the short term seems to be to rely on tactics that promise some impact without requiring external cooperation.

Notes

1. The debate among audit professionals takes place in specialized publications like *International Journal of Government Auditing* and (in Brazil) *Revista do Tribunal de Contas da União*. For a recent discussion of government auditing in Brazil from the viewpoint of auditors, see M. Bugarin, Vieira, and Garcia (2003).

2. Academic journals like the *Journal for Public Administration, Research and Theory, Public Administration Review, Public Administration, Public Administration and Development, International Public Management Review, Public Management Review,* and, in Brazil, *Revista de Administração Pública* include few articles on state auditing. A small group of authors, among them Santiso (2006a, 2006b) and Stapenhurst (Dye and Stapenhurst 1998; Stapenhurst and Titsworth 2001), have published articles on government audit institutions in different periodicals. Searching the SciELO database for Ibero-American academic journals returns only two hits to a search on "tribunal + contas" (Costa, Pereira, and Blanco 2006; C. Freitas and Guimarães 2007). Only a few political scientists, including Speck (2000a, 2008), Speck and Nagel (2002), Pessanha (2007), and Pereira, Melo, and Figueiredo (2009a, 2009b), have published on the Brazilian audit institutions.

3. Research departments of development agencies have produced comparative studies on the role of government auditing: Dye and Stapenhurst (1998); Stapenhurst and Titsworth (2001); Shah (2007).

4. For a typology of different audit systems drawing on the historical background, see Department for International Development (2004). One of the few comparative studies has been published by the National Accounting Office of the United Kingdom (1996). For more information on the historical background and path dependency of the Brazilian TCU, see Speck (2000a, 27–80) or M. Bugarin, Vieira, and Garcia (2003, 57–137).

5. On the issue of standards for the independence of audit institutions and standardized audit procedures, see *The Lima Declaration* (INTOSAI [1977] 1980), a statement worked out by the state audit institutions on their Ninth Congress in Lima, Peru, in October 1977, affirming the principle of independence of government auditing) and *Government Auditing Standards* (the so-called "Yellow Book"), a reference guide to government auditing standards prepared by the Comptroller General of the United States (Comptroller General 2007).

6. The structural-functionalist model of Almond and Powell (1966) sets universal functions as the overarching principle of political systems, while structures (or institutions) come second. This allows us to compare the audit function across political systems. Different structures (or institutional designs) are interpreted in the context of universal functions.

7. Many authors with a background in law answer the question on the role or function of audit institutions by translating the powers and responsibilities of audit institutions into "functions." One example out of many is B. Bugarin (1994),

who lists eight functions for the TCU. This approach is radically different, since it starts with the structure (institutional design) and understands functions as a subordinate category. It highlights the idiosyncrasy of institutions in each country, while the functionalist approach allows for meaningful cross-country comparison.

8. The distinction between sanctions and preventive measures is to a certain extent arbitrary. Sanctions against officeholders also play a preventive role for future behavior. However, they are included in the first category because they refer to past behavior and individual responsibility. Similarly, many preventive measures are based on strengthening the mechanisms of investigation and sanctions. Inasmuch as they do not refer to single cases, they are preventive measures.

9. The discussion on the independence of audit institutions has been central to the audit institutions themselves (see INTOSAI [1977] 1980). In addition, INTOSAI (the global organization of state audit institutions) has developed a project to evaluate the independence of audit bodies, including similar questions on nomination and guarantees for the head of audit institutions and different dimensions of independence of the agency from other powers (INTOSAI 2001).

10. Apart from independence, audit institutions require additional features like professional expertise and the manpower necessary to perform audit tasks. These requirements, however, will not be discussed further in this chapter.

11. However, the power to initiate audits and to conclude with sanctions and recommendations is often shared with other institutions, as indicated earlier.

12. In the Brazilian case, the Fiscal Responsibility Law (Complementary Law 101) is one example where the TCU gained new responsibilities and additional workload, thus limiting its autonomy to implement its own audit policy.

13. Arguably, there might be a cost to extremely long terms for the heads of audit offices from the viewpoint of innovation and accountability. There may be a trade-off between innovation and independence.

14. However, a collegial directorship that might favor the independence of audit agencies can be undermined in practice (by high director turnover, by a political group staying in power over a long time, or by a dominant political group holding sway over all institutions involved in the nomination process), thus resulting in government control of even a collegial directorate. This point has been raised by Speck (2000a) and analyzed empirically by Pereira, Melo, and Figueiredo (2009a).

15. After defining the powers and responsibility of the state audit agencies Tribunais de Contas (TCs) in the Constitution of 1988 and in the Organic Law in 1992 (Law 8.443, of July 16, 1992), the Brazilian TCs have been given several additional tasks. The Law on Public Procurement (Law 8.666, of June 21, 1993) declares that TCs hold the power to receive complaints and follow up on irregularities in processes of public procurement. The Law on Declaration of Assets of Public Officeholders (Law 8.730, of November 10, 1993) states that TCs are in charge of registering and overseeing public servants' asset declarations. The Transparency

Law (Law 9.755, of December 16, 1998) states that the TCU must maintain a Web page on federal, state, and municipal budgets, including updated information on revenue, expenses, and procurement. The Law on Fiscal Responsibility (Complementary Law No. 101, of May 15, 2000, labeled Lei de Responsabilidade Fiscal) defines maximum limits for expenditure on civil servants and for public-sector indebtedness in Brazil. It determines that the TCs are in charge of reviewing the quarterly financial reports by government and alerting the legislative branches of noncompliance. The triennial Budget Guidance Law (Lei de Diretrizes Orçamentarias; Law10.266, of July 24, 2001) stated for the first time the TCU must regularly review all large government projects and report irregularities to the budget commission of the National Congress (Comissão Mista de Orçamento), thwarting further fund transfers to projects with irregularities.

16. The basic legal framework for government auditing is written into the Brazilian Constitution and is mandatory at all three levels of the Brazilian federation. State and local-level government auditing will not be discussed here, however, given space considerations.

17. 1988 Constitution, Art. 71, I, II and III.

18. For an overview of past years, see Speck (2000a, 105).

19. Citizens could report irregularities to the TCU before, and public officeholders are forced by law to do so should irregularities come to their knowledge. However, the creation of ombuds offices has strengthened this interaction with the public.

20. TCU, Resolution 69, 2004.

21. See annual reports of the TCU.

22. 1988 Constitution, Art. 72 IV.

23. 1988 Constitution, Art. 70–75.

24. On different auditing modalities, see Dye and Stapenhurst (1998, 15–16).

25. Gonçalves (1993).

26. Reports on the audit findings are available in publications like *Auditorias do TCU, Sumários Executivos,* and *Revista do TCU.*

27. The annual reports of the TCU for these years show the lowest rate of projects with irregularities in 1998 (32%) and the highest rate in 2007 (77%).

28. The Excelências project developed by Transparência Brasil, a Brazilian nongovernmental organization, for example, published short biographies of candidates running for reelection during the 2006 elections, including information from the TCU list.

29. In the case of municipal governments, the local legislative body needs a qualified majority (two-thirds) to overrule the respective TC.

30. Citadini (1995) notes that the British parliament interrupts its ordinary procedures to receive and debate the National Accounting Office's report evaluating public resource management by the government.

31. Speck (2000a, 210–13).

32. This right to question in courts any decision or action taken by a public institution other than the judiciary is enshrined in the 1988 Constitution.

33. Obviously, these bans have to be complied with by the administration in question. But ignoring the decision of the TCU would be considered an unlawful act.

34. For an analysis of this oversight role of Congress, see A. Figueiredo (2001).

35. For international experiences in this field, see Ramkumar and Krafchik (2005).

36. The TCU created its ombuds office in June 2004, while the program Diálogo Público was started a year earlier.

37. The Web site of the Venezuelan audit institution (www.cgr.gob.ve) states, however, that the current head, Clodosbaldo Russián Uzcátegui, was elected by the Constitutional Assembly in 1999, was confirmed by the National Assembly in 2000, and had his term renewed for another seven years in 2007.

38. This refers to the composition as of September 2008.

Chapter Seven

The Federal Judiciary and Electoral Courts

MATTHEW M. TAYLOR

Sanctioning political wrongdoing provides several important benefits. Sanctioning has both a punitive effect on implicated politicians and a deterrent effect on their colleagues; it improves the answerability of surviving politicians; and it helps build public trust in the public-regardingness of the democratic process (Levi 1999; chapter 1 of this volume). The federal judiciary and the electoral courts are the most important formal institutions in Brazil for imposing legal sanctions. This chapter analyzes their performance and in particular questions their apparent inability to effectively punish political corruption and the broader effects of this weakness on the federal political system as a whole.

As the introduction to this volume points out, there are vital complementarities between the various types of sanctions and between the accountability institutions that impose them, without which the individual institutions in the web of accountability cannot function adequately. An active press corps, for example, may not retain the necessary independence to report scandals if wrongdoers are not removed from positions of power, from which they could otherwise retaliate against journalists, journalists' whistle-blowing sources, or media owners. Likewise, if police or prosecutors find evidence of malfeasance by politicians, the absence of independent media may make it difficult to get information to the public that could otherwise lead to electoral sanctions.[1] Weaknesses in any single link in the web of accountability institutions, in other words, will make the overall system less effective. Further, they may reduce the incentives to pursue and prosecute wrongdoing in the future, especially when the targets are politically powerful and able to shape careers or institutional well-being.

A related argument is that corrupt players who are not held accountable decrease the likelihood of future accountability in the political system. If the web of accountability institutions external to Congress is weak, the dominant strategy in any repeat interaction is for congressional representatives to protect their dirty colleagues from political accountability. In the absence of an external force (jail time, electoral loss, etc.) that permanently removes the "dirty" politician from office, it is not only brave but actually self-endangering for a "clean" congressman to seek accountability against his corrupt colleague. This is especially the case if the "clean" congressman knows that the chances of that colleague returning to office after being sanctioned politically (e.g., forced to resign) are high. Under such conditions, not only are the chances of the corrupt politician remaining in office high, but his permanence (and that of others like him) will also greatly reduce the chances of imposing accountability at any point in the future.

In sum, the overall accountability network is a delicate structure built on mutual supports. The weakness of both electoral and judicial courts is thus a vitally central issue for political accountability in Brazil: first, because of the courts' direct effects in setting the rules and enforcing them via legal sanctions; and second, because of their indirect effects in strengthening the likelihood of the imposition of nonlegal sanctions elsewhere in the political system. As the next section illustrates, legal accountability has been sorely ineffectual in Brazil, with pernicious follow-through effects, both direct and indirect, in the broader political system.

The Accountability Process for Brazilian Politicians

There are three central stages in the accountability process: monitoring, investigation, and sanction. All are weak in Brazil, and the weakness of each of the three undermines the others. But of the three, it is arguably the sanctioning process that is the weakest. Inasmuch as it is possible to separate the three phases, therefore, this chapter focuses primarily on the process of sanction, and specifically legal sanction: the chances of punishment and the ability of federal courts to remove "dirty" politicians from the political process before they contaminate it or other politicians.[2]

How does the evidence stack up? Anecdotal evidence suggests that the view of Brazilian politicians as immune from accountability holds great truth:

1. Ninety incumbent and twenty-five former members of Congress were implicated in the *sanguessuga* scandal that broke in 2006, in which politicians were accused of siphoning off funds from the sale of over-priced ambulances to municipal governments. Although a parliamentary commission of inquiry (*comissão parlamentar de inquérito*, CPI) was convened, and recommended the expulsion *(cassação)* from Congress of seventy-two members, none were expelled. A large number of those implicated were not reelected, but as of this writing, not one of those implicated had faced any penalty in either the electoral courts or the federal judiciary.

2. Of twenty deputies cited by CPIs into the *correios* and *mensalão* scandals, four resigned and three were expelled from Congress. But the remaining thirteen ran for reelection, eight successfully, and one of those who had been expelled nonetheless managed to elect his daughter. Accountability is no better in the courts. Forty defendants—including thirteen politicians—are being tried in the high court on charges related to the *mensalão*. But the slow pace of the courts virtually ensures that none of the defendants' trials will be concluded until after the Lula administration—the alleged beneficiary of the scheme—steps down.

3. Recent studies show that between a sixth and a third of the members of Congress are defendants in criminal suits: 180 of the 594 deputies and senators in 2006; 104 in 2007; and 150 in 2008 (Siqueira and Sardinha 2007; Congresso em Foco 2006; see also Transparência Brasil 2008). During the 2003–7 session of Congress, 105 members of both houses of Congress were reported to the Ethics Committee for unbecoming conduct, and 180 were accused of criminal activity. Of all of these, only four were *cassados* (and this was actually a historically high proportion; Congresso em Foco 2006), and not one has received a definitive, unappealable, conviction.

Scattered data such as these give a flavor of the problem. Unfortunately, more systematic and reliable evidence is hard to come by. One difficulty is that it is hard to figure out how much of the iceberg is above water: that is, how much corrupt activity is in fact being turned up. But it is worth remembering also that it is not always clear that all of those implicated are in fact guilty, much less that all of the guilty are being implicated. Finally, the legal cases presented against corrupt politicians may vary considerably in quality, especially as we compare cases of differing levels of complexity, brought by different prosecutors before different judges and in different courts.

Having noted these shortcomings, however, the examples above suggest there is considerable truth to the view that Brazilian justice convicts only *pés de chinelo*, that is, those too poor to defend themselves adequately. Politicians, meanwhile, seem to be in an entirely different class. Why is their behavior so free of consequences? In trying to answer this question, I turn next to the courts themselves.

The Role of Electoral and Judicial Courts at the Federal Level

Two court systems are central to accountability for political corruption in Brazil. The electoral court system focuses largely on issues related to electoral process, with additional responsibilities for monitoring malfeasance related to campaigns and voting, and imposing political sanctions, such as loss of office. The federal courts, and especially the country's high court, the Supreme Federal Tribunal (STF), are responsible for imposing legal sanctions on federal politicians implicated in corrupt practices.

Both court systems are undergirded by a robust legal framework, including elements of the criminal code and the 1988 Constitution itself.[3] Both institutions are also fixtures in the Brazilian political system: the electoral courts date back to the 1930s, while the STF has been in continuous operation in some shape or form since 1890. In theory, the two court systems help establish the rules governing the political game, oversee the implementation of rules governing political authorities, and punish those who step over these lines. Each institution is addressed in turn below.

Electoral Courts

The electoral courts are largely administrative in nature, with a vital role in maintaining voter and candidate lists, controlling the content of campaign ads, and overseeing campaign spending. They are divided along a federal structure: the Superior Electoral Tribunal (TSE) is the high court and addresses national electoral issues, Regional Electoral Tribunals (TREs) in the state capitals address state issues, and electoral juntas made up of citizens and headed by electoral judges oversee elections at the local level. All electoral laws are valid nationwide,[4] a fact that eliminates local uncertainties and may improve the leverage of electoral judges relative to local politicians.

The electoral court system has a historically distinguished past. The system arose out of the reformist Movimento de 30, whose platform of "representation and justice" included the probity of elections as one of its key planks. The chief aim was to eliminate a key obstacle to broad political representation: it was believed that removing electoral oversight from the hands of the oligarchies that dominated politics would curb their domination of the electoral process (Sadek 1995, 30). The resulting framework, founded on the principle of a neutral and autonomous judicial body with responsibilities only in the electoral process, remains in place today. Although the courts were extremely timid during the military regime, the regime's desire to preserve at least a mask of legality as a way of legitimizing its rule (Skidmore 1988, 51–101) led it to preserve both elections and the electoral courts. Interestingly, although the regime did manipulate elections in its favor, these distortions were largely carried out, not in the electoral process overseen by the electoral courts, but rather through the manipulation of electoral legislation written by the regime itself. This helped to preserve the electoral courts' basic legitimacy and thus enabled them to quickly become an important pillar in ratifying the results of the political process during the uncertain transition to democracy (Sadek 1995, 22; 41; Fleischer and Barreto 2009, 118).

Over the past generation, the electoral court system has effectively addressed the logistical challenge of overseeing elections across the world's fifth-largest country (by area and population) and fourth-largest democracy and has kept up with a steadily expanding electorate that totals more than 130 million. The electoral courts oversaw the registration of twenty-nine political parties and 380,000 candidates in the 2006 national elections. They also carefully monitored the content and scope of campaign commercials aired by candidates and parties. The voting process is highly transparent and procedurally credible, and, after the nationwide introduction of electronic voting machines in 1996, few doubts persist about the manipulation of voting results. Furthermore, blatant contraventions of electoral law have proven consequences: since the 2002 elections, for example, fourteen governors have been judged by the TSE, and, as of this writing, four have been shorn of their offices for illegally using the state bureaucracy to further their election bids.[5]

The electoral courts, in short, are quite effective at overseeing formal aspects of campaigning and voting procedures. Their basic institutional design, with good protections from interference by the elected branches as well as strong potential legal and constitutional powers, enables them to play a significant role in the political process. Most importantly, the electoral courts play an essential and widely accepted role as a neutral arbiter of many basic electoral questions, ranging from how to distribute public campaign funding to how many members municipal councils should have.

Where the electoral courts fall down on the job is precisely in the proactive pursuit of less transparent subterfuges of the electoral process. Although the electoral courts are procedurally quite efficient, and have recently been more proactive about punishing blatant abuses, they are much less effective when it comes to preventing and discovering surreptitious manipulation of the electoral process. The use of so-called *caixa dois*, or off-the-books funds, is widespread. Officially registered campaign expenses may represent no more than half of all spending by candidates and parties, in a country where elections are already comparatively expensive.[6] Other illicit behaviors, such as vote buying, are also believed to occur commonly (a 2002 survey, for example, estimated that one in seven voters had received an offer to sell their vote; Speck 2003).[7] But little is done to monitor such wrongdoing in a comprehensive fashion, and even less to effectively punish it. Indeed, one of the few studies to analyze the actual content of the electoral courts' work found that 70% of a sample of cases before the courts judged the permissible content of free TV and radio spots and that only 0.3% of all cases led to a conviction for electoral crimes (R. Santos 2003).

What contributes to this rather lackluster result? Four weaknesses stand out: the electoral courts' structure, their administration, their place in the political system, and their relation with the regular judiciary.

The first problem is the structure of the electoral courts: they are simply too small to effectively deal with the scope of the job they have been handed. It is already a huge task to oversee the large-scale electoral process, let alone to effectively monitor the thousands of candidates and contributors involved in any election. This is especially the case because of the electoral courts' lean permanent staff and small budgets, but also because the electoral judges who make most decisions about both administrative and legal issues on the electoral courts are not permanent and instead are temporarily allocated from the regular judiciary for periods of two years (with the possibility of renewal for a further two-year term). This impermanence may be helpful in eliminating conflicts of interest, but it undermines the courts' ability to single-mindedly pursue political malfeasance across electoral cycles.

Second, partly as a result of judges' temporary roles, the decisions of the electoral courts have not always been consistent across time, nor has their administration been especially efficient. In administrative terms, spending has frequently been targeted at perks and infrastructure, such as the construction of office space or the upkeep of fleets of official cars, rather than at increasing the staff of auditors or otherwise improving bureaucratic performance. There are only five staff members in the TSE, for example, to audit party expenditures nationwide (Taylor 2006). The turnover in judges has led to a debilitating lack of specialization in electoral matters (Sadek 1995) and, partly as a result, to significant to-and-fro on the rules of the game. Over the past decade, the seven ministers of the TSE have adopted a number of distinct—and even contradictory—positions on important issues such as party loyalty *(fidelidade partidária)*, the uniformity of party coalitions at the state and federal level *(verticalização)*, and thresholds for party representation *(claúsulas de barreira)* (Marchetti 2008). Many of the rule changes can be directly attributed to turnover in the top judges, although they also reflect the poor quality of the legislation the TSE is asked to interpret. And many are stimulated by politicians themselves, through requests for clarification *(consultas)* that can call into question existing jurisprudence and legislation and trigger substantial rule changes.[8]

Third, within the political system as a whole, the gargantuan costs of campaigns encourage a fierce search for both licit and illicit sources of funding, but the electoral courts have proven unable to reliably audit even the officially registered campaign expenditures in real time (or any other time). The auditing process thus relies heavily on whistle-blowers and ad hoc discoveries, with few pretensions to comprehensive monitoring. Although it has been tightened somewhat in the wake of the *mensalão* scandal, electoral legislation remains weak and often seems designed to complicate oversight. In sum, the parties have essentially agreed to turn a blind eye to each other's finance statements (Bohn, Fleischer, and Whitacker 2002, 351). As a recent justice minister noted, the resulting campaign accounts are an "electoral fiction" in which the electoral courts "pretend" they have audited the campaign books, while parties and candidates "pretend" they have been audited (*OESP* 2005b).

The blind eye to politicians' lapses continues in other realms. Although members of Congress are prohibited from holding media licenses by both congressional codes of ethics and the 1988 Constitution, it is estimated that fully half are major shareholders in radio or TV stations in their home states. This has obvious repercussions in terms of the public exposure of political crimes and corruption allegations in those states. Further, it is not clear that removing wrongdoers from office has much effect in raising the level of conduct: under current electoral law, senators are allowed—ahead of their election—to select their substitutes *(suplentes)* should they step down from office for any reason, including if they are forced out of office on ethical grounds. These *suplentes* are often no more law-abiding than the politicians they replace: of fifteen senatorial *suplentes* serving in January 2008, a third were on trial. And of course, as advocates of political-electoral reform frequently point out, the use of open-list proportional representation in large districts to select members of the Chamber of Deputies weakens direct ties between voters and their representatives. Taken together, these broader contours of the political system weaken the ability of voters to make informed judgments about politicians' campaign funding and honesty before they vote and also undermine any effort by the TSE to punish politicians after misbehavior is detected. The STF has never overruled the TSE on an important decision (Marchetti 2008), and in fact, the overlap in the members of the two courts makes any such ruling unlikely. But again, the point is simply that, regardless of the final decision, the numerous avenues for appeal offer considerable room for uncertainty and delay, and thus for keeping corrupt politicians in the game.

Finally, the electoral courts seldom have the last word on any matter. Until recently, federal law prohibited electoral courts from rejecting candidates on the basis of alleged wrongdoing until the suspects had exhausted all potential appeals and received a definitive conviction. This has now changed: a new law called the Lei Ficha Limpa (or clean rap sheet law) was proposed via popular initiative and signed into law in June 2010, barring candidates who had been convicted of any crime in an appeals court. Beyond blocking candidates, however, there is still the issue of removing dirty incumbents. Although in theory the electoral courts can force congressmen out of office and suspend politicians' right to run for office for up to eight years, the glacial pace of the regular courts keeps crooked politicians in the game for years. Even when electoral malfeasance is severe, the possibility of appeal means that cases are often not decided until the accused politician's term is over (a problem the Lei Ficha Limpa will help correct but does not completely eliminate). Further, although the TSE's decisions supposedly cannot be appealed except in rare cases, three broad exceptions exist: they can be contested on constitutional grounds, through habeas corpus requests, or via a writ of mandamus *(mandado de segurança)*. The prevalence of all three avenues of appeal means that the TSE is almost never the final arbiter. This applies as much to allegations against individuals as it does to electoral rules: in all three of the major rules changed by the TSE in recent years (party loyalty, uniformity of party coalitions, and thresholds for party representation), the TSE's decision was challenged on constitutional grounds in the STF. While the STF has delegated increasing powers to the TSE, and has yet to overturn a major TSE decision, this possibility of appeal to a higher authority does weaken the ability of electoral courts to function autonomously and lengthens time to final disposition.

In sum, although the electoral courts provide an important service by guaranteeing the fairness of the voting process, strictly defined, they seldom are able to do much on their own to combat the corruption of political campaigns, much less to remove corrupt politicians from office. Part of the problem lies in their weak internal structure and administration. But equally important is their practical dependence on the follow-through of the judiciary itself, to which I now turn.

The Federal Judiciary

The federal courts' difficulty in holding corrupt politicians accountable is a direct result of the judiciary's broader institutional deficiencies. The system is delay ridden, formalistic, and subject to constant appeal. And yet, and this point needs to be emphasized, the problem is not usually—as in some countries—the willful breaching of the law by judges or prosecutors. Instead, it is precisely the strong adherence to law and procedure as they appear on the books that weakens accountability, by binding the hands of judges.

The rickety legal framework is a first hurdle: the criminal code is nearly seventy years old, dating back to 1940, and it is estimated that there are more than 180,000 federal legal norms on the books, of which 50,000 are currently in force.[9] But a second hurdle relates to the possibility of recurring interlocutory, as well as regular and constitutional, appeals. Cases that begin in the lower trial courts may be decided within a year or two of an indictment. But since every suit can be appealed in up to three other courts on a variety of procedural and substantive grounds, once appealed, cases take an average of eight to ten years to reach a final conclusion in the high courts. Sadly, a great majority of appeals court decisions follow the decision given by the trial court originally (Taylor 2008, 42–43).

The strong rights protection provided to defendants further complicates prosecution. In part because of the country's experience with authoritarian rule, defendants' de jure (but not always de facto) rights are quite well protected under Brazilian law, and a legal discourse of resistance to anything that might undermine those rights is widespread. One right in particular is especially relevant: secrecy. Article 5 of the constitution protects data, telecommunications, and bank secrecy, which cannot be lifted without judicial authorization. This can immensely complicate the tracking of potentially illicit financial flows, especially when the prosecution wishes to avoid alerting targets of an investigation.[10]

For defendants able to afford a good lawyer, rights guarantees are also an effective instrument for delaying punishment, even when guilt is evident. Contrary to the practice prevalent in much of the rest of the world, during the appeals process in criminal prosecutions, a guilty defendant in Brazil with a good lawyer usually can find a way to remain free until a final conviction is handed down.[11] Habeas corpus petitions—including to the high court—are commonly used to keep defendants at liberty, even from preventive imprisonment (used when defendants are judged to pose a flight risk).[12] Furthermore, habeas is often invoked not solely against unjust imprisonment but also in contesting fairly banal procedures such as the lifting of bank secrecy. The exaggerated use and generous interpretation of habeas provisions has led to what one prominent federal judge terms a "cheapening" *(vulgarização)* of the habeas procedure, distorting what was intended to be an extraordinary protection and turning it into a routine defense tactic (Moro 2008).

Procedural delays also facilitate the defense. Defendants, for example, are able to call up to eight witnesses in their defense, a time-consuming process that is further drawn out if the witnesses are abroad and must therefore be heard via letter rogatory. There are few limits to the introduction of delay-inducing evidence, and it is quite commonplace for defendants to request technical or specialized investigations *(perícias)* of evidence such as accounting ledgers, computer records, or phone logs. Most pernicious is the fact that an almost infinite number of appeals on top of appeals are possible: one prominent judge accused of selling court decisions, for example, filed four different legal instruments just to contest the high court's rejection of one of his appeals.[13] Even when they fail on the substance, maneuvers of this sort can draw out trials significantly.

If a conviction is obtained, the period of prescription (the civil code version of what is termed the "statute of limitations" in common-law systems) is another hurdle to effective punishment, since the clock begins to tick from the moment an investigation begins. In other words, from the moment the defendant begins to be investigated, through the prosecutors' opening of a case and the defendant's indictment and subsequent conviction (if guilty), the entire period is counted against the period of prescription.[14] The period of prescription varies according to the length of the prison term, but given that penalties for corrupt activities are usually between one and eight years, the period of prescription in these crimes is often between four and twelve years.[15] Given the typical delays in the judiciary, these are not impossible goals for a defendant and her lawyers to strive for. For defendants above age seventy, furthermore, the period of prescription is cut in half.

In the exceedingly rare cases in which a conviction is in fact obtained and jail time served, parole can begin as soon as one-sixth of the sentence has been served.[16] Although judges theoretically can delay the onset of parole until two-thirds of the sentence has been served, the STF has signaled that, if challenged, such delays will most likely be held unconstitutional. Few judges therefore attempt to delay parole. Except for truly exceptional cases, in practice this means that in corruption cases the longest actual jail term that will ever be served without parole is five years (Brazilian law limits prison sentences to thirty years). Furthermore, even during such prison terms, prisoners with college degrees are guaranteed special jail privileges, such as a separate jail cell;[17] prisoners of means can often obtain substantial perquisites such as visits, weekend furloughs, and so forth. The result is that it is commonplace for the prosecution to win the case without punishment being imposed, or, to use an expression common in the Brazilian legal community, "The prosecution wins but doesn't carry the day" (*A acusação ganha mais não leva;* Moro 2008).

In the case of political corruption, punishment is further hampered by factors specifically related to the treatment of public officials in the legal process. Chief among these is the existence of special standing for some seven hundred officials at the federal level and the related difficulty the STF has in trying crimes by these officials.[18] The so-called special forum (*foro especial*) was created by the military regime and guaranteed in the 1988 Constitution as a way of insulating politicians from frivolous lawsuits. This is a wise protection from a very real threat, but over time it has translated into a practical grant of immunity from prosecution.[19]

Logically, should not the *foro especial,* with its guarantee of direct hearings in a single court (the STF), without possibility of appeal, speed up the judicial process and make politicians more susceptible to punishment? In a word, no. In the first twenty-one years after the Constitution was approved, not a single elected politician at the federal level was convicted in the STF; the very first congressman to be punished by the STF in the post-transition period was convicted for misuse of public funds in May 2010. Of 130 criminal cases filed in the STF between 1988 and 2007 under the guise of the *foro especial,* only six were actually heard, and none resulted in a conviction. Likewise, of 483 cases heard in the *foro especial* of the Superior Tribunal de Justiça (Superior Justice Tribunal, STJ), sixteen were actually heard and only five resulted in conviction (AMB 2007).

One reason for the ineffectiveness of the *foro especial* is the STF's wise trepidation, as an unelected power, about traipsing about in political minefields. But the STF has also been quite ineffective in the case of relatively insignificant politicians caught up in scandal, failing to either convict or absolve them. Why is this the case?

The simplest explanation is that the STF is poorly equipped to hear criminal trials: it is by practice an appellate court and by vocation a constitutional court and as a result is not well organized to hear criminal cases. The court faces on average more than one hundred thousand cases per year, and although only about a tenth of these are heard by the full court *en banc,* this is nonetheless a formidable workload in its own right (Taylor 2008, 40). Perhaps more important, under Brazilian legal procedure there are few available justifications for privileging any particular case over another, except in cases of a clear and present danger from delay *(periculum in mora).* Such a danger is rarely if ever evident in criminal cases, especially because many defendants remain at liberty until final conviction and thus there is no threat of undue punishment.

Because the STF is both cautious about hearing political cases and badly designed to do so, it is easily overwhelmed. In the *mensalão* case, for example, the court has been weighed down by the prospect of hearing forty defendants and a likely total of more than three hundred witnesses.[20] Given the political tensions surrounding the case, furthermore, the court would also prefer to lend legitimacy to its deliberations by holding sessions only when the majority of the court's eleven ministers can attend. The trial process itself will be lengthy even in the unlikely event that no deliberate delay tactics are used: following the court's decision to accept the case against the defendants, (1) the STF receives a list of witnesses and requests all necessary investigations, examinations, and inquests *(perícias);* (2) the defendants and witnesses are each heard individually; (3) lawyers present their evidence and arguments; (4) the judge rapporteur *(ministro relator)* prepares his report and sends the full document to the overseeing judge *(ministro revisor),* and only then (5) the case is included in the STF agenda and (6) judged. The result is that even in the most optimistic scenario the *mensalão* trial is likely to last five years or longer,[21] raising the very real threat that the period of prescription will be breached if any of the accused are found guilty. This futile race of legal procedure against time is not unique to the *mensalão,* although the scale and prominence of that trial are unprecedented.

One final form of accountability that could be forthcoming from courts—and would hit corrupt officials where it hurts most—is seizure of illicit gains and the prevention of money laundering. The record in this regard has not been good: although any count is likely to be at best an approximation, the government estimated that money laundering by Brazilians had totaled US$78 billion between 1996 and 2003 (*OESP* 2005a), and there are more than eighteen thousand cases in federal courts alone to recover stolen assets (*OESP* 2007a). The difficulties in this regard are similar to those already listed: weak legislation and a slow judicial process, for example, but also the complexity of cross-institutional cooperation, often across borders.[22] Creation of specialized federal trial courts that focus on money laundering in 2003 was tacit recognition by the National Judicial Council (CNJ) that the money-laundering law had hitherto been ineffective. But the various legal hurdles listed here greatly complicate investigation, prosecution, and recovery, and as a result, the more complex the transactions involved, the less likely the case will be successfully resolved (Moro 2008).

A final point regards the raw material that reaches the courts themselves. For this I turn to the interaction between the courts and the other accountability institutions they rely upon.

Courts within the Broader Web of Accountability Institutions

A clear lesson of this book is the interactive and cross-institutional nature of the accountability process. This plays out in at least three ways when it comes to the federal judiciary and the electoral court system.

The first relates to inputs in both court systems. In the electoral courts, most allegations refer to simple violations of formal procedure, rather than being the outcome of more complex investigations. Thus most cases are straightforward, relating to how campaign papers were filed, the content of TV ads, or the technicalities of the vote count, rather than more nebulous issues such as the origins of campaign donations or the possible existence of quid pro quo agreements between donors and politicians. Because of rules about litigants' standing, furthermore, the cases that are brought largely pit politicians against politicians. In light of the tacit agreement between politicians to turn a blind eye to most bending of financing rules, violations are thus seldom challenged.

The range of cases heard by the federal courts is much broader, but because corruption cases carry criminal penalties, and criminal cases can be prosecuted only by the Ministério Público, the efficacy of corruption cases is constrained by the Ministério Público's limited resources. Courts' weak performance does nothing to encourage whistle-blowers and others who may be daunted by the unlikely prospect that any good will be accomplished through their efforts. But the Ministério Público's effectiveness is

also restricted by its relatively burdened staff of roughly nine hundred prosecutors at the federal level.[23] Further, a generation after its creation, there is
still considerable question about the extent of the Ministério Público's
powers. A long-running public debate, for example, questions whether the
Ministério Público can actually investigate crimes or whether that power
is restricted to police alone; this debate has been carried all the way to the
top court but remains unresolved.

Second, the quality of the material that arrives at the courts' doorstep
is not always the most propitious to effective prosecution. This is in part a
consequence of the subject matter: as in many countries, charges of corruption are often bandied about irresponsibly in political battles, with or
without good foundation. And, of course, corruption is of necessity hidden from prying eyes, complicating effective prosecution. Perhaps more
important, however, is the performance of the institutions that feed cases
and issues into the electoral courts and the federal judiciary. Particularly
in highly charged political scandals, there is a propensity for numerous
accountability institutions to jump into the game and show their colors
by providing salacious details of their investigations to the media. This
often has a deleterious effect on the quality of the evidence provided to the
courts, and the emphasis on investigation leads to a lot of stepping on toes
without enormous gains in terms of new information or prosecutable evidence. Congressional investigations, in particular, are often of little or no
added legal value and in many cases even undermine evidentiary collection by the Federal Police and prosecution by the Ministério Público (Taylor and Buranelli 2007).

Third, reiterating an earlier point, the rules under which the judiciary
and the electoral courts operate are not always set out with an eye to consistency, efficiency, or even efficacy. In the politically charged realm of electoral law, the rules are often set by politicians in ways that are difficult to
enforce, that purposely generate uncertainty, and that thus provide loopholes for generous interpretation. In the federal courts, the rules governing appeal and the protection of civil liberties are clearly valuable from
the perspective of rights enforcement but are not at all efficiency enhancing. The criminal code itself—written and amended constantly for seven
decades—is so complex as to guarantee some ambiguity in almost all cases.
As a result, courts and judges are forced to work under rules that they themselves find highly unproductive and that often bind their hands.

Finally, courts themselves—and especially the high courts—are often the source of the rules in the accountability system. They have not always performed this role in the most clear or efficient manner. As noted earlier, over the past decade, decisions by the TSE and the STF have significantly shifted rules on party alliances, party loyalty, and party representation. But the STF has also been very active in the accountability processes of other institutions. In the congressional investigations of the *mensalão* and related scandals, for example, the high court was called on nearly fifty times to rule on controversial procedural issues such as whether the investigation could proceed in Congress, what witnesses could testify, which would be given immunity, whose bank secrecy should be lifted, and so forth. And in more administrative matters the STF is often called upon to rule on the constitutionality of bureaucratic rules, such as the Federal Revenue Service's recent internal regulation requiring banks to report financial transactions of a certain size. The STF does not often seek out these cases, but in the course of deciding them it has an important rule-making effect on how the accountability game plays out in the rest of the political system.

Accountability and Reform

In light of the arguments above, it should be no surprise that effective legal punishments for political corruption are largely nonexistent. Even when guilt is clearly evident, impunity seems more likely than not when national politicians are involved, given the tacit privileges they receive under Brazilian law.

What are the implications for accountability more broadly? My broader argument here has been that the direct effect of the courts in punishing corruption is matched by an equally important indirect effect that courts have in buttressing other accountability processes elsewhere in the political system. In other words, a court that effectively punishes wrongdoing is likely to improve the ability of institutions such as Congress to fight corruption, just as it will increase the effectiveness of police, prosecutors, and other state bureaucracies. A congresswoman is far more likely to stick her neck out to punish other politicians if she knows that she will be backed by the courts: that if she votes to expel a peer, electoral courts will then permanently remove that peer from the political game, and that federal courts will follow up with an effective criminal sanction of their own. The implicit privileges that courts provide to political elites thus have clear repercussions in terms of the universality of justice; under current rules, the powerful are largely immune from judicial accountability.

How can the electoral and federal courts be strengthened? Proposals currently under discussion would force defendants to begin their jail time immediately after conviction by both trial and first appellate courts, rather than only after their appeals have been heard in the STJ and STF. Another frequent suggestion is the creation of an ancillary court to the STF, in which lower court judges would oversee the complex trial processes in *foro especial* cases, freeing STF judges to concentrate on other matters and vote on the defendants' guilt only once the ancillary court's proceedings were complete. On the electoral front, a committee of experts convened by the TSE in 2005 advocated the public release of campaign finance statements on the Internet as a way of improving public oversight. The idea of creating a more permanent profession of electoral judge and electoral specialist has also been a constant. Still another proposal would require all official campaign contributions to be deposited at the TSE before being withdrawn and accounted for by candidates, as a way of increasing oversight of the true volume of campaign finances. But so far, these proposals all remain unexamined by Congress itself.

More concretely, a number of proposals have already been approved or are currently being deliberated in Congress. The Lula government in 2007, for example, proposed efficiency-enhancing reforms to the criminal code, including a reduction in the number of possible appeals and the expansion of preventive imprisonment as a means of thwarting witness and evidence tampering.[24] The Senate has approved changes in the way the period of prescription is calculated.[25] The constitutional committee of the lower house in March 2008 approved a proposal (PEC 130/07) that would eliminate politicians' right to the *foro especial* in common crimes (but would maintain it if the crime were of a political nature).[26] Most importantly, after years of debate, a major judicial reform was approved in 2004 that appears to be reducing high court dockets, has marginally increased judicial efficiency, and establishes a Judicial Council that will likely increase the overall rationality (and perhaps even probity) of the federal judiciary. However, this reform process seems to have exhausted the will of reformers, and further large-scale reforms of the courts and legal system—including an oft-discussed massive overhaul of the criminal code—therefore seem unlikely in the short term, suggesting that progress will have to come through small, marginal gains at the fringes.

But all of these changes suggest that there is growing recognition, even among political and judicial elites, of the need for change. Public pressure is a clear driving force in overcoming the many powerful interests that have stymied change for so long, and perhaps as a result of the growing importance of voters in Brazil's political system, the past quarter century has brought the greatest change in judicial institutions of any period in living memory. But time is short, and as this chapter has argued, the continuing weakness of the courts in holding politicians accountable has devastating consequences in terms of ensuring accountability elsewhere in the political system.

Notes

I thank Maria Tereza Sadek, Vitor Marchetti, Tony Pereira, Marco Antonio Lorencini, Judge Sergio Moro, and participants in the workshop on "Accountability Institutions and Political Corruption in Brazil," held at St. Antony's College, University of Oxford, for insightful comments. All errors and opinions are mine alone.

1. McMillan and Zoido (2004) conclude suggestively, "This chain of complementarities means that checks and balances form a package. If one is weak, all are weak" (86). For similar arguments, see Taylor and Buranelli (2007, 63), Bailey and Dammert (2006, 255), and Speck (2002, 481).

2. Throughout this chapter, "federal courts" refers to the STF, the Superior Justice Tribunal (STJ), the regional appellate courts (TRFs), and the lower federal courts. Brazil's STF and STJ are, by the wording of the 1988 Constitution, not strictly part of the "federal" court system, which formally encompasses only the TRFs and federal judges, according to Article 106 of the Constitution. But since the STF and STJ have national jurisdiction (Art. 92, §2), meaning that they often hear appeals rising from the federal courts, it is appropriate to bundle them under this term here.

3. In terms of political corruption, some of the most relevant portions of the legal framework are (1) the criminal code of 1940, in which Articles 317 and 333 set out the rules for active and passive corruption; ancillary articles relevant to the prosecution of corruption are Articles 312–59 (for a detailed explanation, see Junqueira et al. 2002); (2) the 1988 Constitution: Articles 14, 15, 37, 53, 55, and 85, which establish sanctions for illicit and improper actions by civil servants

and politicians; (3) Law 8.429 of 1992, in which Articles 9 and 12 discuss sanctions for illicit actions by public servants and politicians; (4) Law 9.983 of 2000, which greatly expanded the responsibilities of civil servants. Most of the formal legislation governing elections is found in five pieces of legislation: the Constitution, the Electoral Code (Law 4.737 of 1965); the Law of Ineligibilities (Complementary Law 64 of 1990); the Election Law (Law 9.504 of 1997); and the Law of Political Parties (Law 9.096 of 1995).

4. This contrasts with most federal systems, which allow states the ability to pick their own rules (Bohn, Fleischer, and Whitacker 2002, 399).

5. I am grateful to Vitor Marchetti for sharing this information about the TSE, which is part of his broader research on the electoral courts. The four governors who have been removed from office by TSE decisions are Flamarion Portela (Roraima, *cassado* in 2004); Cassio Cunha Lima (Paraiba, 2009); Jackson Lago (Maranhão, 2009); and Marcelo Miranda (Tocantins, 2009). Three other governors elected in 2006 are still awaiting a decision by the TSE: Ivo Cassol (Rondonia), José Anchieta (Roraima), and Marcelo Déda (Sergipe). Two other governors elected in 2006 were tried but found not guilty. Overall, 623 politicians were *cassados* between 2000 and 2007, and there was a continuous increase in the number of politicians removed from office over this period (C. Melo 2008, 377–78, citing data from Movimento de Combate à Corrupcão Eleitoral). It should be noted, though, that 95% were mayors and municipal assembly members rather than state or federal officials.

6. Senatorial campaigns reported official spending of R$91 million in the federal elections of 2006; official spending by all candidates for deputy was R$422 million (Instituto Ethos/Transparency International 2008). Counting all 16,000 candidates nationwide, per candidate spending was thus R$26,600 per candidate for deputy and R$151,000 per candidate for senator. When one looks only at leading candidates, however, spending figures are even higher, on the order of ten to fifteen times greater than the averages above. Note that individual spending is in addition to free radio and TV airtime provided to all candidates (the so-called *horário eleitoral*), a perk that Speck (2005) estimated would be worth R$2.4 billion at the going commercial rates for advertising. Political parties also receive public financing on the basis of past electoral performance, to the tune of R$194 million in 2008 (Instituto Ethos and Transparency International 2008, 16). Adding up the market value of free airtime, the tax breaks given to media companies in exchange for their broadcasts of campaign ads, and the political parties' public financing, Campos (2009) estimates the public contribution to the electoral system at R$6.2 billion.

7. In 1999, a rare popular initiative led by the national bar association (OAB) and the National Council of Brazilian Bishops obtained the one million signatures needed to approve a law increasing the penalties for vote buying (Law 9.840 of 1999).

8. Fleischer and Barreto (2009) express great concern regarding the increasing "judicialization" of politics by the electoral courts since 2002, and espe-

cially the possibility that the TSE's reinterpretation of various laws may weaken its reputation for neutrality and generate political instability.

9. It is estimated that between October 1988 and October 2007 alone, 3.6 million legal norms were written into law at all levels of the federation (*Época* 2008).

10. Recent laws have altered this scenario somewhat: Complementary Law 105, for example, allows for the lifting of bank secrecy as a means of fighting tax evasion. A number of tax laws have also forced banks to provide information about large transactions to the Revenue Service. But the underlying problem remains quite significant.

11. There is a general—but not unanimous—jurisprudential consensus that the 1988 Constitution (Art. 5, LVII) allows anyone whose final appeal has not been heard to request habeas corpus and thus avoid serving a prison sentence until they have received a final conviction, with no possibility of further appeal. For example, Senator Luiz Estevão—who was involved in the massive (roughly US$90 million) fraud surrounding the building of a courthouse in São Paulo—was convicted to three and a half years of prison for use of false accounting documents by the TRF, but was freed on an injunction by the STJ. In April 2006, he was convicted on another count to thirty-one years, but the STJ decision guaranteed he would remain free until a final conviction has been obtained.

12. For example, in the case of Salvatore Cacciola, a prominent banker arrested in 2000 on charges of fraud and embezzlement arising out of his bank's failure, habeas was granted and Cacciatore promptly fled the country. He was extradited from Monaco eight years later, in July 2008.

13. On November 27, 2007, Judge João Carlos da Rocha Mattos filed the following instrument in his defense: "Embargos Declaratórios em Agravo Regimental em Agravo de Instrumento contra Despacho Denegatório de Recurso Especial" (AI-AgR-ED 643632/SP-SÃO PAULO), www.jusbrasil.com.br/jurisprudencia/14724534/embdeclno-agregno-agravo-de-instrumento-ai-643632-sp-stf.

14. Complex rules, however, govern when the period of prescription is counted and when it is not; it need not be continuous. For politicians, the period of prescription is "paused" while they are serving in public office, in accordance with Article 53 of the 1988 Constitution.

15. Prison terms for the most typical forms of corruption are as follows: *corrupção ativa* (roughly, intent to bribe others), two to twelve years; *formação de quadrilha* (roughly, racketeering), one to three years; and *evasão de divisas* (off-shore tax evasion), two to six years.

16. The official term in Portuguese is *progressão de pena para regime semi-aberto*. This is not precisely "parole" in the English meaning of the word, since the criminal still serves jail time alongside periods of furlough.

17. A bill to restrict the privilege of a special jail cell *(prisão especial)* was approved by the Senate in April 2009 (PLC 111 of 2008) but has not received final

congressional approval. But it is worth noting that even if it is approved, although college graduates will no longer have access to a special jail cell, it will be up to the judge overseeing the case or the *delegado* running the prison to decide whether a prisoner is "at risk" and thus requires a special cell. As a result, it is very likely that influential people will be able to count on the privilege in future, and there are already exceptions built into the bill for political figures ranging from mayors through the president.

18. Article 102 of the 1988 Constitution gives the STF original jurisdiction in cases involving the president, the vice president, members of Congress, ministers, the prosecutor general, judges of the high courts and the Tribunal de Contas da União (TCU), chiefs of diplomatic missions, and the chiefs of the army, navy, and air force. This privilege is commonly referred to as the *foro especial* or *foro por privilégio da função*, although at no moment does that phrase appear in the Constitution. Similar forms of special standing exist for state deputies and state judges in appeals courts (Tribunais de Justiça) and for governors in the STJ.

19. Perhaps the most egregious abuse of the *foro especial* was the case of former Paraíba governor Ronaldo Cunha Lima. In 1993, while serving as governor, Cunha Lima walked into a restaurant crowded with witnesses and shot his predecessor three times (the victim survived the shooting, dying a natural death in 2003). Cunha Lima claimed he was defending his family honor, and he was subsequently elected senator and then deputy (twice), guaranteeing that the case against him would be heard by the STF. Fourteen years after the shooting and five years after the case against him began to be heard in the STF, Cunha Lima resigned as congressman in late 2007, just days before the STF was expected to hand down a decision. He claimed that he was stepping down so that the people of Paraíba could judge him. Cunha Lima's lawyers apparently calculated that if he resigned, his case would begin at square one in the state courts and he would not risk the loss of his political rights. Given that Cunha Lima is seventy-one, the period of prescription is likely to expire before he is convicted (or absolved). The Cunha Lima case highlights some important ambiguity in the use of the *foro especial:* Should it apply only to crimes that allegedly occurred while the politician was in office? Should politicians who resign from office continue to be tried in the STF, or should their cases begin from square one in the regular courts? etc. But for now, these questions tend to be settled by offering the most generous interpretation to defendants.

20. In a victory for the defendants, the STF in 2007 invoked the *princípio da conexão* between defendants so as to hear all forty defendants simultaneously, including twenty-seven of them who in principle, as nonpoliticians, would not normally have the right to have their cases heard in the STF.

21. An estimate offered by former STF president Carlos Velloso (*OESP* 2007b).

22. Some examples of weak legislation are the money-laundering law (Law 9.613 of 1998), which is criticized for not being comprehensive, and the law against organized crime (Law 9.095 of 1995), which does not define these criminal

organizations well enough to permit effective prosecution. The judicial process is slow in that, to seize funds, an unappealable final judicial conviction is required, although funds can be frozen in the meantime.

23. By way of comparison, there are ninety-four federal prosecutors in the United States, each overseeing a judicial district with the help of scores of assistant district attorneys. The number of assistants in each district varies, but there are more than 350 in the largest district, Washington, D.C., alone.

24. Among the many elements of the proposed reform are restrictions on habeas corpus petitions; restrictions to judicial review of police investigations *(perícias)*; an increase in the value of bail bonds and a general reduction in the number of chances for defendants to remain free until final conviction; the elimination of a rule requiring new jury hearings for those convicted to more than twenty years of prison time; limits on the length of certain court hearings; and an increase in jail terms for money laundering.

25. The bill was approved in October 2007. The new period of prescription would be counted from the moment the case was filed in court, rather than from when the case began to be investigated.

26. This proposal remains in committee and has not gone to a floor vote as of March 2010.

Chapter Eight

The Federal Police and the Ministério Público

ROGÉRIO B. ARANTES

In the contemporary debate on the "quality of democracy" in Latin America, Norberto Bobbio's diagnosis (in his famous 1984 lecture entitled "The Future of Democracy") remains quite pertinent: the "raw material" of the regime we have succeeded in creating in the past few years is quite distant from the ideal. Among other "unfulfilled promises" of democracy, Bobbio drew attention to the persistence of oligarchies and the issue of "invisible power," power that is not subject to accountability mechanisms. He noted that in Italy "the presence of the *invisible* power (Mafia, *Camorra*, Masonic lodges, secret services that are uncontrollable and cover up the subversive powers they should fight) is highly *visible*" (Bobbio 1986, 29; emphasis and translation mine). Bobbio emphasized that democracy was born with the promise to put an end to these invisible forms of power and create governments whose activities would always be public and subject to public scrutiny. Yet he claimed that Italy remained far from that ideal. This is also an accurate description of Brazil's current situation.

In a country with a patrimonialist history like Brazil's (Faoro [1958] 1996), where economic and state modernization was not preceded or even accompanied by new power relationships based on the liberal principle of contract, the traditional coexists with the modern in what Schwartzman ([1982] 1988) called neopatrimonialism or bureaucratic patrimonialism. In fact, as Nunes (1997) has written, Brazil's incomplete and contradictory modernization has created a set of four "grammars" that structure the relationships between the state and society: clientelism, corporatism, bureaucratic insulation, and universal procedures coexist side by side. In a country with this history, political corruption is endemic in all forms of power and representation. And on the other side of the patrimonialist coin we find a private sector that is strongly dependent on the state and weakly constrained by ethics.

From the standpoint of the political economy of corruption (Silva 1996), Brazil contains many elements favorable to corruption: patrimonialism has given us a strong state, with extensive economic and territorial control. The state commands enormous resources, and its activities directly or indirectly involve a wide array of private-sector agents interested in extracting rents from the state. Although the patrimonialist state is highly centralized and oversees a vast regulatory framework, society has few mechanisms of oversight over the state. In fact, a tradition of centralization and regulation bolsters the power of the state bureaucracy and the political agents who allocate public resources. Opportunities for corruption are numerous in this setting. It is remarkable just how pervasive embezzlement and fraud in Brazilian public bidding and public contracts have been, surviving regime change, institutional innovations, and new accountability technologies. Democracy, the creation of accountability institutions, and mechanisms of electronic government have been unable to eliminate these practices.

But it is worth noting that since the country's redemocratization in the 1980s, the problem of corruption has been at the center of public debate: corruption has drawn the attention of representative institutions, the media, public opinion, civil society actors, and even international bodies. Partly as a result, the country has undertaken legislative changes and signed international agreements and treaties acknowledging the need to fight corruption. Likewise, there is a growing interest in the web of accountability institutions responsible for monitoring, investigating, prosecuting (in both civil and criminal cases), and punishing acts of corruption and administrative malfeasance (Mainwaring and Welna 2003).

This chapter will not comprehensively analyze the fight against corruption by the full set of accountability institutions in Brazil, although I tend to agree with Taylor (2009) that depending on how we look at the situation, the glass of water may appear either half full or half empty. From the half-empty perspective, corruption in Brazil is widely spread among diverse sectors of public administration and political institutions. Although corruption has historical and cultural origins, institutional factors play a central role in its persistence under democracy. Taylor examines particularly

(1) political and electoral factors, especially the problem of financing highly expensive electoral campaigns, the costs of assembling political party coalitions to ensure governability, and the multiplication of these problems at all three levels of federal government; (2) the insufficiency of "social accountability," even by the media, which have proven extremely active in covering corruption-related scandals, but which still have limited influence on public opinion and cannot effectively attribute responsibility; (3) the judiciary's slowness and other difficulties, which contribute to a high level of impunity; and (4) the poor functioning of the web of intrastate accountability institutions, made up of many diverse bodies and agencies that, as a whole, are unable to effectively bite back at corruption given their flawed institutional "orthodontics" (Taylor 2009).

However, if we look at the glass as half full, important advances in the fight against corruption have also been made in the past few years. Influenced by Transparency International's concept of "national integrity systems," Speck (2002) analyzes a wide array of accountability institutions responsible for fighting corruption in Brazil: internal administrative controls, ombuds offices, legislative controls (with emphasis on congressional committees of inquiry, CPIs), Accounting Tribunals (TCs), the judiciary, the Ministério Público (MP), and nonstate actors, such as the media and civil society organizations. All of these institutions are analyzed at the three levels of the federation and across the three branches of power. Though the picture that emerges is promising (the study shows that real progress has been made in fighting issues such as fraud in public tenders, nepotism in the civil service, electoral crimes, and economic crimes), Speck concludes that the proliferation of control institutions is insufficient to ensure an effective "national integrity system." Further, to effectively evaluate the functioning of this system, it is insufficient to examine institutions individually: rather, the cooperation and integration of institutions within the system as a whole must be analyzed.

The work of the Federal Prosecutorial Service (Ministério Público Federal, henceforth MPF; or when referring to the state and federal prosecutorial services in conjunction, MP) and the Federal Police (Polícia Federal) over the past few years offers a very good example of the possibilities of and limits to cooperation and integration among accountability institutions in the fight against corruption and organized crime in Brazil, as the next section illustrates.

The Brazilian "Feds": Ministério Público Federal and Polícia Federal

The MP and the Polícia Federal have taken a leading role in contemporary Brazilian politics. The MP emerged first, gaining new powers—especially with regard to the fight against political corruption—with the 1988 Constitution and especially the Administrative Improbity Law of 1992. More recently, the Polícia Federal has joined the MP's prosecutors in this task. Below we describe these organizations' institutional profile.

The Public Prosecutorial Service (Ministério Público)

The Brazilian MP is a prosecutorial body, like its counterparts in other countries, but it stands out for two reasons: (1) it has a broad array of roles in the defense of society's collective interests; and (2) it has complete institutional independence from the other branches of government. The Brazilian MP has undergone material changes in the past thirty years, and indeed, these represent one of the most significant institutional innovations undertaken since Brazil's redemocratization. The various federal and state MPs today have around ten thousand members and operate in all of Brazil's twenty-seven states, bringing cases before the regular state courts and, at the federal level, also before specialized federal, labor, and military courts.

The Brazilian MP extended the scope of its operations in the civil sphere through three legal-institutional innovations, motivated by a strong ideological component that I label "political voluntarism" (Arantes 2002, 2007). First, the Public Class Action Suit Law (Lei da Ação Civil Pública) of 1985 established the means for legal defense of "diffuse and collective rights." Broadly speaking, these rights may be defined as rights that are indivisible, whether the persons holding title to those rights are indeterminate persons (diffuse rights) or a group of persons linked in some kind of legal relationship (collective rights) (Mancuso 1997). Because of this law, the environment, consumer relations, and historical and cultural heritage are defined in Brazilian jurisprudence as diffuse and collective rights, which can be protected through class-action lawsuits brought by civil society associations and chiefly by the MP. The Constituent Assembly cemented the creation of diffuse and collective rights, writing them into the 1988 Constitution. Since then, the Constitution has provided a generous framework for new laws that replace individual rights with diffuse or collective rights. In the process, the MP has been strengthened in its role as the protector of society and broad diffuse and collective rights. Among many laws created with this intent since 1988, the Administrative Improbity Law (1992) granted the MP greater powers to act against corruption and misuse of public funds. Second, the 1985 law granted the MP important legal advantages over civil society associations, and these have led it to become the principal defender of diffuse and collective rights, to the detriment of civil society associations. Third, with the 1988 Constitution, the MP took the final step toward becoming a "political law enforcer" and a "fourth branch of power": it gained independence from the executive branch and is no longer subordinate to any of the other branches of government.

With the 1988 Constitution, the MP achieved both external and internal independence. Externally, the MP attained functional autonomy, combined with an absolute lack of vertical or horizontal mechanisms of accountability (Kerche 2007).[1] Internally, individual members of the MP are chosen by public examination and are entitled to benefits such as career tenure and guaranteed income, which provides them with a high level of functional independence and policy influence. The autonomy of public prosecutors in Brazil is similar to the autonomy of Brazilian judges. The difference is that judges act only if called upon, while prosecutors are active and have great independence to choose their cases. In sum, the Brazilian MP model is distinct from its counterparts elsewhere around the world because it combines a wide variety of instruments to defend collective rights with high levels of institutional independence and discretion. Since 1988, furthermore, a peculiar definition of "functional independence" has emerged among prosecutors, who perceive themselves subject only to "the law and their own conscience." Madison would add: and to their ambitions.

In addition to these legal-institutional rules, the MP is also marked by what I have termed "political voluntarism." Its main elements are (1) a pessimistic assessment of society's ability to defend itself; (2) a pessimistic view of political representatives and political institutions, which are seen as corrupt and/or unable to fulfill their duties and; (3) an idealized conception of the MP as the preferred representative of a weak society, especially in contrast to inept bureaucracies that fail to enforce the law. This "political voluntarism" is widespread within the MP and has been an important

driver of prosecutors' actions, especially in the fight against political corruption and organized crime (Arantes 2002, 2007).

With this new institutional framework and an ideology of "political
voluntarism," the MP has become the expression of the Madisonian principle that, as far as institutional engineering is concerned, an officeholder's
interest must be aligned with his position's constitutional foundations
and that the ambition to become a kind of fourth branch may be useful to
counterattack the ambition of others. Thus the MP has become a protagonist in numerous attempts to fight corruption at the three levels of government, using both criminal prosecution and civil suits for administrative
improbity against politicians in the executive and legislative branches. This
has led to strong acclaim from the public and especially the media, with
whom the MP has worked closely in several investigations that resulted
in large nationwide scandals. Surveys of public trust in institutions show
the MP in the highest positions, well above electoral institutions and even
the judiciary. Finally, the MP's constitutional status ensures a good budget,
and the salaries of its members are among the highest in government—
presumably a good way to maintain their independence and probity. Data
from 2004 show that state MPs' spending totaled US$1.77 billion; the aver-
age starting monthly salary for prosecutors in 2005 was US$7,279, reaching
US$10,600 by the time they retired (Ministério da Justiça 2006).[2]

However, the MP's great independence and its activism have raised
the old "Who guards the guardian?" dilemma. Ambition, as Madison once
again would have predicted, has counterattacked ambition, and now members of the executive and legislative branches have reacted to the new powers of the MP. Members of the elected branches have sought to impose new
limits on the MP, claiming that prosecutors and attorneys are overstepping
their institutional roles; using the media to inflict reputational costs on the
subjects of their investigations; infringing on and taking over the police's
investigatory powers; and abusing procedures such as civil investigations
to pressure politicians, administrators, and even private citizens to adopt
specific behaviors.[3]

The Federal Police

In comparison with other public bureaucracies, the Federal Police is relatively new. It was first located in the Federal Public Security Department
(Departamento Federal de Segurança Pública, DFSP), created by President

Getúlio Vargas in 1944, at the end of the Estado Novo period.[4] The "federal" in its name did not, however, mean that the DFSP had nationwide jurisdiction but rather referred solely to the DFSP's primary focus: crime in the Federal District. With the country's initial transition to democracy in 1945, the DFSP gained nationwide responsibilities, especially in the fight against drug trafficking and counterfeiting. But the 1946 Constitution adopted a form of federalism with a strong bias toward the states and thus clashed with the idea of a national police body. For this reason, the 1946 Constitution did not include the DFSP as a federal police body, and police activities remained under the control of state governors. When the national capital was moved from Rio de Janeiro to Brasília in 1960, the DFSP practically disappeared, as most of its staff opted to remain in Rio (Rocha 2004). Throughout Brazil's history, the organization of the armed and police forces has always been a delicate matter in the balance between the federal government and the states. The distribution of these forces, and who wields authority over them, has usually pitted the central and subnational governments against each other, and the solutions to that conflict have varied according to regime type (oligarchic, authoritarian, or democratic). In Brazil's federal system, the political elite have always met with reservations the idea of a civilian police force with national jurisdiction and the ability to act in all states. The Federal Police's role over the past few years thus marks a considerable break with tradition.

After the 1964 coup, the military regime granted the Polícia Federal national jurisdiction (through Law 4483). Although this did not imply an increase in personnel or an improved structure, the day the law was passed (November 16, 1964) has been adopted by the Polícia Federal as its founding date (Rocha 2004), reflecting the importance of achieving national jurisdiction. In 1967, in the midst of the regime's reforms to the state security apparatus, the DFSP was renamed the Departamento de Polícia Federal, as it is still known. However, the military regime's investment in political police, public security, and national security was much more targeted toward the unification and strengthening of state military police forces, under the command of the army itself, leaving the Federal Police in a secondary role. During the military regime the "Federal Police operated little and was not a protagonist," except for its work in censoring newspapers and art (Rocha 2004, 91 ff). For political repression, the regime relied more heavily on the Destacamentos de Operações de Informações

(DOIs), which were branches of the National Information Service (SNI), and, in the states, the Departments of Political and Social Order (DOPS) linked to state civil police forces. This secondary role of the Polícia Federal under the authoritarian regime placed it in an ambiguous situation when the country began redemocratizing: it had a less negative image than other state security bodies, but its institutional structure was more precarious.

The 1988 Constitution was written under the shadow of the military, which claimed a whole section for itself. Ironically labeled "Defense of the State and Democratic Institutions," Title V of the Constitution was reserved for the provisions relating to the armed forces, public security, and the definitions of "state of defense" and "state of siege." It was in this section's Article 144 that the Federal Police received a constitutional mention for the first time. Subordinate to the federal executive branch, and specifically to the Justice Ministry, the Federal Police was institutionalized in two ways by the Constitution.[5] First, it is a permanent body that, albeit subordinate to the executive, cannot be dissolved by the government. Second, the Constitution sets clear rules for police careers: how to fill vacancies, overall hierarchy, promotion criteria, and organizational subdivisions.

The Constitution also set forth both general and specific functions for the Polícia Federal. The Polícia Federal is charged with responding to crimes against the "political and social order"—a holdover from authoritarian rule—and also to protect the Union's assets, services, and interests, a role for which there is no equivalent in the state police forces. In other words, the Polícia Federal is considered the federal government's property police. The Constitution also empowers the Polícia Federal to carry out activities to prevent drug trafficking and contraband, attributions that date back to its creation as a department in 1944.

It is worth highlighting that the word *federal* in the name has finally found its etymological roots: the Polícia Federal is now responsible for investigating crimes with interstate (or federal) repercussions. In light of the Polícia Federal's precarious institutional standing before 1988—related to the long-standing difficulty of creating a police corps with national jurisdiction in a federal system with strong states—this constitutional definition is an important development, as it authorized the federal government to create a force capable of acting at the subnational level. Beyond the federal and state levels, the Polícia Federal also has jurisdiction over international law enforcement, performing the role of border police.

The Polícia Federal is responsible for criminal investigations in the cases under its jurisdiction. When the Constitution mentions (Art. 144) the role of "judiciary police," it is not creating another police corps but simply stating that the Polícia Federal shall help the federal courts and the MPF in enforcing warrants and carrying out criminal investigations and legal cases. The fact that it aids judicial institutions, however, does not mean that the Polícia Federal is under their charge. Indeed, in the Brazilian system, neither the judiciary nor the MPF directs the police or their investigations (Santin 2007). The three institutions are independent from each other, and the criminal case progresses *triangularly* among them. For example, only a judge can authorize the tapping of telephones, the breaking of bank and telephone secrecy, or the temporary arrest of people under investigation, upon request from the MP or the police. From the perspective of judicial accountability, it is worth emphasizing that although the Polícia Federal is subordinate to the executive branch (and its activities can thus be curtailed or directed by the Justice Ministry), its main tools for investigating and addressing crimes require the agreement of independent judges and take place under the oversight of the MPF. The Polícia Federal thus has the autonomy to investigate crimes but no authority to adopt extreme measures—such as wiretapping or arresting suspects—on its own.

By all indications, the rising importance of the Polícia Federal cannot be explained, as was the case with the MP, by the emergence of an internal ideology of "political voluntarism." While the Polícia Federal does have an esprit de corps, it is not similar to that of prosecutors, who combine bureaucratic interests with social and political values. In comparison with the MP and the judiciary, furthermore, the Polícia Federal is weakly institutionalized for several reasons, ranging from its subordination to the executive to the fact that police work is the least prestigious government career for young lawyers (after judgeships and prosecutorial appointments). Historically, furthermore, police forces have been more subject than other judicial institutions to corruption and abuse of power. Their public image is thus ambiguous, if not negative. Reports of violence and torture by police officers, involvement with organized crime, and corrupt practices are widespread. The "trust in institutions" surveys carried out by the Brazilian Institute of Public Opinion and Statistics (IBOPE) show police forces at an intermediate level, a little above the very poorly rated political institutions (Senate, Chamber of Deputies, and political parties) but below judicial institutions (judiciary and MP), which are more respected by the public.[6]

The leadership role the Polícia Federal has taken on in the past decade in the fight against corruption and organized crime is as significant as the increasing role played by the MP in previous years. But the causes for its rise are also quite different. The inclusion of the Federal Police in the 1988 Constitution helps explain its new role, as does the police's interest in affirming itself as a bureaucracy, but these elements had already been present since 1988 and only over a decade later did the Federal Police begin to fulfill its promise in the fight against corruption. More important was a new policy adopted by the Justice Ministry at the end of the Cardoso administration (1995–2002) and then strengthened further under the Lula administration (2003–10). One of the key players responsible for a stronger Federal Police was Justice Minister Márcio Thomaz Bastos (2003–7). Soon after he stepped down from the ministry in 2007, Bastos claimed:

> I had a more specific role, which was to rebuild the republican institutions in Brazil. . . . The Federal Police I found [when taking office] was an institution that no longer deserved the respect of Brazilian people. It was ill-equipped, hugely understaffed and underequipped, and they didn't use modern investigative techniques that have now become the norm. . . . Within four years almost four hundred operations were carried out to fight organized crime in all states. And how was this done? Fitting out the police, having systematic meetings . . . , and using modern techniques, such as telephone monitoring, intensive intelligence, strategic planning, temporary arrests. In short, investigation methods that are used all over the world, but here have been used with great care. . . . I think we managed . . . to create a new Federal Police on top of the one that was already there. [When] Paulo Lacerda took office [as director general], [I said] that his job was to build the Brazilian FBI, and I think that is being accomplished. (Gioielli 2007; translation mine)

The Federal Police is run out of a headquarters in Brasília, headed by a director general who is appointed by the justice minister. There are local headquarters in each of Brazilian state and field offices in all of the states. However, despite this nationwide presence, the Federal Police's network of offices is quite limited: in three states (Alagoas, Roraima, and Sergipe) it has only one station in the state capital. Even in some geographically large states (such as Amazonas, Tocantins, Ceará, and Maranhão), the Federal Police has only two stations. On average, if we disregard the headquarters in each state capital, there are only 3.6 stations per state. Some states, such as Rio Grande do Sul and São Paulo, have as many as thirteen to fifteen stations, but otherwise, this is a rather low average when we consider that there are 5,564 towns and cities nationwide.[7]

In addition to administrative personnel, the Federal Police today has 11,022 active staff, divided between detectives, forensics analysts, agents, registrars, and fingerprint experts. At least one-third of these joined the police between 2001 and 2008, and they are relatively young, with new entrants' average age being 31.6 years. Further, Federal Police today have the highest salaries among civilians in the executive branch. Detectives (who must have a law degree) and forensics analysts (who may be engineers, accountants, economists, doctors, systems analysts, dentists, pharmacists, geologists, and even physicists) receive the highest wages among federal civil servants: US$6,500 at the start of their career, rising to a possible maximum of US$9,500. For the purposes of comparison, these salaries are higher than those received by public defense lawyers, union attorneys, and professors at public federal universities (Ministério do Planejamento 2008).

The Federal Police's budget and the size of its staff have grown significantly in recent years. The budget has nearly doubled since Lula took office in 2002, from US$925 million to US$1.5 billion in 2008. And the staff has doubled in size since 2001: thanks to a series of civil service exams for the various posts that make up the Federal Police, 7,841 new posts have been created and 5,260 have been filled. The government has also opened new vacancies for officers to work in specific states, especially in the North and Northeast, where the Federal Police's structure is quite small and where corruption and organized crime are rife. Further, until 2004 the Federal Police did not have its own administrative staff, but since then 1,638 positions have been created in this area. The end result is that there has been a significant renewal in the Polícia Federal, which has also been materially reequipped as never before.

Finally, a civil police force is emerging that is national in nature, something unprecedented in Brazil. Throughout our political history, democratic periods have coincided with a strengthening of state autonomy in the federative setup—concentrating the prerogative of organizing their own justice and police forces, thus inhibiting the appearance of a national police force—and the authoritarian periods have been marked by a central government that had no interest in investing in a civil safety apparatus, only in developing its own military forces. Even after the last redemocratization process in the country, the security agenda was, for quite some time, hostage to the need to disassemble the authoritarian military legacy and conform the police to the principles of the rule of law, as part of the fight for human rights. Only toward the end of the Cardoso administration and the start of the Lula administration did the agenda detach itself from the initial goals of the democratic transition and adopt, more clearly, the idea of expanding and strengthening the police apparatus with a view to fighting organized crime and corruption.

The Struggle against Political Corruption in Brazil: The Institutional Framework

The institutional framework within which the MP and the Polícia Federal fight corruption is quite complex. We have mentioned their triangular relationship with the courts during the investigation, indictment, trial, and sentencing of alleged criminals. In the Brazilian system, judges do not act until called upon by the MP or by lawyers appointed by interested parties. Criminal cases can be brought only by the MP, and they rely in part on investigations carried out by the police, which, in turn, require judicial authorization for many investigatory measures. As this is a federal system and the judiciary has three or four hierarchical levels, such measures can be reviewed and suspended by either state or federal courts, depending on the case.

Since 1988 these institutions—the judiciary, the MP, and lawyers more generally—have grown stronger and more independent. But at a systemic level, cross-institutional integration is weak, and little has been done to reform the overall process in ways that would increase systemic effectiveness. The institutions mentioned are quite activist, and the number of complaints and suits brought is vertiginously high, but so too is the number of court cases that have been dragging on for years without reaching a definitive conclusion. As a result, a sense of impunity pervades society. This paradox has been particularly apparent in cases of political corruption. Brazil has made much progress in the past few years in improving legislation and enhancing the individual performance of accountability institutions, but the end results remain dissatisfying. A more global approach might take into account not just the judicial accountability system but also executive and legislative accountability bodies, such as the Federal Accounting Tribunal (TCU; Speck 2000a; M. Teixeira 2004; Arantes, Abrucio, and Teixeira 2005) or the Federal Comptroller's Office (CGU; Olivieri 2006). In my analysis below, however, I will emphasize recent cases in which judicial and police bodies have held officeholders accountable.

Table 8.1 shows that acts of political corruption by agents of the executive branch can be tackled in at least *three distinct ways*, depending on which of three different juridical definitions of corruption is ascribed to a crime. Corruption is treated differently depending on the location of the proceeding. If it is heard in the legislative branch and thus given "political" treatment, corruption is treated as fraud or embezzlement *(malversação)*. Hearings take place as impeachment proceedings, with the possibility that the accused will lose office and have her political rights suspended. Impeachment proceedings against mayors, governors, and the president are dealt with in the respective legislative bodies at the federal, state, or municipal levels, and as a result they essentially depend on the political balance of power. But impeachment proceedings are judicial in tone (with rules and guarantees for ample defense), and during the proceedings the legislatures resemble regular courts.

There are two ways to address political corruption in the courts themselves: as an ordinary criminal offense or as an act of administrative improbity. In the first case, the act of corruption is defined in the criminal code, and the defendant, if found guilty, may be imprisoned for one to eight years, in addition to losing office and being fined. As in impeachment cases, a defendant charged with corruption as a common crime is entitled to special protections: depending on his or her position in the federal hierarchy, the defendant may not be judged in trial court but rather may have a right to "special standing" *(foro privilegiado):* that is, the right to be tried by an appeals or high court. Such cases are prosecuted by the state attorney general or the federal attorney general. Historically, special standing has been justified as a means of preventing trial court judges from becoming tools in battles between political factions.

The second way of addressing political corruption via the judicial route is a Brazilian innovation: it can be addressed as an act of administrative

Table 8.1. Approaches to Corruption in the Executive Branch

	Political Approach		Judicial Approach
	Crime of Fraud or Embezzlement[a]	Crime of Corruption	Administrative Improbity
Location of judgment	Legislative branch (federal, state, or local, respectively)	Criminal court (allows special standing)	Civil court (no special standing)
Players involved in the investigation and accusation stages	Politicians Ministério Público;	Police; Ministério Público Judiciary[b]	Ministéria Pública
Sentences if found guilty	Impeachment and suspension of political rights	1 to 8 years' imprisonment, and fine; loss of office	Loss of stolen assets; loss of office; suspension of political rights for 8 to 10 years; prohibition from participating in public bidding for 10 years
Costs prior to judicial or semijudicial proceeding	Reputational costs	Reputational costs; temporary arrest; cost of counsel; seizure of documents and invasion of privacy; weakening of criminal organization; blocked bank accounts and other funds	Reputational costs Conduct adjustment

[a] Throughout this chapter, the crime of *malversação* is translated as "fraud" or "embezzlement," although the specific legal treatment of this crime may vary considerably between Anglo and Brazilian judicial systems.
[b] The judiciary may take part in this phase by granting the police search and seizure warrants or authorization for phone tapping and temporary or provisional arrests.

improbity. This way of judging corruption was created in the 1988 Constitution and was enacted by law in 1992. It seeks to curb corruption just as political or criminal proceedings might, but without depending on the contingencies of the former (the balance of political power within the legislative branch) and without being limited by legal prerogatives (such as special standing) that complicate the latter. In administrative improbity cases, prosecutors can file suit against any political authority at any level of the government hierarchy, using the legal instrument of an Ação Civil Pública. If found guilty, the defendant is removed from office, has his political rights suspended for a period of eight to ten years, and must reimburse the public coffers for any losses. Since corruption is not defined as a crime in this case, this third alternative enables those in executive posts—from mayors to the president—to be prosecuted in trial courts without the privilege of special standing.[8] However, because these are civil proceedings, those accused of administrative improbity cannot be preventively arrested, nor can the final judicial decisions send them to jail. Further, the police and the courts do not get involved in the early investigations; prosecutors are the only investigators, since only the civil rather than the criminal aspects of the crime are being investigated.

Brazilian innovations in fighting corruption distinguish the country from other constitutional democracies. The drafting of the Administrative Improbity Law was a condition set down by the 1988 Constitution in response to a succession of political corruption scandals. The law was passed in June 1992, shortly before President Collor's impeachment in late July. In addition to significantly expanding the MP's potential to act as a horizontal *accountability* body, the law sought to speed up the fight against corruption. According to recent data from the MP, in fourteen of the twenty-seven Brazilian states, over four thousand administrative improbity cases were pending against public servants. This avalanche of proceedings is the result of prosecutors' activism in these states: they chose to use administrative improbity suits as an accountability tool, believing that they were a faster and more effective way of fighting corruption, especially when compared to the political and criminal justice approaches.

However, taking stock of fifteen years' worth of experience with administrative improbity cases suggests that they are not entirely effective in the courts, whether as a result of the slowness of proceedings, numerous dilatory appeals, or, frequently, judges' concerns about the MP's authority to act in this arena, as when they fail to recognize the legal legitimacy of suits or the legality of procedures adopted during the investigation. Of 572 suits brought by prosecutors in São Paulo since 1992, for example, fewer than 10 have reached a definitive conclusion *(transit in rem judicatam)* to date. The case of Paulo Maluf, a former governor of the state of São Paulo and former mayor of the city of São Paulo, is exemplary. There are numerous public civil and criminal suits against him, which have even led him to spend a few days in jail. But by continuously appealing his cases Maluf not only has dodged any definitive convictions but also has served as a federal congressman. The only definitive ruling against him so far—which has not yet been fully implemented—concerns the undue use of public funds to prospect for oil in São Paulo during his term as a governor (1979–82).

Such procedural ineffectiveness has led the MP to use pre-judicial procedures, such as investigations, to tackle corruption without being subject to judges' oversight. Investigations of this sort force politicians and administrators to adjust their behavior and impose "reputational" costs, such as negative media exposure. The drive to reduce impunity and achieve quicker results also seems to be at the heart of recent efforts by the MP and Polícia Federal to once again address corruption in criminal rather than civil proceedings. The increase in the number of police operations fighting political corruption and organized crime in the past few years—with participation by prosecutors and endorsement by judges—is in many ways a strategic adjustment to the poor results forthcoming in administrative improbity proceedings. The apparent advantage of administrative improbity hearings—that they require no involvement by the police and avoid problems with special standing or the rigors of the criminal code—has proved to be a key weakness: the excessive formalism of the courts, the number of dilatory appeals, and the various hierarchical avenues for appeal have provided defense counsel with ample opportunity to delay rulings and sometimes even to get cases dismissed. This does not mean that dealing with corruption as a criminal offense will necessarily avoid all of these problems, but the difference is that police investigations can more effectively obtain evidence (e.g., through telephone tapping or search and seizure warrants) and impose costs (e.g., temporary arrest). If both judicial approaches have equally poor end results, which is more likely to impose sanctions or costs on alleged criminals: corruption prosecuted criminally or in civil proceedings, such as in administrative improbity cases? Table 8.1 illustrates that the administrative improbity path imposes reputational costs on defendants and may also lead them to adjust their conduct, including by bargaining with prosecutors (in the cases where this is possible). In the criminal justice approach, phone tapping has proved important not solely in gathering evidence but also in exposing criminal behavior to public opinion before trial. Further search and seizure operations, as well as temporary arrest warrants, not only impose reputational costs but also may weaken criminal organizations. This is especially the case if the evidence is sufficient for a judge to freeze criminal assets before a sentence is handed down.

As we have seen, in civil cases the MP does not require police investigations or judges' authorization to investigate and gather the necessary evidence to file suit. In criminal cases, investigation and accusation require extensive cooperation between police, prosecutors, and judges. If the fight against corruption and organized crime has expanded in recent years as a result of the increasing number of Federal Police operations, it is not only because the institutions involved are each individually more active but also because triangular cooperation among them has improved.

Anticorruption Operations

Federal Police operations against corruption and organized crime represent one of the biggest recent changes in Brazilian accountability processes. The Brazilian press has been filled in recent years with cleverly named police operations, and the number of Federal Police operations has risen nearly continuously, from 15 operations in 2003 to 187 in 2007, with increasing public awareness of the police's work. In most cases what the Federal Police calls an "operation" is the carrying out of arrest or search and seizure warrants, issued by courts after a period of investigation that may last weeks or months and almost always includes participation by the MP or other bodies such as the Revenue Service, the Social Security Ministry, the state police, or regulatory agencies. Though the police phase of the operations is often the most visible one, it is an outcome of extensive cooperation with other institutions in the web of accountability institutions. The operations generally occur only once sufficient evidence has been gathered to lead to temporary arrests and the seizure of assets, funds, and documents; they typically begin at dawn and involve a large number of officers, often flown in from several states.[9]

While the practice of naming its operations is long-standing, the Federal Police began to focus more systematically on its public relations aspects in 2003, an effort that included releasing brief summaries of all its operations.[10] This allowed me to build a database of six hundred operations carried out between 2003 and July 2008. Many operations' names are taken from the Bible or from Greek mythology, others come from Indian languages or local folklore, and many are plays on words that refer to the alleged crime being investigated. By way of example: Operation Fiscal Adjustment cracked down on a gang that had defrauded the pension system of around US$500 million; Operations Ctrl+Alt+Del, Pen Drive, and Trojan Horse arrested cybercriminals who raided Internet bank accounts; Operation Freud uncovered a scheme of fraudulent psychological disability pensions; Operations Aphrodite, Bye-Bye Brazil, Sodom, and Exodus dismantled rings trafficking Brazilian women; Operation Locust (Praga do Egito) dismantled a scheme whereby fraudulently registered civil servants "devoured" the Roraima state payroll; Operation Switzerland cracked down on money laundering; Operation Pinocchio arrested civil servants from the Institute of Environment and Renewable Natural Resources (Instituto Brasileiro do Meio Ambiente e dos Recursos Naturais Renováveis, IBAMA) accused of turning a blind eye to illegal woodcutting; and Operation Vampire revealed fraud in the Health Ministry's bidding for blood by-products.

The symbolic aspect of naming the operations cannot be overstated. In a *democratie du public* (Manin 1995), in which the media plays a crucial role in shaping public opinion, or when political scandals begin to affect the dynamics of the democracy itself (Thompson 2000; Chaia and Teixeira, 2001; Porto, this volume), catchy names play an important role. First, naming engages public and media attention. Second, the operation's name often gives a sense of the result and the likely responsibility of those being implicated. Operation names are an informational shortcut, in other words, for the media and public opinion. This can be useful in addressing some problems of social accountability: the low level of information available to citizens and accountability agencies' inability to keep investigations in the public eye for a long time. Operation names enable interested parties to remember police activity weeks or even months later. They help the press in organizing databases and Internet tags, which enable quick retrieval of information every time new events unfold. Naming also enables the Federal Police itself to monitor the level of media exposure: in 2006, according to the Federal Police's own Communications Division, it was the focus of over fifteen thousand reports in the media, or forty-one references a day. For a recently reformed organization such as the Federal Police, which is seeking recognition from society and other public institutions, naming operations is thus an ingenious strategy.

Public relations aside, what kinds of crimes have effectively been addressed by these operations? At least fifty different types of crimes were addressed in the six hundred operations (table 8.2). The Federal Police has launched operations against corrupt politicians at all levels of the federation and in all branches of government. It has also targeted judges and police officers throughout Brazil, including within the Federal Police itself. From bureaucrats in the Social Security Ministry to members of the environmental agency IBAMA, from accounting tribunals to traffic departments, operations have hit corrupt civil servants throughout public administration. In the private sector, operations have targeted criminal organizations, businessmen, and professionals on a variety of charges, including money laundering, drug trafficking, smuggling, prostitution, infringing on Indian lands, child pornography, medicine counterfeiting, fuel tampering, predatory lobster fishing, irregular land clearing, irregular fossil digs, counterfeiting of powdered milk, fraudulent university entrance examinations, Internet fraud, armed killing squads, illegal gambling, electoral crimes, sexual exploitation of children, piracy, cargo robbery, and traffic in wild animals. The Federal Police has also targeted the highest levels of government: President Lula's brother was investigated in Operation Checkmate, and in other operations various state-level cabinet members have been removed from office, Supreme Court judges have had their telephones tapped, senators and deputies have been caught, and, most remarkably, the number two director of the Federal Police was himself arrested.

The breadth of operations indicates that the Federal Police is using its constitutional mandate to the maximum, if not exceeding it, as some critics allege. But as most operations take place via judicial warrants, any abuse of the Federal Police's mandate necessarily also implicates the federal judiciary and MPF, which are also expanding their anticorruption efforts (albeit more quietly) and thus authorizing the Federal Police to act more compellingly.

Table 8.2 illustrates that 22.7% of Federal Police operations have targeted political corruption. In classifying the operations I have adopted a

Table 8.2. Types of Crimes (Primary) and Number of States Covered in Each Operation (2003–8)

	No.	%	1 State (%)	2 States (%)	3 or More States (%)
Public corruption	136	22.7	67.6	11.8	20.6
Drug trafficking	91	15.2	54.9	14.3	30.8
Smuggling and tax evasion	59	9.8	57.6	15.3	27.1
Environmental crimes	34	5.7	58.8	8.8	32.4
Crimes against the financial system and money laundering	29	4.8	51.7	13.8	34.5
Fraud and swindling	28	4.7	53.6	17.9	28.5
Illegal gambling	24	4	87.5	0	12.5
Online theft from bank accounts	23	3.8	26.1	17.4	56.5
International traffic in persons and illegal emigration	22	3.7	54.5	13.6	31.9
Counterfeiting	17	2.8	47.1	17.6	35.3
Forgery, tampering, illegal manufacturing and commerce of fuels, food, and drugs	16	2.7	50	25	25
Organized crime (several crimes)	16	2.7	56.3	6.3	37.4
Theft	16	2.7	50	12.5	37.5
Irregular telecommunication services (radio, TV, and Internet)	16	2.7	100	0	0
Tax fraud	11	1.8	45.5	9.1	45.4
Piracy	7	1.2	71.4	0	28.6
Other	55	9.1	72	11	17
Total	600	100.0	60.5	12.3	27.2

strict criterion for political corruption, classifying as corrupt only the cases in which the main crime was *direct appropriation and embezzlement of public funds or reiterated and organized fraud in state activities (authorization, granting, and/or inspection of public interests, goods, or economic activities), by public agents (with or without private-sector involvement).*[11] This narrow definition excludes cases in which the corruption of public servants is a secondary dimension of the main crime. For example, one operation against a cross-border smuggling ring led to the arrest of a federal highway police officer on bribery charges. But despite the presence of bribery, the operation was classified in my database under "smuggling and tax avoidance." These secondary cases of corruption are traceable, and thus I found out another ninety-seven operations in which a variety of public agents, bureaucrats, and politicians were caught receiving bribes. If we add up all the cases in which corruption is either the main crime or a secondary crime, corruption rises from 22.7% to 38.8% of the Federal Police operations.

In addition to specific types of crimes such as drug trafficking, smuggling, and tax avoidance (which are indeed among the most prevalent types of crimes targeted by police operations; see table 8.2)—the Constitution grants the Federal Police the authority to act on crimes that have potential interstate or international repercussions. In other words, the cross-border nature of the crime gives the Federal Police jurisdiction and is what justifies police intervention by the federal government in the states, given that the states have their own police officers and judges. From this standpoint, table 8.2 shows a certain stretching of these constitutional principles, with a number of operations in individual states, even when the alleged crimes did not have the interstate character required by the Constitution: no fewer than 60.5% of Federal Police operations took place in a single state, whereas 12.3% took place in at least two states and 27.2% took place in three or more states.

Yet there is some justification for the Federal Police's actions even in these cases, where local institutions are corrupted to such an extent that local actors are no longer able to police themselves. In Operation Taturana (Hairy Caterpillar), for example, 110 defendants allegedly embezzled US$150 million from the Alagoas state legislative payroll. They included fifteen out of the twenty-seven state legislators, members of the state accounting tribunal (TCE), mayors, and a number of civil servants. Four of the eleven members of the state supreme court recused themselves from the case because of their close ties with the defendants. Under such conditions, only intervention by an external force with national jurisdiction can really be effective, even if it risks crossing the lines of state autonomy and rekindling the debate over federalism. Political corruption, as table 8.2 illustrates, is among the crimes that is most likely to force the Federal Police to act in a single state (67.6%).

There is a strong relationship between state GDP and the number of police operations, with an 88.3% correlation. If we consider the level of development and size of the states, it is possible to distinguish three groups of states. The first, in which there have been the most Federal Police operations, includes the most developed states in the Southeast and South of Brazil (São Paulo—the country's economic engine—has been the focus of 182 Federal Police operations, practically twice as many as Rio de Janeiro, which is in second place, followed closely by other wealthy states in the South and Southeast, such as Paraná, Minas Gerais, Rio Grande do Sul, and Santa Catarina). In the second we find the large states—in size and population—of the Midwest, Northeast, and North of the country, where there were, on average, forty operations. The third set of states is made up by the small states of the North and Northeast, where there were twenty operations, on average. Other specific factors could be highlighted, such as the importance of border states such as Paraná and Rio Grande do Sul, where smuggling and drug trafficking are the leading crimes addressed by the Federal Police, or states known for having fragile political institutions but also a much higher GDP than their regional average—such as Amazonas and Pará—where corruption is one of the top crimes.

Cooperation with other institutions in the web of accountability is an important aspect of the Federal Police's work. In at least 43% of the operations, the Federal Police worked with members of the MPF, state MPs, civil and military police officers, Revenue Service inspectors, or agents from the Central Bank, the Social Security Ministry, the Environment Ministry, or other public agencies. Such joint action is tied to the nature of the crime being investigated but also is associated with growing use of joint task forces as a more suitable way of fighting criminal organizations (Arantes 2000, 165).

In their pursuit of more effective ways of fighting corruption and organized crime, the MPF and the Federal Police have been making use of two very effective resources: telephone tapping and preventive or temporary arrest warrants. It is hardly an exaggeration to say that Brazil is "bugland": although the use of phone tapping has led to important evidence gathering, it has also been controversial. Phone tapping enables the police to map criminal networks and to record their members' communications for later use in court. But it is controversial because it has been used to trivial ends, and there has also been a growth in illegal wiretaps. The Federal Police are themselves accused of resorting to "preliminary" (i.e., illegal) phone recordings, and only after significant evidence has been gathered are judges brought in to authorize it. Private and clandestine wiretaps are another problem. According to an investigation by the *Folha de S. Paulo* newspaper, transcripts of public authorities' phone conversations can be purchased in Brasilia for less than US$500 from illegal networks of wiretappers, private investigators, and telephone company staff (L. Souza 2008). Wiretapping is so widespread that Congress set up a congressional committee of inquiry (CPI) to look into the issue in 2008. One of the most amazing revelations came a few months later: summoned to provide data on the matter, telephone companies informed members of Congress that no fewer than 375,633 wiretaps were set up throughout the country in 2007, requested by the police and the MP and authorized by courts. Crossing data from 2007–8 provided to this CPI with data on the location of operations, there is a 72.6% correlation between wiretaps and the number of Federal Police actions.

Provisional and temporary arrests made in the six hundred operations sent 9,255 people to jail. Of these, 14.5% were civil servants and 67.7% private citizens (information was unavailable in 17.8% of the cases). The number of arrests doubled year after year between 2003 and 2006. Growth has slowed down slightly since then, but the number of arrests should reach three thousand a year by the end of 2008, and on average, in 2007, eight people were arrested every day. As these are *special* police operations, aimed especially at fighting organized crime, these figures are quite large.

Although most of those arrested are set free a few days later because of limits on temporary arrest, or because of writs of habeas corpus from higher courts, these arrests can have important effects: they temporarily stymie organized crime networks, lead to media coverage, and expose the accused to public rebuke. But not surprisingly, the large number of arrests has proved controversial, especially among lawyers and politicians who claim abuse of power. In response, the Federal Police published an "etiquette guide" for the operations so as to avoid unnecessary controversy. If there has been lack of oversight in this regard, it has likely been systemic, involving decisions not only by the police but also by the MP and the courts. The Federal Police themselves complain about the 1988 Constitution's prohibition against carrying out search and seizure operations without warrants (Arantes and Cunha 2003). Many police detectives claimed that this prohibition would tie their hands unnecessarily, although it had surely been created to reduce abuse by police forces. Twenty years after the Constitution was written, the prohibition remains in force, but cooperation between the police, the judiciary, and the MP appears to allow the police to overcome the worst constraints on their activity.

Among public servants swept up in Federal Police operations, the highest proportion were federal civil servants, including members of the Social Security Ministry (accused of fraud in granting retirement pensions), staff from the Ministry of the Environment (accused of involvement with environmental crimes), and inspectors from federal agencies such as the Revenue Service and the Ministry of Labor, accused of various corrupt practices.

The second largest public-sector group arrested by the Federal Police were police officers: 22.3% of the operations implicated state police officers and highway police officers, and 8.8% were members of the Federal Police itself. In all, sixty Federal Police officers have been arrested for corruption and involvement with criminal organizations. As Mingardi (1996) points out, organized crime cannot exist on a large scale without some sort of involvement by elements of the state itself, especially the police forces. Corruption is not an isolated occurrence that involves only a few "bad" police officers. "What [the facts] show is that corruption is part of the organization's rules, it socializes its members to act within certain 'standards of corruptibility'" (Mingardi 1996, 63; translation mine). There are several potential degrees of relations between police and crime, from the most minor to the most reprehensible, but all involve some level of corruption of the public agent. Federal Police operations have uncovered everything from the bribery of police officers to ensure that they turn a blind eye to smuggling, illegal gambling, and embezzlement schemes, to police involvement with organized crime groups engaged in drug trafficking and "extermination" of petty criminals and rivals.

Also of interest is the fact that 32.4% of the 238 operations that led to the arrest of politicians and public servants hit state and municipal civil servants—staff, mayors, city councilmen, legislators, judges, and prosecutors—which reinforces the point made earlier that the Federal Police has been working as a national intervention force in subnational governments.

According to Speck (2000b), attempts to measure corruption have most commonly used three types of indicators: cases reported in the media, data produced by the criminal justice system, and data obtained from *surveys*

Table 8.3. Corruption as the Primary and as the Secondary Crime in the Federal Police's Operations (2003–8)

	Freq	*%*
Corruption as the primary crime		
Social Security fraud	45	33.1
Corruption in grants, authorizations, and furnishing of public documents	26	19.1
Fraudulent public tenders	25	18.4
Embezzlement of public funds and resources	21	15.4
Police corruption	11	8.1
Inspection fraud	8	5.9
Total	**136**	**100**
Corruption as the secondary crime		
Smuggling and tax evasion	17	17.5
Environmental crimes	14	14.4
Organized crime (several crimes)	11	11.3
Drug trafficking	8	8.2
Forgery, tampering, illegal manufacturing and commerce of fuels, food, and drugs	6	6.2
Fraud and swindling	6	6.2
Other	35	36.1
Total	**97**	**100**

with citizens. My research on Federal Police operations fits in the second category, although there is some interface with the first, given that media coverage seems to be an essential component of these operations. Looking at the cases of corruption uncovered by these operations (table 8.3)— whether corruption is the main crime or the secondary crime, as defined earlier—provides a good general idea of how severely corruption affects Brazilian public administration. However, Speck's warning that data produced by the criminal justice system perhaps uncover "more on the traits of how the criminal code is applied then on the crime in question" (Speck 2000b, 11; translation mine) is worth noting as we consider just how perfectly Federal Police operations mirror *real* corruption.

The most important target of operations against corruption is fraud in the National Institute of Social Security (INSS) bureaucracy, which accounts for almost one-third of operations in which corruption was the main crime targeted (table 8.3). If the overall rule is that corruption and the sheer volume of public resources involved go together, it is no surprise that social security fraud is at the top of the ranking: social security benefits are the main spending item in the federal budget, totaling approximately US$98.5 billion in 2007. This extraordinary volume of resources is distributed nationally by seventy thousand employees of the INSS to about twenty-six million citizens who no longer work (whether because of age, illness, disability, involuntary unemployment, or even maternity). Indications of corruption in the system have always been high, but when the social security deficit recently started to threaten the Brazilian economy the fight against fraud was intensified.[12] A permanent task force was created, made up of agents from the Federal Police, the MPF, and the Social Security Ministry, and it has acted in all states. The adoption of the task force model aims to improve cooperation among these institutions, thus increasing the efficacy of investigation, criminal indictment, and punishment of corruption.

Regulatory activities are a regular target of fraud in Brazil (as elsewhere): for example, restrictions on the extraction of timber or minerals; regional or sectoral tax benefits or incentives; and even rather simple regulatory activities such as issuing passports or drivers' licenses. Efforts to circumvent regulation often corrupt government agents, and as a result they are the second crime targeted by the Federal Police (table 8.3), appearing under the title "corruption in grants, authorizations, and furnishing of public documents." Operations conducted jointly by the Federal Police and IBAMA against illegal logging, especially in the north of Brazil, have been exemplary in this regard: at least eight major operations were carried out, leading to the arrest of over two hundred people, including IBAMA staff.

Third place in table 8.3 is one of the most common crimes in Brazilian history: fraudulent public tenders. In the twenty-five operations that targeted this offense, federal and state civil servants, police officers, assemblymen, mayors, and federal and state legislators were either arrested or investigated. One of the most well-known of these operations was Operation Sanguessuga ("bloodsucker" or "leech"), which disrupted an alleged scheme for the fraudulent sale of ambulances in over one hundred cities in at least eleven Brazilian states, involving more than sixty federal deputies and one senator.

Embezzlement of public funds is fourth on the list of crimes tackled by the Federal Police. Some cases are circumscribed to particular states, such as the operations known as "Locusts" and "Hairy Caterpillar," both mentioned previously—which cracked down on schemes in the state legislative assemblies in Roraima and Alagoas, respectively. But crimes in one state often spill over to the federal sphere, as in Operation Domino, which initially focused on embezzlement of funds from the state legislature of Rondônia. As the investigation progressed it was discovered that—like dominoes—members of the judiciary, the MP, and Accounting Courts had also fallen down on their professional obligations. Other cases that start at the local level often point to the embezzlement of public funds from large federal programs, such as the FUNDEF fund for elementary school education, the PRONAF program for family agriculture, the FPM fund for sharing income tax revenues with municipalities, and even the Lula administration's most important investment initiative, the Program for Accelerating Growth (PAC), announced in January 2007. Just as there was important cooperation between accountability institutions in the case of social security fraud, so too fraudulent public tenders and embezzlement have led to cooperation between the Federal Police, the MP, and the CGU. At least eight of the large operations against these crimes involved cross-institutional cooperation and began as a result of special audits by the CGU.

The nature of police work makes it especially vulnerable to corruption. Eleven operations have specifically tackled police corruption, especially in the Federal Highway Police, but also among civil, military, and federal police officers.[13] Like police, inspectors are extraordinarily vulnerable and thus have been a target for police operations: Revenue Service inspectors and auditors (responsible for preventing and fighting tax fraud) and labor inspectors (responsible for inspecting labor relations) were the focus of at least eight Federal Police operations for corruption.

Finally, as the second column of table 8.3 shows, corruption as the secondary crime tends to be associated with these inspection and policing activities and so is especially linked to crimes that may rely on the corruption of individual public agents for success (e.g., smuggling, tax avoidance, environmental crimes, drug trafficking, forgery). In these cases the corrupt public servant does not conspire, nor does he carry out the crime itself; rather, he serves as a facilitator in exchange for a bribe.

Final Considerations: Advances and New Challenges

The police operations analyzed here paint a troubling portrait of corruption in Brazil. Beyond the cases that usually concentrate media and public opinion attention, analysis of the operations has shown how corruption remains rooted within the broad state administrative setup and involves civil servants as much as or more than elected politicians. Corruption still takes place in the classic forms, such as tender fraud; embezzlement of public funds and resources; and fraud in grants, authorizations, furnishing of public documents, and regulatory activities. It takes place at federal, state, and local levels and in the executive, legislative, and judiciary branches of power. The volume of funds embezzled reaches, with no exaggeration, the sum of billions of dollars.

That said, it bears repeating again just how novel the Federal Police's work has been and how much more effective the coordinated action by police officers, prosecutors, and judges has become in combating political corruption and organized crime. Further, the shift in how corruption is being tackled—from an act of administrative improbity to an ordinary crime—and the cooperation between component institutions in the web of accountability have produced significant effects in areas as diverse as social security, the environment, oversight of public funds, and even the internal operations of the Federal Police itself.

Emphasis should be given to the novelty represented by cooperation and coordination between accountability institutions. Following the expansion of independent bodies and accountability roles that characterized the period after 1988, at last the players are acting more cooperatively and coordinately among themselves. The police-MP-judiciary triangle seems to be moving away from being a Bermuda Triangle—where cases get lost—and has become more effective, thanks to the greater proximity among them and procedural speed. Bringing together task forces between the Federal Police and independent agencies represents another important introduction. Such a practice has marked almost half of the operations analyzed in this chapter and has been taking place particularly in the areas of social security, taxes, the environment, and public works. Finally, every single day the Federal Police is requested to take part in investigations of internal schemes of corruption and organized crime in public entities.

The downside to these tactics is that turning police operations into media spectacles has triggered harsh reaction from politicians, judges, and lawyers who accuse the police of excess. Media reports seldom distinguish between temporary arrests and in flagrante delicto arrests, so in the public eye many of those arrested before trial are already considered guilty. Everyone from ordinary citizens to high-profile businessmen and public figures has been shoved into a police van, handcuffed and at gunpoint. The footage is aired nationwide and may well boost public support for the police and generate—however temporarily—the feeling that something is being done to fight impunity. But excess is a constant risk.

The cooperation between judges, prosecutors, and police officers has also been a focus of criticism. According to the former president of the highest court in Brazil, the Supreme Federal Tribunal (STF), Minister Gilmar Mendes, "Police officers, prosecutors, and judges cannot work together" without compromising the neutrality of their positions. Mendes even stated that by working jointly they became veritable "militia," a statement for which he was reprimanded by trial court judges and their professional associations (*OESP* 2008).

No operation has put the limits and possibilities of this new form of accountability in starker relief than Operation Satiagraha in 2008. Led by a Federal Police detective who had lost the support of the top echelons of the police in the months prior to the operation, Operation Satiagraha led to the arrest of one of the country's most prominent bankers, Daniel Dantas of Banco Opportunity; Naji Nahas, a well-known financial investor already involved in previous scandals; Celso Pitta, a former mayor of São Paulo; and fourteen other people accused of criminal conspiracy, corruption, money laundering, stock market fraud, and other financial crimes. Suspicion was rife that Dantas had already been involved in past national scandals, but allegations that he was linked to the *mensalão* scandal in 2005 (see Pereira, Power, and Raile, this volume) provided the impetus for this particular investigation.

There is no space to go into the details of Operation Satiagraha here, but the operation was marked by a series of twists and turns involving judicial decisions that had the banker arrested and set free twice. In the process, various confusing but telling details emerged, against both the targets of the investigation and accountability institutions themselves: attempts by Dantas to bribe federal police officers, allegedly offering US$500,000 to suspend the investigation; excessive zeal by the Federal Police officer directing the operation, who sought out the Brazilian Intelligence Agency (Agência Brasileira de Inteligência, ABIN) for unofficial and illegal help; the leaking of the police operation to TV network Rede Globo, whose cameras arrived at the home of one of the accused before the police on the day the secret arrest warrant was to be executed; public disagreements between trial court judges and Supreme Court ministers; divisions within the Federal Police itself, which culminated in the removal of the detective responsible for the operation, who went from being the primary investigator to being investigated by his colleagues; and the reconstruction of the whole police investigation to remove irregularly obtained evidence. These are some of the many dramatic turns that have attracted widespread public attention to the case and to the political, judicial, and police actors involved.

If on the one hand the evidence of crimes committed by gangs such as these has been compelling, on the other hand the STF—especially its president—has tried to put the brakes on federal police officers, prosecutors, and judges responsible for conducting the investigations. Madison wrote that ambition should counter ambition between the branches of government. Operation Satiagraha is a very good example of how, in the absence of strong institutions—capable of finding the correct balance between the fight against crime and the rule of law—personal motivations and ambitions may lead to excesses. In his first decision to set free Daniel Dantas after his arrest, the president of the STF stated that respect for the due process of law is what distinguishes a country with the rule of law from a police state. This has framed the public debate between those who claim to fight impunity by major criminals and those who intransigently defend the rule of law.

While the revelations behind the scenes of Operation Satiagraha would make Madison blush—ambition, betrayal, suspicion, and vengeance have all been factors[14]—institutional adjustments are being made that may improve the balance between legitimate defense and legitimate prosecution. In this regard, it is worth pointing out that the judicial oversight body, the National Judicial Council (Conselho Nacional de Justiça, CNJ), in October 2008 established stricter rules for judges to use when authorizing telephone tapping and harsher punishments for breaches of confidentiality of electronic communications. In addition, the CNJ ruled that whenever information is leaked, the leak must be investigated. The congressional inquiry has completed its work and proposed new legislation on the use of wiretapping, with harsher punishment in cases of abuse and illegal use. In August 2008, the Supreme Court laid down rules for the use of handcuffs in arrests, stating that they are to be used only to protect bystanders or when there is a risk of flight. Not even the symbolic effect of naming Federal Police operations went unnoticed by the CNJ, and recently a determination was made that judges should refrain from using the names given by the Federal Police in their judicial rulings. Once again, according to the president of the STF and of the CNJ, Minister Gilmar Mendes, "We need to end this marketing [by the police] at the expense of the judiciary." The CNJ's decision will not prevent the Federal Police from continuing to name its operations, but such decisions mark an attempt to reestablish a more balanced prosecution of corruption and organized crime.

Another aspect must be highlighted in this conclusion: the accountability system is not static, and interaction among players has often led to corrections to procedures in pursuit of proportionality between the instruments of attack and defense of which Madison spoke. Shifting action in the fight against corruption from the civil to the criminal sphere coincides with the establishment of a civil police force that is national in nature, subject to the political control of the federal government. As we have seen, this is unprecedented in Brazilian political history. It should cause no surprise, therefore, that the concern to adopt measures against abuse of power should arise again in light of the recent expansion of police activism.

The process of institutional adjustment has been ongoing, with the rules of the game shifting as it is played. In terms of the quality of democracy, it seems clear that the best way to understand and predict the path that accountability may take under Brazilian democracy is by analyzing players' individual motives and the effects produced by the institutions they inhabit. Although it is still too early to say how effective the Federal Police's

operations—with support from the web of accountability institutions—
have been, we certainly are more aware today of what Bobbio called the
"invisible power," and perhaps a little closer to fulfilling one of the still unfulfilled promises of democracy.

Notes

1. A 2004 constitutional amendment may change this situation. It created
the National Council of the Ministério Público (CONAMP), which—although it
is largely made up of prosecutors—is nonetheless charged with holding the Ministério Público accountable.

2. In this text, amounts are expressed in U.S. dollars rather than in the local
currency, the *real*, at the exchange rate of US$1 = R$2.

3. The main reforms are (1) a proposal to restrict disclosure of information
about people under investigation. Nicknamed the "gag law," this proposal was approved by the Chamber of Deputies in late 1999 but has been "sitting" unheard in
the Senate ever since, hanging over the MP like Damocles' sword. (2) Given the
MP's greater judicial activism in the past few years, prosecutors and attorneys have
started to conduct criminal investigations with their own tools. Police, politicians,
and even judges have reacted harshly, claiming that under the Constitution it is
the police who must conduct investigations. The STF docket currently includes a
case that will decide whether the MP can continue to carry out such investigations.
(3) Other changes that threaten the work of prosecutors concern the extension of
"special standing" to cases of administrative improbity. This will be discussed in
greater detail later in the next section.

4. Polícia Federal, "Histórico da Polícia Federal," n.d., www.dpf.gov.br/
institucional/historia/, accessed August 13, 2010.

5. The Federal Police appears in the constitutional hierarchy alongside the
state civil and military police and the federal highway and railway police.

6. Instituto Brasileiro de Opinião Pública e Estatística, "Nova pesquisa do
IBOPE Inteligência mostra a credibilidade das instituições brasileiras," press release, November 26, 2009, www.ibope.com.br, under "Pesquisas," "Opinião Pública," 2009.

7. Polícia Federal, "PF pelo Brasil," www.dpf.gov.br/institucional/pf-pelo-
brasil/, data from September 2008.

8. The issue of special standing has become quite controversial, especially
after Congress approved a legislative change (Law No. 10628) extending special
standing from common crimes to acts of administrative improbity carried out
by those in civil service positions. It is frequently argued that special standing

leads to impunity for politicians accused of corruption. Extending it to cases of administrative improbity, which are judged under the civil code and thus do not permit special standing, would be a major step backwards. This change threatened to have a devastating effect on the MP, as it removed prosecutors' ability to use charges of administrative improbity against mayors, governors, and other authorities, who thus could be sued exclusively by the twenty-seven prosecutors general of each state and by the federal prosecutor general. In addition, nearly four thousand existing cases were at risk of being set back by the new law, as they would have to be sent to appeals courts for review. The National Confederation of the Ministério Público (CONAMP) and the National Association of Magistrates (AMB), however, successfully challenged the constitutionality of this law before the STF. The constitutionality ruling, however, did not come down until nearly three years after the law originally went into effect. This delay, and the comings and goings that have characterized the political debate and the STF's decisions on the matter, created strong legal and institutional instability that adversely affected the MP's performance.

   9. The average number of officers involved in each operation is seventy, but this number hides enormous variation across six hundred cases: from as few as six officers to as many as one thousand.

   10. The summaries are available at "Agência de Notícias de Polícia Federal," www.dpf.gov.br/DCS/. Several gaps and inconsistencies have been resolved by means of extensive research on other institutional Web sites connected to the Federal Police (e.g., the Association of Federal Police Detectives, www.adpf.org.br/) and in the press.

   11. Often the operations involved more than one type of crime, but the classification in table 8.2 reflects the main crime in each case.

   12. The numbers provided by the Social Security Ministry are even more comprehensive than those obtained in the official Federal Police listing, on which our data are based: between 2004 and August 2008, no fewer than 171 operations were carried out, with 1,072 arrests: 262 INSS workers and 810 private citizens involved in the most diverse types of social security fraud. Twenty operations carried out by the Social Security Task Force in 2008 interrupted losses to the public coffers estimated at US$60 million. Ministério de Previdência Social, "Força Tarefa Previdenciária: Operações de 2003–2008," www.mpas.gov.br/conteudoDinamico.php?id=658, accessed October 20, 2008.

   13. The results have sometimes been significant: Operation Trânsito Livre (Free Traffic) removed half of the federal highway patrol officers in the border region of Foz do Iguaçu from their posts; Operation Mercúrio removed one-third of the highway officers in the state of Amazonas; and Operation Sucuri, on the border between Brazil and Paraguay, led to the arrest of twenty-three federal police officers, three Revenue Service agents, two highway patrol officers, and eight smugglers. A Federal Police report from 2006 showed that between 2003 and 2006, 719 disciplinary cases were opened and 2,139 inquiries against members of the police itself

were carried out, with 186 agents suspended by Internal Affairs. See Departamento de Polícia Federal, "Relatório de Atividades—2006" [Annual Report 2006], www .dpf.gov.br/institucional/relatorio-anual-pf/RA%202006.ppt/view.

14. A meeting held by the Federal Police to discuss problems with the operation culminated with the decision to remove the detective who had led the investigation. To add to the controversy, the meeting was surreptitiously recorded and a three-hour-long audiotape was leaked to the press. It is available on the Internet at Folha.com, "Reuniao Polícia Federal," November 18, 2008, http://media .folha.uol.com.br/brasil/2008/11/18/reuniao_policia_federal.mp3.

Chapter Nine

Federalism and State Criminal Justice Systems

FIONA MACAULAY

The popular image of corruption as briefcases full of cash changing hands is so way off the mark, it's almost pathetically comic. The backdrop to these briefcases is murder, the collapse of the rule of law, and the involvement of clandestine networks that stretch from the business sector, through the state institutions, right through to armed criminals and police militias, with deadly consequences for the poorest communities.

—Luis Eduardo Soares

The other contributors to this volume focus on federal-level mechanisms of accountability for tackling federal-level political corruption. However, this chapter argues that a key factor behind the persistence of malfeasance among the members of Brazil's National Congress is the array of serious deficiencies in the operation of the criminal justice system at the *subnational* level—that is, within each of Brazil's twenty-seven states.[1] These flaws are, in large part, a function of the administrative matrix of Brazilian federalism. When combined with the opportunities afforded by the political matrix of Brazilian federalism, they have permitted the emergence and rhizomic spread, horizontally and vertically, of a political-criminal nexus that has compromised the capacity of both the state and society to restrain corrupt politicians and officials.

Although Matthew Taylor's and Rogério Arantes's chapters consider the role of the federal-level police and courts in curbing political corruption at the federal level, as in many other federations, the bulk of the activity of the criminal justice system nationwide is conducted by the state police and state-level prosecutorial service and courts. These operate within the structure of the state governments, act largely autonomously of their federal counterparts (and often of each other), and are frequently heavily influenced by essentially local political factors. They are often dysfunctional and rarely pursue investigations of local politicians, either for criminal violence or for political misdoings. Corrupt federal politicians have often attained high office, and have felt free to plunder public resources, precisely because they have been unhindered in such practices in their posts at state and municipal level. Therefore, expecting federal agencies to detect and punish corruption practiced by politicians at the highest levels of a career where advancement is based on bribery, patronage, pork, and, sometimes, old-fashioned intimidation is very often a case of too little, too late.

Many of the shortcomings of the criminal justice system are a consequence of the particular administrative dispositions of Brazilian federalism, which have created what Philip Williams calls "functional holes" in the fabric of the rule of law, holes that are then filled or exploited by a political-criminal nexus (Lahneman and Lewis 2002, 3).[2] The political, criminal, and criminal justice spheres are conjoined and interpenetrated by networks of influence and corruption in terms of both the crimes committed and the institutions implicated, and form an unholy trinity resistant to oversight. The criminal underworld depends on the "upperworld" of politics, business, and the justice apparatus. Increasingly, the opposite is also true (P. Williams 2001, 78). While corruption is often thought of as an essentially white-collar crime (and this volume focuses more on specifically political offenses such as the buying of influence and the misuse of public money), in Brazil as elsewhere, many crooked politicians sustain their impunity by committing more unsavory crimes, including murder, intimidation, and human rights abuses, and distorting the criminal justice system, especially at the local level, to conceal these acts. Police brutality is encouraged, and police, judges, and prosecutors are bought off. Even those corrupt politicians not directly involved in such activities benefit from the impunity resulting from the undermining of the rule of law by their more thuggish colleagues. Violence is the underbelly of political corruption.

Crime and corruption exist on a spectrum whose boundary markers are often culturally, rather than legally, determined. In this vein, Misse (2007) questions whether organized crime corrupts agents of the state or simply co-opts them into becoming trading partners of what he calls "political merchandise": extortion, protection rackets, privileged access to information about police raids, and so forth. These are analogous to more tangible extralegal commodities in which crime syndicates in Rio and elsewhere have traditionally dealt: illegal gambling, drugs, firearms, and, increasingly, commodities on the fringes of legality such as unregistered minibuses and pirated cable TV. Such a political economy approach emphasizes both the continuum across different types of illegal activity and the way in which the protagonists are able to combine interests across the spectrum of political clientelism, corruption, the black market economy, contraband, and criminal violence: "The overlap of two illegal markets—one offering illicit goods and another that lives parasitically off the first through the provision of political merchandise—constitutes one of the main structural axes for the heightened scale of violence in Rio de Janeiro" (Misse 2007, 155). Arias (2006) similarly attributes criminal violence in Rio to the "cross-institutional ties that criminals maintain" and the symbiosis, at a community level, between politicians, local residents, and drug traffickers, all of whom have merchandise—political and tangible—to trade with one another. To understand this complex exchange system he suggests a "networked model of politics" that stresses the "formal and informal ties that bring together like-minded state officials, civil actors and criminals" (Arias 2006, 202), rather than the formal attributes of institutions (Helmke and Levitsky 2004).

These informal political-criminal networks are able to use the formal political arrangements of Brazilian federalism to expand vertically, colonizing and utilizing different levels of government and political representation, and horizontally, infecting all three branches of government in a given location. By focusing both on the state-level criminal justice institutions and on the interactions between political and criminal justice actors across and between all three levels of government, this chapter adds to our understanding of why and how the police and judicial institutions at both the state and federal levels have largely failed in their attempts to investigate and sanction corrupt politicians.

The chapter is organized as follows. Given that federalism is the underlying structural condition, the first section examines how Brazil's administrative and political federal arrangements have been conducive to the emergence of a political-criminal network by providing resources and political opportunities that intersect different levels of government. The second section examines how the structural weaknesses in the state-level criminal justice system—low institutional capacity, resistance to oversight, and "underdeveloped social control institutions" (Lahneman and Lewis 2002, 3)—render it susceptible to penetration by political-criminal networks. The following section analyzes how this in turn prevents the justice system from functioning as a tool of horizontal accountability in the lower echelons of political life, which in turn facilitates the vertical penetration of political-criminal networks into the higher realms. The final section shifts the level of analysis upwards by returning to the federal level of government, the domain that is analyzed by the other contributors to this volume. It explains how the nature of the vertical relationship between the federal bodies responsible for justice and public security, on the one hand, and the state-level criminal justice agencies, on the other, has impeded effective oversight of these agencies and their transformation into instruments of local political accountability. The chapter concludes that a more active use of federal agencies in detecting corruption is positive but that this is still occurring as a compensatory strategy for the failures of subnational criminal justice bodies.

Federalism and Political-Criminal Networks

How does the specific configuration of Brazil's federal system of government and public administration influence the behavior both of potentially corrupt politicians and of the criminal justice system? By considering the relative powers and autonomy of each level of government, as well as the nature of the linkages between them, this section examines how Brazilian federalism affects the incentives governing the political sphere and the criminal justice sphere and creates specific kinds of interactions between them.

In terms of political decision making and representation, Brazil's system may be characterized as one of "cooperative federalism with independent spheres of government" (Broadway and Shah 2009, 7). In this "strong" form of federal settlement, the three levels of government have broadly equivalent structures of political representation: each tier of government and each administrative unit within it has a proportionately elected legislature (federal deputies, state deputies, city councilors) and a popularly elected chief executive (president of the republic, state governor, city mayor) who appoints an executive administrative body (federal ministries, state and municipal *secretarias*). Each is governed by a constitution or organic law (federal constitution, state constitution, municipal organic law).[3]

The first effect of this robust political federalism is that the ills currently afflicting the federal government are also present in lower tiers of government, so that the three tiers cross-infect one another with corrupt practices. The problems of coalitional presidentialism visible on the national stage in the *mensalão* scandal of 2005 (Pereira, Power, and Raile, this volume) are also present as "coalitional gubernatorialism and mayorism" in state and municipal governments.[4] In their 2006 Operation Domino against corrupt politicians in Rondônia, the Federal Police arrested twenty-three of the state's twenty-four deputies after the governor revealed that they had been demanding pork and cash payments in exchange for supporting executive branch projects, just as federal deputies had allegedly done in the *mensalão* scandal. They were also accused of embezzling R$70 million (approximately US$25 million at the time) of public funds over the previous three years. This case underscores the way in which problems of governability, combined with weak rule of law, encourage both legal and illegal rent seeking. Political corruption also often becomes a collective and cooperative (rather than individual and competitive) enterprise, taking hold of entire institutions: in Rondônia, the scam was actually coordinated by the president of the state legislature.

Although, as Arantes's chapter notes, the scheme could not have been successfully uncovered without the reinforcement of the Federal Police under the Lula government, several of these state deputies remained unabashed in their political ambitions and ran for reelection—two even trying for seats in the federal Chamber of Deputies. Vertical accountability in O'Donnell's (1999) terms (by which voters can punish corrupt politicians by not reelecting them) appears weak in Brazil, particularly at lower levels of government, and politicians apparently calculate that they would profit more by using their ill-gotten gains to get reelected than they would lose in reputational costs. When faced with formal limits on reelection, or the threat of punishment by voters, politicians can simply run for another type or level of office.[5] Pereira, Melo, and Figueiredo (2009a) come to the same conclusion in their analysis of audited corruption among mayors in Pernambuco, observing that law enforcement is far more effective than voter displeasure in halting local corruption.[6]

Under Brazilian federalism, all levels of government are deemed autonomous and of equal status and are expected to coordinate with each other within the framework of fiscal interrelationships set out in the federal constitution (Broadway and Shah 2009, 7). The revenue-sharing regime ("fiscal federalism") is one of the factors that drives the interdependence between political actors at all three levels of government, and it has a dual aspect. On the one hand, governors depend on the federal government for resources, and mayors rely on fiscal transfers from both federal and state governments. In such a system, elected politicians act as brokers, leveraging power, votes (from their colleagues as well as from the electorate), and resources, ideally in the service of the needs of the constituency, but often in the service of their own rent seeking.[7] On the other hand, the federal government has relatively weak control over how states and municipalities spend the fiscal transfers they receive and the revenue generated by certain local taxes. Federal funds not only are misused by politicians but also may fund criminal networks: according to the Federal Prosecutorial Service in 2002, for example, half of all federal transfers to the state of Espírito Santo found their way into the pockets of organized crime.

Although the three spheres of government are administratively separate, politicians—partly because of their relationships with political parties, which operate at all three levels of government, and partly because of their roles as public resource brokers—regard them as interlinked. Thus professional politicians move between them, up, down, and sideways, in their political career trajectories (Samuels 2003). While federal funds are disbursed downwards, to subsidize lower levels of government and deliver specific policies (C. Souza 2003), politicians generally move in the opposite direction, rising from municipal to state-level to federal legislative office. Practices of corruption honed in contexts of localized *coronelismo* and clientelism are then reproduced at higher levels of politics.

This strategy creates networks of political finance and support, which politicians seek to reward as they ascend. Some later migrate from high legislative office to lower-level executive positions, as state governors or mayors, in a pattern that Samuels (2000) and Leoni, Pereira, and Rennó (2004) term "progressive ambition," as the financial and status rewards are even greater.[8]

Many politicians build their political careers on the capture of both locally generated and federally allocated resources, either in the legal form of pork barrel or in the illegal form of skimming off public funds through techniques such as overinvoicing and procurement.[9] These funds bankroll selective spending on client groups and illegal funding of their election campaigns, either to gain electoral advantage (coattails and reverse coattails) or to line their own pockets. To do so, politicians have to establish a symbiotic relationship with colleagues in the spheres of government both above and below. Local politicians need political patrons higher up who have access to state and federal funds, while federal and state politicians need local allies to bring in a particular sectoral or territorial vote. Political-institutional factors such as weak party structures and allegiances, the open-list proportional representation electoral system, and large district magnitude oblige federal politicians to adopt such individual strategies to raise funds and win votes (Ames 2000; Samuels 2003). The illegal scheme of the Workers' Party (PT) for raising campaign finance for national presidential elections, allegedly operated through the municipal administrations controlled by the party, illustrates the political interdependence of the three relatively autonomous levels of public administration. The party's *caixa dois* was reportedly filled with kickbacks from concessions of municipal services such as garbage collection and the operation of bus routes.

Some of the presidential hopefuls of recent years have lacked such a party apparatus to generate income but have nonetheless managed to finance their own campaigns through administrative scams run through local government that have often gone uninvestigated or unresolved in the criminal justice system. It was observed of Brazil's first two civilian presidents under the New Republic that "by sheer bad luck [they] . . . came from backward areas where exchange politics is common and elite families break the law with impunity" (Geddes and Neto 1999, 43). However, such practices are certainly not restricted to the Northeast. Paulo Maluf, the former governor of São Paulo State, twice mayor of the state capital, twice federal deputy and presidential candidate in 1989, became a byword in Brazil for large-scale corruption. He has faced innumerable criminal charges, including money laundering and diverting funds from huge municipal and state infrastructural projects such as highways. However, the slowness of the judicial process has left him free at each stage to pursue his political career unobstructed.

The case of Anthony Garotinho illustrates how provincial politicians can use federal transfers for patronage and electoral gain.[10] His name recognition in the evangelical Christian community through his populist radio shows got him elected first state deputy, then governor of Rio de Janeiro State. He then sustained that base by allowing local evangelical churches to disburse funds from the federal government conditional cash transfer program, the Bolsa Escola.[11] Under Lula, this program became the Bolsa Família and the federal government took over from municipalities the responsibility for means-testing recipients, in a move intended to insulate this redistributive policy from clientelism. Thus thwarted, Garotinho's wife, who had succeeded him as governor, declined to disburse the federally controlled funds, preferring instead to distribute Rio's own cash benefits (the Cheque Cidadão) through the evangelical churches, replacing a universal benefit with an electoral tool and conduit for graft: it is alleged that over 10% of registrations were fake (*Istoé* 2000).

In summary, Brazilian federalism offers local politicians a tempting mix of access to federal and state funds and autonomy in local spending. The two types of vertical accountability that might rein in malfeasance— voter power and oversight by the corrective institutions of the federal government (the Federal Prosecutorial Service [MPF], the Federal Police, the Federal Comptroller's Office [CGU], the Audit Court [Tribunal de Contas])—are insufficient and require the enforcement capacity of the state-level criminal justice system, which is a key element in horizontal (interbranch) accountability (or "superintendence," as Moreno, Crisp, and Shugart [2003] would have it).

The Weakness of the Criminal Justice System

If the political arrangements within the Brazilian federal system combine autonomy with fluidity and exchange, how do the administrative dispositions of Brazilian federalism affect the criminal justice system? The fourth "federalism variable" discussed by Samuels and Mainwaring (2004, 90) is the "distribution of government functions across levels of government." In the case of the criminal justice system, the tension between centralization and decentralization creates the dangerous "functional holes" in the rule of law mentioned above.

Brazil is unusual in combining a highly centralized legal framework with a strongly federal system of government. Unlike many other federal systems, penal law and procedure, as with other areas of law, are unitary, legislated at the national level and applied across the entire country.[12] The key structural attributes of the justice system are determined by the federal constitution. Consequently, in terms of overarching institutional architecture, the criminal justice systems of the twenty-six states and the federal district are virtually identical. Although the states and municipalities may pass their own constitutions or legislation, these may not contradict any provision of the federal constitution. However, the day-to-day management of the courts, public prosecutorial service, police, and prison services is decentralized and delegated to the state-level political authorities. This means that control of the criminal justice system is fragmented. It also means, importantly, that different *branches* of government exert influences at distinct *levels* of government.

Impunity at an early stage in many politicians' careers is in large part a function of the weaknesses of the state-level criminal justice system. The horizontal relations between the three major institutions of the criminal justice system (police, prosecutorial service, and courts) and between the separate police forces, both at the state level and across the three branches of federal administration, are characterized by fragmentation, interinstitutional competition, compartmentalization, territorialism, and hyperautonomy. The coordination problem is serious, as the two state police forces and prosecution service hold the investigative function, while the courts determine guilt or innocence, and the appropriate sanction. All of them can be compromised, and all hold veto power over criminal case proceedings. This section examines (1) the capacity of the state-level criminal justice institutions to detect, investigate, and punish political corruption and its cognate activities; (2) the degree to which they themselves are subject to scrutiny by other branches of government and by civil society; and (3) their responses to reform initiatives.

Institutional Incapacity

Many of the dysfunctional attributes of the Brazilian police—inadequate intelligence, institutional incoherence, corruptibility, and lack of over-sight—undermine their ability to prevent and detect criminal activity committed both by the general populace and by politicians. The latter, however, use their privileged position of power and control of public re-sources to take maximum advantage of this institutional fragility and block any reform initiatives aimed at improving police performance. Many Bra-zilian police officers themselves also engage in criminal activity—drug dealing, contraband, extortion, vigilantism—either individually or in or-ganized groups, sometimes in competition, sometimes in collaboration with local crime networks and politicians.

Brazil has four main police forces, with the bulk of policing at the state level conducted by the civil and military police. These have distinct functions, jurisdictions, recruitment processes, training, career structures, and internal cultures, and they tend to compete with one another for re-sources, political influence, and status. The military police, which account for some 80% of the state police, are uniformed, responsible for crime prevention and active on-street policing, and trained and organized along military, hierarchical lines. The civil police are responsible for crime detec-tion and providing evidence for criminal prosecution. One key stumbling block for the detection and prosecution of common or political crimes is that each police force in each state maintains a separate base of crime data, which they generally do not or cannot share between forces or across state borders.[13] Although in 2007 the federal government set up a single data-base, the National System of Statistics on Public Security and Criminal Justice (Sistema Nacional de Estatísticas de Segurança Pública e Justiça Criminal, or SINESP), the states are not obliged to submit data either on reported crimes or on the management and performance of their police forces, and many simply do not do so. The two forces have also functioned with different internal territorial divisions, although a growing number of states and municipalities are now "integrating" their police operations and aligning civil and military police districts.

An additional police force, the municipal police, has been established and run in a number of larger cities. They have a constitutional remit merely to safeguard municipal property, although many town halls are now using them more proactively for community and preventive policing: in reality many end up functionally subordinated to the local state military police.

An added potential bureaucratic fault line emerges as a result of the Federal Police's increasingly prominent role. The federal police's crime-fighting role covers issues of national security, ranging from social order to intrastate and transborder crime. They can be called in to investigate misuse of federal funds and to take over investigations from state police when the latter are deemed incompetent or politically compromised. As Arantes (this volume) details, the federal police force has grown enormously in terms of staff, budget, and capacity, and this, unsurprisingly, has caused some resentment among the state police forces. As he notes, the federal police "has an interest in affirming itself as a bureaucracy." It has wrested a monopoly over two important new pieces of technology, DNA testing and fingerprinting, which it, rather than the Ministry of Justice, now controls, thus denying direct access to the state-level investigative police.[14] It is also subject to less oversight than the state police forces: there exists a Corregedoria-Geral to conduct internal inquiries, but it was not until August 2009 that the federal government submitted a bill to Congress to establish an ombuds office (Ouvidoria Geral) to oversee such inquiries in the federal police, the federal highway police, and the new Força Nacional.

In sum, current institutional arrangements generate incentives for the various police forces to compete rather than cooperate. This leads to inefficiency and ineffectiveness, low crime resolution rates, and misallocation of police resources; it also enables corrupt politicians and public officials to play one force off against another and exploit their lack of communication.

Brazil has two strong and parallel judicial bodies, the court system and the Public Prosecutorial Service (Ministério Público, MP). These judicial institutions are more hierarchically coherent than the police in some respects, although the general characteristics mentioned above still pertain. The court system consists of three tiers. In relation to state criminal justice, at the lowest level are the courts of first instance, although court jurisdictions, or *comarcas,* do not necessarily correspond either to the political-geographic boundaries or subdivisions of the municipalities or to the territorial areas governed by the civil and military police. All the states, and the federal district, have an appeals court (Tribunal de Justiça, or TJ). State level decisions can be further appealed to the national Superior Court of Justice (Superior Tribunal de Justiça, or STJ), and in rarer cases, to the Supreme Court (Supremo Tribunal Federal, or STF). There is a parallel system of specialized labor, electoral, military, and federal courts, the latter dealing with any case involving any federal government, foreign, border, or international questions, among others.

The organization of the Ministério Público corresponds in large part to that of the court system with local, state-level, federal level and specialized prosecutors (Sadek and Cavalcanti 2003: 207). The MP plays an ambivalent role in relation to corruption and politically linked organized crime. As a judicial entity it has two distinct remits. The first is its monopoly over the initiation of criminal prosecutions; the second is its novel power to investigate and prosecute violations of "diffuse and collective rights." The second, as Arantes (2002 and this volume) details, has been associated with a high degree of judicial activism and "political voluntarism" in recent years, as the MP has become zealous in pursuing in both the civil and criminal courts the misuse of public funds by politicians at all three levels of government. Until the advent of an invigorated federal police force, it saw itself as a heroic institution making up for the deficiencies of the state police (incompetence and corruption), state courts (slowness and inability to investigate), and civil society (insufficiently organized). However, in relation to its criminal prosecution function, the institution is visibly neither so independent nor so heroic, inevitably sharing some of the cultural values of the criminal justice milieu in which it operates. In the cases mentioned above, where organized crime and political corruption have taken hold of a state, prosecutors have been inactive and compliant.

In relation to criminal prosecution, the judicial branch suffers many of the maladies common elsewhere in Latin America: long processing delays due to case overloads and complex procedural norms, chaotic record keeping, poor resource allocation, and poor coordination with other links in the criminal justice chain (Hammergren 2007). A successful criminal prosecution of a corrupt politician at the state level should begin with the civil police gathering evidence, passing this on to the MP, which prepares and argues the prosecution case, heard generally before a judge (except in jury trials in homicide cases) using an inquisitorial logic. However, the police and prosecutorial service compete on the terrain of criminal investigation, as the latter may both initiate investigations and oversee the police's gathering of evidence. A strong prosecution case may simply be shelved by the presiding judge or be subject to prolonged procedural delays. In addition, individual criminal justice system operators are accorded excessive personal discretion, either through institutional design, in the case of judges and prosecutors, or because the institutions have failed to produce clear and relevant internal rules for the accomplishment of organizational goals, in the case of the state police. This discretion and autonomy increases their potential corruptibility.

Accountability and Oversight

The criminal justice system needs to be socially accountable precisely so that it may remain immune from political cooptation by government or individuals and avoid becoming embroiled in political-criminal networks.[15] However, oversight over Brazil's bifurcated subnational policing regime, riven by interforce rivalries, is scattered and ineffective. The state police is governed by separate disciplinary rules (the military police by its *regimento interno* and the civil police by the Estatuto do Funcionário Público) and by separate penal codes (the military penal code and the civilian one). There exist, for the state police alone, four distinct police oversight mechanisms, located in three separate branches of government: the military courts; the police internal affairs departments and police ombuds offices, both attached to the executive; and the MP. These agencies replicate each other's work, and none engages in active detection to find out whether the police are colluding with corrupt politicians, failing in their public duty to arrest and investigate them, or indeed are corrupt themselves (and the two tend to go together). They are reactive and focus on investigation and sanction once a complaint of corruption or abuse of power has been received. The oversight agencies with greatest power, such as the military courts and corregedorias, are more secretive, while those more concerned with the public good, that is, the MP and the police ombuds offices *(ouvidorias da polícia)*, find their efforts to exert oversight actively blocked by other institutions or eroded by politicians.

The military courts hold a near-monopoly of oversight over state military police. Barring intentional homicide, all forms of military police misconduct are examined in the first instance by a military *corregedor* and will result either in internal discipline or in a military police investigation.

The case is then passed to the military prosecutor and collegiate *auditoria militar* (military tribunal of first instance) for prosecution. The persistence of these courts represents an enclave of exceptionalism incompatible with creating a culture of police accountability, as they are resistant to civilian scrutiny and maintain the insular, introspective, and defensive corporate culture developed under the military regime.

In each state the civil and military police also have their own internal affairs department, or *corregedoria* (some states have set up a Corregedoria Geral Unificada to oversee the two separate forces), which undertakes all initial investigations of complaints against police. However, they suffer from several structural defects. They are frequently poorly resourced and are housed within police headquarters, making "capture" by the corporation almost inevitable. They also tend to focus on the more extreme forms of police malpractice, such as summary executions, torture, and extortion, rather than on police corruption. They have no review function and do not maintain systematic data on persistent offenders. Although investigators are obliged to open an *inquérito policial* that should be assessed by a prosecutor or judge, in many cases they shelve their own *inquéritos* before they reach the courts, in a ritual that combines the superficial appearance of legitimacy with the internal culture of the police as a parallel legal universe. The *corregedorias,* like the military courts, are slow, secretive, and ineffective, making them essentially "a preemptive institution" that protects officers from prosecution in the courts (Lemos-Nelson 2001).

The seventeen state-level police ombudsman's offices *(ouvidorias da polícia)* initiated in the late 1990s to monitor the *corregedorias* enjoy a higher degree of transparency and public confidence than any other monitoring mechanism (Lemgruber, Musumeci, and Cano 2003). Their remit is preventive: they make their data public and identify systemic trends. They receive complaints about police misconduct, corruption, or omission from the public; prepare an initial case summary; pass on the complaints to the police *corregedorias* or MP; and track the progress of the investigation. However, their weak investigatory power and low capacity to influence the police investigation and prosecution process make them dependent on the cooperation of the *corregedorias,* which engage in forms of passive resistance. They also depend on the backing of the other parts of the justice system (courts and prosecutorial service). Although they should be autonomous and free of hierarchical controls, with their own staff and premises, frequently they are undermined by the executive branch, which houses them alongside the police authorities and starves them of necessary funds. Appointments of the *ouvidor* are often political. As they have no legal power to oblige the police to implement their findings, it is actually the MP that most resembles a true ombudsman.

However, while the MP possesses the necessary institutional capacity to act as an ombudsman, it is constrained in relation to the police by a conflict of interest. On the one hand, the MP needs the cooperation of the police in the production of criminal evidence. However, as a public watchdog, it may investigate any form of police wrongdoing, and there is heated debate between adherents of a minimalist and maximalist view of the MP's role in relation to the police. São Paulo State, for example, accorded its own prosecutorial service wide-ranging powers to inspect police documents, interview prisoners, and check the destination of impounded illegal weapons, money, drugs, vehicles, and other "tradables" within the flourishing illicit police microeconomy, which is inevitably connected to corrupt civilians, including public officials and politicians. This is, however, an exception in Brazil more widely, and the civil police of São Paulo have aggressively fought against the state MP's role as an oversight agency.

While in other countries in Latin America the judicial branch has suffered from a lack of autonomy and has been co-opted and manipulated to political ends, following the promulgation of the 1988 Constitution, Brazil's court system and the MP enjoyed considerable independence. But as a result, both have been rather insular institutions competing with one another in the judicial field. Their hyperautonomy also made them horizontally unaccountable to the executive and legislative branches of government, both for the way in which they managed their own affairs and for their efficiency and effectiveness in dealing with crime, including the misuse of public resources. Vertical accountability was also very low within the judicial branch itself until the 2004 reform, which established the National Judicial Council (CNJ) and the National Council of the Ministério Público (CONAMP) to oversee the administrative and financial affairs of both the courts and prosecutorial service and introduced measures to reduce internal corruption and nepotism.[16] However, the councils cannot tackle the problems of bias in the lower ranks of the judiciary when this is expressed in questionable processing and sentencing of criminal suspects: these are regarded as sovereign functions of *individual* prosecutors and judges, who continue to enjoy a high level of professional autonomy. It was not until late 2004 that the principle of binding precedent was introduced, weakly, into Brazilian law: prior to that, local judges could simply ignore rulings by higher courts. Politicians, if subject to an unfavorable ruling by one level of the judiciary, could simply petition, or exert pressure on, a different level to get the ruling reversed or reconsidered. However, it should be noted that increased activity by other federal accountability agencies is beginning to put pressure on the judiciary. In 2003, an STJ judge was charged with selling habeas corpus decisions to drug dealers, while in 2007 the federal police's Operation Hurricane led to the arrest of three appeals court judges and another STJ judge was charged with selling verdicts to gambling mafia and drug-dealing bosses.

Response to Reform Initiatives

Samuels and Mainwaring (2004, 86) concur with other scholars that federalism generally produces more veto players.[17] In Brazil, all three tiers and branches of government are able to champion or stall reform efforts. In many cases, federal politicians, especially former state governors sitting in the Senate, have close ties with state-level criminal justice actors, to whom they owe favors accrued in the course of their rise to federal office, and whom they need to keep sweet should they lose their office or retreat to a lower level of office. This has enabled a powerful military police lobby in Congress to obstruct reforms that would have directly harmed their interests.[18] Federal deputies and senators have refused to discuss bills proposing deconstitutionalization, demilitarization, or unification of the state police;[19] have dramatically watered down a bill intended to transfer jurisdiction to civilian courts for all crimes committed by the military police; and have maintained spaces of exceptionalism such as the military courts and *prisão especial* for military and police personnel, despite recent reforms such as the 2004 judicial reform bill.

Police also influence political actors at lower levels of government. Although state governors can appoint police chiefs, allocate resources, and set the tone for policing, they also have to take into account the police's own autonomy and ability to resist unwelcome change (e.g., the Garotinho case discussed below). Sometimes one police force may support a reform proposal, whereupon the other will try to sabotage it, depending on the interests at stake. Mayors generally have fewer problems in handling the newer and smaller municipal guards but frequently have to negotiate with the local military police brigade over how the city is policed. Although state deputies and city councilors can interfere only with local operational aspects of policing, such as salaries, resources, oversight mechanisms, policing styles, and so forth, they are also lobbied by the police to resist reform proposals.

The rising number of police officers running successfully for legislative posts in all three tiers of government has increased this spillover between the criminal justice and political spheres and has allowed them to directly defend their corporate interests, embezzle public funds, access networks of political influence, and enjoy parliamentary immunity. In the state of São Paulo, for example, Colonel Ubiratan Guimarães had commanded the 1992 military police operation to quell a riot in the notorious Carandiru Prison, which resulted in the deaths of 111 inmates. Although he was sentenced in 2001 to a 632-year prison sentence for the extrajudicial execution of 102 of these detainees, while his case was under appeal he was elected state deputy for São Paulo in 2002.[20] In that post he served on a state assembly committee of inquiry (*comissão parlamentar de inquérito,* or CPI) on organized crime and was able to campaign against firearms control, leading the so-called *bancada da bala* (the "bullet caucus") in the state assembly. He was thus able to veto any reforms that might harm his personal or corporate interests.

Enough of these police candidates have been successful to begin making a significant change to the composition of local legislatures. In Pernambuco, seven of the forty-nine state deputies (15%) are former police officers, a proportion rising to 20% in Recife's city council.[21] Former police officers now sit as elected representatives in twelve state legislative assemblies and seventeen state capitals. What started as individual police officers' decisions to run for political office has increasingly become a collective strategy on the part of police corporations. In the municipal elections of 2008, across the country 4,144 civil and military police officers ran for office, compared to 3,886 in 2004.[22] In Rio de Janeiro alone, 357 military police officers and 62 civil police officers registered in 2008 as candidates for the 50 city councilor seats, a 35% increase over 2004, attributed to the activism of the police-linked, freelance "militias" taking the law into their own hands against drug traffickers in the favelas.[23] In addition to this, 145 police officers work inside the state assembly, mainly as "parliamentary advisors," creating ideal conditions for promiscuous relations between police and politicians (*O Globo* 2008). In Goiás, the police even formed their own political party, Partido das Polícias Goianas, to support the candidacies of 273 military and 73 civil police officers to municipal posts (*Correio Braziliense* 2008). Recently, the National Federation of Federal Police Officers (FENAPEF) drew up a strategy to encourage its members to run for the posts of state and federal deputy in 2010 (Roncaglia 2008). This suggests that the Federal Police is increasingly conceiving of itself as having an autonomous political role in the widest sense, rather than being merely an operational arm of the Ministry of Justice.

Weak Horizontal Accountability and the Ascendancy of Political-Criminal Networks

The alliances forged between rent-seeking political, criminal, and criminal justice actors, the unhealthy intertwining of branches of government that are supposed to be functionally separate, and the lack of coordination between the institutions of the criminal justice system all combine to prevent the exercise of horizontal accountability. This in turn allows political-criminal networks to vertically penetrate higher levels of government. In particular, oversight is complicated by the inevitably strong attachment of the police to the executive branch and weak ties to the judicial branch, by the lack of vertical oversight by federal justice agencies over their local outposts, and by the legal loopholes that enable politicians to evade prosecution by virtue of their status and ability to take advantage of jurisdictional conflicts in the system.

In some cases it is not clear whether politicians run the police or vice versa because the relationship is so close. For example, following accusations of illegal campaign funding, in May 2008 the Federal Police issued an arrest warrant against former Rio de Janeiro governor Anthony Garotinho. Garotinho was charged with *formação de quadrilha* (racketeering) along with the former chief of the Rio de Janeiro civil police and current state deputy Álvaro Lins. Lins was charged, along with a fellow state legislator and a federal congressman, with using the infrastructure of the civil police over a six-year period for money laundering, criminal association, corruption, and fencing of stolen goods. The irony of Garotinho's association with police corruption is that in 1998 he had run for governor on a platform of police reform, as laid out in a book "coauthored" with the leading sociologist Luis Eduardo Soares, whom he then appointed as subsecretary of public security to carry out these reforms (L. Soares et al. 1998). However, not only was Soares's superior a military police colonel hostile to reform, but Garotinho also refused to back Soares's attempts to remove the *banda podre* (the "rotten apples") within the civil police. The "Astra" group of officers was known for getting results in unconventional ways—through extortion and violence, arresting the small fry and cutting deals with the leaders of the crime syndicates. Through threats of direct violence and the potential to wreak havoc on the public security situation in Rio, they secured Garotinho's cooperation, including his commitment to keep Lins in post throughout his governorship and during that of his wife, when Garotinho served as secretary for public security. Soares was sacked unceremoniously for his insistence on weeding out corrupt police officers (L. Soares 2000). In this case, the executive branch itself acted to veto reforms to the rule of law.

Horizontal and vertical accountability are linked. Santiso (2003, 177) noted prior to the 2004 reform of the judiciary that "the social legitimacy of the judiciary as an institution of 'horizontal accountability' [was] undermined precisely by its lack of 'vertical accountability.'" In Espírito Santo, for example, local-level representatives of the federal judiciary were powerless against corrupt police and politicians. In 1995 federal prosecutors filed a petition to close down an organized crime ring and death squad known as the Scuderie Detetive le Cocq, in which were embroiled police, justice system operators, and politicians. Although a legal entity formed in 1964 as a police mutual society, in the 1990s the Scuderie was notorious for the murder of human rights and land activists and of street children, whose publicly displayed corpses were used as leverage for police pay raises (Global Justice 2002a, 71–79; 2002b).[24] However, it took five years for senior federal judge Ivan Athiê, who had been presiding over the hearings, to decline to issue a ruling on the grounds that it was not a matter for federal jurisdiction. His dilatory handling of the case was due not only to fear of reprisals but also to his own involvement with criminal networks: in 2005 he, a lower-level federal judge, and a federal prosecutor *(procurador regional da república)* were all removed from office by the STJ on charges of racketeering and extortion. It was only after civil society had petitioned the regional federal court (Tribunal Regional Federal, or TRF) that the case was reactivated in 2001 and a decision was finally handed down in 2004 to strip the Scuderie of its legal status and thus shut it down. In the nine years since the initial request, no higher judicial body had intervened to speed up matters. Impartial local judges were intimidated not just by the crime syndicate but also by their colleagues. In 2003, Judge Alexandre Martins de Castro Filho, who had been helping the federal task force, was gunned down because he uncovered evidence that his predecessor in the local sentencing courts *(vara de execução penal)* had been involved in trafficking influence, transferring convicted hit men to open prisons, and issuing favorable parole reports to individuals linked to the Scuderie. Those who allegedly ordered the crime (including his predecessor, Judge Antônio Leopoldo Teixeira, a former military police officer and a former civil police officer) have not yet been convicted. The trial of Teixeira has involved all three levels of the judiciary: the STF has ruled that, as he was forcibly retired and therefore not eligible for *foro privilegiado,* the case should now be tried by jury in the court of first instance, not in the state appeal court, which began handling the case.[25]

Espírito Santo is also an exemplary case of a tightly woven web of collusion between all branches of government and organized crime, leaving civil society as the only mechanism of accountability. The UN Special Rapporteur on Extra-Judicial Executions wrote of her inspection visit there in 2003, "The situation . . . is a particularly striking example of the penetration of death squad activities into the highest levels of legislative, judicial and executive branches of a state" (United Nations 2004, para. 45). The president of the state legislature, José Carlos Gratz, was the kingpin in this schema of graft, network crime, and state-sponsored violence. Gratz was finally arrested in 2003 on charges of paying R$30,000 apiece to twenty-six of the other twenty-nine state deputies to support his reelection as assembly president, a position he used to guarantee his own impunity and that of his associates. He had ensured that a state-level CPI into drug trafficking set up in 1999 concluded that there was in fact no organized crime in Espírito Santo.[26] He also exerted influence over the state electoral court and colluded with the then-governor, the state judiciary, and the police, appointing as the secretary of public security a former head of the Scuderie death squad. A 1999 report on organized crime in Espírito Santo, prepared by the National Congress, implicated a former federal deputy, governor, and senator from the state, Élcio Álvares, who was then serving as minister of defense and was promptly sacked by President Cardoso over the allegations.[27] However, regardless of this reputational tarnishing, in 2006 Álvares, clearly unwilling to relinquish his political networks in the state, was elected state deputy.

Legislators evade horizontal accountability through their legal entitlements to exceptional treatment within the criminal justice system: parliamentary immunity, special legal standing or *foro privilegiado* (the right to trial in a higher court of justice), and separate prison cells while awaiting final conviction and sentence (see discussion in Arantes's and Taylor's chapters, this volume). Until a 2001 amendment, Article 53 of the Constitution gave deputies and senators immunity from prosecution as long as they held public office. Congress would consider the criminal evidence submitted by the STF and normally expel the accused on grounds such as *falta de decoro parlamentar* (conduct unbecoming of a member of Congress) rather than have a serving deputy face criminal charges. Now the STF has only to inform Congress of its intentions and may proceed automatically to prosecute if its request is ignored.

Such a guarantee of impunity gave some rent-seeking politicians perverse incentives. On January 1, 1999, the newly elected federal deputy Ceci Cunha, who had been sworn in just hours earlier, was gunned down with her family, allegedly on the orders of Talvane Albuquerque, who was her runner-up in Alagoas State. He calculated that it was worth having the incumbent murdered in cold blood in order to assume her seat in Congress (which he did), where he would be free from prosecution. He was, however, quickly expelled from the Chamber of Deputies. However, a decade later he has been neither tried nor convicted; indeed, in 2008 he took up a post as secretary of health in a small town in Alagoas. The prosecution process had become lost in the labyrinth of the different branches and levels of the judiciary; until he was expelled from the Chamber, the STF held jurisdiction. Then the state courts of justice concluded that state-level *federal* courts should try him because his motivation was election to the federal legislature. Meanwhile, the actual gunmen waited to be tried in the state courts.

The symmetry of Brazil's federal system ensures that the principle of parliamentary immunity is automatically extended to both state deputies and city councilors, making it possible for individuals to commit serious criminal offences, yet also work their way up the ladder of power, knowing that any criminal process initiated while they were running for office will be suspended once they take office, as was the case with Colonel Ubiratan Guimarães. In perhaps the most egregious case, in September 1999, Federal Deputy Hildebrando Pascoal from Acre was expelled from the Chamber of Deputies under suspicion of being the head of a drug-trafficking ring and death squad responsible for up to 150 murders since the early 1980s.[28] Pascoal was a former state deputy and commander of the Acre State Military Police, and his activities had been investigated by federal prosecutors since at least 1997. However, it was not until a CPI on drug trafficking uncovered allegations against him that action was finally taken. After the issue of a warrant by a federal court in Rio Branco (the capital of Acre State) and arrest by Federal Police, he was first convicted in 2006, by a federal court, for the murder of a former associate.[29] In 2008 he was facing new charges in a jury trial in Acre, this time brought by the state prosecutorial service, related to one of his "trademark" gruesome murders, in which the victims were dismembered with a chainsaw and tossed from a helicopter. However, the case is complicated by the fact that one of the co-accused (Pascoal's cousin, also a former chief of the police in the state) is a state deputy and therefore entitled to *foro privilegiado*. As in the Cunha Lima case cited by Taylor (this volume) and the Talvane Albuquerque case above, jurisdictional confusions caused by politicians' special legal standing often results in them walking free.

This case illustrates several issues already mentioned. The first is the overlap between political corruption, graft, and crimes of violence. Pascoal was charged not only with murder, illegal possession of firearms, and drug trafficking but also with evading taxes, siphoning off public funds, and bribing voters with drugs hidden in food packages. The second is the intersection between politics, crime, and criminal justice institutions. Pascoal rose through the ranks of the state military police, eventually becoming head of the corporation in a border region notorious as a drug transit point. He had been elected state deputy in 1994, running on the ticket of candidates for governor and federal deputy who were already under investigation for corruption. The third is the failure of the state- and federal-level criminal justice institutions to impede his rise to power. As a former military police chief, he was able to call in favors from his colleagues and subordinates. The state government lent him police officers to assist his election campaign in 1997, forming themselves into a death squad at his beck and call.

This raises the question of how such politicians can be stopped when state justice institutions are corrupt. In the Acre case, it was not until the federal courts, federal police, and federal congress joined forces to act promptly and effectively that vertical accountability could be brought to bear. What, however, of "social accountability" (Peruzzotti and Smulovitz 2006) in such cases? In the Alagoas case, Albuquerque was also suspected of having ordered the murder of a radio broadcaster in 1993. Local radio is a major source of information about small-town politics and can be highly influential electorally. Ferraz and Finan (2008, 703) found that when the CGU randomly audited municipalities to detect corruption, where there was a local radio station that publicized its findings, corrupt politicians were punished and clean ones rewarded at the ballot box. However, where the media constitute the only institution demanding accountability, they often pay a very high price. Research by human rights bodies has revealed a pattern of intimidation and killings of journalists investigating alleged corruption by municipal and state-level politicians.[30] Often such journalists are investigating crimes of political corruption that are more properly the purview of the police and prosecutors, or corruption and brutality by the police in states such as Alagoas, where the criminal justice institutions are compromised by local politicians.

The Federal Government and Vertical Accountability

How, then, has the federal government attempted to deal with the weaknesses in the rule of law? Has it been able to strengthen the vertical relationship between the federal executive-branch bodies responsible for justice and public security and the state-level criminal justice agencies?

Two contrary dynamics seem to be at play here. The first strategy open to a federal government is to reform the state-level criminal justice institutions by changing the constitutional framework and exerting pressure, through political or financial leverage, on state governments to do the same. The second available strategy is to bypass the state criminal justice system altogether by introducing new agencies and mechanisms that effectively compensate for the deficiencies of the state-level justice institutions but that leave them largely untouched. Three factors complicate the reform of state-level criminal justice institutions, however, and compensatory strategies have problems of their own.

First, one of the key obstacles to deep structural reform of the criminal justice system has been the federal Ministry of Justice, which was until recently dominated by political rather than judicial concerns, acting as the president's intermediary and broker between the federal and state governments. This resulted in a degree of instability and low technical capacity. Between 1985 and 2003, the ministry had, on average, one minister a year, mainly political appointees with little interest in criminal justice issues. However, a minority were senior jurists with a reform agenda. One, Nelson Jobim, who had the longest tenure under Cardoso, established national commissions to revise the criminal code, the criminal procedure code, and the law governing prison regimes and sentence serving. José Carlos Dias and Miguel Reale Jr., both prominent criminal lawyers, attempted reforms but were thwarted by powerful veto players in the federal government and were forced to resign when political backing was not forthcoming. The former clashed with the military hierarchy when he wanted to transfer primary responsibility for policy on drug trafficking from the army to the federal police. The latter returned to this issue by initiating the expansion of the Federal Police that would occur under the Lula government. However, Reale Jr. was soon toppled by the issue of federal responsibility for corruption and crime at state level, resigning when President Cardoso and the federal attorney general reneged on their commitment to order federal government intervention against the police death squad in Espírito Santo State.

A second reason for neglect of deep structural reforms to the justice sector is that the central government has frequently retreated to the "federal argument" that poor policing, rising crime, and human rights abuses by state agents must be laid at the door of the state governments, which direct the criminal justice agencies on the ground. Delegating responsibility for citizen security and crime prevention to nonstate actors or to agencies in subnational government is often a form of denial in the face of limited federal government capacity (Garland 1996). Here the federal government faces a paradox, for on the one hand Brazil has for decades been an active collaborator in the setting of international norms on human rights, is a signatory to all the relevant regional and international conventions, and participates in the pertinent monitoring bodies. In this universe, the federal argument is irrelevant: as the national government is the state party to the conventions, it is morally responsible for the actions of subnational justice agencies in violating human rights. However, in terms of the efficacy of the criminal justice, the federal government is legally constrained by the constitutional arrangements that make the state-level justice systems autonomous of federal government. The ministry and its dependent agencies have also struggled to impose direction and exercise control over the country's federalized criminal justice system because of a lack of political power and technical capacity. That said, both the Cardoso and Lula governments have been criticized by the reformist policy community that stretches across academia, think tanks, and government for not making use of available leverage by making disbursement of federal funds to the state police forces conditional on improved performance. The Ministry of Justice's National Secretariat for Public Security (SENASP) has had limited technical, political, and financial capacity to generate national policy in these fields, let alone exercise leverage or control over the state-level police forces.

Third, the federal executive branch has chosen not to expend precious political capital on constitutional and legal reform of the state police, the costs of which have been pushed up by the activist entry of police officers into the legislative arena. In addition, under Cardoso and his predecessors, the criminal justice system was simply not accorded much importance in comparison to the need to enact in quick succession the first- and second-generation reforms deemed necessary for market opening. Although the Lula government came into office promising to implement a one-hundred-page blueprint for justice sector reform, it initially retreated into "denial mode." Luis Eduardo Soares was appointed head of the newly established SENASP and led an excellent technical team in an attempt to direct the state governments, over which they had no formal jurisdiction, down a reform path. However, the Lula government realized that the potential cost of failure would far outweigh the possible benefits of success resulting from high-profile activity around law and order issues. It had overplayed its hand by promising major reforms that threatened to attract too much public attention. It therefore remained politically more expedient to blame the inadequacies of the state-level governments. Within months Soares was pressured to step down after what he and his team allege were unfounded and malicious accusations of misconduct from within the ministry.

That said, since 2003 justice sector reform has received more political support and resources than at any other time under the new democratic regime. The Ministry of Justice has refocused on justice sector issues, with just two ministers appointed under Lula.[31] The creation of the Sub-Secretariat for Judicial Reform was successful in driving through the 2004 reform that had staggered directionless through several administrations and congressional committees (Macaulay 2003). In this instance, reform had been blocked by professional legal bodies rather than by federal politicians, and for several years the federal judiciary had managed to resist attempts by both the federal executive and some legislators to increase the institution's transparency, impose external oversight, and democratize its internal processes (Macaulay 2003).[32] In the end, a series of financial scandals involving senior judges and a visit by the UN Special Rapporteur on the Independence of Judges and Lawyers disarmed residual resistance from judges to the reform package and persuaded politicians there was little to be gained by backing a losing horse.

The most notable shift in federal government policy has been the defense of the *res publica* through compensatory strategies driven by the much-bolstered Federal Police force operating in conjunction with activist elements of the MP, often following in the wake of the CGU's investigations. In large part the activism of these federal agencies is a function of the defects of the state-level justice system. The MP has devised ways of "getting around" blockages in the courts, hence its use in recent years first of civil actions (which then failed in the courts) and latterly of the media and criminal prosecution.

Such compensatory action reveals a frequent Brazilian response to problematic areas of public policy or services. When a state institution is failing, the necessary root-and-branch reform is avoided. Instead, new, parallel institutions are added, for example in the case of police oversight, thus sidestepping the problems of removing patronage from existing stakeholders and the creation of any zero-sum dynamics. The old institutions are left to quietly wither and often end up undermining the effectiveness of the new ones. This dynamic of "reform by addition" serves to fragment rather than consolidate information and transparency, to splinter and diffuse control rather than strengthen it, and to undermine rather than reinforce accountability. Accountability mechanisms depend on a clear division of labor, which is muddied by the inappropriate crossover between the political and criminal justice spheres. Congress usurps the functions of the MP each time it assesses the criminal evidence presented by the Supreme Court prior to the prosecution of a deputy or senator. The frequent CPIs held in the nation's legislatures allow elected representatives to usurp the police investigative function, uncovering evidence of criminal activity that has clearly gone undetected or been covered up by incompetent or corrupt local law enforcement agents. It is not yet clear, when federal justice agencies investigate corruption by politicians at all levels of government, whether this will have any beneficial effects on the state-level justice institutions, which still rely on both federal and local political will for root-and-branch reforms, or whether these new agencies will simply overlay and duplicate the existing ones.

Two other "compensatory mechanisms" for tackling local-level political-criminal networks are federal intervention and the federalization of human rights cases. In principle, it is possible for federal justice agencies to intervene in state governments ensnared in organized crime and institutional corruption. The Espírito Santo case shows, however, that local representatives of federal agencies (police, prosecutorial service, or courts) can be as vulnerable to intimidation and corruption as their state justice counterparts. This underscores the importance of top-level federal government commitment to cutting Gordian knots of violence, crime, and graft. However, securing formal federal intervention has been an altogether different political proposition. Authorities and activists tried to get federal action against organized crime in Espírito Santo from 1991 onwards. In 1993, a special committee set up by the governor uncovered the extension of the Scuderie's tentacles into the spheres of justice, politics, and business in the state, findings on which he did not act. Federal prosecutors conducted an investigation and requested the legal dissolution of the Scuderie, but this stalled for several years in the local federal court. The federal congress then took up the baton with a CPI into drug trafficking. By 2002 the breakdown in law and order was so grave that the Brazilian Bar Association made a request to the STF for federal intervention, supported by the government's own Defense of Human Rights Council (Conselho de Defesa dos Direitos da Pessoa Humana, or CDDPH), and then-minister of justice

Miguel Reale Jr. However, neither the federal attorney general nor President Cardoso would back such an intervention six months before general elections. It was not until the new Lula government that a federal task force, consisting of representatives of the Federal Police, the Attorney General's Office, the intelligence service, and the federal tax office, was dispatched and resulted in the arrest of Gratz. In Acre, where the Cardoso administration did act, sending in a task force (which is not the same as federal intervention), Pascoal's mafia was broken because the PT state governor put party competition aside and collaborated fully with the Federal Attorney General's Office, Chamber of Deputies, and Ministry of Justice.

So-called federalization of human rights cases was established by a constitutional amendment in 2004 and can occur in instances of gross violations where the state justice agencies are unwilling or incompetent to investigate properly. The federal attorney general and the STJ may transfer jurisdiction for investigation and trial to the federal justice system, that is, to the hands of federal police, prosecutors, and judges.[33] Such a transfer circumvents the influence of politicians on local judiciaries and allows justice to be pursued in specific cases, but it does not address the underlying structural issues in the state justice system that blocked proper investigation in the first place. Moreover, moving the jurisdictional responsibilities up the federal ladder is not usually effective, as is evident in the case of elected officials who are entitled to trial in higher courts.

WHEREAS WEAK STATES TEND TO BE ENGULFED BY A POLITICAL-CRIMINAL nexus, the Brazilian state is strong, albeit heterogeneous, and therefore has a choice as to whether it colludes with or confronts political corruption and criminal networks. Both reactions are currently evident. On the one hand, many federal politicians have funded their way to the top through collusion with crime networks and corrupted criminal justice actors. Their path has been eased by a lack of cooperation between state and federal agencies and the fragmentation of state-level criminal justice systems. On the other hand, a number of federal agencies have become more determined to tackle political corruption. However, of all the justice institutions operational at state level, only elements of the MP can be said to be proactive in this regard. This, then, is the essential weak link in the chain of accountability, that the state-level police, courts, and criminal prosecutors are separated from the activities of these federal bodies and are prevented from collaborating more with them by direct political influence, lack of institutional reform (in the case of the police), and entrenched, local corporate interests. Not only do the federal institutions not collaborate well with the state-level ones, which remain unreformed and over which they have limited jurisdiction and leverage, but the state criminal justice institutions are also uncooperative. Where there should be interlocking circuits of institutional accountability, there is instead fragmentation and competition.

Corrupt federal politicians have managed to slip through the holes in the net of the state-level justice system. Some are belatedly being caught by the new net of federal criminal justice investigations. However, it is likely that a combination of the privileges they have granted themselves and the influence and veto power they exert over the criminal justice system at the state level will continue to offer them effective escape routes for some time to come.

Notes

The chapter's epigraph is Soares's comment on the arrest of former state police chief and state deputy Álvaro Lins for his involvement in a political-criminal network (*Último Segundo* 2008; my translation).

1. In this chapter, I generally use the term *state* (especially in its adjectival form) to refer to the twenty-seven subnational units: the twenty-six states plus the Federal District, which for most intents and purposes is also a state. To describe the national (central) state, I use the adjective *federal-level.*

2. This is not dissimilar, conceptually, from O'Donnell's (2004) notion of "brown areas" in which the rule of law is absent, or Boaventura de Sousa Santos's (2006) idea of the "heterogeneous state."

3. Federal Constitution, Title III, Chapters 3 and 4.

4. *Coalitional presidentialism* refers to a situation where the president's political party does not hold a majority of seats in the legislature, forcing him or her to govern through a coalition of parties, which requires the distribution of political goods.

5. For example, a state or federal deputy running for city mayor, or vice versa.

6. The CGU found in its spot checks that second-term mayors, emboldened by success and impunity, were more corrupt than first-term mayors in terms of both the quantity of resources misappropriated and the number of irregularities (Ferraz and Finan 2005).

7. The changing brokerage role of the governors is discussed by Abrucio (1998) and Cheibub, Figueiredo, and Limongi (2002). Samuels and Mainwaring (2004) examine the fiscal consequences of "strong" federalism in Brazil.

8. Some 20% of federal deputies in each legislature run for mayor or vice mayor in the middle of their term of office. Around a quarter to a third get elected (Samuels 2000).

9. The independent monitoring bodies Congresso em Foco and Transparência Brasil maintain a Web site listing of all the federal deputies and senators currently facing criminal charges. See "Mapa da Mina: Processos," congressoemfoco .ig.com.br/noticia_list.asp?ct=46, and "Ocorrências na Justiça e Tribunais de Conta," www.excelencias.org.br/@casa.php?pr=1. Many are accused of crimes against the law on tendering *(lei de licitações)* and various forms of misappropriation of public money.

10. Garotinho ran for the presidency in 2002 on the Brazilian Socialist Party (PSB) ticket, receiving 18% of the first-round vote.

11. At the end of Cardoso's second administration, this scheme, first implemented in a number of municipalities and states, was rolled out nationally. However, the responsibility for identifying beneficiaries was left in the hands of municipalities.

12. In Mexico, Argentina, the United States, and Canada, each state or province has its own penal code.

13. Only a minority of states, such as São Paulo and Minas Gerais, have set up an integrated crime data system, based on the latest Geographic Information Systems.

14. Information from an anonymous source in the Ministry of Justice, June 2009. The Federal Police run a National Identification Institution (Instituto Nacional de Indentificação, or INI) and a National Crime Institute (Instituto Nacional Criminalística, or INC). In 2004 the INI acquired the Automatic Fingerprint Identification System. In March 2009 the Federal Police signed an agreement with the FBI to use the Combined DNA Index System, the largest database in the world. They will use this to integrate and standardize the DNA databanks that as of September 2009 exist in fifteen Brazilian states (*Istoé* 2009).

15. This section draws heavily on Macaulay (2002) and Lemgruber, Musumeci, and Cano (2003).

16. The fifteen-member CNJ and CONAMP, which have a remit to demand or oversee disciplinary inquiries into particular judges as well as to monitor the management of the courts, include two lawyers and two independent citizens appointed by Congress. The state appeals courts now also have ombudsmen's offices *(ouvidorias)*. Other measures include a quarantine period for judges wanting to return to private practice.

17. Here I disagree with the finding of Andrews and Montinola (2004, 55) that "systems with multiple veto players have higher levels of the rule of law," as they restrict their analysis to executive-legislative relations at the federal level.

18. The Web site run by Transparência Brasil gives the number of former police officers as 14 out of 512 federal deputies, and one out of eighty-one senators, but this underestimates the number of police sympathizers in Congress. See Projeto Excelências, "Policiais," www.excelencias.org.br/@casa.php?bc=policia, accessed August 24, 2009.

19. The 1988 Constitution states that every state must have a military and a civil police force. Removing such a prescriptive constitutional reference to these two forces would gives states flexibility to organize their police as they wish.

20. Proud of his actions in Carandiru, he ran, provocatively, on the electoral number "14111." His conviction was overturned, on a technicality, by a special session of the twenty-five most senior judges in the state court of appeal (Tribunal de Justiça).

21. This move by the police into politics has had a more localized effect on the rule of law: it left fifty-seven small towns in the interior of Pernambuco without police chiefs.

22. In 2008, forty civil police officers and forty-five military police ran for mayor, while 1,022 civil police and 2,937 military police officers ran for seats on the city council. More officers may have run, but registered themselves as "public employees." Data from the Tribunal Superior Eleitoral, reported in Daniel Roncaglia, "Mais de 4 mil policiais são candidatos nessas eleições," October 2, 2008, www .conjur.com.br/2008-out-02/mil_policiais_sao_candidatos_nessas_eleicoes.

23. This compared to only around sixty officers running in São Paulo City, according to the state association of civil police scribes.

24. Its logo—a skull and crossbones—gave a clue as to its more unsavory activities.

25. In the Rondônia case cited earlier, the state judiciary had been similarly implicated through the involvement of a state appeals court judge, guaranteeing that any investigations could be blocked in the courts.

26. Gratz had invited one of the few uncompromised state legislators, Claudio Vereza, to head the commission, but he withdrew the invitation when Vereza and his PT colleagues set out the conditions under which they wished to conduct the inquiry (Global Justice 2002b, 41).

27. The report, a quarter of it focused on Espírito Santo, was conducted by the Chamber of Deputies' CPI on Drug Trafficking.

28. He was also accused of the political murder in 1992 of state governor Edmundo Pinto.

29. Pascoal was tried in the first instance federal court in the Federal District: the trial was not held in Acre because of lack of security.

30. Annual reports issued by Reporters without Borders (http://en.rsf.org/) note that eight journalists were killed between 2002 and 2008. Many more have received death threats, been assaulted, or had their offices ransacked.

31. Márcio Thomaz Bastos, Lula's personal criminal lawyer from his trade union days, and Tarso Genro, former mayor of Porto Alegre and PT grandee, who led the internal party protests against the corruption scandals in which the party found itself embroiled.

32. Judges even went on strike over antinepotism proposals to prevent them from employing relatives.

33. Paragraph 5 of Article 109 of the Constitution was amended in 2004 to read, "In order to comply with the obligations imposed by international treaties to which Brazil is party, the Federal Attorney General has the power, in the event of gross human rights violations, to ask the Supreme Court of Justice to shift the competence from the state to the federal justice system at any stage of the investigation or trial" (my translation).

Chapter Ten

Conclusion

The Web of Accountability Institutions in Brazil

TIMOTHY J. POWER & MATTHEW M. TAYLOR

This project embarked from the now ubiquitous assumption that corruption is a destabilizing force in transitional democracies. In contrast to the "functionalist" assumptions of a half century ago that saw corruption "greasing" the wheels of development (Huntington 1968; Leff 1964; Nye 1967), we follow more recent findings that illustrate that corruption is pernicious: corruption distorts policy making, lessens the public-regardingness of government action, and undermines the trust essential to democracy. Our second starting point was that accountability is therefore a public good. There is room for complaints that accountability processes gum up the works and unreasonably burden public bureaucracies and that there may be a trade-off between the pursuit of efficiency and the quest for probity (e.g., Light 1993; Behn 2001; Philp 2009). But the salience of political corruption on the Brazilian public agenda, and its enormous human and political costs, suggest that for the time being, at least, probity is the greater worry.

In the course of the past century, political corruption has frequently been a focal point of Brazilian politics: the military revolts of the 1920s justified themselves in part by allusion to the corruption of the First Republic; Getulio Vargas's suicide in 1954 was a desperate response to an opposition campaign against the "sea of mud" in his government; Juscelino Kubitshek's "fifty years of progress in five" was marred by accusations of grand corruption; Jânio Quadros came to office using a broom as his campaign symbol; and the military seized power in 1964 promising to "stamp out communism and corruption" (Fleischer 1997, 298; Carvalho 2008). More recently, as the Introduction pointed out, corruption has been a persistent theme of political life under the post-1985 democratic regime.

What is different this time around? Is the seemingly renewed interest in accountability anything more than a convenient tactic for bashing one's political opponents and weakening them at the ballot box? While we have been cautious in our interpretations, we do not believe that contemporary attention to corruption is purely instrumental. In large part, this is because the accumulated experience of the past two and half decades of Brazilian democracy suggests a genuine collective interest in improving accountability, a drive within bureaucracies for gains in this regard, and—most important—real improvements. During the transition to democracy in the 1980s, few analysts paid much attention to corruption per se, and of those who did, few placed accountability high on the agenda. Over the past generation, the rising international prominence of the anticorruption agenda, stimulated by the creation of Transparency International and the assimilation of its core message by multilateral organizations and national governments, has slowly pushed corruption to the forefront. Within Brazil, deepening democratic practices, greater media freedoms, and growing citizen activism have also all increased awareness of the issue. And exhaustion with the seemingly unending string of scandals is pervasive: even before the *mensalão* scandal struck, Brazilians surveyed for Transparency International's 2004 Global Corruption Barometer ranked corruption alongside crime and violence, poverty and unemployment, as one of the most important issues facing the nation.

Despite the prominence of corruption on the public agenda, however, the essays in this book point to the difficulty of combating it effectively. In part this is an outcome of institutional weaknesses—budgetary shortfalls, incomplete or purposefully weak laws, staffing limits, internal inefficiencies, and so forth—that are considerable. But the challenge of controlling corruption is also a more broadly systemic issue, driven in two ways by the interdependence of all the component institutions in the broader web of accountability: first, by the web's magnification of the *weaknesses* of individual institutions, and second, by the *interdependence* of component institutions in the web. In this concluding chapter, we draw on both phenomena to advance some preliminary conclusions about the possibilities for effective accountability in Brazil. Working from the analyses in this volume as well as lessons from the international experience, we then discuss possible policy recommendations for the future and, finally, lessons for scholars working on similar issues in other democracies.

Institutions, Institutional Interdependence, and the Web of Accountability

The Weakness of Individual Agencies

A first problem—the weakness of some (but by no means all) of the key accountability institutions—is relatively simple, but it is compounded and magnified as the effects of individual, poorly functioning institutions ripple through the web of accountability. Individual institutions' weaknesses are retransmitted throughout the web and undermine even those institutions that are working reasonably well, forcing them to adopt strategies and tactics that are not necessarily first-best, as well as to privilege certain stages of the accountability process and certain types of sanctions over others.

To give just one example, the slow judicial system has an effect that extends beyond courts to other institutions. Corruption scandals tend to follow a well-rehearsed and disheartening script. Corruption is initially exposed in a cacophony of revelations coming from multiple, overlapping and sometimes competing investigations, amplified by the reporting of an eager media. Eventually, the tide of revelations subsides as investigations peter out for lack of further evidence and media attention turns elsewhere. If the amount of evidence and public pressure is great enough, political institutions may do their part to punish offenses before the legal cases begin their tortuous and lengthy route through the courts. And from that point on, the media will only occasionally return to the figures at the center of the scandal—such as Fernando Collor, Paulo Maluf, P. C. Farias, Marcos Valério, José Dirceu, or Roberto Jefferson—chronicling the curious paths their political and personal lives have taken, with occasional reference to how their appeals are faring in the courts. These "where are they now?" stories rarely detect evidence of accountability. The result is a generalized feeling of impunity, as well as a significant loss of confidence not only in the courts but also in the political system and the bureaucracies that were at the center of the initial investigations. The weakness of the courts also leads other institutions to compensate in various ways, privileging their own weaker sanctions (such as leaks to the media or administrative fines) over more punitive but highly uncertain judicial punishments.

We pointed at the outset of this volume to how the characteristics of individual institutions in the web of accountability—scope, autonomy, proximate institutions, and activation—influence their potential roles. As we think about discrete institutions, the first two characteristics are particularly relevant. Some institutions are greatly limited in what they can do by the scope of their institutional mandate. But the autonomy of individual agencies from political pressures also varies greatly and can substantially alter the course of the accountability process. In the cases of the Federal Police, the executive branch task force on financial transactions (Council for the Control of Financial Activities, COAF), and the Federal Accounting Tribunal (TCU) especially, the considerable political pressures to which members of the bureaucracy are submitted clearly influence the course of their work. COAF, for example, is able to investigate fewer than 1% of the irregular bank transactions to which it is alerted. It has considerable discretion in choosing which cases to investigate and has been accused of making this choice largely on the basis of political criteria.[1] Equally troubling are the feuding cliques within the Federal Police, who sometimes appear to choose their battles in calculated ways aimed at the political patrons of other cliques or simply at a given partisan grouping. Such politicization influences the strength of investigations as well as public perceptions of the motivations behind them; in this way, individual institutional frailties may weaken the entirety of the web of accountability.

Weaknesses within particular institutions are also clearly an issue. Some institutions are simply too politicized: congressional committees of inquiry (CPIs) are not especially effective, for example, and a vast majority of them close without a final report (A. Figueiredo 2001; *O Estado de São Paulo* 2005c) or fail to bring prosecutable charges. Some bureaucracies are just too small to do everything they are tasked to do: the federal Ministério Público, for example, has roughly nine hundred prosecutors charged with pursuing a wide range of cases in the public interest.[2] Perhaps more damaging is the fact that the autonomy of individual prosecutors means that there is little central coordination of the overall direction of the Ministério Público's anticorruption strategies (although internal groups often do set their own priorities). Similar problems of scale or direction plague a number of federal accountability institutions: the Federal Police, the Federal Comptroller's Office (CGU), the TCU, and the electoral courts among them. The size and allocation of budgets is a contentious issue in any government, and although many federal agencies are well funded in Brazil, these budgets are not always sufficient for all the tasks the agencies are asked to fulfill. Nor are scarce resources always funneled most effectively to the most central tasks, rather than to civil service pay and benefits, fancy equipment, or perks.

Finally, it will come as no surprise that perhaps the most dangerous weakness of individual bureaucracies is susceptibility to corruption itself, which can undermine even the most successful efforts and weaken trust in the accountability process. As both Rogério Arantes and Fiona Macaulay warn in this volume, the police, at both the federal and state levels, have been among the most vulnerable institutions in this regard: the record-breaking 2005 theft of more than R$150 million from the Central Bank's offices in Fortaleza, for example, set off a cinematic chase by rival police forces seeking to extract the proceeds of the heist from the original thieves. There was "accountability" for the original thieves, several of whom paid for the theft with their lives and others of whom were forced to ransom family members kidnapped by rogue police agents, but this "accountability" was of course completely at odds with any reasonable democratic conception of the rule of law. The central point is that the web of accountability is not autonomous from society or immune to its pressures; rather, it is tied to society in ways that both enhance and at times undermine its ability to effectively pursue rule breakers. If rule breakers find their way into accountability institutions, the effects on the overall accountability process can be catastrophic.

Frictions and Problems in Institutional Interaction

The second element of the accountability process has been reiterated so often that it requires little elaboration here: the natural interdependence between what we have called "proximate institutions" in the web of accountability would be a concern even if all the component institutions were individually strong and robust. Five issues of institutional interaction are worth considering as we reflect on accountability in Brazil: friction between bureaucracies; the length of the chains between proximate institutions; the effects of second-best compensatory mechanisms; the emphasis on investigation over effective monitoring or sanction; and corruption itself.

Public bureaucracies naturally generate some friction whenever they are forced to work in concert. In part because of the newness of the institutional structure—much of which was created or significantly overhauled in the 1980s and some of which was only added in the last decade—this friction has been an important feature of the Brazilian federal accountability system. Recurring tensions between immediately proximate institutions such as branches of the state (subnational) police, between police and prosecutors at all levels of the federation, and between congressional committees of inquiry and prosecutors, among others, have hampered cooperation and even led to unproductive cross-agency competition.[3]

Second, the length of the chains between proximate institutions is an important consideration. The institutional scope of some institutions places them further from the application of actual sanctions than others, and they thus must rely on more than one proximate agency if their work is to result in any reasonable degree of accountability. The CGU, for example, cannot prosecute wrongdoing on its own. Any suspicious activity its audits turn up is forwarded to the TCU, which then investigates further before sending the cases to the Ministério Público, which then must decide whether to prosecute the case in the courts. Given this lengthy and uncertain chain of events, it is not surprising that the CGU has frequently turned to public "naming and shaming" of the politicians it audits as a way of achieving a form of nonlegal, reputational accountability on its own, long before legal sanctions are even contemplated.

This brings us to a third issue: compensatory strategies adopted either formally or informally, wittingly or unwittingly, in response to the perceived weaknesses of the rest of the web of accountability. As Speck's chapter illustrated, the slow pace of the courts has meant that the TCU has increasingly given pride of place to alternative sanctions (such as fines or the firing of corrupt civil servants) that do not require it to wait on judges and the judicial process. Sidestepping the courts is a way of guaranteeing that the TCU's work leads to some sort of accountability. Few would begrudge the decisions by CGU or TCU staff to adopt second-best strategies in order to secure a few immediate results. The question, however, is to what extent such compensatory strategies are a first-best outcome for the political system as a whole. Macaulay (this volume) similarly points to the federalization of anticorruption efforts as a recent phenomenon aimed at circumventing the influence of local politicians on state accountability networks. On the one hand, this compensatory action by federal agencies helps to root out state corruption networks; less positively, however, it does nothing whatsoever to improve the underlying state institutions, thus removing incentives for state institutions to become more effective or assiduous in tackling corruption. A third example of compensatory mechanisms is the Ministério Público's use of the media to name and shame politicians outside the courts (Macaulay, this volume; Porto, this volume; Arantes, this volume; Arantes 2002). Not surprisingly, such efforts have led to considerable conflict, culminating in the push to create external controls over the Ministério Público in the form of the National Council of the Ministério Público (CONAMP).

In terms of political competition, the chapters in this volume point to at least two compensatory mechanisms through which scandal imposes electoral costs on politicians. As Lucio Rennó shows quite clearly, the multidimensionality of preferences means that corruption will not always be the central issue driving voters. But in double-ballot majoritarian elections, at least, disgruntled voters can punish politicians by making them sweat in the first round of voting. In a second vein, Carlos Pereira, Rennó, and David Samuels (this volume) illustrate that although there is indeed evidence of voter retribution for some scandals (especially if voters have been "primed" by the media), electoral accountability can be further enhanced through elite-controlled mechanisms, such as withdrawal of campaign financing. While neither first-round electoral punishment nor withholding of campaign contributions is, strictly speaking, electoral accountability in the sense of "throwing the bums out," both chapters illustrate the important costs they can impose on politicians believed to have abused the public trust.

A fourth, related concern is the interaction of institutions at each stage of the accountability process. In part because of the weakness of the courts, but also because of the weakly institutionalized relations between accountability agencies, the Brazilian web of accountability gives considerable emphasis to investigation over monitoring or sanctioning processes (Taylor and Buranelli 2007). Again, this may be in large part be due to the weakness of the judicial system: in the absence of credible or likely legal sanctions, there is little alternative but to punish wrongdoers via reputational sham-ing or political punishments such as expulsion from Congress, while hoping that voters will turn out tainted politicians in the next election. But it is also the case that when scandal breaks, most agencies jump into the investiga-tion in often chaotic and sometimes unproductive competition to demon-strate their prowess and perhaps justify their bureaucratic mandates.

The result does not always get to the bottom of the scandal at hand, nor do the competing investigations usually lead to efficacious account-ability holding. A classic example comes from the pursuit of the São Paulo politician Paulo Maluf's alleged offshore bank accounts: after five years of separate investigations, various Brazilian agencies—including the fed-eral Ministério Público, the São Paulo State Ministério Público, the Min-istry of Justice, and the COAF—began to cooperate only after foreign bank oversight officials expressed concern about the multiple requests for in-formation they were receiving from Brazil (Taylor 2009, 161–62). Such cross-bureaucracy coordination is not a problem unique to Brazil (Key Centre 2001, 109), nor would centralizing all investigations necessarily solve the problem: in fact, there may be gains from accountability insti-tutions approaching corrupt networks from various angles and in over-lapping fashion. But an absolute lack of cooperation can be remarkably counterproductive in terms of duplicated efforts and wasted resources, and there is no evidence that it leads to more effective accountability.

Finally, once again returning to the issue of corruption, the constant in-teraction between accountability institutions means that, once introduced, dirty practices can easily spread across the entire web. As Macaulay (this volume) illustrates forcefully, this problem is particularly complex when it comes to the linkages between state and federal bureaucracies. Local-level practices are often introduced—together with corruption—into federal policy making and into the accountability process at the federal level. This problem of contagion between bureaucracies is an issue even if we focus solely on the federal level, where it clearly matters which institutions are in-volved in the accountability game: some agents and some agencies are more likely to lead to effective sanctioning than others, in part because they are less susceptible to either corruption or political manipulation.

Where do these broadly systemic observations leave us? In the next section, we look first at how cross-national prescriptions for accountability might be adopted in Brazil, before reflecting more specifically on the advances of the past twenty-five years and country-specific recommendations for improvement.

Innovations Drawn from the Cross-National Literature

A common starting point in many diagnoses of the absence of accountability is structural-cultural, blaming poverty or culture for the failure of some nations to actually succeed in curbing corruption or impunity. Many structural problems undergird political corruption in Brazil, most notably inequality, and particularly its perverse effects on social structure— including through elitism and the possibilities for clientelism (Silva 2001, 14–18). Related is the problem of wealth and education. Poor countries may be more corrupt than rich countries for a number of reasons, not least the fact that citizens' ability to influence politics requires solid education, both to adequately assess what is going on and to take effective action (Almeida 2008). Wealth also makes it easier to find time to devote to the pursuit of active citizenship, which in turn "empower[s] citizens to engage with government institutions" (Glaeser et al. 2004, 3; Glaeser and Saks 2004).

Not surprisingly, research finds that anticorruption programs work best where corruption is lowest (Shah and Huther 2000; Steves and Rousso 2005). Or to put the point another way: "Accountability . . . feeds on itself. . . . The more accountability one has, the more one can get" (Morris 2009, 233; Fox 2007). The paradoxical result is that underlying structure and culture both bind our hands—they are difficult to change—yet at the same time they promise rapid change. If society can break out of a low-level equilibrium in which corruption makes sense to the corruptible and the noncorrupt are unable to devote time to combating it or see little reason to do so given low levels of interpersonal trust (Morris 2009, 201, 237), the improvements may be very quick.

For this reason, and given that we have no credible prescription for addressing such issues, we have largely foresworn cultural or structural prescriptions in this volume. Over the past three decades, democracy's equalizing tendencies have significantly altered Brazil's prevailing political culture and economic structure, giving us reason to believe that an improved institutional framework may have even more "bite" in the future, and leading us to privilege institutional explanations. This is not to say that we discount the culturalist perspective, only that because we are uncertain of how to measure culture or change it we have focused on institutional aspects that have more directly tangible effects on both accountability and, to a lesser extent, corruption. But we recognize that culture remains "a consequence, facilitator, and cause of corruption, and . . . a critical factor conditioning reformist efforts" (Morris 2009, 214).

From an institutional perspective, the existing international literature is somewhat disappointing. Lists of cross-national recommendations for fighting political corruption typically include a number of bland and often infeasible suggestions, "folk remedies," or one-size-fits-all approaches (Shah 2007, 234). Given the overall approach of this volume, targeted to understanding the interaction between specific institutions in a famously idiosyncratic national setting, it will come as no surprise that we find many of the prescriptions (e.g., creating the rule of law, reducing the size of the public sector, decentralizing government, or increasing public-sector wages; Shah and Huther 2000)—either too broad, too bland, too obvious, or too focused on alternate policy objectives to be of much use. Further, much of the legislation that is prescribed as helpful in curbing corruption, such as laws governing the civil service, financial disclosure, public procurement, freedom of information, party financing, and money laundering (Steves and Rousso 2005), already exists in Brazil.

It is encouraging, we suppose, that many of the prescribed laws and institutions are already in place. This suggests that the issue is less one of creating new institutions from whole cloth than one of tinkering with the extant institutions and streamlining both their individual performance and their interaction with others (the devil, however, will be in the details). It is also somewhat encouraging—and frequently forgotten by those studying Brazil—that in comparison with many other countries Brazil has relatively strong federal institutions that are clearly imperfect but that rise far above many of the most discouraging cases described in the literature. Indeed, the somewhat impressionistic conclusion one is left with after analyzing other countries experiences is that Brazil not only is doing fairly well but may be on the cusp of a very positive equilibrium, if it can push itself over the hump and improve the overall performance of its web of accountability.

But what can the vast international literature and experience offer us that is of specific relevance to Brazil's web of accountability? Perhaps the most important warning is that fighting corruption may not be the best way to, in fact, fight corruption (Kaufmann 2006; Shah 2007). Indeed, large-scale, top-down, highly visible public efforts that garner enormous public attention may backfire by exhausting public support, by politicizing the anticorruption effort, and, most of all, by suggesting that all it takes to defeat corruption is concentrated political will. Given the persistence of political corruption in even the most propitious economic and political settings, accountability processes require sustained, long-term effort and commitment. As Morris (2009) illustrates so convincingly in his analysis of Fox's anticorruption efforts in Mexico, the klieg-light focus of public attention on anticorruption measures is no guarantee of success, especially if leadership falters or the government's credibility suffers. In such cases, in fact, the effect may be exactly the opposite of desired. In sum, the lesson seems to be: fight corruption, but do so in ways that do not rely on a single leader, that institutionalize accountability efforts, and that are broad based, involving civil society without boosting expectations for the rapid resolution of long-standing and deep-rooted problems of inadequate accountability.

The second lesson is related: augment the information available to the public, thus increasing the ease with which potential citizen "fire alarms" can be set off, rather than relying solely on "police patrols" by specific accountability institutions.[4] In other words, make it possible for the millions of citizens to raise the alarm when things are not going well, rather than relying solely on costly and uncertain audits or other investigations by bureaucracies that may face mixed incentives. This is not to suggest investments in huge media awareness campaigns, or workshops on corruption for the media or civil servants, which have largely been shown to be a fools' errand (Shah 2007, 244). Rather, the idea is to get credible information into the public domain—not necessarily solely as an anticorruption measure, but rather as a way of allowing citizens to monitor their own government and their own representatives. Brazil does fairly well on some measures of bureaucratic transparency already: the Bellver and Kaufmann Index of Transparency (2005), for example, places the country between the seventy-fifth and ninetieth percentile cross-nationally, and the International Budget Partnership's 2008 Open Budget Index places Brazil's federal government in its second-best category ("provides significant information"), alongside

Norway, Sweden, and Germany and ahead of all other Latin American nations surveyed.

This is very encouraging, but such measures obscure significant subnational variation, as well as perhaps misrepresent the utility and accessibility of much of the available information. The quantity of data provided is not sufficient in its own right, since much of it is incomprehensible to the average citizen, and some of the available information is not necessarily accurate. As Taylor's chapter notes, much of the publicly disclosed electoral finance data, for example, is an elaborate ruse. Recent scandals have shown, furthermore, that publicly disclosed information on politicians' finances hides significant public perks (such as congressional representatives' "travel" budgets and access to public housing in Brasília). There are also many ways to shift records of illegal income from officeholders to relatives or *laranjas,* the term given to the often unwitting accomplices whose names are used to register property actually owned by corrupt public officials.

In sum, while public disclosure is not anemic in Brazil, there is room for improvement. Publicly disclosed assets and incomes, as well as campaign finance data, for both officeholders and their families could be significantly strengthened. A good model in this regard is the British House of Commons, which in the past two decades has implemented rigorous new requirements for disclosure, including regular publication of Members of Parliament's (MPs') financial interests, a code of conduct, a self-regulating Committee on Standards and Privileges, and an independent parliamentary commissioner for standards who is largely independent and charged with monitoring and investigating complaints about MPs' misconduct (Andersson and Cousinou 2009). Not only are MPs required to register their interests, but the registry—which is overseen by a select parliamentary committee—must be updated every six to eight weeks. To add greater bite to public disclosure laws, a further possibility would be to create a system of random audits of members of Congress (Azfar 2007, 264), whereby some small proportion of representatives would be chosen by lottery each year for an extensive audit led by an external commission of notable citizens, with assistance from civil servants from the TCU, the CGU, the Polícia Federal, the Ministério Público, and other public bureaucracies. If properly insulated, such a commission would not only confirm that politicians' registered data are correct but also look beyond them to relatives' stated income and assets, campaign finance registries, and so forth. Such randomized checks would hopefully engender greater honesty and completeness in the disclosure of existing data, although under Brazilian law, legislator participation would most likely need to be voluntary.[5]

There are also many examples of ways to encourage greater public participation in setting off "fire alarms" and setting priorities for accountability actions. India, for example, has a central telephone number to which members of the public may text details of corruption, which are then followed up on by the Indian equivalent of the Polícia Federal. Perhaps more productive in the long term is involving the public and civil society organizations in trying to more systematically define what the "corruption danger zones" are in any given public policy or public process (Andersson and Cousinou 2009). As Shah and Huther (2000) note, public opinion surveys have been very useful in articulating precisely citizens' concerns about corruption, from Argentina to Bangalore. Creating incentives for further research, as we will note later, is another important way of involving academics and civil society organizations. In particular, establishing regular diagnostics to set cross-temporal benchmarks of patterns of corruption or the success of accountability programs, as well as to evaluate evolving institutional performance, have been helpful tools in countries ranging from Japan to Lithuania (Transparency International 2002).

Third, the international experience suggests that "mutually antagonistic surveillance" (Gillespie and Okruhlik 1991) between government agencies should be encouraged. Given the problems of "coalitional presidentialism" described below, and the resulting dominance of the Congress by the executive branch, this is not always possible in Brazil: the interests of the executive and the dominant congressional coalition are too closely aligned, with perverse effects on supposed oversight agencies like the TCU or the CGU in overseeing corrupt practices horizontally, across the branches of government. However, with some changes, it may be possible to "destabilize corrupt agreements" (Lambsdorff, Taube, and Schramm 2004, quoted in Shah 2006, 28 n. 4) between or across branches of government. Giving current members of the opposition greater representation on congressional committees of inquiry, for example, or allowing the TCU or CGU to define some of the Ministério Público's priorities for investigation and prosecution, might help to destabilize cozy arrangements and set the branches to actually check each other.

A final, related suggestion is to increase active auditing. There is considerable proof that auditing decreases corrupt behavior, both abroad (e.g., Olken 2007 on Indonesia) and within Brazil (Ferraz and Finan 2008, forthcoming). But these efforts could be more deeply institutionalized. The use of public expenditure tracking systems (PETS), which track how money is disbursed in policy implementation from its origin through its destination (Dehn, Reinikka, and Svensson 2003), could be implemented as a rule for all federal programs. Undercover revenue service agents could imitate Mexico's Usuario Simulado program, whereby officers solicit government services to verify their quality and check for probity in their provision (Morris 2009, 97). And to keep the auditors themselves diligent, civil society organizations and private firms could be encouraged (and empowered) to reaudit existing audits, potentially receiving some type of remuneration if they uncover malfeasance where official audits did not (Azfar 2007, 272). This might go a long way to ensuring that audits by government agencies would be rigorous rather than pro forma and that they would receive the public attention that would make them effective accountability instruments.

Innovations Drawn from Brazil's Own Experience

The literature on political corruption in Brazil almost invariably returns to three central issues—the process of coalition formation, the electoral system, and the courts—to which Macaulay's chapter adds a fourth, federalism. With regard to the first, concerns with so-called *presidencialismo de coalizão* (Abranches 1988) and the unwieldiness of multiparty presidentialism (Mainwaring 1995) are long-standing, even though the system has permitted a degree of governability that has exceeded many observers' expectations (A. Figueiredo and Limongi 1999). The question that arises with regard to accountability and corruption, however, is: At what cost does this coalitional governing system work?

At the most general level, as the literature on Brazil's coalitional presidentialism shows, the strong correlation of interests between the majority coalitions in Congress and the executive branch means that checks and balances are weak (Power 2010). The Congress does not act as a particularly hard-nosed monitor of executive behavior, and even in cases of extreme wrongdoing executive influence over the majority coalition means that congressional inquiries seldom get very far in their investigations of the incumbent. Meanwhile, in the effort to facilitate cooperation with congressional allies, the president has little incentive to monitor Congress or point to legislative wrongdoing. In 2009, this point became disturbingly apparent in the scandal surrounding Senate president José Sarney, which highlighted a noxious combination of nepotistic appointments to unelected sinecures on the Senate staff, cozy relations between private-sector companies and legislators, and, perhaps most damaging, the use of "secret" regulations to distribute jobs and resources from the gargantuan Senate budget (roughly US$1.2 billion in 2008). Far from decrying these behaviors, the executive branch worked hard to protect its legislative allies, including Sarney, and even pushed coalition members—including the Workers' Party, which had once campaigned on a proethics platform—to quash Senate hearings on the matter.

Further, the process of coalition formation has frequently led to the "auctioning off" of ministries and state enterprises for legislative support; politicians take charge of these public agencies with a view not necessarily to serving the public good but to raising campaign funds and building or strengthening clientelistic networks. As the Federal Police report on the *mensalão* noted, for many years resources from public bureaucracies have been "funneled to political parties infiltrated in public enterprises [to] the ruin of taxpayers . . . through frauds of all types" (*Veja* 2008, our translation).[6] Pereira, Power, and Raile (this volume) point out, furthermore, that if for whatever reason the executive cannot provide sinecures in public agencies to legislative allies, it may resort to equally unsavory compensatory arrangements, such as "cash for policy" schemes like the *mensalão*, to ensure coalition support. To aggravate matters, coalition building follows a similar pattern at the state level, leading the authors to conclude that "we have not seen the last of this volatile connection between corruption and coalition building."

Second, the electoral system is widely believed to pose a fundamental problem, especially in proportional representation electoral contests (e.g., for congressional deputy), where the districts are statewide and the electoral lists are open. The large size of districts and the sheer number of parties and candidates mean that it is notoriously difficult for individual voters to monitor and hold congressional representatives clearly accountable, leading to some of the compensatory punitive strategies described earlier.

Third, the judiciary is an extraordinarily ineffective institution when it comes to addressing political corruption. Not only do the prevailing rules provide considerable privileges to politicians, such as a tradition of deference by justices and concrete privileges like the *foro privilegiado,* but the court system is also plagued by remarkable procedural delays (Arantes, this volume; Taylor, this volume). Even though judges are highly trained and selected from the most talented echelons of the legal community, these privileges and inefficiencies in the court system greatly complicate the task of effectively and efficiently imposing legal sanctions on the guilty or, just as importantly, of clearing the names of those who are not guilty.

Finally, as Macaulay points out, the complexities of federalism mean that corrupt political actors can find shelter from accountability at various levels of government—federal, state, and municipal—as well as obtain support from political allies across the three branches of government. The result is not only that political corruption spreads "rhyzomically" up and across government but also that accountability suffers correspondingly. Compensatory federal accountability efforts are helpful but will ultimately be insufficient—and may even be undermined—if they do not tackle the weakness of state and local institutions.

Could these four sources of political corruption and weak accountability be eliminated? It seems doubtful, at least in the short term, in large part because the current players in this system are the very same players whose support would be needed to approve any meaningful change. The judicial reform of 2004 was a step in the right direction,[7] but it was rather lackluster in improving aspects of the courts that would most contribute to anticorruption efforts, such as efficiency, which it addressed only timidly, and politicians' privileges, which it touched not at all. Furthermore, the effort seems to have exhausted the political initiative for further judicial reform, at least for the time being. Electoral reforms, meanwhile, have had a troubled past: most recently, a law that would have created minimum thresholds for party representation in Congress (and thus, it was hoped, reduce the extraordinary fragmentation of the party system) was overturned by the Supreme Federal Tribunal (STF). The law had been approved in

1996 for implementation one decade later, a delay aimed at getting it past the self-interest of incumbent politicians. But the STF overturned the law when it went into effect in 2006 on an appeal by small parties, who argued that it would hurt minority rights (Marchetti 2008). Partly as a result, there seems to be little likelihood of any major overhaul in the electoral system in the near future. Without either electoral or judicial reforms, furthermore, it seems unlikely that the prevailing pattern of coalition formation will change on its own. The executive branch simply has too much at stake: coalition support is essential to governability, and the incumbent members of the coalition do not want to overturn the formal and informal rules that got them where they are. Finally, the weaknesses of subnational accountability processes can be helped along with occasional federal interventions, but changes in Brazil's long-standing federal structure seem unlikely, and the enormous quantity of veto players mean that reforms to eliminate or significantly overhaul lower-level justice institutions are also a nonstarter.

The result is that realistically, barring a cataclysmic scandal that dwarfs all those that have come before, accountability reforms will not be momentous or regime altering but instead small-bore, incremental, and ongoing. While less satisfying in the short run, the results of incrementalism may well be better tailored to the Brazilian political system and will allow for useful experimentation and review. Further, useful ideas for incremental reform are already circulating widely in the public domain (e.g., Nicolau and Power 2007; F. Santos and Vilarouca 2008).

Before moving to some of these ideas, it is worth pausing to reiterate again just how far Brazil has come in the past generation. New institutions such as the CGU and COAF have been created from scratch. Others, such as the Ministério Público, the Polícia Federal, and the Federal Revenue Service (Receita Federal), have seen their powers expanded considerably. New legislation has also been written that greatly clarifies the rules and thereby facilitates the accountability process, such as the so-called Law of Administrative Improbity, which sets out the rules for civil service behavior (Law 8429 of 1992), a law on public bidding procedures (Law 8666 of 1993), and a law on money laundering that created the COAF and established a national registry of clients of the financial system to facilitate money tracking (Law 9613 of 1998), among many others.[8] Meanwhile, Brazil does very well on many measures of transparency and bureaucratic quality. Brazil's banking regulations meet or exceed top-notch international standards. Its federal civil service is considered the most developed and functionally capable in Latin America (Stein et al. 2005, 68–69). And as noted earlier, it has many of the institutions the cross-national literature finds desirable, from an independent judiciary to an anticorruption agency, the CGU.

Further, individual agencies have strengthened their own internal rules and tried to improve their oversight in many different ways. Sometimes, agencies have smuggled helpful changes into legislation that seemingly has little to do with accountability: the CPMF tax on financial transactions was created largely to provide the fiscal solvency needed to combat inflation, for example. But the enabling legislation permitted the Receita Federal to evaluate individuals' tax declarations against the size of their financial flows and thus to target those whose transactions far outstripped their declared income. Other relatively straightforward bureaucratic innovations also have considerable effect, such as the creation of the SIAFI and SISBACEN systems, which permit the tracking of financial transactions across financial institutions. If nothing else, these innovations disrupt the business of corruption by forcing transgressors into ever more byzantine arrangements for hiding and laundering their ill-gotten gains.

Sometimes scandals themselves contribute to policy change, as when the National Monetary Council (CMN) in 2005 restricted access to one of the most used means of transferring illicit gains abroad (so-called CC-5 accounts), in the wake of several scandals early in Lula's term, or when President Cardoso created a Code of Public Ethics by executive decree in 2000, as two simultaneous congressional investigations threatened his administration's public image (Fleischer 2002, 27). Likewise, the affair that led to Collor's impeachment resulted in a more realistic electoral finance system in which private donations are no longer banned. Instead, they are accepted but monitored, and there has been a concomitant and quite substantial real increase in the volume of public campaign financing (Speck 2005, 130–32). In response to the *mensalão* scandal, the TSE proposed and the Congress approved greater penalties for off-the-books campaign finance, increasing jail time and fines for scofflaws. And in an unprecedented action, in December 2007, the Federal Revenue Service followed up on the TSE's recommendation and suspended the tax exemption of seven major political parties, arguing that because they had cooked their books they had forfeited their constitutionally guaranteed tax exemption. These innovations point to one frequent benefit of scandal in democracy: the possibility of retroactive corrective measures aimed at tackling systemic weaknesses.

Government agencies have also worked to reach out and incorporate citizens in the pursuit of corrupt players, through instruments such as the CGU's Portal de Transparência, which allows anyone with access to the Internet to track federal spending in great detail. The media have gained importance, and their "bark" has helped to expose corrupt officials, impose reputational costs on wrongdoing, and push anticorruption agencies to prosecute dishonest officials (Porto, this volume).

Civil society groups active in fighting corruption have expanded remarkably in recent years, to great effect. One of their greatest triumphs came in 1999, when a proposal for a law increasing the penalties for vote buying obtained the signatures of 1% of the voting population (the proportion needed to propose a law to Congress under a rarely used article of the Constitution that permits "popular initiatives"). With such strong popular pressure—a million signatures—it was perhaps inevitable that the law (Law 9840 of 1999) would be approved by Congress. Similarly, in 2010 Congress approved a law proposed via popular initiative that would bar candidates who have been convicted of any crime in an appeals court from running for office (the so-called Lei Ficha Limpa). This corrects the previous practice, whereby politicians' electoral rights could be suspended only if they had received a final conviction, without possibility of any further appeal. Citizen efforts have sometimes been helped along by seemingly extraneous factors: for example, transparency and citizen participation have been greatly improved by the stabilization of the economy, which has permitted comparison of government spending across time and thus rapid "reality checks" without the need for daily currency adjustments, a price index, and an accountant.

All of these changes point to the sorts of shifts at the margin that over time may add up to great progress. What other changes might be helpful?

The individual chapters in this volume have already pointed to some suggestions for individual institutions. Within the judiciary, for example, despite its timidity, the 2004 reform was an important starting point because it demonstrated great concern for making the courts more rational, responsive, and efficient. It created a National Judicial Council (CNJ) and a National Council of the Ministério Público (CONAMP) to oversee judges and prosecutors: these are likely to curb some of the worst abuses within these institutions, such as nepotism, abusively high salaries, and individual corruption. But from the perspective of holding accountable actors outside the judiciary, the reform appears to have brought only marginal gains in efficiency and perhaps rationality.

Incremental reform proposals for the courts, then, include efforts to restrict the number of appeals, or at the very least to ensure that once convicted of common crimes in an appeals court, criminals would be able to appeal only from behind bars. This contrasts with the current practice, where the requirement of a final, unappealable conviction provides great incentives for protracted legal wrangling and in the process generates a volume of appeals that engenders systemic delays. This also suggests the need for a deeper review of the criminal code,[9] with an eye to fighting corruption specifically. Further, a change in the period of prescription for many crimes would be useful to dissuade defendants from delaying tactics aimed only at "running out the clock."[10]

Within Congress, one upside of the many scandals since the transition has been a number of corrective measures that would otherwise have been extremely unlikely. In the wake of the *mensalão,* as noted above, Congress approved more stringent punishments for illicit campaign finance. Similarly, in the wake of the congressional budget scandal of the early 1990s, it approved changes in the legislative process to circumscribe the discretionary powers of the congressional budget committee (Praça 2007, 15) and to modify bidding processes for public procurement (Fleischer 1997, 305–9). And perhaps most important, Congress in 2001 approved a constitutional amendment that allows the STF to hear cases against politicians without first obtaining the authorization of both houses of Congress (a protection written into the 1988 Constitution as a defense against potential authoritarian abuses). Incremental reform proposals that might deepen these gains include greater tracking of representatives' claimed sources of wealth, along the lines described in the previous section; a deepening of incipient efforts against nepotism in Congress; and further restrictions on politicians' "right" to the *foro especial* in all but the most clearly political of charges.[11]

Specific reforms to the various bureaucracies discussed in this book include an increase in the proportion of TCU ministers chosen from within the TCU bureaucracy (or at least, from outside the world of electoral politics); the tightening of laws such as the money-laundering law to better define crimes and facilitate their prosecution; a concerted effort to create and expand the powers and autonomy of ombuds offices within all ministries and state enterprises; further reductions in bank secrecy; the elimination of secrecy in some court cases, especially those related to corruption; stronger freedom-of-information laws, so as to increase public oversight and decrease journalists' reliance on leaks from officialdom; stronger oversight of public servants' income and wealth; and, especially crucial to the success of accountability efforts, strong and credible protections for whistle-blowers, witnesses, prosecutors, and judges.[12] It is perhaps imprudent to go into more specifics—those must come from within the various bureaucracies and be guided by practitioners—but the point is that many of the bureaucracies in the web of accountability have given considerable thought to how to improve their work and its outcomes. With high-level political leadership and coordination, this wellspring of ideas could be readily tapped.

One of the most promising interactive efforts to generate practical solutions in this regard has come from the National Strategy for Combating Corruption and Money Laundering (ENCCLA), which since 2004 has brought together representatives of a large number of institutions—including the Ministério Público, the Central Bank, TCU, CGU, AGU, and the Revenue Service, among others—for annual meetings to discuss reform proposals and attempt to prioritize them with an eye to curtailing money laundering and corruption. The ENCCLA is coordinated through the Ministry of Justice, but despite the potentially weaker autonomy this suggests, it is a valuable effort to extend cross-institutional cooperation in considering and implementing incremental reforms and increasing communication and information sharing between distinct institutions. The exercise allows individual bureaucrats to better comprehend the constraints their peers in other agencies work under, as well as to evaluate specific reform recommendations backed by their expert analysis from the inside. Such regular brainstorming, if backed by high-level political support, is likely to be the source of considerable innovation and, equally important, critical appraisal of the effectiveness of ongoing reform efforts and reform priorities.

We conclude this section with three additional, if rather imprecise, proposals. The first would be an effort to prioritize punishments against corruptors as well as the corrupt. This is a complicated task, given that the line between being a corruptor and being shaken down by corrupt public officials can be very tenuous. Is a firm that makes illegal campaign contributions doing so to achieve legislative gains, or is it being forced to do so to prevent greater legislative losses? Perhaps more to the point, these ambiguities, combined with weak and vaguely written legislation, set high hurdles for prosecutors trying to convict. That said, there have been plenty of unambiguous cases of the corruption of public agents in which it was clear that the two sides were actively complicit. It is also clear that the demonstration effect from effective prosecution of corruptors would be enormous and would provide a useful argument for businesspeople to employ against shakedowns in the future.

The second proposal is for greater and more systematic research. We know very little about some institutions that are either secretive (e.g., the Brazilian Intelligence Agency, ABIN), relatively new (e.g., the CGU), or simply understudied (e.g., the Ministry of Justice and the Revenue Service). We know even less about subnational agencies, subnational webs of accountability, or the interactions between corrupt networks at the state and federal levels. Prizes for research on country-specific corruption are a useful way of encouraging academics and civil society organizations to engage the issue. The CGU already gives awards for some types of research, but these could arguably be extended; currently, too much academic research and policy prescription seems to be focused on responding to the latest scandal, rather than analyzing underlying patterns of corruption or corrective measures. And civil society organizations could be more actively involved in the development of anticorruption strategies, their implementation, and their evaluation (Steves and Rousso 2005), rather than leaving the work solely to civil servants who do not always have all the information or autonomy they need to proceed effectively. Prizes for actual proposals of effective anticorruption legislation, programs, or projects might be very effective in coaxing academia and civil society toward pragmatism (Azfar 2007, 272).

A third proposal is to highlight even more widely the danger and the costs posed by political corruption. Corruption is not simply bribe taking or a wink-wink, nudge-nudge form of campaign finance. As Macaulay argues, the protagonists of political corruption are often involved in a host of illegal transactions "across the spectrum of political clientelism, corruption, black market economy, contraband, and criminal violence." For the public, awareness of high-level political-criminal networks may be discouraging and even frightening. But the fact that such networks can be tackled from a variety of angles offers reason for hope. As the famous story of Al Capone's conviction for tax evasion illustrates, so long as *some* way of disrupting the network is available, it does not matter greatly what instrument is used. Furthermore, by removing the network from power, it may be possible to achieve great marginal gains in fighting a host of criminal activities, of which political corruption is only one.

Final Thoughts

Throughout this volume, we have focused on the Brazilian case, partly to reduce the effects of cultural or historical variance, but mainly because it is very difficult to think in configurational terms about the interactions between institutions while also comparing these institutions and interactions across national boundaries. A single-country study has allowed us to delve more deeply into the individual institutions with an eye to the complex ways they interact in the overall accountability process. As Paul Pierson stated in another context, this has enabled us to gain "an appreciation of institutional complementarities—the ways in which multiple, interacting institutions and policies can come to constitute distinctive regimes that facilitate particular kinds of political action and generate divergent social outcomes" (2004, 8).

Future researchers might well extend this single-country case study approach to other nations, which would produce useful thick description and provide the local-level insights that might permit later, cross-national comparison of specific interactions between accountability institutions or specific types of webs of accountability. Future research also seems likely to gain greatly from comparing not only distinctive accountability regimes but also the various types of corrupt processes—cash for policy, for example, or grand corruption—so as to better understand how these processes function in cross-national perspective and thus how they can be effectively disrupted and uprooted.

For now, perhaps the clearest lesson for comparative scholars is that Brazil's democratic accountability institutions have required time to settle into place, to learn how to work on their own and then jointly, and to find ways of cooperating to develop corrective improvements. This experience offers further backing to the argument that it may take some time for democracies to ramp up their anticorruption efforts, although there is also reason to suspect that they may be more effective over the long haul in providing accountability than other regime types (Thacker 2009).

Like other forms of human cooperation, accountability holding relies heavily on four basic elements: coercion, interests, values, and personal bonds (B. Williams 1988). In this volume, we have focused largely on the institutional aspects of the first element: how institutions work together to ensure that corrupt processes are rooted out, that sanctions are imposed, and that wrongdoers are removed from positions of power. Certainly the coercive function of the web of accountability—which influences the perceived costs and benefits of political corruption—has a large role to play in dissuading corruption. But shared interests, values, and personal bonds are likely to drive the integrity system to become truly self-sustaining: to operate in a self-correcting fashion, with an eye to collective well-being. Indeed, this is the central reason why it seems to us that the consolidation of Brazilian democracy has sparked a genuine interest in accountability and why, despite many scandals, there have also been so many genuine improvements in accountability over the past quarter century. The most important force driving the ongoing process of tinkering and incremental adjustment has been the broad societal consensus that corruption—and especially political corruption—is a major problem. This consensus, and the shared interests and values that undergird it, keeps corruption on the public agenda and drives accountability institutions forward in an ongoing process that seems likely to deepen alongside democracy itself. The more that can be done to improve the performance of these accountability institutions, the more likely that cooperation and consensus between Brazilians will grow, deepening the societal underpinnings for enhanced accountability.

Notes

1. One prominent example of the political use of the COAF was the ill-considered decision to look into the bank accounts of a house caretaker, Francenildo Santos Costa, when he blew the whistle on the comings and goings of Finance Minister Palocci at a private home in Brasília. The uproar over this meddling

in Francenildo's private finances led directly to Palocci's resignation in March 2006. (In August 2009, Palocci was absolved of wrongdoing in this matter by a 5–4 vote of the STF).

2. These are not the only prosecutors at the federal level, however. A number of *procuradores* act on behalf of the federal government: the Procuradoria Geral da Fazenda Nacional has roughly one thousand lawyers who defend the Federal Revenue Service (Receita Federal) in tax cases, and the INSS social security agency has roughly seven hundred lawyers that work on its behalf. But the work of prosecutors in the Ministério Público is qualitatively different from that of prosecutors subordinated to the executive branch, and it tends to be much more focused on tasks related to accountability per se.

3. Ongoing relations between proximate institutions are not the only forms of interaction or the only sources of cross-agency friction. Institutions that are not usually proximate often interact in ad hoc ways. In the case of congressional committees of inquiry, for example, a relatively recent phenomenon is the intervention of the STF to protect the rights of those being investigated by Congress. In the case of the *mensalão,* for example, the STF intervened in the congressional inquiries on multiple occasions at the behest of those being investigated. This is not to impugn such interference by the high court, which actually may enhance the legitimacy of congressional proceedings and the accountability process overall. But it does introduce elements of delay and uncertainty that have ambiguous effects on public sentiment, and the novelty of the court's intervention can lead to incredulity, especially if coverage of the scandal is extensive.

4. The concept of "police patrols" and "fire alarms" was developed by McCubbins and Schwartz (1984), who argued that the way in which oversight safeguards operate influences their effectiveness in U.S. executive-legislative relations. Police patrols, whereby bureaucratic agencies created by Congress "patrol" the executive, are considered less effective and more costly than "fire alarms," whereby citizens and interest groups keep a looser watch over issues that concern them directly, raising an alarm if things are not going as they wish.

5. We are grateful to Claudio Weber Abramo for noting, in a seminar presenting our research at the University of São Paulo, that random auditing of Brazilian members of Congress without their prior consent would most likely be considered an unconstitutional violation of the right to secrecy. This is an important and probably realistic caveat, but such audits might nonetheless be possible on a voluntary basis, with the "naming and shaming" of legislators who refused to participate in the audits.

6. "Ao longo dos anos vem ocorrendo, tanto nos correios quanto em outras empresas estatais do país, uma espécie de 'loteamento' dos cargos em comissão. . . . Através desse instrumento censurável, busca-se angariar recursos financeiros junto às empresas privadas. . . . Esses recursos, geralmente provenientes de 'caixa dois', são, em parte, destinados aos partidos políticos infiltrados nas empre-

sas públicas à custa da dilapidação do erário levado a cabo por meio de fraudes de toda ordem."

7. As chapter 7 noted, the constitutional reform to the judiciary approved in 2004 required a major political investment by the Lula government and followed years of debate over how to improve the courts.

8. Despite its important contributions, the money-laundering law has been criticized, including by some of the very agencies that were behind its creation, for failing to set rules that are specific enough to permit effective prosecution.

9. The Lula administration in 2007 proposed changes in the criminal code that include a reduction in the number of possible appeals and the expansion of preventive imprisonment, but these have not been approved by Congress and do not seem to be a high political priority.

10. The Senate has approved a proposal that would change the way the period of prescription is calculated; it has not been approved in the Chamber, however.

11. Congress in 2001 reduced (but did not completely eliminate) congressional immunity from prosecution for "common crimes," but the right to the *foro especial* for elected representatives remains in place, even in such crimes. There are good arguments for preserving the *foro especial* in cases where authorities are being sued for choices made in their role as public servants (e.g., for building a dam or rescuing a bank); there are seemingly fewer justifications for its use when a politician commits a crime unrelated to his or her position, such as murder. The constitutional committee of the Chamber in March 2008 approved a proposal (PEC 130/07) that would eliminate politicians' right to the *foro especial* in common crimes but not in political disputes. This has not gone to a floor vote as of this writing.

12. In the past decade, both criminal plea bargaining and witness protection have been introduced into the Brazilian legal system. However, the protections are not yet sufficiently credible to lead to the types of high-level defections that are needed to effectively target organized political-criminal networks.

References

Abramo, Claudio Weber. 2006. "Percepções pantanosas." *Revista da CGU* 1 (1): 117–21.

———. 2007. "Brazil: A Portrait of Disparities." *Brazilian Journalism Research* 3 (1): 93–107.

Abranches, Sérgio Henrique de. 1988. "Presidencialismo de coalizão: O dilema institucional brasileiro." *Dados* 31:5–38.

Abreu, Alzira. 2002. "Imprensa e responsabilidade política." Paper presented at the XI Encontro Nacional da Associação Nacional dos Programas de Pós-Graduação em Comunicação, Rio de Janeiro, Brazil.

Abrucio, Fernando Luiz. 1998. *Os barões da federação: Os governadores e a re-democratização.* São Paulo: Hucitec.

Albuquerque, Afonso de. 2005. "Another 'Fourth Branch': Press and Political Culture in Brazil." *Journalism* 6 (4): 486–504.

Almeida, Alberto Carlos. 2001. "A esquerda dos números à direita dos fatos." *Insight Inteligencia,* no. 15:112–28.

———. 2007. *A cabeça do brasileiro.* Rio de Janeiro: Editora Record.

———. 2008. "Core Values, Education, and Democracy: An Empirical Tour of DaMatta's Brazil." In *Democratic Brazil Revisited,* ed. Peter R. Kingstone and Timothy J. Power, 233–56. Pittsburgh: University of Pittsburgh Press.

Almond, Gabriel A., and G. Bingham Powell Jr. 1966. *Comparative Politics: A Developmental Approach.* Boston: Little, Brown.

Alston, Lee J., and Bernardo Mueller. 2006. "Pork for Policy: Executive and Legislative Exchange in Brazil." *Journal of Law, Economics, and Organization* 22 (1): 87–114.

Alves, Rosental. 2005. "From Lapdog to Watchdog: The Role of the Press in Latin America's Democratization." In *Making Journalists,* ed. Hugo de Burgh, 181–202. New York: Routledge.

Amaral, Oswaldo. Forthcoming. "PT, um outro partido: As tranformações do Partido dos Trabalhadores entre 1995 e 2006." PhD diss., University of Campinas.

Amaral, Roberto, and Cesar Guimarães. 1994. "Media Monopoly in Brazil." *Journal of Communication* 44 (4): 26–38.

AMB. See Associação dos Magistrados Brasileiros.

Ames, Barry. 1995a. "Electoral Rules, Constituency Pressures, and Pork Barrel: Bases of Voting in the Brazilian Congress." *Journal of Politics* 57 (2): 324–43.

———. 1995b. "Electoral Strategy under Open-List Proportional Representation." *American Journal of Political Science* 39 (2): 406–33.

———. 2000. *The Deadlock of Democracy in Brazil.* Ann Arbor: University of Michigan Press.

Ames, Barry, Andy Baker, and Lucio R. Rennó. 2008. "The Quality of Elections in Brazil: Policy, Performance, Pageantry or Pork?" In *Democratic Brazil Revisited,* ed. Timothy J. Power and Peter R. Kingstone. Pittsburgh: University of Pittsburgh Press.

Amorim Neto, Octávio. 2002. "Presidential Cabinets, Electoral Cycles, and Coalition Discipline in Brazil." In *Legislative Politics in Latin America,* ed. Scott Morgenstern and Benito Nacif, 48–78. Cambridge: Cambridge University Press.

———. 2007. "O poder executivo, centro de gravidade do sistema politico brasileiro." In *Sistema político brasileiro: Uma introdução,* 123–33. Rio de Janeiro: Fundação Konrad Adenauer.

Amorim Neto, Octávio, and Carlos Frederico Coelho. 2008. "Brasil en el 2007: El desencuentro entre la economía y la política." *Revista de Ciencia Política* 28 (1): 81–102.

Amorim Neto, Octavio, Gary W. Cox, and Mathew D. McCubbins. 2003. "Agenda Power in Brazil's *Câmara dos Deputados,* 1989–98." *World Politics* 55 (4): 550–78.

Andersson, Staffan, and Gloria Martínez Cousinou. 2009. "A Framework for the Comparative Analysis of Measures to Curb Political Corruption." March 20. Social Science Research Network Working Paper Series. http://papers.ssrn.com/sol3/papers.cfm?abstract_id=1366035.

Andrews, Josephine T., and Gabriella R. Montinola. 2004. "Veto Players and the Rule of Law in Emerging Democracies." *Comparative Political Studies* 37 (1): 55–87.

Arantes, Rogério Bastos. 2000. "Ministério Público e corrupção política em São Paulo." In *Justiça e cidadania no Brasil,* ed. Maria Tereza Sadek, 39–156. São Paulo: Editora Sumaré.

———. 2002. *Ministério Público e política no Brasil.* São Paulo: Editora Sumaré.

———. 2007. "Ministério Público na fronteira entre a justiça e a política." *Justitia* 197 (July–December): 325–35.

Arantes, Rogério B., Fernando Abrucio, and Marco Teixeira. 2005. "A imagem dos Tribunais de Contas subnacionais." *Revista do Serviço Público* 56 (1): 57–83.

Arantes, Rogério B., and Luciana Cunha. 2003. "Polícia Civil e segurança pública: Problemas de funcionamento e perspectivas de reforma." In *Delegados de polícia,* ed. Maria Tereza Sadek. São Paulo: Editora Sumaré.

Araujo, Luis, Carlos Pereira, and Eric D. Raile. 2008. "Bargaining and Governance in Multiparty Presidential Regimes." Paper presented at the annual meeting of the International Society for New Institutional Economics, Toronto, Canada.

Arias, Enrique Desmond. 2006. *Drugs and Democracy in Rio de Janeiro: Trafficking, Social Networks and Public Security.* Chapel Hill: University of North Carolina Press.

Associação dos Magistrados Brasileiros. 2007. *Juízes contra a corrupção.* Brasilia: AMB.

Avritzer, Leonardo. 2008. "Índices de percepção da corrupção." In *Corrupção: Ensaios e Críticas,* ed. Leonardo Avritzer, Newton Bignotto, Juarez Guimarães, and Heloisa Maria Murgel Starling. Belo Horizonte: Editora UFMG.

Azevedo, Fernando. 2006. "Mídia e democracia no Brasil: Relações entre o sistema de mídia e o sistema político." *Opinião Pública* 12 (1): 88–113.

Azfar, Omar. 2007. "Disrupting Corruption." In *Performance Accountability and Combating Corruption,* ed. Anwar Shah, 255–84. Washington, DC: World Bank.

Bailey, John. 2009. "Corruption and Democratic Governability." *Corruption and Democracy in Latin America,* ed. Charles H. Blake and Stephen D. Morris, 60–76. Pittsburgh: University of Pittsburgh Press.

Bailey, John, and Lucía Dammert, eds. 2006. *Public Security and Police Reform in the Americas.* Pittsburgh: University of Pittsburgh Press.

Bailey, John, and Pablo Paras. 2006. "Perceptions and Attitudes about Corruption and Democracy in Mexico." *Mexican Studies/Estudios Mexicanos* 22:57–82.

Baker, Andy, Barry Ames, and Lucio Rennó. 2006. "Social Context and Campaign Volatility in New Democracies: Networks and Neighborhoods in Brazil's 2002 Elections." *American Journal of Political Science* 50 (2): 382–99.

Bardhan, Pranab. 1997. "Corruption and Development: A Review of Issues." *Journal of Economic Literature* 35 (3): 1320–46.

Behn, Robert D. 2001. *Rethinking Democratic Accountability.* Washington, DC: Brookings Institution Press.

Blake, Charles H., and Stephen D. Morris, eds. 2009. *Corruption and Democracy in Latin America.* Pittsburgh: University of Pittsburgh Press.

Bobbio, Norberto. 1986. *O futuro da democracia.* Rio de Janeiro: Paz e Terra.

Bohn, Simone Rodrigues da Silva, David Fleischer, and Francisco Whitaker. 2002. "A fiscalização das eleições." In *Caminhos da transparência,* ed. Bruno Speck. São Paulo: Editora da UNESP.

Booth, John A., and Mitchell A. Seligson. 2009. *The Legitimacy Puzzle in Latin America: Political Support and Democracy in Eight Nations.* New York: Cambridge University Press.

Broadway, Robin, and Anwar Shah. 2009. *Fiscal Federalism: Principles and Practices of Multi-order Governance.* Cambridge: Cambridge University Press.

Brunetti, Aymo, and Beatrice Weder. 2003. "A Free Press Is Bad News for Corruption." *Journal of Public Economics* 87 (7–8): 1801–1924.

Bugarin, Bento José. 1994. "Controle das finanças públicas." *Revista do Tribunal de Contas da União* 25 (6): 2.

Bugarin, Maurício Soares, Laércio Mendes Vieira, and Leice Maria Garcia. 2003. *Controle dos gastos públicos no Brasil: Instituições oficiais, controle social e um mecanismo para ampliar o envolvimento da sociedade.* Rio de Janeiro: Konrad Adenauer Stiftung.

Câmara dos Deputados. 2003–6. "Emendas orçamentárias." Computer files obtained from the Secretaria-Geral da Mesa.

Campbell, Angus, Philip Converse, Warren Miller, and Donald Stokes. 1960. *The American Voter.* New York: Wiley.

Campello de Souza, Maria do Carmo. 1989. "The Brazilian 'New Republic': Under the Sword of Damocles." In *Democratizing Brazil,* ed. Alfred Stepan, 351–94. New York: Oxford University Press.

Campos, Mauro Macedo. 2009. "Democracia, partidos e eleições: Os custos do sistema partidário-eleitoral no Brasil." PhD diss., Universidade Federal de Minas Gerais.

Carreirão, Yan. 2007. "Relevant Factors for the Voting Decision in the 2002 Presidential Elections: An Analysis of the ESEB (Brazilian Electoral Studies) Data." *Brazilian Political Science Review* 1 (1): 70–101.

Carreirão, Yan, and Pedro Alberto Barbetta. 2004. "A eleição presidencial de 2002: A decisão de voto na região da Grande São Paulo." *Revista Brasileira de Ciencias Sociais* 19 (56): 56–79.

Carreirão, Yan, and Maria D'Alva Gil Kinzo. 2004. "Partidos políticos, preferência partidária e decisão eleitoral no Brasil (1989/2002)." *Dados* 47 (1): 131–67.

Carvalho, José Murilo de. 2008. "Passado, presente e futuro da corrupção brasileira." In *Corrupção: Ensaios e críticas,* ed. Leonardo Avritzer, Newton Bignotto, Juarez Guimarães, and Heloisa Maria Murgel Starling. Belo Horizonte: Editora UFMG.

Cavalcanti, Rosângela. 2006. "The Effectiveness of Law: Civil Society and the Public Prosecution in Brazil." In *Enforcing the Rule of Law,* ed. Enrique Peruzzotti and Catalina Smulovitz, 34–54. Pittsburgh: University of Pittsburgh Press.

Cervellini, Silvia. 2006. "Corrupção na política: Eleitor vítima ou cúmplice?" Paper presented at the annual meeting of the World Association for Public Opinion Research, Colonia del Sacramento, Uruguay.

Chaia, Vera. 2004. *Jornalismo e política: Escândalos e relações de poder na Câmara Municipal de São Paulo.* São Paulo: Hacker.

Chaia, Vera, and Marco A. Teixeira. 2001. "Democracia e escândalos políticos." *São Paulo em Perspectiva* 15 (4): 62–75.

Cheibub, José Antonio, Argelina Figueiredo, and Fernando Limongi. 2002. "The Politics of Federalism in Brazil: The Role of Governors in the Brazilian Congress." Presented at the Seminar on Taxation Perspectives: A Democratic

Approach to Public Finance in Developing Countries, Institute of Development Studies, University of Sussex, October 28–29.

Chowdhury, Shyamal. 2004. "The Effect of Democracy and Press Freedom on Corruption: An Empirical Test." *Economics Letters* 85 (1): 93–101.

Citadini, Antonio Roque. 1995. *O controle externo da administração pública.* São Paulo: Max Limonad.

Comptroller General of the United States. 2007. *Government Auditing Standards* (July revision). Washington, DC: General Accounting Office.

Congresso em Foco. 2006. "Quase um terço do Congresso está sob suspeita." September 20. http://congressoemfoco.ig.com.br.

Conti, Mario Sergio. 1999. *Notícias do Planalto.* São Paulo: Companhia das Letras.

Correio Braziliense. 2008. "Dos quartéis e delegacias aos palanques." August 30.

Costa, Armindo Fernandes da, José Manuel Pereira, and Sílvia Ruíz Blanco. 2006. "Auditoria do setor público no contexto da nova gestão pública." *Revista de Estudos Politécnicos* 3 (5–6): 201–25.

Da Matta, Roberto. 1979. *Carnavais, malandros e heróis: Para uma sociologia do dilema brasileiro.* Rio de Janeiro: Zahar Editores.

Dehn, Jan, Ritva Reinikka, and Jakob Svensson. 2003. "Survey Tools for Assessing Performance in Service Delivery." http://siteresources.worldbank.org/INTPEAM/Resources/PETS1.pdf.

Della Porta, Donatella, and Alberto Vannucci. 1997. "The 'Perverse Effects' of Political Corruption." *Political Studies* 45:516–38.

Delli Carpini, Michael X., and Scott Keeter. 1996. *What Americans Know about Politics and Why It Matters.* New Haven: Yale University Press.

Department for International Development. 2004. *Characteristics of Different External Audit Systems.* DFID Policy Division Series, PD Info 021. London: DFID.

Desposato, Scott W. 2006a. "How Informal Electoral Institutions Shape the Brazilian Legislative Arena." In *Informal Institutions and Democracy: Lessons from Latin America,* ed. Gretchen Helmke and Steven Levitsky. Baltimore: Johns Hopkins University Press.

———. 2006b. "Parties for Rent? Ambition, Ideology, and Party Switching in Brazil's Chamber of Deputies." *American Journal of Political Science* 50 (1): 62–80.

Dimenstein, Gilberto. 1988. *A república dos padrinhos: Chantagem e corrupção em Brasília.* São Paulo: Editora Brasiliense.

Domingues, José Maurício. 2008. "Patrimonialismo e neopatrimonialismo." In *Corrupção: Ensaios e críticas,* ed. Leonardo Avritzer, Newton Bignotto, Juarez Guimarães, and Heloisa Maria Murgel Starling. Belo Horizonte: Editora UFMG.

Dye, Kenneth, and Rick Stapenhurst. 1998. *Pillars of Integrity: Importance of Supreme Audit Institutions in Curbing Corruption.* Washington, DC: World Bank Institute.

Época. 2008. "Lugar de corrupto não é na cadeia." Special "Debate" supplement, March 17, 59–82.

Faoro, Raymundo. [1958] 1996. *Os donos do poder: Formação do patronato político brasileiro*. São Paulo: Editora Globo.

Fausto Neto, Antônio. 1995. *O impeachment da televisão*. Rio de Janeiro: Diadorim.

Federação de Indústrias do Estado de São Paulo. 2006. "Relatório corrupção: Custos econômicos e propostas de combate." Report, Questões para Discussão. www.fiesp.com.br/competitividade/downloads/custo%20economico%20da%20corrupcao%20-%20final.pdf.

Feldman, Stanley, and John Zaller. 1992. "The Political Culture of Ambivalence: Ideological Responses to the Welfare State." *American Journal of Political Science* 36:268–307.

Fernandes, Florestan. 1975. *A revolução burguesa no Brasil*. Rio de Janeiro: Zahar.

Fernández-Kelly, Patrícia, and Jon Shefner. 2006. *Out of the Shadows: Political Action and the Informal Economy in Latin America*. University Park: Penn State University Press.

Ferraz, Claudio, and Frederico Finan. 2005. "Reelection Incentives and Political Corruption: Evidence from Brazil's Municipal Audit Reports." Unpublished paper, www.ie.ufrj.br/eventos/seminarios/pesquisa/reelection_incentives_and_political_corruption.pdf.

———. 2008. "Exposing Corrupt Politicians: The Effects of Brazil's Publicly Released Audits on Electoral Outcomes." *Quarterly Journal of Economics* 123 (2): 703–45.

———. Forthcoming. "Electoral Accountability and Corruption: Evidence from the Audit Reports of Local Governments." *American Economic Review*.

FIESP. See Federação das Indústrias do Estado de São Paulo.

Figueiredo, Argelina Cheibub. 2001. "Instituições e política no controle do executivo." *Dados* 44 (4): 689–727.

Figueiredo, Argelina Cheibub, and Fernando Limongi. 1999. *Executivo e legislativo na nova ordem constitucional*. Rio de Janeiro: Editora FGV.

———. 2000. "Presidential Power, Legislative Organization, and Party Behavior in Brazil." *Comparative Politics* 32 (2): 151–70.

Fiorina, Morris. 1981. *Retrospective Voting in American National Elections*. New Haven: Yale University Press.

Fisman, Ray, and Edward Miguel. 2006. "Cultures of Corruption: Evidence from Diplomatic Parking Tickets." National Bureau of Economic Research, Working Paper No. 12312. www.nber.org/papers/w12312.

Fleischer, David. 1997. "Political Corruption in Brazil: The Delicate Connection with Campaign Finance." *Crime, Law and Social Change* 25:297–321.

———. 2002. *Corruption in Brazil: Defining, Measuring, and Reducing*. Washington, DC: Center for Strategic and International Studies.

Fleischer, David, and Leonardo Barreto. 2009. "El impacto de la justicia electoral sobre el sistema político brasileño." *América Latina Hoy* 51:117–38.

Flynn, Peter. 1993. "Collor, Corruption and Crisis: Time for Reflection." *Journal of Latin American Studies* 25:351–71.

———. 2005. "Brazil and Lula, 2005: Crisis, Corruption and Change in Political Perspective." *Third World Quarterly* 26:1221–67.

Fox, Jonathan. 2007. *Accountability Politics: Power and Voice in Rural Mexico.* New York: Oxford University Press.

Fraga, Plínio. 2009. "Ninguém é inocente." *Folha de São Paulo,* October 4.

Freille, Sebastian, M. Emranul Haque, and Richard Kneller. 2007. "A Contribution to the Empirics of Press Freedom and Corruption." *European Journal of Political Economy* 23 (4): 838–62.

Freitas, Carlos Alberto Sampaio de, and Tomás de Aquino Guimarães. 2007. "Isomorphism, Institutionalization, and Legitimacy: Operational Auditing at the Court of Auditors." *Revista de Administração Contemporânea* 11:153–75.

Freitas, Janio de. 1987. "Concorrência da Ferrovia Norte-Sul foi uma farsa." *Folha de São Paulo,* May 13, A-1.

Garland, David. 1996. "The Limits of the Sovereign State." *British Journal of Criminology* 36 (4): 445–71.

Geddes, Barbara, and Artur Ribeiro Neto. 1999. "Institutional Sources of Corruption in Brazil." In *Corruption and Political Reform in Brazil: The Impact of Collor's Impeachment,* ed. Keith S. Rosenn and Richard Downes, 21–48. Miami: North-South Center Press.

Gerring, John, and Strom C. Thacker. 2004. "Political Institutions and Corruption: The Role of Unitarism and Parliamentarism." *British Journal of Political Science* 24:295–330.

Giannetti, Eduardo. 1993. "Ética e inflação." *Braudel Papers* 1:1–12.

Gillespie, Kate, and Gwenn Okruhlik. 1991. "The Political Dimensions of Corruption Cleanups: A Framework for Analysis." *Comparative Politics* 24 (1): 77–95.

Gioielli, Vicente. 2007. "Márcio Thomaz Bastos: O advogado de Lula." Interview. *O Povo: O Jornal do Ceará,* December 17. http://iddd.org.br/imprensa/show/84.

Glaeser, Edward L., Rafael LaPorta, Florêncio Lopes-de-Silanes, and Andrei Shleifer. 2004. "Do Institutions Cause Growth?" June. National Bureau of Economic Research, Working Paper 10568. www.nber.org/papers/w10568.

Glaeser, Edward L., and Raven Saks. 2004. "Corruption in America." October. Harvard Institute of Economic Research Discussion Paper 2043. http://papers .ssrn.com/sol3/papers.cfm?abstract_id=599042.

Global Justice. 2002a. *Front Line Brazil: Death Threats and Other Forms of Intimidation of Human Rights Defenders, 1997–2001.* Rio de Janeiro: Global Justice.

———. 2002b. *The Human Rights Crisis in Espírito Santo: Threats and Violence against Human Rights Defenders*. Rio de Janeiro: Global Justice.

Gonçalves, Fernando. 1993. "Auditoria operacional." *Revista do Tribunal de Contas da União* 24 (55): 11–21.

Grant, Ruth W., and Robert O. Keohane. 2005. "Accountability and Abuses of Power in World Politics." *American Political Science Review* 99:29–43.

Green, Donald, and Bradley Palmquist. 1994. "How Stable Is Party Identification?" *Political Behavior* 16:437–66.

Grupo de Mídia. 2006. *Mídia dados 2006*. São Paulo: Porto Palavra Editores.

Hall, Anthony. 2006. "From *Fome Zero* to *Bolsa Família:* Social Policies and Poverty Alleviation under Lula." *Journal of Latin American Studies* 38 (3): 689–709.

Hamilton, Alexander, John Jay, and James Madison. [1787–88] 1902. *The Federalist, and Other Constitutional Papers*. Chicago: Scott, Foresman.

Hammergren, Linn. 2007. *Envisioning Reform: Improving Judicial Performance in Latin America*. University Park: Pennsylvania University Press.

Helmke, Gretchen, and Steven Levitsky. 2004. "Informal Institutions and Comparative Politics: An Agenda for Research." *Perspectives on Politics* 2 (4): 725–40.

———, eds. 2006. *Informal Institutions and Democracy: Lessons from Latin America*. Baltimore: Johns Hopkins University Press.

Herscovitz, Heloísa. 2004. "Brazilian Journalists' Perceptions of Media Roles, Ethics, and Foreign Influences on Brazilian Journalism." *Journalism Studies* 5 (1): 71–86.

Heywood, Paul. 1997. "Political Corruption: Problems and Perspectives." *Political Studies* 45:417–35.

Holanda, Sergio Buarque de. [1936] 1971. *Raízes do Brasil*. 6th ed. Rio de Janeiro: José Olympio.

Holbrook, Thomas. 1994. "Campaigns, National Conditions, and U.S. Presidential Elections." *American Journal of Political Science* 38:973–98.

Hunter, Wendy. 2007. "The Normalization of an Anomaly: The Workers' Party in Brazil." *World Politics* 59 (3): 440–75.

Hunter, Wendy, and Timothy J. Power. 2007. "Rewarding Lula: Executive Power, Social Policy, and the Brazilian Elections of 2006." *Latin American Politics and Society* 49 (1): 1–30.

Huntington, Samuel. 1968. *Political Order in Changing Societies*. New Haven: Yale University Press.

Instituto Ethos. 2006. "Pacto empresarial pela integridade e contra a corrupção." June 22. by Instituto Ethos. www.empresalimpa.org.br/temos_adesao.aspx.

Instituto Ethos and Transparency International. 2008. *A responsabilidade social das empresas no processo eleitoral*. São Paulo: Instituto Ethos.

International Monetary Fund. 2008. World Economic Outlook Database, April 2008 ed. www.imf.org/external/pubs/ft/weo/2008/01/weodata/index.aspx.

International Organization of Supreme Audit Institutions. [1977] 1980. *Lima Declaration of Guidelines on Auditing Precepts.* Vienna: INTOSAI.

———. 2001. *Independence of SAIs Project: Final Task Force Report.* March 2001. http://intosai.connexcc-hosting.net/blueline/upload/1indepe.pdf.

INTOSAI. See International Organization of Supreme Audit Institutions.

Istoé. 2000. "Cheque-Voto: Garotinho e evangélicos manipulam programa que dá R$ 100 a carentes." May 21. www.istoe.com.br/reportagens/37619_CHEQUE +VOTO?pathImagens=&path=&actualArea=internalPage.

———. 2009. "A ciência dá a pista." June 3. www.istoe.com.br/reportagens/ 19621_A+CIENCIA+DA+A+PISTA.

Jacobson, Gary, and Michael Dimock. 1994. "Checking Out: The Effects of Bank Overdrafts on the 1992 House Elections." *American Journal of Political Science* 38 (3): 601–24.

Jambeiro, Othon. 2001. *A TV no Brasil do século XX.* Salvador: Editora UFBA.

Johnston, Michael. 2005. *Syndromes of Corruption: Wealth, Power, and Democracy.* New York: Cambridge University Press.

José, Emiliano. 1996. *Imprensa e poder: Ligações perigosas.* São Paulo: Editora Hucitec.

Junqueira, Aristides, Denise Frossard, Rodrigo Janot Monteiro de Barros, and José Roberto Santoro. 2002. "O direito penal e o combate à corrupção." In *Caminhos da transparência,* ed. Bruno Speck. São Paulo: Editora da Universidade Estadual de Campinas.

Kapiszewski, Diana, and Matthew M. Taylor. 2008. "Doing Courts Justice? Studying Judicial Politics in Latin America." *Perspectives on Politics* 6 (4): 741–67.

Kaufmann, Daniel. 2006. "Myths and Realities of Governance and Corruption." In *World Competitiveness Report, 2005–06,* 81–98. World Economic Forum Reports. New York: Palgrave Macmillan.

Kaufmann, Daniel, Aart Kraay, and Pablo Zoido-Lobaton. 1999. "Governance Matters." World Bank Policy Research Working Paper No. 2196. Washington, DC.

Kerche, Fábio. 2007. "Autonomia e discricionariedade do Ministério Público no Brasil." *Dados,* no. 50:259–79.

Key Centre for Ethics, Law Justice, and Governance, Griffith University, and Transparency International Australia. 2001. *Australian National Integrity Systems Assessment: Queensland Handbook.* Brisbane: Key Centre.

Kinder, Donald R., and D. Roderick Kiewiet. 1981. "Sociotropic Politics: The American Case." *British Journal of Political Science* 11:129–61.

Kitschelt, Herbert, and Steven J. Wilkinson. 2007. *Patrons, Clients, and Policies: Patterns of Democratic Accountability and Political Competition.* New York: Cambridge University Press.

Krieger, Gustavo, Fernando Rodrigues, and Elvis Cesar Bonassa. 1994. *Os donos do Congresso: A farsa na CPI do Orçamento.* São Paulo: Editora Ática.

Kunicová, J., and Susan Rose-Ackerman. 2005. "Electoral Rules and Constitutional Structure as Constraints on Corruption." *British Journal of Political Science* 35:573–606.

La Pastina, Antônio. 2004. "Selling Political Integrity: Telenovelas, Intertextuality, and Local Elections in Rural Brazil." *Journal of Broadcasting and Electronic Media* 48 (3): 302–25.

Lahneman, Bill, and Matt Lewis. 2002. "Summary of Proceedings: Organized Crime and the Corruption of State Institutions." Conference at the Center for International and Security Studies at Maryland, University of Maryland, College Park. www.cissm.umd.edu/papers/files/organizedcrime.pdf.

Lambsdorff, Johann Graf, Markus Taube, and Matthias Schramm. 2004. *The New Institutional Economics of Corruption*. London: Routledge.

Lattman-Weltman, Fernando. 2003. "Mídia e transição democrática: A (des)institucionalização do pan-óptico no Brasil." In *Mídia e política no Brasil*, ed. Alzira Abreu, Fernando Lattman-Weltman, and Mônica Kornis, 129–83. Rio de Janeiro: Editora FGV.

Lattman-Weltman, Fernando, José Carneiro, and Plínio Ramos. 1994. *A imprensa faz e desfaz um presidente*. Rio de Janeiro: Nova Fronteira.

Lederman, Daniel, Norman V. Loayza, and Rodrigo R. Soares. 2005. "Accountability and Corruption: Political Institutions Matter." *Economics and Politics* 17 (1): 1–35.

Leff, Nathaniel. 1964. "Economic Development through Bureaucratic Corruption." *American Behavioral Scientist* 8:11–22.

Lemgruber, Julita, Leonarda Musumeci, and Ignácio Cano. 2003. *Quem vigia os vigias: Um estudo sobre controle externo da polícia no Brasil*. Rio de Janeiro: Editora Record.

Lemos-Nelson, Ana Tereza. 2001. "Judiciary Police Accountability for Gross Human Rights Violations: The Case of Bahia, Brazil." PhD diss., University of Notre Dame.

Lemos-Nelson, Ana Tereza, and Jorge Zaverucha. 2006. "Multiple Activation as a Strategy of Citizen Accountability and the Role of Investigating Legislative Commissions." In *Enforcing the Rule of Law*, ed. Enrique Peruzzotti and Catalina Smulovitz, 75–114. Pittsburgh: University of Pittsburgh Press.

Leoni, Eduardo, Carlos Pereira, and Lucio Rennó. 2004. "Political Survival Strategies: Political Career Decisions in the Brazilian Chamber of Deputies." *Journal of Latin American Studies* 36:109–30.

Levi, Margaret. 1999. "A State of Trust." In *Trust and Governance*, ed. Valerie Braithwaite and Margaret Levi. New York: Russell Sage Foundation.

Lício, Elaine, Lucio Rennó, and Henrique Castro. 2009. "Bolsa família e voto nas eleições presidenciais de 2006: Em busca do elo perdido." *Opinião Pública* 15 (1): 31–54.

Light, Paul C. 1993. *Monitoring Government: Inspectors General and the Search for Accountability.* Washington, DC: Brookings Institution.

Lijphart, Arend. 1999. *Patterns of Democracy: Government Forms and Performance in Thirty-six Countries.* New Haven: Yale University Press.

Lima, Venício. 1988. "The State, Television, and Political Power in Brazil." *Critical Studies in Mass Communication* 5 (2): 108–28.

———. 1993. "Brazilian Television in the 1989 Presidential Election: Constructing a President." In *Television, Politics and the Transition to Democracy in Latin America,* ed. Thomas Skidmore, 97–117. Baltimore: Johns Hopkins University Press.

———. 2001. *Mídia: Teoria e política.* São Paulo: Editora da Fundação Perseu Abramo.

———. 2006. *Mídia: Crise política e poder no Brasil.* São Paulo: Editora da Fundação Perseu Abramo.

Lins da Silva, Carlos Eduardo. 1988. *Mil dias: Os bastidores da revolução em um grande jornal.* São Paulo: Trajetória Cultural.

———. 2000. "Journalism and Corruption in Brazil." In *Combating Corruption in Latin America,* ed. Joseph S. Tulchin and Ralph H. Espach, 173–92. Baltimore: Woodrow Wilson Center Press.

Luca, Tânia de. 2008. "A grande imprensa no Brasil da primeira metade do século XX." Paper presented at the annual meeting of the Brazilian Studies Association, New Orleans, March 27–30.

Lupia, Arthur. 1994. "Shortcuts versus Encyclopedias: Information and Voting Behavior in California Insurance Reform Elections." *American Political Science Review* 88 (1): 63–76.

———. 2001. "Delegation of Power: Agency Theory." In *International Encyclopedia of the Social and Behavioral Sciences,* ed. Neil Smelser and Paul Baltes. Oxford: Elsevier.

Lupia, Arthur, and Mathew D. McCubbins. 2000. "Representation or Abdication? How Citizens Use Institutions to Help Delegation Succeed." *European Journal of Political Research* 37:291–307.

Luskin, Robert. 2002. "From Denial to Extenuation (and Finally Beyond): Political Sophistication and Citizen Peformance." In *Thinking about Political Psychology,* ed. James Kuklinski. Cambridge: Cambridge University Press.

Macaulay, Fiona. 2002. "Problems of Police Oversight in Brazil." Working Paper CBS 33–2002, Centre for Brazilian Studies, University of Oxford.

———. 2003. "Democratisation and the Judiciary: Competing Reform Agendas." In *Brazil since 1985: Economy, Polity and Society,* ed. Maria D'Alva Kinzo and James Dunkerley. London: Institute of Latin American Studies.

Macdonell, Rod, and Milica Pesic. 2006. "The Role of the Media in Curbing Corruption." In *The Role of Parliament in Curbing Corruption,* ed. Rick Stapenhurst, Niall Johnston, and Riccardo Pellizo, 111–27. Washington, DC: World Bank.

Mainwaring, Scott. 1991. "Politicians, Parties, and Electoral Systems: Brazil in Comparative Perspective." *Comparative Politics* 24 (1): 21–43.

———. 1995. "Brazil: Weak Parties, Feckless Democracy." In *Building Democratic Institutions: Party Systems in Latin America*, ed. Scott Mainwaring and Timothy R. Scully 354–398. Stanford: Stanford University Press.

———. 1999. *Rethinking Party Systems in the Third Wave of Democratization: The Case of Brazil.* Stanford: Stanford University Press.

———. 2003. "Introduction: Democratic Accountability in Latin America." In *Democratic Accountability in Latin America*, ed. Scott Mainwaring and Christopher Welna, 3–33. New York: Oxford University Press.

Mainwaring, Scott, and Timothy R. Scully, eds. 1995. *Building Democratic Institutions: Party Systems in Latin America.* Stanford: Stanford University Press.

Mainwaring, Scott, and Christopher Welna, eds. 2003. *Democratic Accountability in Latin America.* New York: Oxford University Press.

Mancuso, Rodolfo C. 1997. *Interesses difusos: Conceitos and legitimação para agir.* São Paulo: Editora Revista dos Tribunais.

Manin, Bernard. 1995. *Principes du gouvernement représentatif.* Paris: Calmann-Lévy.

Manin, Bernard, Adam Przeworski, and Susan C. Stokes. 1999. Introduction to *Democracy, Accountability, and Representation,* ed. Adam Przeworski, Susan C. Stokes, and Bernard Manin, 1–26. Cambridge: Cambridge University Press.

Manzetti, Luigi, and Charles Blake. 1996. "Market Reforms and Corruption in Latin America." *Review of International Political Economy* 3:671–82.

Manzetti, Luigi, and Carole J. Wilson. 2008. "Why Do Corrupt Governments Maintain Public Support?" In *Corruption and Democracy in Latin America,* ed. Charles H. Blake and Stephen D. Morris. Pittsburgh: University of Pittsburgh Press.

Marchetti, Vitor. 2008. "Poder judiciário e competição política no Brasil: Uma analise das decisões do TSE e do STF sobre as regras eleitorais." PhD diss., Pontifícia Universidade Católica de São Paulo.

Martínez, Juan, and Javier Santiso. 2003. "Financial Markets and Politics: The Confidence Game in Latin American Emerging Economies." *International Political Science Review* 24 (3): 363–95.

Matos, Carolina. 2008. *Journalism and Political Democracy in Brazil.* Lanham, MD: Lexington Books.

Mattos, Sérgio. 2000. *A televisão no Brasil.* Salvador: Edições Inamã.

Mauro, Paolo. 1995. "Corruption and Growth." *Quarterly Journal of Economics* 110:681–712.

Mazzilli, Hugo Nigro. 1993. *Regime jurídico do Ministério Público.* São Paulo: Editora Saraiva.

McCubbins, Mathew D., and Thomas Schwartz. 1984. "Congressional Oversight: Police Patrols versus Fire Alarms." *American Journal of Political Science* 28 (1): 165–79.

McMillan, John, and Pablo Zoido. 2004. "How to Subvert Democracy: Montesinos in Peru." *Journal of Economic Perspectives* 18:69–92.

Melo, Carlos Ranulfo. 2004. *Retirando as cadeiras do lugar: Migração partidária na Câmara dos Deputados (1985–2002)*. Belo Horizonte: Editora UFMG.

———. 2008. "Corrupção Eleitoral." In *Corrupção: Ensaios e críticas,* ed. Leonardo Avritzer, Newton Bignotto, Juarez Guimarães, and Heloisa Maria Murgel Starling. Belo Horizonte: Editora UFMG.

Meneguello, Rachel. 1994. "Partidos e tendências de comportamento: O cenário político em 1994." In *Os anos 90: Política e sociedade no Brasil,* ed. Evelina Dagnino, 151–71. São Paulo: Editora Brasiliense.

Mingardi, Guaracy. 1996. "O estado e o crime organizado." PhD diss., University of São Paulo.

Ministério da Justiça, Secretaria de Reforma do Judiciário. 2006. *Diagnóstico do Ministério Público dos Estados.* www.mp.sc.gov.br/portal/site/conteudo/noticias/cao/pgj/diagnostico_mp.pdf.

Ministério do Planejamento. 2008. *Boletim Estatístico de Pessoal,* no. 145, May. www.servidor.gov.br/publicacao/boletim_estatistico/bol_estatistico_08/Bol145_mai2008.pdf.

Misse, Michel. 2007. "Illegal Markets, Protection Rackets, and Organized Crime in Rio de Janeiro." *Estudos Avançados* 61:139–57.

Mochel, Marília, Barry Ames, Andrew Baker, and Lucio Rennó. 2006. "Party Identification in Third Wave Democracies: Brazil's 2002 Elections." Paper presented at the annual meeting of the Midwest Political Science Association, Chicago, April 20–23.

Moisés, José Álvaro. 2008. "Cultura política, instituições e democracia: Lições da experiência brasileira." *Revista Brasileira de Ciências Sociais* 23 (6): 11–43.

———. 2009. "Political Corruption and Democracy in Today's Brazil." Paper presented at the Latin American Studies Association (LASA) Congress, Rio de Janeiro, June.

Moisés, José Álvaro, and Gabriela Piquet Carneiro. 2008. "Democracia, desconfiança política e insatisfação com o regime: O caso do Brasil." *Opinião Pública* 14 (1): 1–42.

Montinola, Gabriella R., and Robert W. Jackman. 2002. "Sources of Corruption: A Cross-Country Study." *British Journal of Political Science* 32 (1):147–70.

Moreno, Erika, Brian F. Crisp, and Matthew Soberg Shugart. 2003. "The Accountability Deficit in Latin America." In *Democratic Accountability in Latin America,* ed. Scott Mainwaring and Christopher Welna 79–131. Oxford: Oxford University Press.

Moro, Sergio Fernando. 2008. Interview by Matthew M. Taylor, February 20.

Morris, Stephen D. 2009. *Political Corruption in Mexico: The Impact of Democratization.* Boulder, CO: Lynne Rienner.

Morris, Stephen D., and Charles H. Blake. 2009. "Introduction: Political and Analytical Challenges of Corruption in Latin America," in *Corruption and Democracy in Latin America*, 1–24. Pittsburgh: University of Pittsburgh Press.

———, eds. 2010. *Corruption and Politics in Latin America: National and Regional Dynamics*. Boulder, CO: Lynne Rienner.

Motter, Paulino. 1994. "O uso político das concessões de rádio e televisão no governo Sarney." *Comunicação e Política* 1:89–115.

Nascimento, Solano. 2007. "Jornalismo sobre investigações: Relações entre o Ministério Público e a imprensa." PhD diss., University of Brasília.

Nassif, Luis. 2003. *O jornalismo dos anos 90*. São Paulo: Editora Futura.

National Accounting Office of the United Kingdom. 1996. *State Audit in the European Union*. London: NAO.

Nicolau, Jairo. 2007. "An Analysis of the 2002 Presidential Election Using Logistic Regression." *Brazilian Political Science Review* 1 (1): 125–35.

Nicolau, Jairo, and Timothy J. Power. 2007. *Instituições representativas no Brasil: Balanço e reformas*. Belo Horizonte: Editora UFMG.

Nunes, Edson. 1997. *A gramática política do Brasil: Clientelismo and insulamento burocrático*. Rio de Janeiro: Jorge Zahar.

Nye, Joseph S. 1967. "Corruption and Political Development: A Cost-Benefit Analysis." *American Political Science Review* 61:417–27.

O Estado de São Paulo. 2005a. "Carta anticorrupção vigora hoje." December 14.

———. 2005b. "Justiça eleitoral finge que fiscaliza, diz Bastos." October 6.

———. 2005c. "Maioria das comissões não conclui trabalhos." June 5.

———. 2007a. "AGU monta operação para recuperar R$40 bilhões." December 5.

———. 2007b. "Ex-ministro vê risco de prescrição." August 29.

———. 2008. "Crise na Justiça." September 10.

O Globo. 2008. "Rio tem dois policiais para cada deputado." July 7.

O'Donnell, Guillermo. 1994. "Delegative Democracy." *Journal of Democracy* 5:55–69.

———. 1999. "Horizontal Accountability in New Democracies." In *The Self-Restraining State: Power and Accountability in New Democracies*, ed. Andreas Schedler, Larry Diamond and Marc Plattner. Boulder, CO: Lynne Rienner.

———. 2004. "Why the Rule of Law Matters." *Journal of Democracy* 15 (4): 32–46.

OECD. See Organization for Economic Cooperation and Development.

OESP. See *O Estado de São Paulo*.

Oliveira, Francisco de. 2006. "Lula in the Labyrinth." *New Left Review* 42:5–22.

Olivieri, Cecília. 2006. "O controle interno como instrumento de accountability horizontal: Uma análise exploratória da Controladoria Geral da União." Encontro de Administração Pública e Governança, São Paulo (National Conference on Public Administration and Governance).

Olken, Benjamin A. 2007. "Monitoring Corruption: Evidence from a Field Experiment in Indonesia." *Journal of Political Economy* 115 (2): 200–249.

Olsen, Tricia. 2007. "A Latin American Paradox? Democratic Quality and Endurance." Latin American Public Opinion Project, Americas Barometer Small Grants Research Series, Paper No. 6. http://sitemason.vanderbilt.edu/files/lnsleo/OLSEN_LAPOP_Paper.pdf.

Opinião Pública. 2006. "Encarte Tendências." *Opinião Pública* 12 (1): 189–209.

Organization for Economic Cooperation and Development, Working Group on Bribery in International Business Transactions. 2007. "Report on the Application of the Convention on Combating Bribery of Foreign Public Officials in International Business Transactions and the 1997 Recommendation on Combating Bribery in International Business Transactions." December. www.oecd.org/dataoecd/61/30/39801089.pdf.

Panizza, Ugo. 2001. "Electoral Rules, Political Systems, and Institutional Quality." *Economia Política* 13 (3): 311–42.

Pappi, Franz U. 1996. "Political Behavior: Reasoning Voters and Multiparty Systems." In *A New Handbook of Political Science,* ed. Robert Goodin and Hans-Dieter Klingemann, 255–75. Oxford: Oxford University Press.

Pereira, Carlos, Marcus André Melo, and Carlos Mauricio Figueiredo. 2009a. "The Corruption-Enhancing Role of Re-election Incentives? Counterintuitive Evidence from Brazil's Audit Reports." *Political Research Quarterly* 62 (4): 731–44.

———. 2009b. "Political and Institutional Checks on Corruption: Explaining the Performance of Brazilian Audit Institutions." *Comparative Political Studies* 42 (9): 1217–44.

Pereira, Carlos, and Bernardo Mueller. 2004. "The Cost of Governing: Strategic Behavior of the President and Legislators in Brazil's Budgetary Process." *Comparative Political Studies* 37 (7): 781–815.

Pereira, Carlos, Timothy J. Power, and Lucio Rennó. 2005. "Under What Conditions Do Presidents Resort to Decree Power? Theory and Evidence from the Brazilian Case." *Journal of Politics* 67 (1): 178–200.

———. 2008. "Agenda Power, Executive Decree Authority, and the Mixed Results of Reform in the Brazilian Congress." *Legislative Studies Quarterly* 33 (1): 5–33.

Pereira, Carlos, and Lucio Rennó. 2003. "Successful Reelection Strategies in Brazil: The Electoral Impact of Distinct Institutional Incentives." *Electoral Studies* 22:425–48.

Pérez-Liñán, Aníbal. 2007. *Presidential Impeachment and the New Political Instability in Latin America.* New York: Cambridge University Press.

Persson, Torsten, Guido Tabellini, and Francesco Trebbi. 2003. "Electoral Rules and Corruption." *Journal of the European Economic Association* 1:958–89.

Peruzzotti, Enrique. 2006. "Media Scandals and Social Accountability: Assessing the Role of the Senate Scandal in Argentina." In *Enforcing the Rule of Law: Social Accountability in the New Latin American Democracies,* ed. Enrique Peruzzotti and Catalina Smulovitz, 249–71. Pittsburgh: University of Pittsburgh Press.

Peruzzotti, Enrique, and Catalina Smulovitz, eds. 2006. *Enforcing the Rule of Law: Social Accountability in the New Latin American Democracies*. Pittsburgh: University of Pittsburgh Press.

Pessanha, Charles. 2007. "Accountability e controle externo no Brasil e na Argentina." In *Direito e cidadania: Justiça, poder e mídia*, ed. Angela de Castro Gomes, 139–67. Rio de Janeiro: Editora FGV.

Philp, Mark. 2009. "Delimiting Democratic Accountability." *Political Studies* 57:28–53.

Pierson, Paul. 2004. "Why Americanists Should Be Buyers in the Marketplace of Ideas." *APSA-CP: Newsletter of the American Political Science Association Organized Section in Comparative Politics* 15 (2): 6–8.

Pope, Jeremy. 2000. *Confronting Corruption: The Elements of a National Integrity System*. London: Transparency International.

Porto, Mauro. 2000. "La crisis de confianza en la política y sus instituciones: Los medios y la legitimidad de la democracia en Brasil." *Ameria Latina Hoy* 25:23–33.

———. 2003. "Mass Media and Politics in Democratic Brazil." In *Brazil since 1985: Economy, Polity and Society*, ed. Maria D'Alva Kinzo and James Dunkerley, 288–313. London: Institute of Latin American Studies.

———. 2005. "Political Controversies in Brazilian TV Fiction: Viewers' Interpretations of the Telenovela *Terra Nostra*." *Television and New Media* 6 (4): 342–59.

———. 2006. "Political Advertising and Democracy in Brazil." In *The Sage Handbook of Political Advertising*, ed. Lynda Kaid and Christina Holtz-Bacha, 129–42. Thousand Oaks, CA: Sage Publications.

———. 2007a. *Televisão e política no Brasil*. Rio de Janeiro: E-Papers.

———. 2007b. "TV News and Political Change in Brazil: The Impact of Democratization on TV Globo's Journalism." *Journalism* 8 (4): 381–402.

———. 2008. "Democratization and Election News Coverage in Brazil." In *Handbook of Election News Coverage around the World*, ed. Jesper Stromback and Lynda Kaid, 252–72. London: Routledge.

Powell, G. Bingham, Jr. 2000. *Elections as Instruments of Democracy: Majoritarian and Proportional Visions*. New Haven, CT: Yale University Press.

Power, Timothy J. 2010. "Optimism, Pessimism, and Coalitional Presidentialism: Debating the Institutional Design of Brazilian Democracy." *Bulletin of Latin American Research* 29 (1): 18–33.

Power, Timothy J., and Jennifer M. Cyr. 2009. "Mapping Political Legitimacy in Latin America: A Multidimensional Approach." *International Social Science Journal* 60 (196): 253–72.

Power, Timothy J., and Julio González. 2003. "Culture, Values, and Perceptions of Corruption: A Cross-National Analysis." In *Democracy and Development: New Perspectives on an Old Debate*, ed. Jeffrey Cason and Sunder Ramaswamy. Boston: University Press of New England.

Praça, Sérgio. 2007. "Corrupção no processo orçamentário brasileiro." *Revista Getúlio* 1 (2): 11–15.

Przeworski, Adam, Susan C. Stokes, and Bernard Manin. 1999. *Democracy, Accountability, and Representation*. Cambridge: Cambridge University Press.

Raile, Eric D., Carlos Pereira, and Timothy J. Power. 2011. "The Executive Toolbox: Building Legislative Support in a Multiparty Presidential Regime." *Political Research Quarterly*, early online publication March 4, 2010, accessible for download at http://prq.sagepub.com/content/early/2010/03/04/1065912909355711 .abstract.

Ramkumar, Vivek, and Warren Krafchik. 2005. *The Role of Civil Society Organizations in Auditing and Public Finance Management*. Washington, DC: International Budget Initiative.

Rêgo, Patricia. 2004. "A Battle Arena on TV: A Study of the Journalist's Authority." Paper presented at the conference of the International Association for Media and Communication Research, Porto Alegre, Brazil, July 25–30.

Reis, Fábio Wanderley. 2008. "Corrupção, cultura e ideologia." In *Corrupção: Ensaios e críticas*, ed. Leonardo Avritzer, Newton Bignotto, Juarez Guimarães, and Heloisa Maria Murgel Starling 291–398. Belo Horizonte: Editora UFMG.

Rennó, Lucio. 2007a. "Escândalos, desempenho parlamentar e Reeleição: a Câmara dos Deputados de 2003 a 2007." Unpublished manuscript, University of Brasília.

———. 2007b. "Escândalos e voto: As eleições presidenciais brasileiras de 2006." *Opinião Pública* 13:260–82.

———. 2007c. "Notes on the 2006 Brazilian Presidential Elections: The Winding Road to Democratic Consolidation." *Colombia Internacional* 64:154–65.

Ribeiro, Lavina. 2004. *Imprensa e espaço público: A institucionalização do jornalismo no Brasil, 1808–1964*. Rio de Janeiro: E-Papers.

Roberts, Kenneth, and Erik Wibbels. 1999. "Party Systems and Electoral Volatility in Latin America: A Test of Economic, Institutional, and Structural Explanations." *American Political Science Review* 93 (3): 575–90.

Rocha, Bruno L. 2004. "A Polícia Federal após a Constituição de 1988: Polícia de governo, segurança de estado and polícia judiciária." M.A. thesis, Federal University of Rio Grande do Sul, Porto Alegre.

Roett, Riordan. 1999. *Brazil: Politics in a Patrimonial Society*. 5th ed. Westport, CT: Praeger.

Roncaglia, Daniel. 2008. "Mais de 4 mil policiais são candidatos nessas eleições." *Consultor Jurídico*, October 2.

Rosa, Mário. 2004. *A era do escândalo*. São Paulo: Geração Editorial.

Rose-Ackerman, Susan. 1999. *Corruption and Government: Causes, Consequences, and Reform*. Cambridge: Cambridge University Press.

———. 2000. "Is Leaner Government Necessarily Cleaner Government?" In *Combating Corruption in Latin America,* ed. Joseph Tulchin and Ralph Espach. Baltimore: Woodrow Wilson Center Press.

Rosenn, Keith S. 1984. "Brazil's Legal Culture: The Jeito Revisited." *Florida International Law Journal* 1 (1): 1–43.

Rosenn, Keith S., and Richard Downes, eds. 1999. *Corruption and Political Reform in Brazil: The Impact of Collor's Impeachment.* Boulder, CO: Lynne Rienner.

Sadek, Maria Tereza. 1995. *A justiça eleitoral e a consolidação da democracia no Brasil.* São Paulo: Konrad Adenauer Stiftung.

———. 2008. "Ministério Público." In *Corrupção: Ensaios e críticas,* ed. Leonardo Avritzer, Newton Bignotto, Juarez Guimarães, and Heloisa Maria Murgel Starling 543–550. Belo Horizonte: Editora UFMG.

Sadek, Maria Tereza, and Rosângela Batista Cavalcanti. 2003. "The New Brazilian Public Prosecution: An Agent of Accountability." In *Democratic Accountability in Latin America,* ed. Scott Mainwaring and Christopher Welna 201–227. New York: Oxford University Press.

Samuels, David. 2000. "Ambition and Competition: Explaining Legislative Turnover in Brazil." *Legislative Studies Quarterly* 25:481–98.

———. 2001a. "Does Money Matter? Campaign Finance in Newly Democratic Countries: Theory and Evidence from Brazil." *Comparative Politics* 34:23–42.

———. 2001b. "Incumbents and Challengers on a Level Playing Field: Assessing the Impact of Campaign Finance in Brazil." *Journal of Politics* 63 (2): 569–84.

———. 2001c. "Money, Elections, and Democracy in Brazil." *Latin American Politics and Society* 43:27–48.

———. 2002. "Pork-Barreling Is Not Credit-Claiming or Advertising: Campaign Finance and the Sources of the Personal Vote in Brazil." *Journal of Politics* 64 (3): 845–63.

———. 2003. *Ambition, Federalism, and Legislative Politics in Brazil.* New York: Cambridge University Press.

———. 2006a. "Informal Institutions When Formal Contracting Is Prohibited: Campaign Finance in Brazil." In *Informal Institutions and Democracy: Lessons from Latin America,* ed. Gretchen Helmke and Steven Levitsky 87–105. Baltimore: Johns Hopkins University Press.

———. 2006b. "Sources of Mass Partisanship in Brazil." *Latin American Politics and Society* 48 (2): 1–27.

———. 2008. "A Evolução do Petismo (2002–2008)." *Opinião Pública* 14 (2): 302–18.

Samuels, David J., and Scott Mainwaring 2004. "Strong Federalism, Constraints on the Central Government, and Economic Reform in Brazil." In *Federalism and Democracy in Latin America,* ed. Edward Gibson. Baltimore: Johns Hopkins University Press.

Santin, Valter F. 2007. *O Ministério Público na investigação criminal.* Bauru: Edipro.

Santiso, Carlos. 2003. "Economic Reform and Judicial Governance in Brazil: Balancing Independence with Accountability." *Democratization* 10 (4): 161–80.

———. 2006a. "Banking on Accountability? Strengthening Budget Oversight and Public Sector Auditing in Emerging Economies." *Public Budgeting and Finance* 26 (2): 66–100.

———. 2006b. "Improving Fiscal Governance and Curbing Corruption: How Relevant Are Autonomous Audit Agencies?" *International Public Management Review* 7 (2): 97–109.

Santos, Boaventura de Sousa. 2006. "The Heterogeneous State and Legal Plurality." In *Law and Justice in a Multicultural Society: The Case of Mozambique,* ed. Boaventura de Sousa Santos, João Carlos Trindade, and Maria Paula Meneses. Dakar: Council for the Development of Social Science Research in Africa.

Santos, Fabiano, and Márcio Grijó Vilarouca. 2008. "From FHC to Lula: Changes and Continuity in Political Institutions and Impact upon the Political Reform Debate." In *Democratic Brazil Revisited,* ed. Peter R. Kingstone and Timothy J. Power, 57–80. Pittsburgh: University of Pittsburgh Press.

Santos, Pedro. 2008. "Punishing Corruption: The Impact of Corruption Allegations in the 2006 Brazilian Congressional Elections." Paper presented at the conference of the Brazilian Studies Association, New Orleans, March 27–30.

Santos, Reinaldo dos. 2003. "Mídia e democracia na legislação eleitoral brasileira: Um levantamento dos mecanismos legislativos de controle e compensação do uso dos meios de comunicação em contextos eleitorais (1974–2000)." Paper presented at the 26th Congresso Brasileiro de Ciências da Comunicação, Belo Horizonte, September 3–7.

Santos, Suzy dos, and Sérgio Capparelli. 2005. "Coronelismo, radiodifusão e voto: A nova face de um velho conceito." In *Rede Globo: 40 anos de poder e hegemonia,* ed. Valério Brittos and Cesar Bolaño, 77–101. São Paulo: Paulus.

Schedler, Andreas. 1999. "Conceptualizing Accountability." In *The Self-Restraining State,* ed. Andreas Schedler, Larry Diamond, and Marc F. Plattner, 13–28. Boulder, CO: Lynne Rienner.

Schedler, Andreas, Larry Diamond, and Marc F. Plattner, eds. 1999. *The Self-Restraining State.* Boulder, CO: Lynne Rienner.

Schilling, Flávia. 1999. *Corrupção: Ilegalidade intolerável? Comissões Parlamentares de Inquérito e a luta contra a corrupção no Brasil (1980–1992).* São Paulo: Instituto Brasileiro de Ciências Criminais.

Schneider, Ben Ross. 2004. *Business Politics and the State in Twentieth-Century Latin America.* New York: Cambridge University Press.

Schwartzman, Simon. [1982] 1988. *Bases do autoritarismo brasileiro.* Rio de Janeiro: Editora Campus.

Seligson, Mitchell A. 2002. "The Impact of Corruption on Regime Legitimacy: A Comparative Study of Four Latin American Countries." *Journal of Politics* 64:408–33.

———. 2006. "The Measurement and Impact of Corruption Victimization: Survey Evidence from Latin America." *World Development* 34:381–404.

Shah, Anwar. 2006. "Corruption and Decentralized Public Governance." January. World Bank Policy Research Working Paper 3824. http://info.worldbank.org/etools/docs/library/239565/corruptionandDecentralized.pdf.

———, ed. 2007. *Performance Accountability and Combating Corruption.* Washington, DC: World Bank.

Shah, Anwar, and Jeff Huther. 2000. "Anti-Corruption Policies and Programs: A Framework for Evaluation." December. World Bank Policy Research Working Paper 2501. http://papers.ssrn.com/sol3/papers.cfm?abstract_id=632571.

Silva, Marcos Fernandes Gonçalves da. 1996. "A economia política da corrupção." *Estudos Econômicos da Construção* 2:71–96.

———. 2001. *A economia política da corrupção no Brasil.* São Paulo: Editora Senac, 2001.

Singer, André. 1999. *Esquerda e direita no eleitorado brasileiro: A identificação ideológica nas disputas presidenciais de 1989 e 1994.* São Paulo: Edusp.

Siqueira, Ana Paulo, and Edson Sardinha. 2007. "Muito além do mensalão." Congresso em Foco, September 4. www.congressoemfoco.com.br.

Skidmore, Thomas E. 1988. *The Politics of Military Rule in Brazil, 1964–1985.* New York: Oxford University Press.

Smulovitz, Catalina, and Enrique Peruzzotti. 2000. "Societal Accountability in Latin America." *Journal of Democracy* 11 (4): 147–58.

———, eds. 2006. *Enforcing the Rule of Law: Social Accountability in the New Latin American Democracies.* Pittsburgh: University of Pittsburgh Press.

Soares, Gláucio Ary Dillon, and Sonia Luiza Terron. 2008. "Dois Lulas: A geografia eleitoral da reeleição (explorando conceitos, métodos e técnicas de análise geoespacial)." *Opinião Pública* 14 (2): 269–301.

Soares, Luis Eduardo. 2000. *Meu casaco de general: Quinhentos dias no front da segurança pública do Rio de Janeiro.* Rio de Janeiro: Companhia das Letras.

Soares, Luis Eduardo, Barbara Musumeci Soares, João Trajano de Lima Sento-Sé, Leonarda Musumeci, Silvia Ramos, and Anthony Garotinho. 1998. *Violência e criminalidade no Estado do Rio de Janeiro: Diagnóstico e propostas para uma política democrática de segurança.* Rio de Janeiro: Editora Hamas.

Soares, Sergei, Rafael Guerreiro Osório, Fábio Veras Soares, Marcelo Medeiros, and Eduardo Zepeda. 2007. "Conditional Cash Transfers in Brazil, Chile and Mexico: Impacts upon Inequality." International Poverty Center Working Paper No. 35 (April).

Souza, Celina. 2003. "Federalismo e conflitos distributivos: Disputa dos estados por recursos orçamentários federais." *Dados* 47 (4): 345–84.

Souza, Leonardo. 2008. "Sigilo telefônico é vendido a menos de R$ 1000 no Brasil." *Folha de S. Paulo*, September 14, A-4.

Spanakos, Anthony, and Lucio Rennó. 2006. "Elections and Economic Turbulence in Brazil: Candidates, Voters, and Investors." *Latin American Politics and Society* 48 (4): 1–26.

Speck, Bruno W. 2000a. *Inovação e rotina no Tribunal de Contas da União: O papel da instituição superior de controle financeiro no sistema político-administrativo do Brasil.* São Paulo: Fundação Konrad Adenauer.

———. 2000b. "Mensurando a corrupção: Uma revisão de dados provenientes de pesquisas empíricas." In *Cadernos Adenauer 10: Os custos da corrupção.* São Paulo: Fundação Konrad Adenauer.

———, ed. 2002. *Caminhos da transparência.* Campinas: Editora Universidade Estadual de Campinas.

———. 2003. "A compra de votos: Uma aproximação empírica." *Opinião Pública* 9 (1): 148–69.

———. 2005. "Reagir a escândalos ou perseguir ideais? A regulação do financiamento político no Brasil." *Cadernos Adenauer* 6:123–59.

———. 2008. "Tribunais de contas." In *Corrupção: Ensaios e críticas,* ed. Leonardo Avritzer, Newton Bignotto, Juarez Guimarães, and Heloisa Maria Murgel Starling, 551–58. Belo Horizonte: Editora UFMG.

Speck, Bruno W., and José Nagel. 2002. "A fiscalização dos recursos públicos pelos Tribunais de Contas." In *Caminhos da transparência,* ed. Bruno W. Speck, 227–57. São Paulo: Editora Universidade Estadual de Campinas.

Stapenhurst, Rick, and Jack Titsworth. 2001. *Features and Functions of Supreme Audit Institutions.* Washington, DC: World Bank Institute.

Steibel, Fabro. 2007. *Feios, sujos e malvados: Políticos, juízes e a campanha eleitoral de 2002 na TV.* Rio de Janeiro: E-Papers.

Stein, Ernesto, Mariano Tommasi, Koldo Echebarría, Eduardo Lora, and Mark Payne. 2005. *The Politics of Policies: Economic and Social Progress in Latin America. 2006 Report.* Washington, DC: Inter-American Development Bank.

Steves, Franklin, and Alan Rousso. 2005. "The Effectiveness of Anti-Corruption Programmes: Preliminary Evidence from the Transition Countries." Paper presented at the annual meeting of the American Political Science Association, September 1–4.

Stokes, Susan. 2001. *Public Support for Market Reforms in New Democracies.* Cambridge: Cambridge University Press.

———. 2005. "Perverse Accountability: A Formal Model of Machine Politics with Evidence from Argentina." *American Political Science Review* 99 (3): 315–26.

Taschner, Gisela. 1992. *Folhas ao vento: Análise de um conglomerado jornalístico no Brasil.* Rio de Janeiro: Paz e Terra.

Taylor, Matthew M. 2006. "Justiça Eleitoral." In *Reforma política no Brasil,* ed. Leonard Avritzer and Fátima Anastasia. Belo Horizonte: Editora UFMG.

———. 2008. *Judging Policy: Courts and Policy Reform in Democratic Brazil.* Stanford: Stanford University Press.

———. 2009. "Corruption, Accountability Reforms and Democracy in Brazil." In *Corruption and Democracy in Latin America,* ed. Charles H. Blake and Stephen D. Morris. Pittsburgh: University of Pittsburgh Press.

———. 2010. "Brazil: Corruption as Harmless *Jeitinho* or Threat to Democracy?" In *Corruption and Politics in Latin America: National and Regional Dynamics,* ed. Stephen D. Morris and Charles H. Blake. Boulder, CO: Lynne Rienner.

Taylor, Matthew M., and Vinicius Buranelli. 2007. "Ending up in Pizza: Accountability as a Problem of Institutional Arrangement in Brazil." *Latin American Politics and Society* 49 (1): 59–87.

Teixeira, Carla. 2004. "The Price of Honor: The Press versus Congress in the Rhetoric of Brazilian Politics." *Public Culture* 16 (1): 31–46.

Teixeira, Marco A. 2004. "Entre o técnico and o político: O Tribunal de Contas do município de São Paulo e o controle financeiro das gestões Luiza Erundina (1989–1992) e Paulo Maluf (1993–1996)." PhD diss., Pontifícia Universidade Católica de São Paulo.

Thacker, Strom C. 2009. "Democracy, Economic Policy, and Political Corruption: Latin America in Comparative Perspective." In *Corruption and Democracy in Latin America,* ed. Charles H. Blake and Stephen D. Morris. Pittsburgh: University of Pittsburgh Press.

Thompson, John. 2000. *Political Scandal: Power and Visibility in the Media Age.* Cambridge: Polity.

Transparência Brasil. 2008. *Projeto Excelências.* Online database, www.excelencias.org.br; accessed January 15, 2008.

Transparency International. 2002. *Corruption Fighters' Tool Kit: Civil Society Experiences and Emerging Strategies.* Berlin: Transparency International.

———. 2004. *Report on the Transparency International Global Corruption Barometer 2004.* Berlin: Transparency International. www.transparency.org/policy_research/surveys_indices/gcb/2004.

Treisman, Daniel. 2000. "The Causes of Corruption: A Cross-National Study." *Journal of Public Economics* 76:399–457.

———. 2007. "What Have We Learned about the Causes of Corruption from Ten Years of Cross-National Empirical Research?" *Annual Review of Political Science* 10:211–44.

Tribunal Superior Eleitoral. 2002a. "Eleições 2002: Prestações de Contas Eleitorais." www.tse.gov.br/internet/eleicoes/pretacao_2002.htm.

———. 2002b. "Resultados das eleições gerais." www.tre-df.gov.br/default/eleicoes/elei_2006.jsp.

———. 2007. "Prestações de contas das eleições de 2006." www.tse.gov.br/internet/eleicoes/pretacao_2006.htm.

TSE. See Tribunal Superior Eleitoral.

Tsai, Kellee S. 2006. "Adaptive Informal Institutions and Endogenous Institutional Change in China." *World Politics* 59 (1): 116–41.

Tsebelis, George. 1990. *Nested Games: Rational Choice in Comparative Politics.* Berkeley: University of California Press.

———. 2002. *Veto Players: How Political Institutions Work.* New York: Russell Sage Foundation.

Tulchin, Joseph, and Ralph Espach. 2000. *Combating Corruption in Latin America.* Baltimore: Woodrow Wilson Center Press.

Último Segundo. 2008. "Luiz Eduardo Soares afirma que prisão de Álvaro Lins tem 'impacto enorme.'" Interview with Luiz Eduardo Soares, May 29.

United Nations. 2004. *Extrajudicial, Summary or Arbitrary Executions: Report of the Special Rapporteur, Asma Jahangir, Addendum Mission to Brazil.* UN Economic and Social Council Commission on Human Rights, E/CN.4/2004/7/Add.3.

Veja. 2008. "Autópsia da corrupção." January 28.

Vieira, Fabiano Mourão. 2008. "Cultura brasileira e corrupção." *Revista da CGU* 4 (1): 46–62.

Waisbord, Silvio. 1996. "Contando histórias de corrupção: Narrativa de telenovela e moralidade populista no caso Collorgate." *Comunicação e Política* 3 (2): 94–110.

———. 2000. *Watchdog Journalism in South America.* New York: Columbia University Press.

———. 2006. "Reading Scandals: Scandals, Media, and Citizenship in Contemporary Argentina." In *Enforcing the Rule of Law,* ed. Enrique Peruzzotti and Catalina Smulovitz, 272–303. Pittsburgh: University of Pittsburgh Press.

Warren, Mark E. 2004. "What Does Corruption Mean in a Democracy?" *American Journal of Political Science* 48 (2004): 328–43.

———. 2006. "Political Corruption as Duplicitous Exclusion." *PS: Political Science and Politics* 39 (2006): 803–7.

Weyland, Kurt. 1998. "The Politics of Corruption in Latin America." *Journal of Democracy* 9:108–21.

Whitehead, Laurence. 2000. "High-Level Political Corruption in Latin America: A 'Transitional' Phenomenon?" In *Combating Corruption in Latin America,* ed. Joseph S. Tulchin and Ralph H. Espach. Baltimore: Woodrow Wilson Center Press.

Wiesehomeier, Nina, and Kenneth Benoit. 2007. "Presidents and Parties in Policy Space: Expert Surveys of Policy Positions in 18 Latin American Countries." Unpublished paper, University of Konstanz.

Williams, Bernard. 1988. "Formal Structures and Social Reality." In *Trust: Making and Breaking Cooperative Relations,* ed. Diego Gambetta, 3–13. Oxford: Basil Blackwell.

Williams, Philip. 2001. "Transnational Criminal Networks." In *Networks and Netwars: The Future of Terror, Crime and Militancy,* ed. John Arguilla and David Ronfeldt, 61–97. Santa Monica, CA: Rand.

Zaller, John R. 1992. *The Nature and Origins of Mass Opinion.* Cambridge: Cambridge University Press.

Zucco, Cesar. 2008. "The President's 'New Constituency': Lula and the Pragmatic Vote in Brazil's 2006 Presidential Elections." *Journal of Latin American Studies* 40:29–49.

Contributors

Rogério B. Arantes is Assistant Professor of Political Science at the University of São Paulo. A specialist in judicial institutions, he is the author of *Ministério Público e política no Brasil* (Sumaré/Educ, 2002) and *Judiciário e política no Brasil* (Sumaré/Educ, 1997). He is currently studying the relationships among constitutional politics, democracy, and decision-making processes in Brazil. He is coauthor of the article "Constitution, Government and Democracy in Brazil" (*World Political Science Review,* 2008), which won the Brazilian Political Science Association's Olavo Brasil de Lima Junior Prize for the best article in political science and international relations in 2008.

Fiona Macaulay is Senior Lecturer in Development Studies at the Department of Peace Studies, University of Bradford, and a former Research Fellow in Human Rights at the Centre for Brazilian Studies, University of Oxford. Her research focuses on gender policies and politics, as well as criminal justice reform and human rights, in Latin America. Her work has been published in *Bulletin of Latin American Research, Journal of Latin American Studies, Latin American Perspectives, América Latina Hoy,* and *Social Policy and Society,* among other journals. She is the author of *Gender Politics in Brazil and Chile: the Role of Political Parties in Local and National Policy-Making* (Palgrave Macmillan, 2006) and is coeditor of the *Journal of Latin American Studies.*

Carlos Pereira is Assistant Professor of Political Science at Michigan State University and also Assistant Professor at the School of Economics at the Fundação Getúlio Vargas in São Paulo. From 2000 to 2002 he was a Research Fellow in Politics at the Centre for Brazilian Studies, University of Oxford. His major research interests are political institutions in comparative perspective and the positive political economy of regulation. He has also studied public policy making, executive-legislative relations, coalition formation, agenda setting, and congressional organization in comparative perspective. His work has been published in *Journal of Politics, Political Research Quarterly, Comparative Political Studies, Journal of Latin American Studies, Governance, Latin American Politics and Society, Legislative Studies Quarterly,* and *Electoral Studies,* among other journals. He has also published a coauthored book (with Paulo Correa, Bernardo Mueller, and Marcus Melo) entitled *Regulatory Governance in Infrastructure Industries* (World Bank Press, 2006). He is currently preparing a coauthored book-length manuscript, tentatively entitled *Brazil on the Road to Good Governance.*

Mauro P. Porto is Assistant Professor in the Department of Communication at Tulane University, where he is also affiliated with the Stone Center for Latin American Studies and the Brazilian Studies Program. He is currently on leave at the Ford Foundation in Rio de Janeiro, as Program Officer for Media Rights and Access. His main research interests are political communication and democratization, with a focus on the relationship between media and politics in Brazil. His work has been published in *Political Communication, Critical Studies in Media Communication, Journalism, Television and New Media,* among others. He is the author of *Televisão e política no Brasil: A Rede Globo e as interpretações da audiência* (E-Papers, 2007).

Timothy J. Power is Director of the Latin American Centre at the University of Oxford, where he is also a fellow of St. Cross College. A former president of the Brazilian Studies Association, he conducts research on democratic institutions in Brazil. His most recent book, coedited with Cesar Zucco Jr., is *O Congresso por ele mesmo: Autopercepções da classe política brasileira* (Editora UFMG, 2011). His work has been published in *Journal of Politics, Political Research Quarterly, Comparative Political Studies, Political Science Quarterly, Party Politics, Studies in Comparative International Development,* and *Electoral Studies,* among other journals. He is an associate editor of the *Journal of Politics in Latin America.*

Eric D. Raile is Assistant Professor of Political Science at North Dakota State University. His research examines how political actors build support for policy initiatives within particular institutional and cultural environments.

He has worked on issues of corruption prevention for the U.S. government, including work related to the anticorruption monitoring mechanism administered by the Organization of American States. He has presented his research at institutions such as the World Bank, the Organization for Economic Cooperation and Development, and Asia-Pacific Economic Cooperation.

Lucio R. Rennó is Associate Professor in the Research Center and Graduate Program on the Americas at the University of Brasilia. His research on legislative politics, voting behavior, and public opinion has been published in the *American Journal of Political Science, Legislative Studies Quarterly, Latin American Politics and Society, Journal of Politics, Journal of Latin American Studies, Journal of Legislative Studies, Electoral Studies, Dados,* and *Opinião Pública.* He is coeditor of *Reforma política: Lições da história recente* (Editora FGV, 2006), *Reforma política em questão* (Editora UnB, 2008), and *Legislativo brasileiro em perspectiva comparada* (Editora UFMG, 2009).

David J. Samuels is Benjamin E. Lippincott Professor of Political Science at the University of Minnesota. His research and teaching interests include Brazilian and Latin American politics and the empirical implications of democratic theory in comparative politics. He is the author of *Ambition, Federalism, and Legislative Politics in Brazil* (Cambridge University Press, 2003) and coauthor (with Matthew Shugart) of *Presidents, Parties, and Prime Ministers* (Cambridge University Press, 2010). His articles have appeared in the *American Political Science Review, Journal of Politics, Comparative Politics, Comparative Political Studies, Legislative Studies Quarterly,* and the *British Journal of Political Science,* among others.

Bruno W. Speck is Assistant Professor of Political Science at the University of Campinas. His main research areas are party and campaign finance, diagnostic surveys on corruption, national integrity systems, and government audit institutions. Prior to his current position, he worked as a researcher at the Arnold Bergstraesser Institut (ABI), as a fellow at the Max Planck Institute for Foreign and International Criminal Law, as a visiting professor at the Freie Universität Berlin, and as Senior Advisor for Transparency International, a nonprofit organization fighting corruption and promoting good governance.

Matthew M. Taylor is Assistant Professor of Political Science at the University of São Paulo. His research on judicial politics, political economy, and corruption has been published in *Comparative Politics, Journal of Latin American Studies, Perspectives on Politics,* and *World Politics,* among others. He is the author of *Judging Policy: Courts and Policy Reform in Democratic Brazil* (Stanford University Press, 2008), which was awarded the Brazilian Political Science Association's Vitor Nunes Leal Prize in 2008 as best book in political science and international relations.

Index

accountability. *See also* electoral
accountability; web of
accountability institutions
benefits of, 8–9
central issues of, 263–65
compensatory strategies, 255–57
criteria of, 26n1
cross-national innovations,
258–63
defined, 1, 56
delegation in tension with, 59
democracy and pressures for, 6
importance of, 6–9
improvements
—Brazil, 265–70
—interest in, 251
—suggestions for, 268–72
legislating, 169–72, 176–78, 198,
265–66, 268
media role in, 111–19, 122–24
reform and, 177–79
requirements for, 9–10, 80
rights guarantees restricting, 171
sanctions for
—effectiveness, 163–65
—TCU, 140t, 141–43, 149
vertical and horizontal dimensions
of, 60
accountability process
court systems central to, 165
cross-institutional nature of,
175–77

federal-level institutions, 18
interdependence in the, 13–16
stages in the, 13, 163–65
accountability reforms, 265–68
activation, 17t
Administrative Improbity Law, 188,
198, 266
Advocacia Geral da União (AGU), 18
Albuquerque, Alfonso de, 121, 240
Alckmin, Geraldo, 64, 66, 67–78, 97
Alencar, Chico, 64
Álvares, Élcio, 238
Amaral, Delcídio, 34
Americas Barometer, 4, 5t
anticorruption approaches
judicial, 196, 197t, 198–200
law enforcement, 223
political, 196, 197fig
anticorruption bureaucracies, 4
anticorruption institutions,
framework of, 195–200
anticorruption practices. *See also*
Federal Police; Ministério
Público (MP)
advances in, 186, 211–15
legal-institutional innovations,
187–89
new challenges, 211–15
anticorruption strategies
cross-institutional, 270
effective, 260
improvements in, 96